Dynamics of Asian Development

The series situates contemporary development processes and outcomes in Asia in a global context. State intervention as well as neoliberal policies have created unusual economic and social development opportunities. There are also serious setbacks for marginalized communities, workers, the environment, and social justice. The rise of China, India, and new dynamism of South Korea, Indonesia, and Vietnam in East and South East Asia have given a new meaning to Asian development dynamics. Japan's energetic ties with India and Vietnam, Korea joining the OECD's Development Assistance Committee, and China and India's investments and foreign aid in Africa and Latin America are some of the new processes of development whose impact transcends the vast Asian region. Globalization compounds uneven development, affecting macroeconomic stability, internal and international migration, class and caste dynamics, gender relations, regional parity, education and health, agriculture and rural employment, informal sector, innovation possibilities, and equity. Thus the series views development studies as an unfinished agenda of economic, social, political, cultural interactions, and possible transformations in a fluid policy and global contexts. The editor, with the assistance of a distinguished group of development scholars from Asia and elsewhere specializing in a variety of disciplinary and thematic areas, welcomes proposals that critically assess the above-mentioned wide-ranging developing issues facing Asian societies. With Asia's contemporary transformation, the series promotes the understanding of Asia's influence on the prospects of development elsewhere. The editor encourages interdisciplinary, heterodox approaches within the social sciences, and comparative work with solid theoretically informed empirical research. Critical development policy debates in Asia and regional governance issues that have a bearing on development outcomes are also sought.

More information about this series at https://link.springer.com/bookseries/13342

Rajah Rasiah · Kamal Salih · Cheong Kee Cheok
Editors

Malaysia's Leap Into the Future

The Building Blocks Towards Balanced Development

Springer

Editors
Rajah Rasiah
Asia-Europe Institute
University of Malaya
Kuala Lumpur, Malaysia

Cheong Kee Cheok
Asia-Europe Institute
University of Malaya
Kuala Lumpur, Malaysia

Kamal Salih
Malaysian Institute of Economic Research
Kuala Lumpur, Malaysia

ISSN 2198-9923 ISSN 2198-9931 (electronic)
Dynamics of Asian Development
ISBN 978-981-16-7044-2 ISBN 978-981-16-7045-9 (eBook)
https://doi.org/10.1007/978-981-16-7045-9

This Springer imprint is published by the registered company Springer Nature Singapore Pte Ltd.
The registered company address is: 152 Beach Road, #21-01/04 Gateway East, Singapore 189721, Singapore

Foreword

ISTANA ISKANDARIAH

Kuala Kangsar, Malaysia

When we find ourselves embroiled in such challenging and uncertain times as we are currently experiencing, with the immediate and unremitting impacts of the Covid-19 pandemic, ever-turbulent national and international politics, let alone the medium-term challenges posed by climate change, it can be easy to lose sight of the longer term. Books such as this one, which remind us of the vital importance of planning carefully for the future, are particularly valuable in this context. "Leap into the Future: the building blocks" thus proves a very timely contribution indeed.

This task of casting a critical eye on our present and past, before setting out some possible future directions for our nation, is difficult enough. This challenge is amplified by the wide-ranging scope of this volume's subject matter, which covers a multitude of topics that are all highly pertinent to understanding our nation's prospects and trajectory. The editors, Rajah Rasiah, Kamal Salih, and Cheong Kee Cheok, have met this demanding objective most admirably with this book. It offers not only a detailed critical appraisal of where we are as a nation and how we got here, but also a credible vision of our route forward, as well as a wealth of closely argued and well-informed analysis of some of the key aspects of our socio-economic condition and path.

I commend the three editors for the laudable job they have done in bringing together in this way so many crucial elements of the state we are in, and the challenges we face in our ongoing journey towards sustainable development and advanced country status. Their well-curated selection of writers on the various subjects complements their own specialist contributions most effectively. The range of topics covered by the editors themselves adds to the sense throughout that we are in highly capable hands here, in relation to both the bigger picture and the specifics. The page of contents, incidentally, is a good place to start to work one's way through what is undeniably a hefty tome, which requires quite some investment in order to reap the many rewards it contains.

The editors and other writers tackle in depth a wide range of relevant topics and themes. They cover the core economic sectors of agriculture, manufacturing, and knowledge-based services. They address the multiple challenges associated with the further development of our human capital, in relation to everything from the necessary changes in our approach to education, to future-proofing employment and the labour market. They also consider the continued challenges posed by poverty and inequality, and the intensifying ones concerning our natural environment. Throughout, sensible and credible analysis is put forward, with clear and well thought out options for our way forward. This thorough and enlightening survey of our socio-economic past, present, and future, thus sets out a robust and credible analysis of our nation's path and of how it may unfold, given our heritage and structural constraints.

I want to congratulate the editors and authors for the insight and erudition they have bought to so many urgent issues and commend them for having produced such convincing diagnoses and prognoses of our strengths and weaknesses across so many areas. I urge everyone interested in these important questions to keep a copy of this book close to hand, to read, reread, and refer to at leisure, according to relevant events and individual interests. This book contains a multitude of different facets far beyond what is apparent on an initial quick glance through, and I have no doubt that it will prove a highly useful reference work long into the future which it also ambitiously aims to shape.

Kuala Kangsar, Malaysia

Sultan Nazrin Shah
HRH

Preface

This book was conceived following the submission of the economics chapter of the Project, *Envisioning Malaysia in 2050* in 2017 that Academy of Science, Malaysia (ASM) was preparing for the Malaysian government. Invariably it brought together different aspects of what constitutes socio-economics for a national economy. It is then that we recognized the need to put together a seriously researched book with all the critical pillars of socio-economics in the broadest sense not just to serve as a base but also as a roadmap on how countries should plan their future. The approach taken in the book takes a critical assessment of the Malaysian economy, as well as what, how, and why the building blocks proposed are necessary to achieve a better future.

While it is difficult to provide a thorough critical assessment of an economy at any one point in time, (including its different aspects), the task this book has taken, is daunting as the future is uncertain. As in Karl Popper's book, *The Open Society and Its Enemies*, he makes it clear that however much one plans there are limits imposed by the unknown. Nevertheless, the book is the result of a profound set of critical discussions between the authors of the individual chapters that were carried out between 2015 and 2019, which includes a strong interface with members from government, the private sector, and civil society officials.

In doing so, the book adopts a novel approach by starting with what are the critical pillars of a sound national economy. Each chapter draws on an incisive screening of related theories before the empirical evidence is examined. Consequently, the first pillar of the book discusses Malaysia's economic growth and structural change, including how it has evolved the way it has in comparison with some of the Northeast East Asian and Southeast Asian countries, and why it is trapped in the middle-income group. This chapter is then, followed by projections of population and demographic change as it will have a bearing on the nature of policies that the government should pursue. Chapter 4 assesses government finances to focus on how the economic development of the country can be financed. Chapter 5 examines the reasons behind a declining contribution of the agricultural sector in the national economy with an emphasis on food security.

Chapter 6 dissects the performance of the manufacturing sector, which the government had identified as the engine of growth in 1971, to argue that Malaysia has been experiencing premature deindustrialization since 2000. This chapter offers three strategies on how industrial upgrading should be promoted. Chapter 7 follows by discussing why knowledge-based services are important to synergize the Malaysian economy, and how they should be promoted. Chapter 8 evaluates in detail the education sector in the country, arguing with evidence on why Malaysia must rethink some of its strategies to improve the role of education in the country. Chapter 9 explains why the human capital and talent development policies in Malaysia have not achieved their desired success, and what should be done to position them to propel the country's development in future.

Chapter 10 examines urbanization and infrastructure, and its socio-economic consequences highlighting in the process the importance of sound urban planning to accommodate encroachment of concentrated cities on one hand, and to support key economic thrusts on the other hand. Chapter 11 addresses the future of labour, arguing strongly for the need to train the labour force alongside the introduction of automation to move away from low wage labour activities. Chapter 12 discusses poverty and inequality. While acknowledging the contributions of the New Economic Policy, the chapter firmly argues that the future direction must replace ethnic-based approaches with a needs-based approach to not only contain poverty effectively but to build a plural Malaysia. Chapter 13 discusses environmental practices and standards the young Malaysians now wish to have in future. Chapter 14 discusses the state of healthcare in Malaysia, contending that there must be strategies to absorb new technologies while at the same time strategies to solve access problems faced by the poor.

It is our belief that the building blocks presented in this book will initiate further deliberations among the stakeholders with a view towards contributing to constructing a better Malaysia. We take this opportunity to thank the management of the ASM, Johan Merican from the Economic Planning Unit of Malaysia, private sector officials, civil society members, colleagues at the faculty of Economics and Administration, University of Malaya, and Malaysian healthcare officials for graciously contributing to this exercise. We wish to thank Datuk Professor Dr Mazlan Othman and Professor Dr Tengku Azman Sharifuddin for the many incisive meetings and discussions we had with ASM officials. A special thanks to High Royal Highness Sultan Nazrin Shah for generously contributing the foreword to this book. Finally, we wish to acknowledge the generous support from the Ulung *grant (Project No: MO004-2018) awarded to Rajah Rasiah, which was used to finance, inter alia,* this book project.

Kuala Lumpur, Malaysia

Rajah Rasiah
Kamal Salih
Cheong Kee Cheok

Endorsement for "Malaysia's Leap into the Future: The building blocks"

Long version (105)

Malaysia is one of Southeast Asia's star economies with an enviable growth record. It is poised to make the transition to a high-income nation even as the share of manufacturing shrinks and services take the lead. The contributors to this volume demonstrate with admirable clarity, analytic rigor and empirical detail that knowledge and technology-driven, productivity-led growth is within reach, but Malaysia must strengthen the multi-faceted, institutional scaffolding, which invigorates a knowledge economy, and make haste to improve the quality of its human capital. It is one of the several virtues of this volume that it clearly spells out how this could be done.

Shahid Yusuf
Chief Economist, Growth Dialogue, Washington DC

Contents

Editors and Contributors

About the Editors

Rajah Rasiah Ph.D., is Distinguished Professor of Economics at the Asia-Europe Institute, University of Malaya. His research interests include technology and international development, foreign investment, human capital, public health, and environment. He holds external positions at UNU-MERIT, Oxford University, Cambridge University, and Universiti Tenaga Nasional. He is the 2014 recipient of the Celso Furtado Prize awarded by the World Academy of Sciences for advancing the frontiers of social science thought.

Kamal Salih Ph.D. is an Executive Chairman of Ankar Corporation and Chairman of Malaysia Institute of Economic Research (MIER). He has served as Senior Technical Advisor to UNDP Malaysia and was Adjunct Professor of Economics and Development Studies and Senior Advisor to Asia Europe Institute in University Malaya.

Cheong Kee Cheok is currently Senior Research Fellow, Institute of China Studies, and Senior Advisor, Asia Europe Institute, University of Malaya. As a graduate of the University of Malaya, he obtained his Ph.D. at the London School of Economics. Upon his return from studies, he joined the Faculty of Economics and Administration, University of Malaya, where he held the positions of Deputy Dean and Dean of Faculty. After a decade at UM, he spent 16 years at the World Bank in the capacity of Economist and subsequently Senior Economist. At the Bank, he was Coordinator for China and Vietnam in the Economic Development Institute, now the World Bank Institute. After returning to Malaysia in 2000, he has continued as Consultant for the Bank and UN agencies. Back with the University of Malaya since 2010, he has coauthored books, book chapters, and published numerous papers in top-tier academic journals as well as successfully supervised Ph.D. students, both international and local.

Contributors

V. G. R. Chandran Faculty of Business and Economics, University of Malaya, Kuala Lumpur, Malaysia

Yong Chen Chen Faculty of Business and Economics, University of Malaya, Kuala Lumpur, Malaysia

Cheong Kee Cheok Asia-Europe Institute, University of Malaya, Kuala Lumpur, Malaysia

Yap Su Fei Faculty of Business and Economics, University of Malaya, Kuala Lumpur, Malaysia

Rospidah Ghazali Institute for Environment and Development (LESTARI), Universiti Kebangsaan Malaysia, Bangi, Selangor, Malaysia

Melvin Terry Gumal Kuching, Malaysia

Mohammed Ibrahim Institute for Environment and Development (LESTARI), Universiti Kebangsaan Malaysia, Bangi, Selangor, Malaysia

Wee Yeap Lau Faculty of Business and Economics, Universiti Malaya, Kuala Lumpur, Malaysia

Than Lee Lee Faculty of Business and Economics, University of Malaya, Kuala Lumpur, Malaysia

Sylvia Ng Kuching, Malaysia

Dwight Heald Perkins Littauer Center M-14, Department of Economics, Harvard University, Cambrdige, USA

Rajah Rasiah Asia-Europe Institute, University of Malaya, Kuala Lumpur, Malaysia

Elvinson Rosedy Kuching, Malaysia

Kamal Salih Malaysian Institute of Economic Research, Bukit Petaling, Kuala Lumpur, Malaysia

Viswanathan Selvaratnam Kuala Lumpur, Malaysia

Sharifah Muhairah Shahabudin Faculty of Business and Economics, University of Malaya, Kuala Lumpur, Malaysia

Kuppusamy Singaravelloo Faculty of Business and Economics, University of Malaya, Kuala Lumpur, Malaysia

Chamhuri Siwar Institute for Environment and Development (LESTARI), Universiti Kebangsaan Malaysia, Bangi, Selangor, Malaysia

Douglas Tan Kuching, Malaysia

Nai Peng Tey Faculty of Business and Economics, University of Malaya, Kuala Lumpur, Malaysia

Wing-Thye Woo Jeffrey Cheah Institute On Southeast Asia, Sunway University, Sunway, Selangor, Malaysia

Yunus Yasin Petaling Jaya, Malaysia

Christina Yin Kuching, Malaysia

List of Figures

List of Tables

Chapter 1
Introduction: Problematizing the Building Blocks

Rajah Rasiah, Cheong Kee Cheok, and Kamal Salih

Abstract Using largely foresight analysis by taking stock of Malaysia's existing key development pillars, the chapter attempts to orientate how these pillars should be planned over the period from now until 2050 taking account of sustainability. The critical building blocks problematized in the chapter are population and demography, the financing of development, agriculture and food sufficiency, manufacturing, knowledge intensive services, education, talent and human capital, urbanization and infrastructure, future of labour, poverty and inequality, the environment, and health and wellness. The chapter lays the groundwork for the presentation of the building blocks in the subsequent chapters.

Keywords Foresight analysis · Building blocks of sustainable development · Malaysia

Smith (1776) arguably wrote the first account of how a range of factors stimulate the accumulation of wealth in nations. Whereas Smith's work was both inductive and instructive using examples to demonstrate his points, it was not seriously historical. It was Toynbee (1934–1960) who in a twelve volume series used history to explain the rise of civilization, which to him was among other challenges, "the stimulus of hard countries", i.e. the ability of groups to overcome harsh environments, the triumph of human resourcefulness (resources) over what was often a lack of physical resources. More recently, Landes (1999) wrote about the rise of Europe because of its culture and Protestant ethic—again, the effective deployment of human resources.[1]

[1] Weber (1958) had initiated the cultural argument on how the positivist Protestant ethics supported capitalist accumulation.

R. Rasiah (✉) · C. K. Cheok
Asia-Europe Institute, University of Malaya, 50 603 Kuala Lumpur, Malaysia
e-mail: rajah@um.edu.my

K. Salih
Malaysian Institute of Economic Research, JKR 606, Jalan Bukit Petaling, 50 460 Bukit Petaling, Kuala Lumpur, Malaysia

R. Rasiah et al. (eds.), *Malaysia's Leap Into the Future*, Dynamics of Asian Development, https://doi.org/10.1007/978-981-16-7045-9_1

However, there has been a long but circular debate on the importance of natural resources, and colonial structures in economic development. Prebisch (1949) and Singer (1950) had initiated the argument on how colonial structures had turned post-colonial states into producing a narrow range of commodities for exports to industrial countries. This fallacy of composition argument posited that specialization of large numbers of countries on a narrow range of commodities that is characterized by long gestation periods subjected them to falling terms of trade to undermine their development potential. Corden and Neary (1982) subsequently advanced the Dutch Disease argument to show how volatile swings in commodity demand have undermined the economic growth of countries heavily reliant on natural resources. High commodity prices generate balance of payments surpluses but consequent rising exchange rates end up crippling the real sectors of manufacturing and agriculture. A slightly different argument on the curse of resources focused on complacency that comes with being resource rich (Sachs & Warner, 1997).[2] Fortunately for Malaysia, none of these arguments has seriously dominated economic growth and structural change as the respective governments addressed initially overdependence on rubber and tin exports by diversifying into oil palm, and cocoa cultivation, and subsequently by introducing export-oriented industrialization.

Narrowing the narrative from world systems to development economics, the discussion is focused on the effective use of scarce (capital) and abundant (labour) resources (Hirschman, 1958; Lewis, 1954; Nurkse, 1961) to first escape from the poverty trap and move to higher income, although this has been tempered by arguments on the need to take into account the role of institutions (Geertz, 1963; Myrdal, 1968; Veblen, 1915). Hirschman (1958, 1970) had argued lucidly on how and why it is important to integrate into the world economy, and what role national governments should play to engender the conditions for national development.

The optimistic among development thinkers see development as a staged process (Akamatsu, 1962; Rostow, 1960). Whereas Akamatsu (1962) worked on regional synergies between investment and trade, and along with that a sequential flight of a gaggle of geese through a value added defined division of labour, Rostow (1960) argued over the movement of development forces initially from the creation of development conditions through concentration of capital among the capitalist class to eventually mature economies characterized by mass consumption. There were also models that called for delinking from capitalist structures to promote egalitarian national development (Lenin, 1917; Mao, 1957). These stylized frameworks did not gain much traction as several shortcomings diminished their importance. Indeed, with the exception of Cuba and North Korea, the other socialist experiments all collapsed from their own international [internal?] contradictions, as well as rivalry from superior capitalist organizations (Ellman & Kontorovich 1991).

Disputing the view of orderly staged growth, and more relevant to countries already at the middle-income level, others argue that the history of countries that have enjoyed sustained economic growth and structural change to move from poor

[2] Anita (2015) uses the resource curse framework to examine the political economy of oil revenue management and expenditures in Malaysia.

to rich nations is associated with deliberate catching up and leapfrogging strategies implemented by governments (Reinert, 2007). Hamilton (1791) had advised the American government to introduce industrial policy after discovering how backward his country was against British manufacturing. List (1886) subsequently wrote the economic catch-up experience of several European economies along similar lines. The early advocates promoting this approach, i.e. Gerschenkron (1952) and Abramovitz (1956), had argued that late movers enjoy certain advantages that offer them the opportunity to catch up and leapfrog the first movers. Latecomers learn from the achievements of incumbents, including skipping the mistakes and switching from past novelty to new novelty to cheapen and quicken the catch-up process (Rasiah, 2015). Kim (1997) outlined the early strategies of firms' to creatively change starting with a duplicative learning process before shifting to innovations at the frontier. Indeed, Rasiah (2016) posited that the distinction between copying and creating is borderless in this process, and it is how latecomers appropriate innovation synergies through creative destruction that distinguishes firms that move up in the technology ladder and those that either stagnate or fall behind.

Britain was arguably the first nation to develop modern industrialization to achieve economic prosperity but it took place over a period from 1485 till 1750 (Reinert, 2007). The newcomers, such as the United States, Germany, South Korea, and Taiwan shortened that period. Indeed, South Korea and Taiwan developed in one generation between the 1960s and 1990s (Amsden, 1989; Chang, 1994; Wade, 1990).[3] South Korea's per capita income in 2005 prices rose by around 22 times from US$1,107 in 1960 to 23,893 in 2013.[4] The other rapid industrializers of Malaysia, Thailand, and China have also managed impressive growth rates. Malaysia's GDP per capita in real prices grew by 7 times from US$987 in 1960 to US$6,998 in 2013. Thailand's GDP per capita in real prices grew by 8 times from US$437 in 1965 to US$3,348 in 2013. China's GDP per capita growth in real prices significantly surpassed that of Malaysia and Thailand as it grew by 15 times from US$246 in 1982 to US$3,567 in 2013.

Whatever the debates and arguments highlighted above, there can be little dispute that economic development is a complex, multi-dimensional process, encompassing institutions, their governance, growth strategies and policies, as well as specific contexts that can either promote or hinder growth. Given this complexity, a single country's experience and prospects make for a more concrete analysis that may also provide insights for other countries in a similar situation.

Six reasons explain why Malaysia is an excellent laboratory to explore how a middle-income country can eventually become a developed country. Firstly, Malaysia has largely eliminated absolute poverty and have kept unemployment and inflation to low levels since the 1990s, all these hallmarks of sound macroeconomic management. Absolute poverty of 49.3% in 1970 has been reduced to 0.4% in 2016 (Malaysia,

[3] This "Eurocentric" view of development is, however disputed by Frank (1998) and Pomeranz (2000), among others.

[4] Computed from World Bank (2020).

2020).[5] Unemployment and inflation have hovered below 4% since 1990. Secondly, Malaysia's export structure has evolved from specialization in primary raw materials in the 1960s to specialization in high tech exports from the 1990s. Thirdly, Malaysia shows strong education and health indicators. Education enrolment levels in secondary and tertiary education have risen, while access to healthcare is comparable to that in developed countries. Fourthly, Malaysia's innovation indicators of scientific publications and citations, and patent filing, have improved strongly since 2005. Fifthly, Malaysia enjoys basic infrastructure with access to modern roads, internet access and security comparable to developed countries. Malaysia's success in achieving growth and distribution led the World Bank (1993) to classify it as a high performing economy. Indeed, the World Bank (1993) considered Malaysia and the other fast-growing Southeast Asian economies of Indonesia, the Philippines and Thailand as better examples to imitate than South Korea and Taiwan on the basis of their more open economic approach than the interventions that characterized the Northeast Asian economies. Sixthly, existing accounts of catch-ups are focused on successful developers, such as the United States, Germany, Japan, South Korea and Taiwan. The assessment of Malaysia, which some consider as on the brink of achieving such a status, will offer an opportunity to debate whether indeed Malaysia is poised to become developed. In addition, a study of Malaysia will offer the opportunity to examine if economic development can go alongside a green development trajectory.

The above positives notwithstanding, Malaysia is still struggling to graduate from middle to high-income status. It faces challenges ranging from deficient human capital to low value added exports. Some have even argued that the country is facing a middle-income trap (Anita, 2015). Hence, while Malaysia has come a long way to be an upper middle-income country from specialization in the production of raw materials (especially tin and rubber) to electronics, oil and oil palm exports, for the country to qualify as a successful latecomer a number of developments are necessary. Also, in contrast to the early movers Malaysia's pursuit has to negotiate the difficult task of achieving growth and structural change through increasing use of green technologies.

In this introduction, we discuss the building blocks of Malaysia's leap into the future. The next section presents the arguments behind the selection of the building blocks followed by the outline of the book. The final section presents the summary.

---

[5] However, one can contest these achievements as the figures presented by the government of Malaysia have retained the basket of goods and services that constitutes the poverty line income, i.e. the figure of MYR980 in 2016 will fetch the same goods as MYR50 in 1970. Also, the Malaysian data has not taken account of address-less Malaysians, and that poor families tend to have larger family sizes than rich families.

Building Blocks

It is critical that Malaysia moves to a high growth path so as to support improvements in the standards of living of its population, and the capital and labour sources that Malaysia must achieve to become developed status by 2050. Hence, it is important to estimate reasonable achievable economic growth projections for the country until 2050. These projections must address growth in gross fixed capital formation and the supply of human capital. In light of the uncertainty associated with the external environment and with the future in general, these projections will need review and readjustments every five years.

Poverty and Inequality

Central to the achievement of economic development is its objective of alleviating poverty and redressing economic inequalities. Indeed, while governments have often targeted economic growth by enabling selected strategic sectors, poverty alleviation has always been a key objective of the economic development of most countries.

The original argument on causes of poverty advanced by Malthus (1798) was posited using the argument that population growing faster than resource supply (see also Ehrlich, 1971). Using longitudinal data on the OECD countries Kuznets (1955) found an inverted "U" shaped relationship between income inequality and per capita GDP (Logarithm) growth. Singh (1976) and Robinson (1976) subsequently misled us by running cross-sectional regressions to claim that this relationship is a law. This argument, however, was convincingly dismissed following Rasiah, Ishak, and Jomo's (1996) empirical work on East Asia that turned Kuznets on his head. Also, Anand and Segal (2008), Fields (2001) and Palma (2006, 2011) found no such evidence using global data. Palma (2014) went further to argue that the most significant relationship to observe was the Palma ratio, which is the trend movements in wealth between the top 10% and bottom 40% in particular countries.

Another significant note to examine is the measurement of poverty incidence. Countries such as Malaysia have yet to address the following three problems associated with poverty line measurements: one, changes in the composition of goods used to measure poverty line as countries become more affluent; two, enumeration of households without address and the homeless; and three, household size. These are some of the criticisms that have been levelled in Malaysia where official records show a trend fall in poverty incidence from 49.3% in 1970 to 0.4% in 2016 (Malaysia, 2020). Hence, this building block will seek to review the measurement instruments to ensure that projections are scientifically robust, as well as, policy directions to reduce absolute and relative poverty over the future.

Population, Demography and Urbanization

The Malthusian debate on overpopulation has long been laid to rest among developed economies as using longitudinal evidence Kuznets (1950) convincingly debunked the notion that countries will eventually be trapped by rowing deficit between food production and population growth. What came to be famously known as the inverted Kuznets "U-shaped" curve, the demographic transition was for a long time used to explain per capita income growth against income inequality. Among the developed economies falling mortality rates tended to be equalled or superseded by falling birth rates. This phenomenon has persisted despite some countries introducing incentives to raise birth rates. Malaysia's population growth rates have slowed down since the 1980s but the population has continued.

Demographic change has also seen the world characterized by a mad rush by people to live in urban locations because of the infrastructure available there *vis-a-vis* rural locations. The World Bank (2009), Young et al., (1980) and Krugman (1999) had argued over the economic rationale for humans to live in high rise buildings and cities owing to agglomeration economies. Urbanization has resulted in both positive and negative consequences. While the costs for providing public utilities per household has generally fallen during early urbanization it tends to reverse once cities become too big or when rural–urban migration has not been matched by a rise in economic opportunities (McGee, 1971). While the early town planners had focused on the provision of public utilities without sufficient consideration for the environment and health, major developments since the 1990s have opened up the debate on urban planning to include the environment as a global common.

As climate change and global warming reached crisis proportions since the 1990s there is recognition that urbanization will have to handle not only the effective provision of essential public utilities, which include housing, power, water, health, and education but also to avoid over-concentrations of humans. Hence, high-speed rail networks have sprung up in different parts of the world to disperse populations.

Growth and Technological Progress

Malaysia aimed to become developed by 2020 when the Vision 2020 blueprint was launched in 1991 (Malaysia, 1991). The aim then was to achieve a per capita income of USD15,000 (in constant 2010 prices) and along with it achieve developed country levels in a number of areas, such as health, education, and the environment, though no clear targets were defined for the nongrowth pillars. However, the country had fallen behind the growth path required to achieve that goal since 2000. Consequently, the government deferred the target of becoming developed to 2030 following the launching of the Shared Prosperity Vision blueprint in 2018. Malaysia's GDP per capita was USD12,478 (in constant 2010 prices) in 2019. Since economic growth is essential to support wage rise and improvements in living standards the envisioned future for Malaysia should attempt to target at least the per capita income of developing countries, such as South Korea, which enjoyed a GDP per capita of USD28,606 (in constant 2010 prices) by 2050. South Korea is a good example to follow as its GDP per capita in 1995 was USD12,163 (in 2010 prices), which is close to Malaysia's USD12.478 in 2019. In addition, South Korea' population in 2019 was 51.7 million against Malaysia's population of 20.5 million in 1995, 31.9 million in 2019 and a projected population of 40.6 million in 2050 (World Bank, 2020; see Tey, 2022). South Korea's population was 45.1 million against Malaysia's population of 20.5 million in 1995 (World Bank, 2020).[6]

While GDP per capita projections require recalibration over time, the sources of growth have to be located in deliberate technological catch-up strategies, which constitute the critical building block. Regardless of the methodology deployed to estimate technical change, there is consensus that technical change is the path countries must take to stimulate rapid economic growth and structural change (Lucas, 1988; Luxembourg, 1967; Marx, 1957; Rasiah & Pietrobelli, 2012; Rasiah et al., 2016; Romer, 1986; Rosenberg, 1976, 1982; Schumpeter, 1930, 1943; Solow, 1957). While the country can target several industries for catch up, the principle behind successful catch-up strategies achieved by the developed countries need addressing. Where necessary and possible interventions accompanied by stringent monitoring and performance standards to prevent rent dissipation need to be articulated well. Institutions—social, political, and economic—are important (Veblen, 1915; Nelson & Winter, 1982; North, 1994).

In terms of the trajectory of economic development, structural economists have argued that economies begin with primary sectors first (Kaldor, 1967). Whereas mining is wholly reliant on finite resource supplies, agriculture, especially oil palm has evolved through massive technological change. These primary sectors have stimulated growth not only in their own sectors but also in the emergence of the secondary and tertiary sectors. Successful economies have shown that the primary sectors first act as the engine of growth until manufacturing matures to take leadership as the engine of growth. It is only subsequently that services driven by knowledge-based activities eventually propels its own growth and that of the other sectors (Rowthorn & Wells, 1987). Especially because of food security countries undergoing a fall in the contribution of agriculture in the overall economy still enjoy productivity growth in these sectors with manufacturing and services stimulating technical change in the sector. The same happens when countries confront deindustrialization. Positive deindustrialization is associated with a fall in the relative contribution of the sector to economic growth but it remains characterized by strong productivity increments that is supported by continuous technological change. The current Malaysian manufacturing experience, which is facing premature deindustrialization (Rasiah, 2011), requires a reinvigoration through technological catch up.

[6] It is also noteworthy to state that Malaysia's Look East Policy that was launched in 1981 used South Korea as one of its main model (Malaysia, 1981).

In light of the above arguments, while knowledge-based services are expected to be the engine of growth in the future as Malaysia becomes a developed country, agriculture and manufacturing shall remain as major contributors to economic growth and structural change. Hence, services, agriculture and manufacturing constitute important building blocks to fashion Malaysia's leap into the future.

Fundamental to ensuring that Malaysia continues to record economic growth to fuel its developmental initiatives is the need to establish a reasonable set of scenarios, which must be grounded on initial conditions and the economic structure of the country. For this purpose, it will be important to project in dynamic terms long run catch-up scenarios using input–output tables. Being a latecomer Malaysia's task will be easier than the early movers as the paths tracked by the latter will become important lessons to track. Since technological progress is the driver of economic growth an additional chapter will examine the organization of Malaysia's engine of growth to fuel rapid economic growth.

Education, Human Capital, and Skills

Education inevitably has to be divided into two. The first shall deal with the expansion of schooling and university education, including the increasing emphasis on science education. Education is, after all, a basic human right that the state is obliged to provide. Thus UNESCO in its website (http://www.unesco.org/new/en/social-and-human-sciences/themes/fight-against-discrimination/role-of-education/) defines the role of education thus:

> Education should be a means to empower children and adults alike to become active participants in the transformation of their societies. Learning should also focus on the values, attitudes and behaviours which enable individuals to learn to live together in a world characterized by diversity and pluralism.

In other words, education provides the foundation for a society to be governed by the rule of law. Also, it is a public good as its non-excludable and non-rivalrous properties ensure that its provision publically will generate greater synergies for society than its provision privately.

Although there is much more to education than solely as an input to the production process, this role, cast by economists as producing human capital (Becker, 1994) has dominated the education discourse as countries advance up the income ladder. Thus, both neoclassical and evolutionary economics has made human capital the cornerstone of the drive for competitiveness and growth.

Most neoclassical arguments have tended to focus on its importance in driving economic growth, including explaining when latecomers are ready to include a focus on secondary and tertiary education (Mincer, 1958). Past developers have demonstrated that the development of a strong school and university education, especially in the fields of science and technology have served well to provide the reservoir for labour force participation in high value added activities (Arkerlof & Kranton,

2002). Vogel (1991) and Perkins (2013) discussed succinctly how Japan, South Korea and Taiwan evolved a strong technical labour force through supporting science and technology education both domestically and abroad.

In the arena of evolutionary economics, there is also consensus over the importance of human capital in supporting technological catch-up and by and large this group is uniquely different from the minor innovators (UNESCO, 2015). Schumpeter (1943) had argued that entrepreneurs as innovators only generated innovations through minor changes achieved through incremental engineering and adaptations to existing technologies. In successful industrializers, such as Germany, the dual training system offers high competency in technical and vocational education that enables apprentices but more importantly the master craftsmen innovative competencies to appropriate minor innovations through incremental engineering (Womack et al., 2007). The subsequent introduction of kaizen (Imai, 1995) that attracted the introduction of Just-In-Time inventory control systems by Toyota (Schonberger, 1988), rapid product launches by Canon (Best, 2001) and integrated materials requirement planning using cellular and parallel manufacturing systems are developments engineered by small group activities comprising personnel interaction across departments that are largely associated with entrepreneurial and technical synergies evolved at the workplace.

In discussing the development of human capital it is pertinent to distinguish human capital that is critical for stimulating radical innovations and new cycles of innovation from those capable of generating incremental innovations through the generation of new stocks of knowledge. Schumpeter glorified such human capital as he regarded them to initiate business cycle recoveries through the introduction of new technologies (see also Perez, 1980). Firms and organizations in Malaysia will have to be able to shape the globe's technology frontier in selected sectors and fields as the country becomes developed. Such competencies typically come from well-qualified R&D scientists and engineers. The sequence of development paths advocated by Penrose (1959) and Polanyi (1967) also show that experiential and tacit knowledge is critical in guiding R&D into commercializable areas. Etzkowitz and Leydesdor (1995), and Etzkowitz (2002) advanced the "triple helix" to argue for the critical role of university, industry and government relationships to stimulate innovation. The Vinnova model went a step further to advance the important role of stakeholders, which include the incisive role of civil society (Rasiah, 2019).

While the emphasis on human capital and entrepreneurship is key to economic development, labour force participation rates have largely increased as countries industrialize, not just through rural–urban migration but also following increasing enrolment in education. The old debate had focused extensively on the Keynesian kinked Phillips curve relationship between inflation and unemployment and the Lewis (1962) turning point as labour flows from agriculture helped support industrialization. While these debates have continued to re-emerge during moments of boom and busts, the discussion has moved on to the creation of an educated labour force that can support rapid growth and structural change. Saxenian (1994, 2006), and Rasiah (2004), and Rasiah, Lin, and Muniratha (2015) showed how such human capital evolved from the world's leading national innovation systems were accessed by some governments to lead technological catch-ups. While this segment of labour is generally acknowledged as a necessary force in economic development, several countries have also been characterized by formal and informal inflows of less-skilled labour, such as maids, construction and restaurant helpers, and agricultural labourers. Hence, inevitably any efforts to conceive a prosperous and peaceful Malaysia over the future must address such labour force issues.

In the discussion on human capital and its impact illustrated by the analysis above, how human capital is acquired is typically given scant attention, it is assumed that human capital is created primarily by education. This is a major oversight. Globalization has increased the mobility of and competition for talent and skilled labour. Attracting talent from other countries represents a viable alternative to educating the local population, as Singapore has shown. Arguably, an even more attractive strategy may be to attract diaspora home with the right incentives or to promote networking through "brain circulation" and "brain gain" initiatives (Saxenian, 2006). Rasiah (1994) and Saxenian (1994) had already showed evidence of how firms act as invisible colleges to generate experiential and tacit knowledge embodied in humans. While only a few countries have witnessed success in pursuit of these strategies, Korea, Taiwan, and increasingly China being prime examples, the experience garnered by both successes and failures points to growing prosperity at home complemented by attractive policy packages that can make the difference in drawing the diaspora or diasporic brains. For Malaysia, this discussion is particularly relevant, given the sizable talent outflow that has taken place (World Bank, 2011). In addition, Malaysia is home to a large pool of international students mostly in private tertiary institutions who can be tapped to augment the supply of domestically produced human capital.

Also, important on training and skilling is the link between formal skills and workplace practices. Whereas Taylorist division of labour typical of sweatshops that reduced workers to execution skills under the control of supervisors while leaving concept and cognitive tasks in the domain (Braverman, 1974), Fordist work organizations gave specialized technical skills a special place among engineers and technicians while automation replaced physical and precision skills of direct workers (Best, 1990). Specific conveyor belts carried specific models in the Fordist system. The introduction of Just-In-Time by Toyota transformed work organization further as Toyota integrated production layouts to singular multiple product lines (Best, 2001). These developments benefited enormously from the introduction of kaizen (continuous improvement) as production and process operations experienced constant change to eliminate defects and shorten throughput time (Rasiah, 1988). Demand for technical and vocational education training (TVET) increased as firms sought precision engineering and automatic machinery to undertake high precision manufacturing to raise yields and eliminate defects. These dimensions have since undergone massive changes as robotization, digital infrastructure and big data has started to drive the replacement of mass production with mass customization (Dayita, Rasiah, & Sameer, 2020). These Industry 4.0 features are now promising a major pillar that will shape the building block of entrepreneurship and human capital development over the next fifty years.

Finance

Finance is a major topic in economic development. Four main models have evolved to explain the financing of economic growth among countries starting from the bottom of the technology trajectory. Feldman's (1928) and later Mahalanobis' (1953) focused on targeting capital goods production to support the production of domestic consumption goods. The focus here was on domestic accumulation based on a closed economy and without a significant assessment of savings, which explains why such models have generally disappeared since.

The Solow (1956, 1957) and later the Solow-Romer (1986) neoclassical model of relative prices determining the choice between capital and labour in production, and existing demand patterns. Capital accumulation is the basis of economic growth but is driven by factor endowments with technical change captured in static terms. Capital market convertibility and flexible exchange rates are critical in such models. The International Monetary Fund (IMF) and the World Bank largely follow such prescriptions by arguing that it not only offers economies the right direction to stimulate economic growth with little factor distortions but also keeps such economies away from the balance of payments problems and debt overhang.

The McKinnon–Shaw model of financial repression became famous following the South Korean experience as the government introduced high arbitrage differentials to penalize the savers and reward the investors (McKinnon, 1989). It also allowed the government through government-owned banks till 1985 to service its huge external debt borrowed to finance economic development. However, such a financial regime required a strong state to prevent nationals from transferring money out, and also to ensure that the subsidized interest rates facing targeted chaebols were governed carefully to prevent rent dissipation. The Won's exchange rate with the USD was also fixed between the late 1960s and 1985s (Chang, 1994). Rodrik (2006) argued that capital accumulation, which easily solved balance of payments and debt service problems. was the basis of economic growth. Rodrik (2012) subsequently argued that such a framework also explains the rapid economic growth achieved by Taiwan and China. Summers (2002) had argued that domestic savings need not be an essential requirement (as capital can come from abroad) while making the case that integration into the global economy is a major requirement. Both Summers and Rodrik argue that it is important to address how capital was sought, and how growth was managed. However, none of these works addresses technological progress as they claim that latecomers can simply purchase or absorb technology from abroad.

It is in this context, that Schumpeterian notions of state intervention to support innovative activities become crucial. The subsidization of funds driven at the catch-up experiences in Japan (Johnson, 1981), South Korea (Amsden, 1989), Taiwan (Wade, 1990), and the knowledge networks that evolved as with the American Silicon Valley and Route 128 models (Best, 2001), the Technopolis framework of France, Taiwan's ITRI framework, and the Vinnova models (Rasiah, 2019) are important examples of how small firms and start-ups have managed to connect to knowledge networks to innovate at the frontier. Arguments to support catch up and leapfrogging, which is critical when countries, such as Malaysia develop, are central to the allocation of capital.

Labour

Labour is a critical component of economic development. Not only that development eventually is targeted at the upliftment of living standards of the people with labour being a key component, but the process itself is largely also driven by labour. As countries undergo a transition from labour surplus to labour scarce economies, wages rise. However, economies tend to face overheating if the technology levels cannot support improvements in wages to reflect the relative demand for labour. In other words, real wages should rise if such economies are to remain competitive globally.

Typical of early developers the government in Malaysia imposed draconian laws to favour capital over labour right through colonial and independent Malaysia. Unions were suppressed and laws were enacted to restrict pickets, undermine labour sympathizers, as well as prevent all together in pioneering industries (Rasiah, 1993; 1989).

Environment

The fifth building block deals with the environment, which the early movers did not focus on. Clearly, Malaysia's leap into the future must be achieved through an increasing switch from environment unfriendly to environment-friendly technologies. The Limits to Growth exponents had argued that the world is largely a finite body that cannot accommodate unlimited growth over the short and medium term (Meadows et al., 1972). This argument follows from Malthus' (1798) argument about the poverty trap envisaged through the arithmetic projection of food production against the geometric projection of population (see also Erhlich, 1971). While Penayatou (1995) helped surmount the problem of the population bomb by introducing the environmental Kuznets curve that posited improvements in environmental standards once a certain threshold of per capita income is reached as the marginal utility for the environment equals and exceeds the marginal utility for material growth, it still left behind the problem of how much more environmental damage the world will have to face for every country to develop. This argument remained a problem as the environment is a global common that if damaged will have serious repercussions for all inhabiting the earth (Hardin, 1968).

Nevertheless, following the convincing evidence advanced by Stern (2007) and Nordhaus (2008) it is now increasingly clear that latecomers need not slow down economic growth as climate change and global warming are consequences of human activity that destroys the ozone layer. Indeed, it is in recognition of these facts that 195 of the 196 United Nations members signed the Paris Declaration in 2015 to cap temperature rise over the next century to 1.5 °C (COP21, 2015). Malaysia subsequently submitted its Intended Nationally Determined Contribution (INDC) to the UFCCC (2015) to reduce carbon emissions by 35% on its own, and an additional 10% through technology transfer from the developed countries by 2030. Hence, institutions through the introduction of an incentive framework (perhaps a carbon tax) must guide economic agents in the country to step up the introduction of and utilization of backstop technologies. Mathews (2015) offers a lucid account of how China and India have been switching to green energy to power their economic growth.

Healthcare

Efforts to transform Malaysia into not just a prosperous location but also one that will be liveable and enjoyable requires addressing important social planks. Healthcare is one of them. The current trend of increased commercialization cannot be viewed as the solution (Rasiah, Tumin, Latifa, & Ndoma, 2016). First, a developed country must offer this utility to all with minimal costs. Second, a developed country must enable its research faculties to anticipate and overcome deadly diseases and other unwanted ailments. Thus, it is important for this building block to envisage how healthcare should be structured and delivered to Malaysian citizens as a whole over the future.

An ageing population brings further challenges to strengthening the country's healthcare services. While the quantum and nature of health services must necessarily change as the population ages, the resources for healthcare provision will also come under pressure as the proportion of contributors to social protection schemes diminishes while that of beneficiaries of social protection grows.

This book will focus on not just the direction of healthcare, by way of services delivery and the production of health goods and services through R&D, but also the nature of financing is critical to ensure that it is provided to all citizens as it is a public utility. Unlike public goods, public goods are excludable and rivalrous but being a basic essential of life healthcare should reach all of them.

Reaching the Envisioned Future

The attempt to achieve the envisioned future by 2050 would require a transformation in three national elements, viz., institutions, organizations, and firms, and individuals. As defined by North (1994), institutions and the "rules of the game", while organizations, firms, and individuals are the players. Social, political, and economic institutions mould the conduct of organizations, firms, and individuals (see also Veblen, 1915; Nelson & Winter, 1982). The government is obviously the most complex and important super-organization that will play a critical role in the transformation.

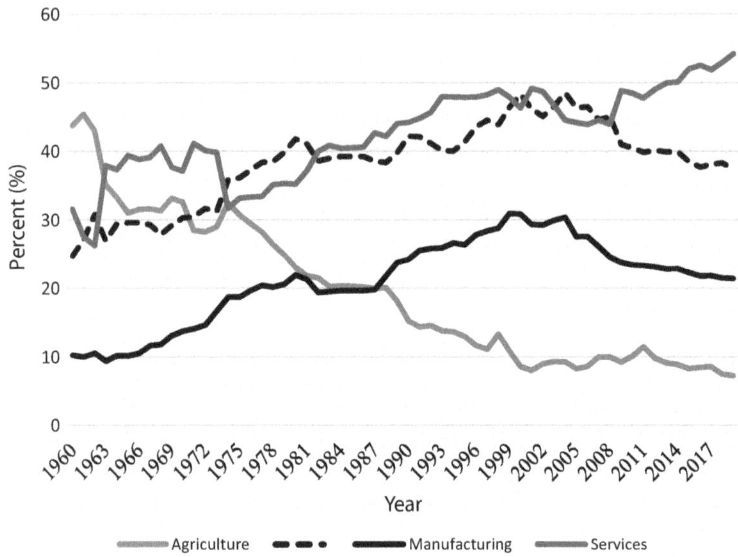

Fig. 1.1 GDP by sectors, Malaysia, 1960–2019. *Notes* Industry constituted by manufacturing, mining and construction. *Source* World Bank (2020); Bank Negara Malaysia (various reports)

The critical economic building block shall emphasize structural change. While typical economies undergo a transformation in specialization from primary sectors (especially agriculture) to secondary sectors (especially manufacturing), and eventually to services, the arguments on their dynamics emphasize that each of these sectors and their components undergo a shift from low to high value added activities. Hence, although the Malaysian economic structure experienced a gradual fall in the share of agriculture in GDP since the 1960s, and manufacturing in GDP since 2000 as services have taken over the leading sector in the country (Fig. 1.1) there are questions over whether both sectors have continued to enjoy a rise in productivity and wages. Yusof and Nabeshima (2009) address some of the policy shortcomings faced by the tiger economies of Southeast Asia with a focus on Malaysia. Rasiah and Salih (2019) showed evidence to argue that agriculture enjoyed productivity growth from the 1970s until the early 1980s in rural small-scale farming and plantation agriculture, but the former has gradually stagnated since the mid-1980s so much so that net food trade has worsened over the period 1989–2019.

Concerns over whether the Southeast East Asian second-tier economies of Indonesia, Malaysia, the Philippines, and Thailand can still compete internationally were raised by, among others, Yusof and Evenett (2002), and Rasiah (2010), arguing that major changes in innovation capacity will be necessary to sustain further expansion especially in manufacturing. Meanwhile, Rasiah (2011) offered evidence to argue that Malaysia has been facing premature deindustrialization with productivity and wages growing slowly since 2000. Besides, the services sector has grown without a significant rise in productivity and wages. These arguments were reinforced by Hill et al. (2014) who consider Malaysia as a country facing the middle-income trap. In doing so, the subsequent chapters start first with a comparative assessment of Malaysia's economic performance against the Northeast and Southeast Asian countries. This shall then be followed by an attempt to examine the future with a profound understanding of population growth trends and changes in demographic structure, and subsequently existing and required development financing. Consequently, the subsequent chapters will address not only the problems facing agriculture, manufacturing and services but also the path the country should take to stimulate technological upgrading to support productivity and wage growth.

While economic development is important, a vibrant and developed Malaysia in the future will also require the essence of planning to address population projections, the financing of the economic transformation and sustenance issues. Critical in future Malaysia will be for economic development to enjoy a balance with environmental harmony, access to education and health, elimination of poverty, and socioeconomic equality. The subsequent chapters seek to the state of these issues but with a strong focus on how planning should shape the desired future for the country.

Thus, each of the building blocks will focus on changes in the institutional setting necessary to stimulate Malaysia's leap into its desired future (see Fig. 1.2). In doing so, the desired goals will be presented taking account of opportunities and threats, arising from domestic and international fronts. In the first part, the emphasis will be on technological catch-up and leapfrogging in the sectors that will propel and sustain high wages and competitiveness of Malaysia's exports, viz, agriculture, manufacturing and services. In the second part, the focus will be on the evolution expected

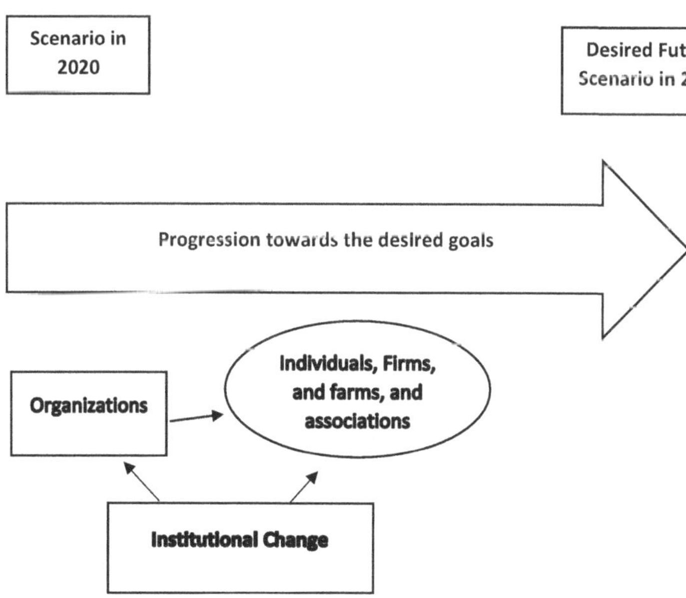

Fig. 1.2 Planning the future

of living conditions through changes in population and demography, urbanization, education, and labour markets. The third part will address essential welfare elements, such as socio-economic equality, healthcare, and environment.

All chapters discuss changes in institutions necessary to govern and sustain changes in the respective focal areas, followed by changes in organizations' collective actions. Organizations, (which are necessary to solve collective action problems), will serve to deliver output essential for supporting the activities of firms, individuals and associations, (such as R&D services, education and training), which in some cases can also be delivered directly (e.g. universities and hospitals).

Outline of Book

Following this introductory chapter, Perkins, Rasiah, and Woo (2021) evaluate Malaysia's economic growth, and the key drivers of innovation and education comparatively to locate the country against similar countries but with a special focus on the Northeast and Southeast Asian countries. While acknowledging the remarkable success Malay has achieved, they point out that Malaysia has largely underperformed against the Northeast Asian countries and Singapore. In addition, they also argue that the innovation capabilities and education output of Malaysia require a significant overhaul to catch up with these countries.

In Chap. 3, Tey (2022) discusses the gradual slowing down of population growth in Malaysia, and the consequent changes in the demographic structure of the country. The demographic transition was not uniform across the various sub-groups of the population, with significant changes in the population composition. He argues that more population research is required in future for Malaysia to address better the specific issues facing the country regionally, ethnically and socially.

Lau (2022) examines in Chap. 4 the key issues on financing development in Malaysia. He argues that the evolving financial system must drive future growth through innovation and exploit to the fullest current and future financial technology through the industry 4.0 technologies that require the increasing deployment of the digitalized infrastructure, data-driven financing, Crypto currencies, big data analytics, crowdfunding and e-wallets. In doing so, the financial system should become an enabler of future inclusive growth to drive Malaysia's financial architecture.

Chamhuri, Rospidah, and Mohamad (2021) discuss in Chap. 5 the trend fall in the contribution of agriculture in Malaysia in Malaysia's GDP. They argue that the extensive focus on industrialization, and rapid encroachment of industrial and commercial interests have combined to squeeze agriculture. In addition to calling for intensive farming and the introduction of high technology, the chapter addresses a number of issues pertinent to reinvigorating food crops and animal farming to raise self-sufficiency levels.

Rasiah (2021a) starts Chap. 6 by contending that Malaysia is facing premature deindustrialization, pointing to a trend fall in manufacturing's contribution to GDP since 2000 before the sector has graduated to high value added activities to support high wages. He argues that a reinvigoration of the sector is critical through stimulating innovation-driven industrial upgrading with a focus on the electric and electronics, and palm oil industries. Three different models are presented in the chapter to show how firms can upgrade to power value added growth, which is important to drive Malaysia into a developed nation, namely, one, incremental innovations for new product proliferation, catching up and leapfrogging, and the blue ocean strategy of integrating markets and expanding product functions.

In Chap. 7, Chandran (2021) assesses the knowledge-intensive services industry in Malaysia, tracks the contribution and progress of the industry, and assesses its future prospects. While acknowledging the progress made in the industry, the chapter notes that its contribution to value added activities and exports remain low. Despite Malaysia's agenda for a knowledge-based economy, he provides evidence to show that it lags behind the levels seen in other emerging countries. Given the important role of the knowledge-intensive services sector in catalyzing the productive transformation of other sectors, he argues that efforts must be taken to upgrade the industry to spur inter-industry knowledge spillover.

Selvaratnam (2021) discusses in Chap. 8 critical education policies and their consequences on the labour force of Malaysia. While acknowledging the massive funding education has received over the decades, he argues that a lack of emphasis on the critical drivers, such as merit and reach has undermined the quality of graduates at all levels, including primary, secondary and tertiary. In addition to calling for the use of instruments that raise quality, he also argues that emphasis on the English language must be brought back for the labour force of the future to be competitive internationally.

Following the discussion in Chap. 8, Cheong and Lee (2022) take up the issue of talent acquisition, retention, and management. The discussion context is framed in the context of a "talent war" in which the advanced countries have a clear advantage and in which Malaysia also have an important stake as it strives to become an advanced country. Beginning with a clarification of talent development, this chapter proceeds to examine where Malaysia is today, using aggregate indices and international education benchmarks. Malaysia's quality deficits are clearly displayed, made worse by a sizeable "brain drain" from a relatively narrow human capital base. And it has not been helped by the country's unfocused efforts to develop talent. Yet, as the chapter shows, ways to develop talent do exist through education supported by a strong Technical and Vocational Education and Training (TVET) system, attracting talent, and retaining talent. This chapter concludes with the observation that talent development can be achieved; the question is whether the commitment exists.

Chap. 10 Kuppusamy and Salih (2021) examine in Chap. 10 urbanization, the growth of cities and infrastructure in Malaysia, contending that its governance has been uneven with little coordination between the different stakeholders. They call for renewal and modernization of the infrastructure over the next three decades. The future governance of urbanization and infrastructure, they argue, must be proactive with the deployment of accountable city managers and councillors who should be made answerable to the people rather than to political masters.

In Chap. 11, Cheong and Yong (2022) take up the challenges of the country's labour force. Starting with the reliance on low-skill immigrant labour, the legacy of Malaysia's early labour-intensive industrialization that has militated against industrial through technology, they noted other forms of industrial malaise such as premature deindustrialization, abetted by the shift to services. Structural issues also dogged Malaysia's social system, resulting in low participation rates of females in the workforce, as well as gender discrimination at work. As alluded in Chap. 2, pervasive affirmative action in education has led not only to the unintended consequence of disincentivising the production of science and technology graduates but also brain drain, the latter greatly facilitated by the geographical proximity of high-income Singapore and Malaysia's tradition of sending students overseas to pursue their studies.

To the extent that many of the damages to the country's labour force are self-inflicted, Cheong and Yong (2022) are hopeful that by the year 2050, leaders with vision can put things right. While as Doner and Schneider (2016) predicted, that problems leading to the "middle-income trap" are "more politics than economics", this chapter concludes with the optimistic view that an idealized long-term scenario for Malaysia's labour force is achievable.

Rasiah (2021b) reviews Chap. 12 the policies and the critical pillars that helped reduce poverty and inequality in Malaysia. While he acknowledges the importance of the New Economic Policy of 1971 in driving rural development and export manufacturing, he argues that the ethnic restructuring policies were largely counterproductive. In fact, he contends that ethnic restructuring beyond its elimination from occupational polarization in estates, mines, and businesses has been compromised by the heavy concentration of Bumiputeras in the civil service. He also provides evidence to show that both absolute and relative poverty only improved from 2012 following the distribution of cash vouchers. He calls for all future policies in the country to shed ethnic colouration to promote ethnic integration, which has been the rallying call of the country's single most important national integration blueprint, i.e. the *Rukun Negara.*

In Chap. 13, Melvin, Yin, Yunus, Elvinson, Tan, and Ng (2021) use a case study of both youngsters and experts to envisage the environment they desire in Malaysia's future. Unlike typical works on the environment that focus on addressing climate change and global warming from the perspective of climate change scientists, they take on an inclusive approach to let the potential future inhabitants of Malaysia address these issues. While respondents call for awareness creation through education, stringent curbs on environment abuse through stricter laws and exposure to environmental issues, they argue that these efforts will have to be taken in the coordination of a wider set of management and administrative procedures, focus on concentrations of human settlements, and community groups, including non-government organizations and government agencies dealing with them.

Chapter 14 by Muhairah and Yap (2021) examine the Malaysian public and private health systems, together with the issues arising therefrom and analyses the opportunities and threats facing the sector. It notes that the public healthcare system, being the main provider, has increasingly encountered difficulties in providing adequate delivery of healthcare, (including on geriatrics), while lacking basic medical programmes for immigrants. Acknowledging that the private healthcare providers are profit-driven and largely cluster around large towns and cities, they argue that Malaysia's future healthcare sector should be upgraded through adapting the intermediate pathway of the Australian health system. They also propose that every person residing in Malaysia should be entitled to enjoy the maximum life expectancy and an advanced level of healthcare through the provision of both primary and secondary preventive care.

References

Abramovitz, M. (1956). Resource and output trends in the United States since 1870. In *Resource and output trends in the United States since 1870* (pp. 1–23). NBER.

Akamatsu, K. (1962). A historical pattern of economic growth in developing countries. *Journal of Developing Economies, 1*(1), 3–25.

Amsden, A. (1989). *Asia's next giant: South Korea and late industrialization*. Oxford University Press.

Anand, S., & Segar, P. (2008). What do we know about global income inequality? *Journal of Economic Literature, 46*(1), 57–94.

Anita, D. (2015). Has Malaysia escaped the resource curve? *A Closer Look at the Political Economy of Oil Revenue Management and Expenditures. Resources Policy, 45*, 98–108.

Arkelof, G. A., & Kranton, R. E. (2002). Identity and schooling: Some lessons for the economics of education. *Journal of Economic Literature, 40*(4), 1167–1201.

Becker, G. (1994). *Human capital: A theoretical and empirical analysis with special reference to education*. University of Chicago Press.

Best, M. H. (2001). *The new competitive advantage*. Oxford University Press.

Braverman, H. (1974). *Labor and monopoly capital*. Monthly Review Press.

Chang, H. J. (1994). *The political economy of industrial policy*. Macmillan.

Cheong, K. C., & Yong, C. C. (2022). In R. Rasiah, K Salih, & K. C. Cheong, (Eds.), *Malaysia's Leap into the Future: The Building Blocks for Balanced Development*. Singapore: Springer.

Corden, W. M., & Neary, J. P. (1982). Booming sector and de-industrialisation in a small open economy. *Economic Journal, 92*(368), 825–848.

Doner, R., & Scheider (2016). The middle income trap: more politics than economics. *World Politics, 68*(4), 608–644.

Ehrlich, P. R. (1971). *The population bomb*. International Publishers.

Ellman, M. & Kontorovich, V. (Eds.) (1991). The Disintegration of the Soviet economic system, London: Routledge.

Etzkowitz, H. (2002) Technology transfer: The second academic revolution. *Technology Access, 6*, 7–9.

Etzkowitz, H., & Leydesdor, L. (1995) The Triple Helix—University-Industry-Government Relations: A Laboratory for Knowledge Based Economic Development, Rochester: Social Science Research Network.

Feldman, G. A. (1928). On the theory of growth rates of national income. Translated into English in 1964 in Spulber, N. (Eds.). *Foundations of soviet strategy for economic growth*. Bloomington: Indiana University Press.

Fields, G. (2001). *Distribution and development: A new look at the developing world*. MIT Press.

Frank, A. G. (1998). *Reorient global economy in the Asian age*. University of California Press.

Geertz, C. (1963). *Agricultural involution: The process of ecological change in Indonesia*. University of California Press.

Gerschenkron, A. (1952). Economic backwardness in historical perspective'. In B. F. Hoselitz (ed), *The progress of underdeveloped areas* (pp. 3–29). Chicago: University of Chicago Press.
Hamilton, A. (1791). Report to congress on the subject of manufactures. Accessed 23 September 2020. http://nationalhumanitiescenter.org/pds/livingrev/politics/text2/hamilton.pdf.
Hardin, G. (1968). The tragedy of commons. *Science, 162*(3859), 1243–1248.
Hill, H., Tham, S. Y., & Ragayah, M. Z. (2014). *Malaysia's development challenges: Graduating from the middle*. Routledge.
Hirschman, A. (1970). *Exit, voice, and loyalty: Responses to decline in firms, organizations, and states*. Harvard University Press.
Hirschman, A. O. (1958). *The strategy of economic development*. Yale University Press.
Kaldor, N. (1967). *Strategic factors in economic growth*. Cornell University Press.
Kim, L. (1997). *Imitation to innovation: The dynamics of Korea's technological learning*. Harvard business press.
Krugman, P. (1999). The role of geography in development. *International Regional Science Review, 22*(2), 142–161.
Kuznets, S. (1955). Economic growth and income inequality. *American Economic Review, 45*(1), 1–30.
Landes, D. S. (1999). *The wealth and poverty of nations: Why some are so rich and some so poor*. Abacus.
Lau, W. Y. (2022) Financing Development. In R. Rasiah, K. Salih, & K. C. Cheong (Eds.), *Malaysia's Leap Into the Future: The Building Blocks for Balanced Development*, Singapore: Springer.
Lenin, V. I. (1917). The tasks of the proletariat in the present revolution. *Lenin's Collected Works*, 19–26.
Lewis, W. A. (1954). Economic development with unlimited supplies of labour. *The Manchester School, 22*(2), 139–191.
List, F. (1886) The national political economy system.
Lucas, R. (1988). On the mechanics of economic development. *Journal of Monetary Economics, 22*(1), 3–42.
Luxembourg, R. (1967). *The accumulation of capital*. Progress publishers.
Mahalanobis, P. C. (1953). Some observations on the process of growth of national income. *Sankhyā: The Indian Journal of Statistics (1933–1960), 12*(4), 307–312.
Malaysia. (1981). *Fourth Malaysia plan 1981–1985*. Kuala Lumpur: Government Printers.
Malaysia. (1991). The Sixth Malaysia Plan 1991–1995, Kuala Lumpur: Government Printers.
Malaysia. (2020). National Fourth Industrial Revolution (4IR) Policy, Putrajaya: Economic Planning Unit.
Malthus, T. R. (1798). *An essay on the principle of population*. Chapter V, (pp. 39–45). Oxford: Oxford World's Classics reprint.
Mao, Z. D. (1957). *On the correct handling of contradictions among the people*. Foreign Languages Press.
Marx, K. (1957). *Capital: Critique of political economy* (Vol. One). Foreign Languages Press.
Mathews, J. A. (2015). *Greening capitalism: How Asia is driving the next great transformation*. Stanford University Press.
McGee, T. (1971). *The urbanization process in the third world*. G. Bell & Sons.
McKinnon, R. I. (1989). Financial liberalization and economic development: A reassessment of interest-rate policies in Asia and Latin America. *Oxford Review of Economic Policy, 5*(4), 29–54.
Meadows, D. H., Meadows, D. L., Randers, J., & Behrens, W. W. (1972). *A report for the club of Rome's project on the predicament of mankind*. Universe Books.
Mincer, J. (1958). Investment in human capital and personal income distribution. *Journal of Political Economy, 66*(4), 281–302.
Myrdal, G. (1968). *Asian drama—An inquiry into the poverty of nations*. Penguin.
Nelson, R. R., & Winter, S. G. (1982). *An evolutionary theory of economic change*. Harvard University Press.

Nordhaus, W. D. (2008). *A question of balance—Weighing the options on global warming policies*. Yale University Press.
North, D. C. (1994). Economic performance through time. *American Economic Review, 84*(3), 359–368.
Nurkse, R. (1961). *Problems of capital formation in underdeveloped countries*. Oxford University Press.
Palma, J. G. (2006). Globalizing inequality: 'Centrifugal' and 'centripetal' forces at work. In *Working Papers 35*. New York: United Nations, Department of Economics and Social Affairs.
Palma, J. G. (2011). Homogeneous middles versus heterogeneous tails, and the end of the 'Inverted-U': It's all about the share of the rich. *Development and Change, 42*(1), 87–153.
Palma, J. G. (2014). Has the income share of the middle and upper-middle been stable around the '50/50 Rule', or has it converged towards that level? The 'Palma Ratio' revisited. *Development and Change, 45*(6), 1416–1418.
Penrose, E. (1959). *The theory of the growth of the firm*. John Wiley & Sons.
Perkins, D. H. (2013). *East Asian development: Foundations and strategies*. Harvard University Press.
Polanyi, M. (1967). Sense-giving and sense-reading. *Philosophy, 42*(162), 301–325.
Pomeranz, K. (2000). *The great divergence: China, Europe, and the making of the modern world economy*. Princeton University Press.
Prebisch, R. (1949). Growth, disequilibrium and disparities: interpretation of the process of economic development. *Economic Survey of Latin America, 1949-E/CN. 12/164/Rev. 1-1951 p.* 3-85.
Rasiah, R. (1988). The semiconductor industry in Penang: Implications for the new international division of labour theories. *Journal of Contemporary Asia, 18*(1), 24–46.
Rasiah, R. (1993). Free trade zones and industrial development in Malaysia. In K. S. Jomo (Ed.), *Industrializing Malaysia: Policy, performance, prospects*. London: Routledge.
Rasiah, R. (1994). Flexible production systems and local machine tool subcontracting: Electronics transnationals in Malaysia. *Cambridge Journal of Economics, 18*(3).
Rasiah, R., Ishak, S., & Jomo, K.S. (1996). Globalizationand Liberalization: Implications for Growth, Inequality and Poverty in East and Southeast Asia. In A. Woodfield, (Ed.), *Globalization and Liberalization and its Implications for Growth, Poverty and Inequality*. Geneva: UNCTAD.
Rasiah, R. (2010). Industrialization in the second tier NIEs. In R. Rasiah, & J. D. Schmidt (Eds.), *The new political economy of Southeast Asia*. Cheltenham: Edward Elgar.
Rasiah, R. (2011). Is Malaysia facing negative deindustrialization? *Pacific Affairs, 84*(4), 714–735.
Rasiah, R., & Pietrobelli, C. (2012). Sanjaya Lall: A consummate development theorist and policy advocate. In C. Pietrobelli, & R. Rasiah (Eds.), *Evidence-based development economics: Essays in honor of Sanjaya Lall*. Kuala Lumpur: University of Malaya Press.
Rasiah, R., Al-Amin, A. Q., Adeel, A., Filho, W. L., & Calvo, E. (2016). Climate mitigation roadmap: Assessing low carbon scenarios for Malaysia. *Journal of Cleaner Production, 133*(10), 272–283.
Rasiah, R., Lin, Y., & Muniratha, A. (2015). The role of the diaspora in supporting innovation systems: The experience of India, Malaysia and Taiwan. In P. Shome & P. Sharma (Eds.), *Emerging economies* (pp. 353–373). New Delhi: Springer.
Reinert, E. (2007). *How the rich became rich ...*. Anthem Press.
Robinson, S. (1976). A note on the U hypothesis relating income inequality and economic development. *American Economic Review, 66*(3), 437–440.
Rodrik, D. (2006). Goodbye Washington consensus, hello Washington confusion? A review of the World Bank's economic growth in the 1990s: Learning from a decade of reform. *Journal of Economic Literature, 44*(4), 973–987.
Rodrik, D. (2012). Why we learn nothing from regressing economic growth on policies. *Seoul Journal of Economics, 25*(2), 137–151.
Romer, P. M. (1986). Increasing returns and long-run growth. *Journal of Political Economy, 94*(5), 1002–1037.
Rosenberg, N. (1976). *Perspectives on technology*. Cambridge University Press.

Rosenberg, N. (1982). *Inside the black box*. Cambridge University Press.
Rostow, W. W. (1960). *The stages of economic growth: A non-communist manifesto*. Cambridge University Press.
Rowthorn, R. E., & Wells, J. R. (1987). *De-industrialization and foreign trade*. Cambridge University Press.
Sachs, J. D., & Warner, A. M. (1997). Fundamental sources of long-run growth. *The American Economic Review, 87*(2), 184–188.
Saxenian, A. L. (1994). *The regional advantage*. Harvard University Press.
Saxenian, A. L. (2006). *The New Argonauts: Regional advantage in a global economy*. Harvard University Press.
Schumpeter, J. A. (1930). *Theory of economic development*. Harvard University Press.
Schumpeter, J. A. (1943). *Capitalism*. Harvard University Press.
Singer, H. W. (1950). The distribution of gains between borrowing and investing countries. *American Economic Review, 40*(2), 473–485.
Singh, M. A. (1976). Inequality, poverty and development. *Journal of Development Economics, 3*, 307–342.
Smith, A. (1776). *Wealth of nations*. London: Strahan and Cadell.
Solow, R. M. (1956). A contribution to the theory of economic growth. *The Quarterly Journal of Economics, 70*(1), 65–94.
Solow, R. M. (1957). Technical change and the aggregate production function. *The Review of Economics and Statistics, 39*(3), 312–320.
Stern, N. (2007). *The economics of climate change: Stern Review*. Cambridge University Press.
Tey, N. P. (2022). Population and Demography. S. Rasiah, K. C. Cheong (Eds.), *Malaysia's Leap into the Future: The Building Blocks for Balanced Development*. Singapore: Springer.
Toynbee, A. (1934–1960). *A study of history* 1934–1960 (Vol. 1–12). Oxford: Oxford University Press.
Veblen, T. (1915). *Imperial Germany and the industrial revolution*. Macmillan.
Vogel, E. F. (1991). *The four little dragons: The spread of industrialization in East Asia*. Harvard University Press.
Wade, R. (1990). *Governing the market: Theory and the role of government in East Asian industrialization*. Princeton University Press.
Weber, M. (1958). *The protestant ethic and the spirit of capitalism*. Scribner Publications.
Womack, J. P., Jones, D. T., & Roos, D. (2007). *The machine that changed the world: The story of lean production—Toyota's secret weapon in the global car wars that is revolutionizing world industry*. Free Press.
World Bank. (2009). *World Development Report 2010: Development and Climate Change*. New York: Oxford University Press, published for the World Bank.
World Bank. (2011). *Malaysian economic monitor April 2011—Brain drain*. World Bank.
World Bank .(2020). *World development indicators*. Washington D.C.: World Bank Institute.
Young, K., Bussink, W. C. F., & Parvez, H. (1980). *Malaysia: Growth in a Multiracial Society*. Baltimore: Johns Hopkins University Press for the World Bank.
Yusof, S., & Evenett, S. J. (2002). *Can East Asia compete?: Innovation for global markets*. Washington D.C.: World Bank.
Yusof, S., & Nabeshima, K. (2009). *Tiger economies under threat*. Washington D.C.: World Bank.

Rajah Rasiah is Distinguished Professor of Economics at Asia-Europe Institute, Universiti Malaya, and visiting Professor at the Institute of Energy Policy and Research, UNITEN. He received the 2014 Celso Furtado Prize from the World Academy of Sciences for advancing the frontiers of social science (Economics) thought.

Cheong Kee Cheok is currently Senior Research Fellow, Institute of China Studies, and Senior Advisor, Asia Europe Institute, University of Malaya. As a graduate of the University of Malaya, he obtained his Ph.D. at the London School of Economics. Upon his return from studies, he joined the Faculty of Economics and Administration, University of Malaya, where he held the positions of Deputy Dean and Dean of Faculty. After a decade at UM, he spent 16 years at the World Bank in the capacity of Economist and subsequently Senior Economist. At the Bank, he was Coordinator for China and Vietnam in the Economic Development Institute, now the World Bank Institute. After returning to Malaysia in 2000, he has continued as Consultant for the Bank and UN agencies. Back with the University of Malaya since 2010, he has coauthored books, book chapters, and published numerous papers in top-tier academic journals as well as successfully supervised Ph.D. students, both international and local.

Kamal Salih Ph.D. is an Executive Chairman of Ankar Corporation and Chairman of Malaysia Institute of Economic Research (MIER). He has served as Senior Technical Advisor to UNDP Malaysia and was Adjunct Professor of Economics and Development Studies and Senior Advisor to Asia Europe Institute in University Malaya.

Chapter 2
Explaining Malaysia's Past Economic Growth

Dwight Heald Perkins, Rajah Rasiah, and Wing-Thye Woo

Abstract Post-independence Malaysia has achieved significant economic growth: faster than that of most of the developing countries of Africa and Latin America, slower than the tiger economies of Northeast Asia, and similar to the growth rates of several Southeast Asian neighbouring countries. Manufacturing quickly replaced rubber and tin as the dominant growth engine of the country. Government policies particularly with respect to physical infrastructure contributed to manufacturing growth but other government policies, notably the new economic policy of 1971 and the heavy industry policies of the 1980s and 1990s were a drag on overall economic performance. Requirements designed to promote the Bumiputera ownership share of business played a central role in limiting the contribution of domestic manufacturers to Malaysia's rapidly growing manufactured exports. Manufactured exports as a result came mainly from foreign direct investment that were not subject to the ownership requirements. A careful analysis of the innovative capacity of the key sectors of manufacturing indicates some areas where Malaysian firms were innovative, but the rate of innovation in most of the leading sectors has been modest. Limited domestic innovation capacity also helps explain the country's slow total factor productivity growth. Weaknesses in the Malaysian education system are an important component particularly at the tertiary level of why innovation has not progressed more rapidly. Government's pursuit of social goals in the education sector is one part of why the country has not produced enough innovators to support more robust innovative capacity in the country.

D. H. Perkins (✉)
Littauer Center M-14, Department of Economics, Harvard University, Cambrdige, USA
e-mail: dwight_perkins@harvard.edu

R. Rasiah
Asia-Europe Institute, University of Malaya, 50603 Kuala Lumpur, Malaysia
e-mail: rajah@um.edu.my

W.-T. Woo
Jeffrey Cheah Institute On Southeast Asia, Sunway University, 5 Jalan Universiti, 47500 Sunway, Selangor, Malaysia
e-mail: wtwoo@ucdavis.edu

R. Rasiah et al. (eds.), *Malaysia's Leap Into the Future*, Dynamics of Asian Development, https://doi.org/10.1007/978-981-16-7045-9_2

Keywords GDP growth · Bumiputera Ownership · Manufacturing · Productivity · Innovation · Education

Did Malaysia's or any other country's economy perform well or poorly relative to that of other countries? One could also ask whether Malaysia made full use of its potential in promoting growth but a country's potential must also be looked at by comparing it to the highest performing economies at particular times in history. In Malaysia per capita incomes have risen much faster since independence in 1957.[1] Per capita GDP in 2019 was 9.2 times what it was in 1960 in constant prices.

But how does Malaysia's growth performance compare to that of other countries in the world? Compared to the average growth performance of Latin America and Sub-Saharan Africa, Malaysia has done much better. Between 1960 and 2019, the GDP per capita of the Latin American countries taken together increased by 2.5 times and Sub-Saharan Africa by only 1.5 times. Put differently, Malaysia's annual average per capita has grown at 3.8% over the last six decades since independence while that of Latin America and Sub-Saharan Africa have grown at 1.6% a year and 0.7% a year.

The difference between Malaysia's economic growth and that of the other members of ASEAN is less dramatic than the Latin American and Sub-Saharan African comparisons. Malaysia's per capita income is higher than that of other ASEAN members except for Singapore but in terms of growth rates Malaysia's performance exceeded that of Indonesia but was lower than that of Thailand over the entire 1960–2018 period (Table 2.1).

When one compares Malaysia with its Northeast Asian neighbours, the story is quite different (Table 2.2). Japan, South Korea, Taiwan, and Hong Kong all performed at levels comparable to Singapore and China for the past three-plus decades has done comparably well but from a much lower per capita income base.

Table 2.1 Annual average GDP per capita growth, selected countries, 1961–2018 (%)

	1961–70	1971–80	1981–90	1991–2000	2001–10	2011–18	1961–2018
Indonesia	1.8	5.4	4.4	2.7	4	3.9	3.2
Vietnam	NA	NA	NA	5.9	5.9	5.7	NA
Philippines	1.8	3.1	−0.9	0.8	2.8	4.9	1.8
Thailand	5.1	4.3	5.9	3.5	3.4	2.5	4.2
Malaysia	3.4	5.3	3.1	4.4	2.7	3.7	3.8
Cambodia	NA	NA	NA	NA	6.1	5.5	NA
Singapore	4.4	7.2	4.9	4.6	3.4	2.5	5.0

Source Computed from World Bank (2020)

[1] For Malaysia's economic performance before independence, and its comparison with the period after independence see Sultan Nazrin Shah (2017, 2019).

Table 2.2 Annual average GDP per capita growth, selected countries, 1961–2018 (%)

	1961–70	1971–80	1981–90	1991–2000	2001–2010	2011–2018	1961–2018
China	1.0	4.3	7.7	9.3	9.8	6.6	6.7
Hong Kong	7.7	6.9	5.4	2.3	3.5	1.9	4.4
Taiwan	7.0	7.9	6.4	5.7	2.3	2.4	NA
Japan	9.8	3.3	4	0.9	0.8	1.6	5.7
Republic of Korea	5.7	5.4	7.5	5.1	3.7	2.4	6.0
Malaysia	3.4	5.3	3.1	4.4	2.7	3.7	3.8

Source Computed from World Bank (2019); National Statistics Republic of China (Taiwan) (www.eng.stat.gov.tw) August 27, 2020

A reasonable question to ask is why did Malaysia not grow as rapidly as its Northeast Asian neighbours? Was there something fundamentally different about the Malaysian economy that prevented it from doubling per capita income every seven or eight years as happened in Northeast Asia and Singapore? Malaysia like Northeast Asia had peace and comparative political stability throughout this six-decade period, it had natural resources that were far superior to those of Northeast Asia, and it started from a per capita income base comparable at least to South Korea and Taiwan and considerably higher than that of China. Was Malaysia instead held back by specific government policies? And if government policies inhibited growth, how was it that Malaysia's economy still performed far better than the economies of most of Latin America and Sub-Saharan Africa?

The challenge of this chapter is to provide answers for these questions to offer the platform for speculating about the future, and suggestions of how Malaysia could eventually catch up with the high-income countries of the world. The term "middle-income trap", while is widely used is seldom defined. We will define it as experiencing a decline in the country's GDP per capita growth rate to a degree where a country is no longer catching up with high-income countries. The CUI or Catch-up Index measures the degree to which a country's per capita GDP falls short of that of the United States.[2]

The evidence for the middle-income trap for Malaysia from the movements in their CUIs are mixed depending on the data source; the original 2010 Maddison dataset which ends in 2008, the revised 2018 Maddison Project dataset which ends in 2016, and the 2020 World Bank dataset which begins in 1990 and ends in 2019.[3] The CUI increased by an annual average of 0.28% points with a range of 0.16–0.49

---

[2] The CUI Index was first used to our knowledge by Woo (2011) to express the standing of living in a country as a percentage of the US standard of living, with GDP measured in PPP$. Woo (2012) applied this concept to analyze the growth prospects of China, and Woo (forthcoming) applied it to Malaysia.

[3] The two Maddison datasets (which begins in 1 A.D.) are from https://www.rug.nl/ggdc/historicaldevelopment/maddison/releases/; and the Word Bank dataset (which begins in 1990) is the 2020

for the 1996–2008 period; and 0.47% point with a range of 0.26–0.67 for the longer 1996–2016 period.[4] The higher catch-up rate after 2008 had more to do with the economic recovery of Malaysia from the 2008 Global Financial Crisis being faster than that of the United States, and not because of a new higher trend growth rate in Malaysia after 2008.

Comparing the catch-up growth in Malaysia in the 1996–2019 period with those of its East Asian neighbours, Malaysia performed marginally better than Thailand but markedly worse than South Korea. Malaysia closed its development gap with the United States by 6.5% points, Thailand closed it by 5.2% points, and South Korea reduced it by 16.9% points.[5] This much higher speed in catch-up growth in South Korea (being two and half times larger than Malaysia and Thailand) is certainly impressive and raises many troubling questions about possible growth inhibitors within Malaysia and Thailand.[6]

The data clearly indicate that the CUI for Malaysia has not been stagnant through 2019 at least, and this was also the case for most of the other nations of Southeast Asia, suggesting that Southeast Asia has not been caught in the strictest version of the middle-income trap where the value of the CUI had stayed unchanged over time (Myanmar was in a low-income trap for several decades, however). Much of Latin America, in contrast, has been in the middle-income trap for decades. For example, CUI for Mexico stood at 25.9% in 1970, 37.9% in 1980, 26.4% in 1990, 24.7% in 2000, 29.0% in 2010, and 29.8% in 2016.

To show the comparative picture more starkly, the GDP per capita in 2011US$ in Thailand was $2,720 in 1976 and $14,341 in 2016 (an increase of 5.3 times), South Korea was $5.478 and $36,151, respectively (6.6 times), Malaysia was $5,488 and $22,687, respectively (4.1 times), Mexico was $8,696 and $15,803, respectively (1.8 times), and the United States was $27,059 and $53,015 respectively (2 times).[7] In short, Mexico has not been closing its developmental gap with the rich countries and can be clearly described as caught in the middle-income trap, while South Korea has leaped over the middle-income trap and moving decisively to equal Japan and Western Europe in prosperity. As Malaysia is growing much slower than South

World Development Indicators at https://data.worldbank.org/indicator/NY.GDP.PCAP.PP.CD?locations=MY. The three datasets were accessed on 15 September 2020.

[4] The estimates for the 1996–2008 period were computed from the three datasets; and the ones for the 2006–2016 period were calculated from the last two datasets. The CUI is based on World Bank data stood at 38.8% in 1996, 40.7% in 2008, 44.1% in 2016, and 45.3% in 2019.

[5] The World Bank-based CUI value for Malaysia was at 38.8% in 1996 and 45.3% in 2019; Thailand was 24.4 and 29.5%; and South Korea was 49.1 and 66.1%. Averaging the 2018 Maddison data and 2020 World Bank data. The CUI for Thailand grew at annual average of 0.25% in the 1996–2016 period with a range of 0.22 to 0.29; while the CUI for South Korea grew an annual average of 0.94% point with a range of 0.93 and 0.96 (compared with 0.47 and a range of 0.26–0.67 for Malaysia).

[6] Further examination of the data confirms that this conclusion about the difference in catch-up growth performance between Malaysia and Thailand being small and the difference between Malaysia and South Korea being very large is a robust conclusion. The 2018 Maddison-based CUI index reports a 1976–2016 gain of 22.5% points for Malaysia, 17.0% points for Thailand, and 47.9% points for South Korea.

[7] Data in this sentence and in the previous sentence are from the revised 2018 Maddison Project.

Korea and Taiwan out of the middle-income phase, in fact, moving even slower than Thailand, there are reasons to be concerned about whether the pace of its crawl could slow down to be closer to that of Mexico. It is the most important question that this chapter seeks to answer.

To answer the questions about Malaysia's overall economic performance we start with an analysis at an economy-wide level looking at some of the characteristics of Malaysian society and institutions that have influenced growth. We then turn to a quantitative analysis of the degree to which Malaysian growth resulted mainly from high levels of investment or whether it also enjoyed rising productivity. These macro-level analyses, however, take us only a limited distance towards an answer so we then turn to an in-depth analysis at a more micro level of Malaysia's industrial and service sector performance. That analysis provides a basis for an analysis of the prospects for Malaysia avoiding the "middle-income trap" and moving steadily up to high-income status.

Sources of Growth

In a period of nearly six decades Malaysia has risen from a country where a large majority of the population was quite poor and the average per capita income of the entire population calculated at the official exchange rate with the US dollar was US$1400 (in 2010 prices). The structure of the Malaysian economy has been transformed from one dependent on agriculture and tin mines to one dominated by the growth and share in GDP of industry by the 1990s. That transformation was followed by a second shift where growth since 2000 is driven more by services. The share of manufacturing in GDP levelled off and then in 2006 began to slowly decline. Agriculture, despite being a country covered with palm oil plantations and small holders, has fallen to only 10% of GDP (see Chamhuri, Rospidah, & Mohamad, 2021). Mining has remained a large share of GDP at 16% largely because of the rise of the petroleum sector beginning in the 1980s.

Malaysia's growth, however, has been quite volatile at least in comparison with the Northeast Asian economies that were going through a similar transformation of their economic structure and doing so at roughly the same time. Both Southeast Asia and Northeast Asia promoted manufacturing expansion. Figure 2.1 shows, the contribution of manufacturing to the GDP of Malaysia and some Southeast Asian countries. Whereas deindustrialization in Singapore has emerged after it had long become developed, the remaining countries have been facing it when they are still in the middle-income category. The rising role of manufactured exports, however, has made Malaysia dependent on income fluctuations in high-income countries that buy most of Malaysia's exports, which accounts for recessions in Malaysia in 1975, 1985–86, and 2008–09. Although a cyclical downturn in the electronics industry caused a sharp fall in manufactured exports (Rasiah, 1988), the sharp downturn in 1985–86 was primarily caused by government austerity policies made necessary by the rapid buildup of debt resulting from the heavy industry programme as the prices

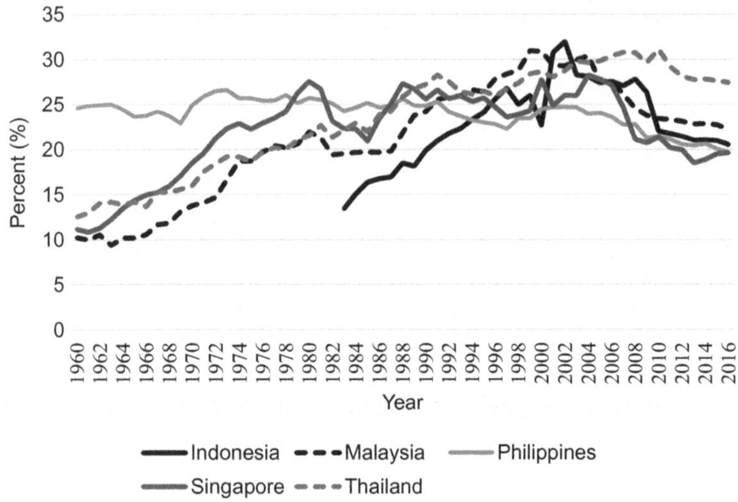

Fig. 2.1 Manufacturing value added share in GDP, selected economies, 1960–2017. *Source* Plotted from World Bank (2020) data

of commodities fell. The much sharper recession of 1998 was driven by policies of government and business that made Malaysia subject to the panic that also engulfed a number of other financially vulnerable countries in East Asia. Malaysia recovered quickly from the two recessions of 1985 and 1998 that largely resulted from its own policies. Recessions in Malaysia generated by global recessions largely reflect the fact that it is difficult to increase exports rapidly if global incomes are stagnant or falling. Put differently, Malaysia's potential growth rate as well as its actual growth rate fell in such circumstances.

The fact remains that the GDP growth rate of Malaysia since independence has been slower than that of the northeast Asian economies by a substantial margin (see Fig. 2.1). In the 1970s alone, Malaysia did not match the 5–9% per capita GDP growth rates that characterized the northeast Asian counties. At the beginning of the 1960s, Malaysia had roughly the same per capita GDP at constant 2010 USD prices as Taiwan and Korea while by 2018 Korea and Taiwan's per capita income was 2.4 times higher. Hong Kong (3.8 times) and Singapore (4.8 times) had even higher per capita income in 2018 relative to Malaysia, but their income in 1960 was already roughly 2.5 times higher.

But we still do not have an explanation for why Malaysia's growth was significantly slower than the Northeast Asian countries. For that purpose, there are several different methodologies that can get us to a tentative if far from a definitive answer. Those methodologies are,

(a) There have been many attempts to run regressions where GDP per capita is the dependent variable explained by a number of independent variables. These equations have tested a wide variety of variables using this approach. Many of the results are not robust but they do give some indication of what is important for growth.

(b) There have also been many calculations using the methodology first developed by Solow (1956, 1957) that attempt in what is basically a growth accounting exercise to differentiate the sources of growth between those brought about by increases in capital and the labour force from those brought about by increases in the productivity of those inputs, what is called total factor productivity.

(c) Because productivity growth has been a central element in GDP growth, it is important to understand the nature of that productivity growth. Productivity growth in high-income countries is largely driven by technological innovation. In middle-income countries the role of technological innovation becomes increasingly important as a nation approaches high-income status and is in fact essential to attaining that status. Malaysia is near to becoming a high-income economy and thus understanding innovation there is essential for understanding not only its growth performance during the last two decades, but also understanding whether or not the country has the innovation potential to continue growing rapidly as it approaches high-income status. To understand innovation in Malaysia one must not only understand Research and Development (R&D) in the country and the quality of the institutions doing R&D, but one has to go beyond this to an understanding of the educational institutions that are producing the people who are carrying out innovation through R&D. The discussion of these issues will make up the last part of this chapter since it is not only necessary for understanding past performance but is essential for understanding Malaysia's future prospects.

Econometrically Identified Variables that Explain GDP Growth

The challenge in using regression techniques to identify the sources of GDP growth is that there are a great many policies and institutions that have some influence on growth and they interact with each other as well as independently. That said, the method does allow one to identify key policies and institutions that are likely to influence growth either positively or negatively. Our approach here will be to discuss Malaysia's performance with respect to the variables that have proved to be the most robust in explaining the growth of those estimated by the many scholars who have run these regressions. In deciding which variables have been the most robust, we will follow the work of Xavier Sala-i-Martin who tested these variables against thousands of different combinations.[8]

---

[8] Sala-i-Martin (1997b) "I Just Ran Four Million Regressions", In this work he uses three different criteria for judging. The extreme bounds calculation in essence produces no significantly robust variables, but the methods that use more conventional methods such as 95 or 99% probability of being different from zero do produce over 60 variables. These more conventional criteria in this essay start with three fixed variables (level of income in 1960, level of education in 1960, and life

We will begin with the political variables, variables that cover a wide range of different political activities and institutions and include the rule of law, political rights, civil liberties, and the number of revolutions, military coups, and wars. These are significant contributors to growth when the investment rate as a fixed variable is left out of the equation and some are not significant when the investment rate is included. This latter estimate results from the fact that the investment rate is a clearly endogenous variable because the investment rate is determined mainly by the opportunities for profitable investment in the country and that in turn is heavily influenced by the other variables including the level of per capita income, the dependent variable being estimated. We will ignore this statistical problem and discuss the level of investment separately and use the results mainly from the regressions that were run without the investment rate variable.

Malaysia has had a stable government throughout most of its independent history. There have been no wars, coups, or revolutions and the only major political disturbance that influenced the nation in a major way were the riots of May 13, 1969. Those riots, while they did lead to major policy changes, they did not lead to a change in government other than the retirement of one Prime Minister and succession by the Deputy Prime Minister. Elections in Malaysia have been relatively free and the votes counted as accurately as in many other democratic countries although incumbent governments also use their power and resources to tip the scales in the government's favour. Civil liberties and political rights are not as respected as in say the Scandinavian countries or Western Europe more generally, but they are as or more protected than in a wide spectrum of developing countries. Malaysia also began independence with a strong legal system and, while the rule of law in the country was clearly weakened during the 1980s and 1990s, the Malaysian legal system in 2020 is still much stronger than that in most other ASEAN countries with the exception of Singapore.

The one political variable that was not tested by Sala-i-Martin but is almost certainly significant in the Malaysian case is that the country has deep ethnic divisions and the government has been dominated throughout post-independence by a majority that is among the economically disadvantaged groups. There have been regressions run with ethnic differences as a variable, but there are only a few where the disadvantaged ethnic group ruled the country. This variable has clearly shaped much of Malaysian economic policy as our brief review of Malaysia's growth history will make clear.

The second set of significant variables that also clearly helps explain Malaysian growth are those that deal with a country's approach to policies that make markets work efficiently and avoid policies that distort market signals in a major way. Those variables include "real exchange rate distortions", "deviations of black markets" from legal markets, and the "number of years the economy has been open" (meaning mainly that international trade has not been restricted by major barriers to imports or foreign investment). Malaysia has been relatively open throughout its history in part no doubt because it began independence as a country with strong exports and

expectancy in 1960). One additional fixed variable (the investment rate) is included in one set of regressions and excluded in another.

foreign exchange earnings and has continued to actively promote exports ever since. Malaysia has also had a Central Bank and Ministry of Finance that for the most part have conducted stable macroeconomic policies that avoided major government deficits and high inflation that in turn would have been likely to lead to distortions in the exchange rate and other markets.

Malaysia has also to a substantial degree remained a country that has relied on the private sector rather than on state-owned enterprises and thus scores relatively well on the "degree of capitalism" variable. There have been notable exceptions such as the early years of the heavy industry drive that relied on state-owned enterprises but these periods were relatively brief. In addition, as we shall see later the government has played a very large role in the economy even if much of the ownership remains private.

A variable that has a clear negative impact on growth is the "fraction of primary products in exports" or the "fraction of mining in GDP". The larger the fraction, the lower is the growth rate. This is the "resource curse" that has been written about for many decades and has often been labelled the "Dutch disease" because of the impact large oil discoveries in the North Sea had on Dutch manufacturing (Corden and Neary, 1982). Natural resources or commodities are a problem mainly because their prices fluctuate widely rising and falling. When prices are high a country's exchange rate tends to strengthen thus weakening the competitive position of manufactured and agricultural exports. More importantly, high prices, particularly if the profits or rents go directly into government coffers, lead to booms in spending that are often poorly planned. Booms also tend to generate corruption opportunities as government officials and companies close to them take steps to move the surpluses into their own pockets. When prices fall, the boom comes to an end and half-finished projects often have to be stopped but corruption remains even though the returns are lower.

Because Malaysian macroeconomic policies have generally been well managed, the exchange rate has not been a major problem and manufactured exports, notably electronics, have remained highly competitive (Rasiah et al., 2015). High oil prices, in contrast, have created large rents that have helped fuel such problematic policies as the heavy industry drive. More importantly, they have to some degree been indirectly siphoned off to pay for many of the large subsidies to Bumiputera and the goal of increasing Bumiputera ownership that among other things made Malaysia vulnerable to the 1997–1998 financial crisis (Rasiah, 1998). Whether the impact of oil rents in Malaysia was positive or negative for growth depends on what would have happened if the rents had not existed. Would the large subsidies to Bumiputera have been pursued with equal vigour in which case the oil rents helped relieve what otherwise might have been a large budget deficit or cuts in essential investments and services. If those Bumiputera subsidies had been cut back, such events such as the 1997–1998 financial crisis might have been avoided although the political implications of those cutbacks could have led to other unpredictable and possibly damaging directions. Overall one can clearly state that the handling of Malaysia's resource wealth in general and petroleum rents in particular may have been flawed but not to any degree comparable to what happened in Nigeria or in Iran among many other countries that have mismanaged their resource wealth.

In the Sala-i-Martin analysis, there were also three fixed variables that had a significant relationship with growth: the per capita GDP at the beginning of the growth period (1960), the level of education in 1960, and life expectancy in 1960. The lower is the level of per capita GDP, the faster is the rate of growth relative to high-income countries. This may explain in part why China grew more rapidly since it had a much lower level of income in 1960 (or 1978) than did Malaysia. On the other hand, Korea and Taiwan had incomes similar to those of Malaysia in 1960 but they also grew much faster. Furthermore, growth rates do not come down gradually in most cases as the typical regression implies, they come down more abruptly as in Japan in the 1970s, and Korea in the 2000s, and China in 2014 and 2015.

A country with a higher level of education at the beginning of the period being measured clearly has an advantage over a country with a lower level of education and the faster the quantity and quality of education increases over subsequent years give even greater advantages. The regression equations, however, can only measure the impact of the initial level of education because the increase in the quality of education is clearly endogenous. A similar situation exists with the life expectancy variable. Healthy individuals clearly are more effective members of the workforce both physically and mentally and the healthier the better, but only the initial level is measured. Malaysia by the standards common in the world in 1960 had both a fairly high level of education and health, but not the level and quality of education found in Korea, Taiwan, Hong Kong, and Singapore in 1960. We shall return to Malaysia's education situation at length later since it is almost certainly even more important for the country's future performance than it has been for its performance over the past half-century.

Finally, a few variables, such as religion and whether a country was a former colony of Spain rather than Britain or France have some significant influence on economic growth. The Confucian religion variable is in fact the only variable that is significant using the extreme bounds test. It is highly unlikely that the religious variables have anything to do with the actual content of the religion for reasons that would sidetrack us from the main purpose of this essay. Religion is probably in this context a proxy for the overall culture of a society and culture does affect politics often in significant ways and politics in turn affects such things as economic policies. But one cannot talk of a single religion in Malaysia since there are Confucians (which is more a philosophy than a religion), Buddhists, Taoists, Moslems, Christians, and Hindus among others. There are certainly substantial differences between the cultures of Malaysian Malays, Chinese, and Indians and how they interact but the regression analysis is of no help in assisting us to understand how these differences and interactions affect growth. For that purpose, in-depth historical analysis is far more useful.

To sum up this discussion of where Malaysia fits into the cross-country regression analysis of economic growth, overall Malaysia has performed favourably in the dimensions measured by these equations. The political institutions, the lack of major distortions in key prices such as the exchange rate, the reliance on the private sector rather than state enterprises, and the level of education and health all help explain why Malaysia has experienced a level of sustained economic growth far above that of most of Sub-Saharan Africa and also above that of most countries in Latin America. These equations, however, do not provide much of a guide as to why Malaysia has performed substantially less well than most of the northeast Asian economies or Singapore. They also tell us little about what Malaysia should do if it wanted to accelerate growth closer to the levels of the northeast Asian economies.[9]

It is also the case that the significant variables in these regressions were important for a particular moment in time, the last half of the twentieth century and the beginning decade of the twenty-first. There is no reason to believe that these same variables would apply equally well to explaining growth, such as it was, in the first half of the twentieth century that was dominated by two world wars and the great depression. Nor are they necessarily the right variables to explain growth over the next several decades if those decades turn out to include long periods of economic stagnation in most of the high-income countries together with rapidly ageing populations in those same countries. We will return to this subject at the end of the chapter.

Growth Accounting Explanations

A very different approach to explaining how countries achieve higher growth is the growth accounting method pioneered by Robert Solow. The basic idea of this method, as explained earlier, is to separate the contributions to the growth of inputs of capital and labour from the contribution of the productivity of these inputs termed total factor productivity. One virtue of this methodology is that it brings investment back into the discussion, and, more importantly, it brings back technological change including improvements in management efficiency and government policies. The central question Solow attempted to answer for the United States and the one that we are most interested in is whether Malaysian economic growth has been determined by large levels of investment and a rapid increase in the labour force or has it been largely driven by increases in productivity. For Solow higher productivity largely meant improvements in technology, but for developing economies such as Malaysia it clearly includes much more than technology such as improvements in management practices within firms and government policies towards the economy.

In the cases of Korea, Taiwan, and China, there is no question that what led them to decades of near double-digit growth started with major changes in government policies that in turn led to a large jump in total factor productivity (TFP). Over time the impact of major policy reforms tapers off and capital investment plays a larger role. In the cases of South Korea and Taiwan, the large jumps in TFP occurred first in the early 1960s when both economies went from inward-looking policies and overvalued exchange rates to open economies, at least for exports, including

[9] The variables used in the regressions confirm that certain approaches, such as reliance on state-owned enterprises, large restrictions on international trade, or low levels of education are bad for growth. But they do not give much guidance as to how to improve policies and performance if the desired general approaches are in place.

major devaluations of their currency. As time passed the role of TFP fell and that of investment or capital formation rose until the mid-1980s when there was a major effort to further open and liberalize the two economies and there was another jump in TFP followed by another tapering off of the role of TFP. For China, the late 1970s was a major turning point as China began to abandon the policies and institutions of a Soviet-type economy in favour of opening up the economy and relying more on market forces. The investment rate before and after these radical reforms was much the same but the growth rate roughly doubled initially because of the large jump in productivity. The large jump in productivity, as in Korea and Taiwan, created more and better investment opportunities and over time the contribution of investment capital rose until the next major reform.

Many growth accounting exercises simply mechanically measure the contributions of capital, labour, and TFP over a long period of time and reach conclusions about the nature of growth from whether the long term contribution of capital or TFP is higher or lower than some other country or that the contribution of capital is larger or smaller than the contribution of TFP. These calculations often ignore data from earlier years when major reforms were undertaken usually because the data for those earlier years are not as reliable as for later years. There seldom is any effort to relate the periods covered by the calculations to major changes in policies or other conditions that could have a major impact on economic performance.

In the case of Malaysia, there are three major changes in policies, institutions, or the stage of development that plausibly could have a significant impact on the sources of growth. They are first, the introduction of the New Economic Policy (NEP) after the riots of May 13, 1969, that coincided with the beginning of a larger effort to promote manufacturing and manufactured exports mainly by foreign direct investment (FDI) firms. The second major policy change was the push to develop a heavy industry that began with Prime Minister Mahathir's term in office that started in 1981. That term ended in 2003 but by then Malaysia's per capita GDP was at a level where the period of catch-up growth largely had come to an end and growth from then on was likely to slow down and future Malaysian growth would depend increasingly on innovation. Another large influence that should affect the relative role of capital and TFP was the price of natural resources, notably the price of petroleum in the years after the 1960s. A major jump in prices of natural resource exports, other things being equal, will lead to higher growth even if the rate of investment does not itself increase.

Figure 2.2 presents one estimate of the contributions of TFP to Malaysian growth and Fig. 2.3 shows the rate of gross capital formation (GCF) as a share of GDP. Both the rate of gross investment and the level of total factor productivity began rising in the early 1970s despite the introduction of the NEP which many probably expected would both hurt investment and lower productivity. This is also a period when FDI rose from two percent of GDP to six percent in 1974 and then fell in the mid-1970s no doubt mainly because of the OPEC generated increased prices of oil and the resulting global recession (Malaysia was not yet a large producer or exporter of petroleum), but these investments quickly renewed their rise.

Total factor productivity continued its rise peaking in 1980 but staying at that level until it plunged in 1985 and the rate of gross capital formation rose similarly

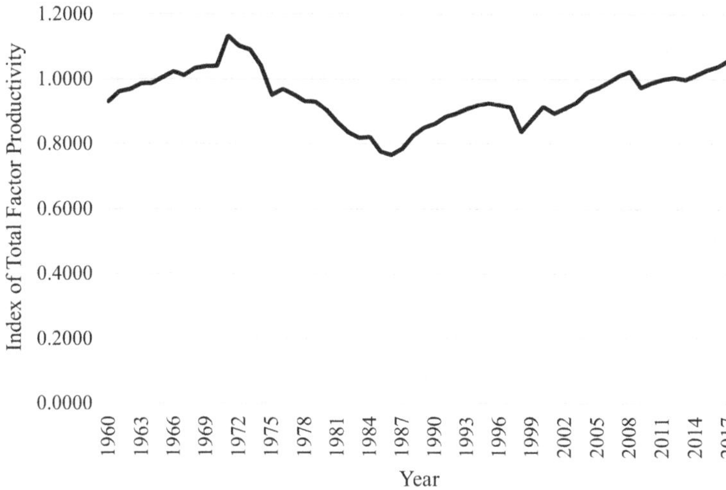

Fig. 2.2 Total Factor Productivity Index, 1960–2017. *Source* Feenstra et al. (2013); Shah (2019: 273)

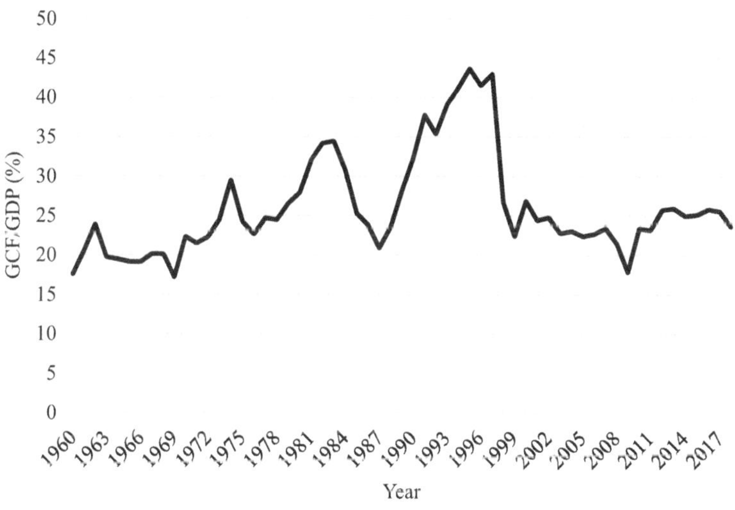

Fig. 2.3 Gross Capital Formation, Malaysia, 1960–2018. *Source* Plotted from World Bank (2020) data

but began falling a bit earlier. Gross capital formation then rose to its highest level either before or since of over 40% of GDP before plunging in the 1997–1998 financial crisis to 18% (in 1999) and has hovered mostly just below 25% in the years since then although it rose to 26% in 2012 and 2013. The pattern of TFP was similar except for the investment boom of the 1990s when TFP rose only modestly before falling

Table 2.3 Total factor productivity, Malaysia, 1960–2017

Period	Annual average growth (%)
1960–1969	1.5
1970–1979	−1.1
1980–1989	−0.9
1990–1999	0.3
2000–2009	1.1
2010–2017	1.0
1960–2017	0.3
1971–1989 (*NEP*)	−1.1
1990–2017 (*Post-NEP*)	0.8

Source Shah (2017: 272)

during the financial crisis. Net FDI peaked earlier in 1992 then fell sharply and has averaged below 4% of GDP ever since.

Basically, these patterns are consistent with the view that the initial drive for manufactured exports in the 1970s made possible rises in both investment and TFP but while investment during the activist government industrial policies of the 1980s and 1990s rose for a brief time to a very high level, productivity first levelled off and then fell sharply in the mid-1980s and stayed down although it remained positive. With the end of the activist industrial policies, productivity did rise and did so despite the global recession that began in 2007–2008. Apart from the blip in 1997–98 arising from the Asian financial crisis, TFP grew since till 2017, albeit at very low rates. Oil prices it should be noted remained relatively low from the mid-1980s until just after the late 1990s when they began rising rapidly.

The TFP growth of Malaysia has been carefully explored in Sultan Nazrin Shah (2017), and Table 2.3 reports his estimates, which shows a decline in TFP in the 1970s and 1980s, with the latter capturing the impact of the first years of the heavy industry campaign. There also appears to be a modest pickup in TFP growth over the period 2000–17. As Shah (2017: 270) has observed, factor accumulation rather than TFP has accounted for most of Malaysia's growth since 1960 with TFP growth averaging 0.3% per annum in 1960–2017. Importantly, TFP declined on average by −1.1% per annum over the NEP period (1971–90), while it only grew on average by 0.8% per annum in 1990–2017.

Is one percent a high or low rate of productivity growth? It is lower than that of China in recent decades or South Korea and Taiwan during their high growth decades, but it is higher than that of Africa where TFP growth has been negative throughout the post-independence period, and of Latin America which averaged only 0.2% per year from 1960 through 2000.[10]

It is impossible to attribute causality to these correlations although the domestic investment boom of the 1990s was clearly driven mainly by domestic forces including the government. Overall TFP was positive and improved since 1990 but modestly so.

[10] Bosworth and Collins (2003).

How that compares with other developing countries requires explicitly comparative estimates using similar methodologies.

The overall conclusion from this brief look at the growth accounting literature for Malaysia, therefore, is that Malaysia's productivity performance has been consistent with its GDP growth rate performance. Malaysian has done better than large parts of the developing world but has fallen short of the high performance of the Northeast Asian economies during their high growth period. TFP growth during a country's rise from low income to lower middle income and then to higher middle-income status is driven by improvements in policies, incentives, and management that accelerate the adoption of well-known technologies and uses them with increasing efficiency. It is largely not due to the development of major advances in that technology. To understand how Malaysia has performed in that regard, however, this aggregate analysis is inadequate. We need to look more closely at a more micro level as to just what Malaysian technology upgrading has involved particularly in the manufacturing sector. Before looking in depth at the micro level at Malaysia's technological performance, it is first necessary to review the fundamental changes in development policy over the past decades and in the structure of ownership of Malaysia's modern sector.

Economic Growth and Shifts in Ownership

At the time of independence in 1957 and throughout the 1960s Malaysia was a classic natural resource-dependent economy. Tin had been discovered long before independence and had been developed at first by Chinese miners using the chain pump followed by gravel pumping and hydraulic sluicing technologies and then since 1912 increasingly by large mostly British owned dredges (Thoburn, 1977). Demand for tin rose rapidly with the development of such products as tin cans used by the Western food processing industries. The development of the automobile and the resulting need for rubber for tires led to the rapid development in Malaysia of large rubber plantations, mostly British owned, and also many Malaysian small holder rubber planters. GDP growth was higher when rubber and tin prices were higher and slowed when these prices fell. Private investment fluctuated with tin and rubber prices with a one-year lag. There was a modest effort to develop manufacturing following the enactment of the pioneer industry ordinance that involved some restrictions on trade designed to promote infant industries and was also in part designed to attract FDI. Overall, however, the economy was generally open with few restrictions on imports thanks in part to the large foreign exchange earnings from rubber and tin.

Urban businesses were largely in the hands of foreigners, mainly British, or local Chinese-Malaysians. Agriculture was primarily a Malay occupation of small holders some of whom owned their land but many who rented from mainly Malay landlords. Occupations generally were closely associated with ethnicity with Chinese-Malaysians dominating most urban commerce, construction, and what little industry existed, foreigners dominating the large rubber estates and tin mines, and Malays dominating government employment, food-based agriculture, and most smallholder rubber. Politically the country was ruled by an alliance of the United Malay National Organization (UMNO) (the dominant partner representing the Malays), the Malaysian Chinese Association (representing the Chinese), and the Malaysian Indian Congress (representing the Indians) and was friendly to private business and foreign investors. This alliance mainly carried on the economic policies of the past but with some modest efforts to improve the low economic status of the majority Malay population. Singapore, Sarawak, and Sabah joined Malaya to form Malaysia in 1963, but Singapore left to become independent in 1965. Since that time there have not been any changes in the boundaries of the Malaysian state.

The elections of 1969 brought about a fundamental political change that had immediate and large ramifications for economic policy and ownership of the economy. The change, however, was not through the ballot box but resulted from the large-scale riots and killings caused mainly by the response to the elections in the state of Selangor. The fear that the violence connected with these riots instilled in all parts of the population led to a consensus or at least acquiescence on the part not only of the Malay majority, but also the Chinese-Malaysian minority, that a major effort needed to be undertaken to deal with the disadvantaged economic position of the Malays. This took the form of the New Economic Policy (NEP) that was designed not just to raise the economic position of the poorer parts of the Malay population (hereafter referred to as Bumiputera) but also had the stated goal of eliminating the relationship between ethnicity and occupation. Introduced in 1971, the NEP controversially called for the elimination of the relationship between ownership of business assets and ethnicity since most of these assets up to that time had been in the hands of foreigners and Chinese-Malaysians (Malaysia, 1971).

The NEP itself was eventually replaced by other programmes and laws but the principles it enunciated have remained in force up to the present. Some of the provisions of NEP were not particularly controversial. Affirmative action and outright quotas designed to hire more Bumiputera in manufacturing and in urban business fit well with the boom in labour-intensive manufacturing that was getting underway in earnest in the 1970s. Young Bumiputera women, for example, were quite suitable for the kinds of assembly jobs then opening up in export-oriented manufacturing firms (Lim, 1978; Salih et al., 1988).

The great expansion of Bumiputera education at the primary and secondary level was not an issue either although there was some controversy over the increased use of the Malay language in instruction at those levels. The Chinese and Indian minorities, however, had little difficulty mastering Bahasa Malaysia when required. There were complaints that the less well-educated Bumiputera experienced a decline in English language proficiency, but, even if true, it is unlikely to have affected economic growth in a major way at least initially. Education policies at the tertiary level were a bigger issue but they will be discussed in a later part of this essay. The main negative aspect of policies concerning the public universities since was the lowering of qualifications for admitting Bumiputera using the argument that their performance would only be better if they had enjoyed the same resources. Once weak Bumiputera students were admitted into university, especially in the professional disciplines of medicine, engineering, and business the pressure to pass them was considered to have undermined standards of graduates entering the job market in Malaysia (Rasiah et al., 2015; Selvaratnam, 2015).

The ownership component of the NEP was not only controversial but had a direct and more or less immediate impact on the structure of the industry. It became official when the Industrial Coordination Act was promulgated in 1975 (Chee, 1986). The provision required firms with a certain size, which was raised from RM100,000 in 1975 to RM1 million in 1986 when they invested in new capacity to set aside 30% of the shares generated to finance the expansion for sales to Bumiputera. Initially, this meant subsidized selling of shares to the few rich Bumiputera who could afford them but the Bumiputera who received the shares often simply then sold the shares on the market at market prices taking their profits and leaving the firm's owner to find another group of Bumiputera shareholders. That problem was remedied by creating unit trusts that would buy shares for the Bumiputera who would be given shares in the unit trusts. The unit trusts were managed by PNB, a generally well-run public company. Still, the incentives for Chinese-Malaysian owned firms were clearly negative although it would require large-scale micro analysis of firm behaviour if one were to attempt to measure the impact of this ownership measure on the level of investment by private non-Bumiputera firms.

Firms that exported at least 80% of their output were exempt from this ownership provision (Rasiah, 1995). Few domestically owned firms in Malaysia, however, were exporters. This provision was mainly designed to avoid scaring off FDI in manufacturing for export. Also, the government created Free Trade Zones and Licensed Manufacturing Warehouses to attract foreign export-oriented firms who largely exported. The purpose was to create jobs as Malaysia's market was too small for these firms. Examples include National Semiconductor, Intel, Texas Instruments, Penfibre, and Penfabric (Rasiah, 1995). The location choice of foreign export-oriented firms also was determined by ease of policing tariff-free operations (Malaysia, 1971). Foreign investors in rubber and tin and later palm oil were of less concern to the government but the Bumiputera ownership objective for some of the large estates and mines was handled differently. The Malaysian government itself together with private domestic firms took the initiative to transfer these assets to domestic ownership with such actions as the Dawn Raid on Guthries where the government bought majority shares in a number of major plantations. Seizing these assets by legal means probably had little impact on their contribution to economic growth because they were commodities that sold on world markets at world prices and the technology of production was well understood locally. There was no particular benefit to Malaysia of foreign ownership in these areas by the 1970s.

For manufacturing, it was a very different story. Malaysian businesses on their own neither had easy access to foreign markets nor did they have much experience producing manufactured products for foreign markets. Domestic firms could have made arrangements to work with foreign buyers to gain access to markets in the US and Europe and they could have bought the necessary technology and management expertise as happened in South Korea and Taiwan. But, for the most part, Malaysia did not do so. Most domestic manufacturing firms around the world first develop products for their local markets often behind trade barriers that protect them from outside competition. Some import-substituting firms of this sort remain content behind these barriers, but if the incentives are right as they were in South Korea, Taiwan, and later China, they expand to overseas markets as their increasing efficiency and falling costs make them internationally competitive. Any measure that inhibits steady expansion, and Malaysia's NEP ownership provisions certainly did inhibit expansion, makes it that much more difficult for domestic firms to become exporters. Also, institutional change, especially in education and R&D support, facilitated technological upgrading in South Korea and Taiwan (Vogel, 1991). Despite aggressive efforts, investment into such activities failed to provide the same support for Malaysian firms.

Whatever the cause, most manufactured exports coming from Malaysia have from the beginning been dominated by foreign firms. Malaysia was attractive to foreign investors for a number of reasons. It had inherited a comparatively good physical infrastructure from the colonial period, most educated people were fluent in the English language, and the economy was open and the repatriation of profits was not difficult. Over the next several decades Malaysia has steadily improved its physical infrastructure particularly in the transport area, and the economy including capital markets has remained open with the notable exception of the immediate aftermath of 1997–1998 financial crisis.

As the data in Figs. 2.4 and 2.5 make clear, Malaysia's value added rose rapidly in constant dollar terms in 1970–1997 dipping modestly in 1999–2002 and then, after recovering and growing rapidly, dipped more sharply during the global economic

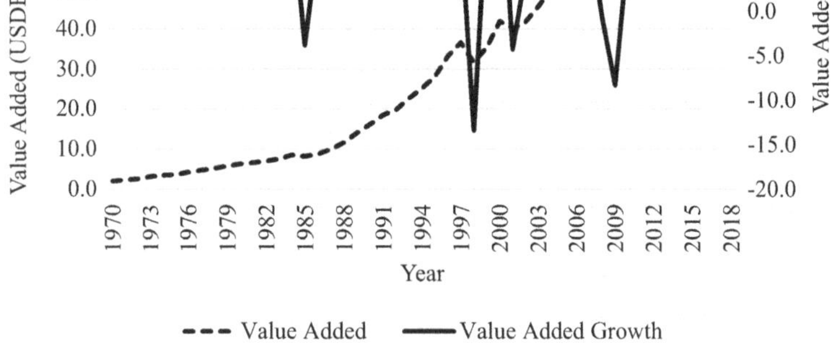

Fig. 2.4 Manufacturing value added, Malaysia, 1960–2018. *Source* Computed from World Bank (2020) data

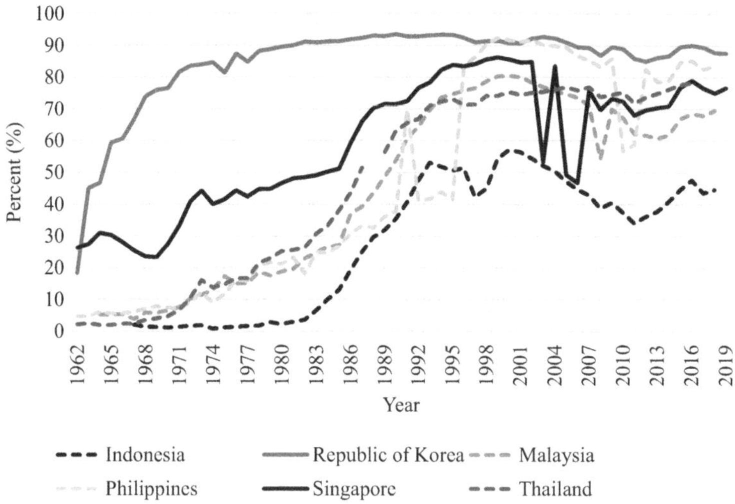

Fig. 2.5 Manufactured exports in total exports, selected countries, 1960–2018. *Source* Plotted using World Bank (2020) data

recession of 2007–2009 before rising again. Manufactured exports rose from a minuscule 5% or less of total merchandise exports in the 1960s to over 20% by the end of the 1970s and to exceed 80% in 1998 before falling gradually in 2014 with a dip in 2008, and then rising slightly after 2015 (Fig. 2.5). Malaysia's shares compare well with its Southeast Asian neighbours. Resource scarce Korea has consistently managed higher share of manufactured exports though. With the exception of petroleum and palm oil exports, most of Malaysia's export growth in constant prices over four-plus decades (2018/1970) resulted from FDI and not domestic manufacturers. In the absence of this rapid FDI-generated growth in manufactured exports, Malaysia's overall economic growth would almost certainly have been much slower and there is no reason to think that domestically owned manufacturers would have been in a position to step in and replace the FDI exporting firms.

There is nothing inherently wrong with an economy relying to this degree on FDI if the investors are committed to staying with the local economy indefinitely into the future or alternatively if they take steps to replace themselves over time with domestic managers and investors who could continue development of manufacturing and modern sector services (such as information technology) after the FDI has left. FDI also has to be a large and growing share of total investment in the country if it is to have a major continuing influence on growth. Hong Kong and Singapore have basically risen to high-income status relying to a large degree on FDI fuelled growth.

FDI in Malaysia up to this time has held up. In the 1970s, as Fig. 2.6 indicates, it fluctuated by around 3–4% of GDP or roughly one-sixth of total gross capital formation, rising well above that level in the early 1980s but coming back to that level since the financial crisis of the late 1990s. Whether it is likely to continue at that level as a share of GDP and the total investment will be discussed later in this essay. There

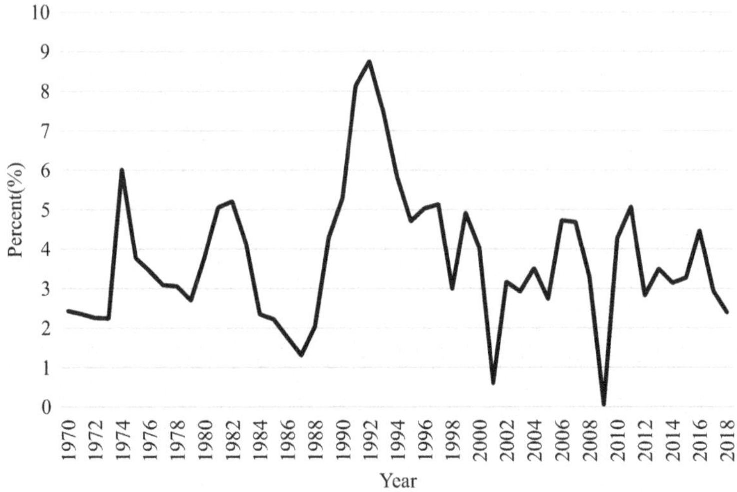

Fig. 2.6 Net foreign direct investment inflows in GDP, Malaysia, 1970–2018. *Source* World Bank (2020) data

was a big jump in FDI in 1986–91, then a falling trend followed by a rising trend again in 2001–2005 as FDI entered services and consumer markets. The sharp rise in FDI was also felt by Indonesia, the Philippines, and Thailand following the Plaza Accord of 1985 and the withdrawal of GSP from the NIEs in 1988 (Rasiah, 1989). To a large extent, Malaysia's competitiveness declined eventually in these years as the rising national currencies during that period exacerbated current account deficits while squeezing manufacturing. Malaysia and Thailand imported cheap foreign labour to sustain manufactured exports (Rasiah, 2011, 2020a, b).

There have been Malaysian firms that have developed activities outside of Malaysia, but for the most part this has involved investing in enterprises located elsewhere rather than exporting goods and services from Malaysia. YTL has built power plants and hotels outside the country and Petronas, the state oil company, has also invested extensively abroad. Berjaya Holdings has large investments in property and hotels around the world. United Engineers Malaysia (UEM) has successfully built highways abroad, including in India. Malaysian clothing firms have successfully relocated to Cambodia to export. In electronics, Globetronics has successfully started a subsidiary in Singapore to manufacture semiconductors for export.

The Malaysian government attempted to build a manufacturing base where ownership is locally owned. The major activity of this sort was the heavy industry drive initiated by Prime Minister Mahathir in the early 1980s and continued through the 1990s. The way that was carried out is instructive as to why Malaysian-owned manufacturers have had trouble becoming exporters. The Proton automobile was the centre piece of the heavy industry drive together with a number of machinery manufacturing firms designed to provide inputs to Proton. Subsequent national automotive firms such as Perodua, Naza Motors and Inakom have followed less indigenization to supply largely the domestic market. The other enterprises supported included Perwaja Steel and cement producers. The objective was to assist Malaysia to move up the manufacturing ladder to more sophisticated industries and to do so under Malaysian ownership. Up to that point, automobile producers in Malaysia were foreign automobile firms many of which assembled cars in Malaysia but almost entirely with imported components, what is known as CKD or complete knockdown kits. Their contribution to Malaysian GDP was negligible and in some cases their value added to Malaysia was negative. YTL's acquisition of Perak Hanjoong (Korean owned) and further downstream integration allowed the firm to produce high quality klinker and cement, but only for the domestic market.

The heavy industry effort began as an import-substituting programme. Unlike the South Korean heavy industry drive of the 1970s, there was no expectation that Proton or the other heavy industries would become exporters within a short span of time such as five years. Proton and its component manufacturers received a high level of protection and that protection continued into the twenty-first century. Furthermore, the ownership goal was to have domestic Bumiputera ownership, not just Malaysian ownership. To that end, these heavy industries began as state-owned firms in a state that had little experience with manufacturing of any kind. The problems that caused led the government to privatize these enterprises (together with several other large state-owned firms not involved in the heavy industry drive) but to do so in a way that would ensure Bumiputera ownership even though there was virtually no Bumiputera experience with manufacturing. Since there were also few Bumiputera that had the personal resources to purchase a major or controlling share in these privatized enterprises, the government made sure that the banking system lent them the money. The privatized ownership was thus both relatively inexperienced in managing these large enterprises and highly leveraged. This situation was to contribute to Malaysia being hit hard by the 1997–1998 financial crisis.

Well before the 1997–1998 crisis in the mid-1980s, however, the heavy industry programme had caused a fiscal crisis. The first years of the programme in the early 1980s involved large government expenditures paid for in part out of the revenues from petroleum, but these revenues were not sufficient and so the government began borrowing heavily against future oil revenues. But in 1985–1986 the price of oil plunged to half and less of the price spike caused by OPEC in the 1970s. The then finance minister, Tun Daim Zainuddin, introduced a major austerity programme to rein in the growing debt and GDP growth became negative. Thus the heavy industry programme during the 1980s was producing little but became a drag on the economy. The drag on the economy was short-lived, however, and during the rest of the 1980s through the mid-1990s Malaysia experienced both an investment boom and enjoyed its highest rates of GDP growth averaging 6–7% a year. The rate of investment rose to over 40% of GDP before plunging in 1999 to 22%.

The biggest problem of the heavy industry programme, however, was that it was both expensive and the social returns on the investment were low or negligible when one removes the large subsidies provided by high tariff protection. Proton automobiles as well as Perodua, Naza and Inakom are not internationally competitive 34 years after the heavy industry programme was initiated. Furthermore, far from being a truly made in Malaysia automobile, many of the key more sophisticated components had to be imported from Japan and elsewhere. Proton has localized substantially but its sales among national producers have plunged. Perodua is the leading seller of national cars now but its components are largely supplied from abroad, including its model designs. By the twenty-first century, the whole idea of a national automobile was obsolete since most automobile manufacturers around the world now get their parts from many different countries.

The Proton effort, however, at least did produce a large share of the cars on Malaysian roads beginning from 1985. Even that cannot be said about Perwaja Steel that went from one large loss to another despite government bailouts and high protection from imports. Could Malaysia have produced a large and successful steel company if the sole goal had been to produce steel in Malaysia? There were and are private steel mills in Malaysia run by experienced people which do make money much of the time all be it with the help of import restrictions. If these firms had been helped by the government to reach a scale that would make them internationally competitive, Malaysia might have been able to create a modern steel industry, not unlike Korea's Pohang Iron and Steel that also started and was for a long time a state-owned enterprise. But the builders of Pohang knew they had to become internationally competitive in a relatively short time and the government helped them get started but Pohang mostly got there on its own. Unlike Proton's subsidies and protection in the domestic market, POSCO's access to these benefits was stringently tied to performance (Amsden, 1989). Pohang, however, was not expected to serve major social goals.

Despite the drag on growth of the heavy industry programme, Malaysia's economy grew rapidly in 1988–1996 with GDP per capita averaging nearly 7% per year. Net FDI was at its highest levels ever as a share of GDP and partly as a result exports as a share of GDP also rose substantially from 62% of GDP in 1987 to 91% in 1996 (Fig. 2.7). But then in 1997–1998 the economy crashed as Malaysia became embroiled in the Asian financial crisis, which also hit hard Thailand, Indonesia, the Philippines, and Korea), largely because the policies of the 1980s and 1990s had led to many highly leveraged companies that were particularly vulnerable to the crisis (Fig. 2.7).

The dependence of the economy on portfolio equity investment in Malaysia also played a role as it plunged during the crisis (Rasiah, 1998). Banks from Korea (since 1985), and Thailand had borrowed extensively from abroad (appreciating national currencies drew them to make money from arbitrage differentials). Banks in Malaysia borrowed mainly from domestic sources in Ringgit and that is why the country still had huge international reserves against current account payments and short-term debt service commitments. The foreign payment commitments of Indonesia (136%), the Philippines (149%), and Thailand (153%) exceeded their international reserves, while that of Malaysia only reached 55% of international reserves in 1996 (Rasiah, 1999: 367). As the ringgit fell owing to both an unsustainable build-up in current account deficits and the speculative contagion from the Baht, defaulters (NPLs) mounted. However, Malaysia was fortunate to have much of its debt domestically denominated, which allowed the government to restructure the debt without foreign

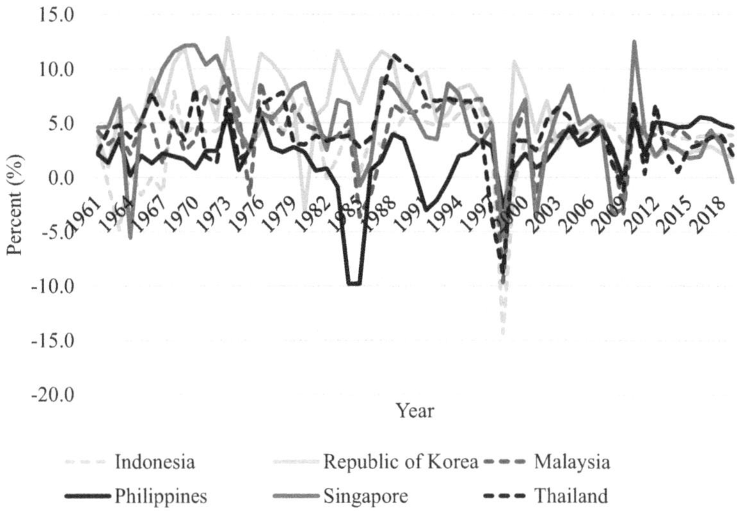

Fig. 2.7 GDP per capita annual growth rates, selected countries, 1961–2019. *Source* World Bank (2020) data

pressure. The booming US market also quickened recovery as electronics exports rose strongly (Rasiah et al., 2014).

Since the 1997–1998 crisis there have been two further downturns in the Malaysian economy, in 2001 and 2009. Both resulted from global recessions that did not originate from conditions within Malaysia. These two recessions largely account for the slower average growth rate of GDP during the first decade of the twenty-first century. By the middle of that decade, oil and palm oil prices together with the prices of other natural resource products rose rapidly and then, with the exception of the financial crisis years, stayed up through most of 2014. Manufactured exports in real terms grew briskly for several years after the 1997–1998 financial crisis at 6.1% a year (2003/1999) then slowed to 3.1% for the next eight years (2010/2003) and actually declined at 1.5% per year from the end of 2010 through 2013.[11] Total exports in current US dollar prices did much better growing at 4.1% a year (2014/2010) but that was thanks largely to high oil and palm oil prices. Malaysian GDP growth in the second decade of the twenty-first century to date has depended on the growth rate in services that in turn has depended at least in part on the high natural resource prices, high prices that fell dramatically in 2015.

By the 1990s government efforts had transformed the ownership structure of the Malaysian economy, which has since persisted into the twenty-first century. In agriculture, food products and smallholder palm oil and rubber acreages are mainly in Bumiputera hands, either those working these farms or landlords. Many of the largest plantations formally owned by foreigners have been taken over by the government.

---

[11] These figures were derived from the export volume index and the share of manufacturing in total exports in World Bank, WDI online January 2016.

In the service sector, a large portion of small shops are in Chinese-Malaysian hands as in the past. It is among the larger firms, the kind that is listed on the Kuala Lumpur Stock Exchange (KLSE), where the transformation in ownership has been most profound. The data on ownership in 1974 before the NEP had much impact and 1993 are presented in Table 2.4. By 1993 (and likely much the same today), foreign ownership had been reduced from 49.11 to 10.7% and Chinese-Malaysian private ownership from 27 to 13.9%. The government controlled 40.5% directly and Unit Trusts another 17.6%. The government was dominated by UMNO politically and by Bumiputera in the civil service. The major Bumiputera unit trusts were managed by PNB, a government company set up for that purpose.

The leading firms of the Malaysian economy over the past two decades, therefore, have largely been firms dominated by the government either directly or indirectly. The major exceptions are the foreign-owned firms that provide most of Malaysia's exports and Malaysian-Chinese owned firms that mainly provide goods and services for the domestic market particularly in such areas as housing and hotels. Together these latter two groups account for just over a quarter of the capital of the firms listed on the Kuala Lumpur stock exchange and probably an even smaller share of GDP.

Table 2.4 Market capitalization of top KLSE firms by ownership, 1974 and 1993

Nationality or ethnicity	1974	1993
Foreign controlled companies	49.1	10.7
Malaysian controlled companies		
Government A	6.3	40.5
Government C		17.7
Chinese (private local)	27.0	13.9
Bumiputera (private local)		6.3
Indian (private local)		0.1
Institutions		10.4
Unit trusts	–	17.6
Nominees	–	0.7
Total	100.0	100.0

Note Foreign controlled companies in 1974 do not include Singapore controlled companies. If Singapore companies were included, the foreign share would be 61.1% of a larger total. Singapore companies are excluded because of the complications connected with the way Singapore and Malaysian companies were cross-listed in the early years in both Singapore and Kuala Lumpur
Government A companies were those under government control in 1974. Government C companies were those under foreign control in 1974 but were taken over by the government in 1977; Private local ownership in 1974 was mostly Chinese-Malaysian
Sources The data for 1974 come originally from Tan (1982), The 1993 data were constructed by Ms. Veena Loh under the supervision of Dr. Tan Tat Wai; This table as presented was taken from Perkins and Woo (2000: 234)

The question this ownership structure raises is whether it is an appropriate structure for an economy that needs to rely increasingly on innovation and global competitiveness if it is to sustain steady and fairly rapid growth towards high-income status? Government-controlled enterprises have not often been seen as either innovators or even firms capable of competing internationally in fields such as manufacturing or business services. Alternatively, can the remaining private sector firms that compete on the open market for business carry the innovation and global competitiveness load? To begin to answer these questions we need to look in greater depth into the performance of the manufacturing and modern service sectors. In the section that follows we will focus mainly on manufacturing. A study of the technological sophistication of the service sector is a research project for the future.

Growth and Structural Change in Manufacturing

Any discussion of rising technological sophistication and increasing efficiency in the Malaysian economy must focus on those sectors where major changes in those areas have been achieved at a rate that will, if continued, support Malaysia's rise to high-income status. That emphasis does not necessarily eliminate a discussion of palm oil and rubber but the main focus looking backward has to be on manufacturing and particularly the manufacturing sectors that to date have carried Malaysia to upper middle-income status and that means the major manufacturing export sectors. Thus, we compare the experience of the manufacturing sector of Malaysia with that of the Northeast Asian and Southeast Asian countries' manufacturing sectors in this section.

Manufacturing

Since the East Asian economies grew rapidly on the back of manufacturing expansion, we examine in detail Malaysia's record here against the other economies. Over the period 1960–2019, South Korea (11.0%) experienced the highest average annual growth in real manufacturing value added (see Table 2.5). Malaysia (8.4%) enjoyed the same average annual growth rate as Singapore (8.4%), though Malaysia's starting year is 1970. Indonesia (7.4%), Thailand (7.4%), and the Philippines (4.2%) were the next fastest industrializers among these countries.

Manufactured exports have been the most important export of Malaysia since the 1980s, which grew from MYR548 billion in 2013 to MYR137 billion in 2019 (Malaysia, 2020). Agricultural exports have shown a trend fall in their percentage contribution to GDP since 1970. In fact, its absolute exports fell from MYR147 billion in 2013 to MYR137 billion in 2019. Other exports rose slightly from MYR25 billion to MYR41 billion during the same period. Malaysia's manufacturing expansion has largely been spearheaded by exports of electric and electronics goods, which over

Table 2.5 Manufacturing value added, annual average growth rates, 1960–2019

	1960–70	1970–80	1980–90	1990–2000	2000–10	2010–19	1960–2019
Indonesia	5.3	13.5	12.3	8.0	5.1	4.7	7.4
Korea	18.5	18.0	12.2	10.8	8.0	3.9	11.0
Malaysia		11.8	10.9	11.8	5.6	5.0	8.4*
Philippines	6.5	7.0	1.5	2.9	4.1	5.8	4.2
Singapore	15.4	13.2	8.2	8.4	7.8	5.7	8.4
Thailand	12.9	11.7	10.3	5.9	5.9	2.5	7.4

Note *Malaysia—1970–19
Source Computed from World Bank (2020) data

the period 2013–19 even exceeded the primary exports associated with petroleum and palm oil (Fig. 2.8). Metals and machinery, and transport equipment have been the next biggest manufactured exports from Malaysia.

Given the dominance of electric and electronics products in Malaysia's manufactured exports, we compare the innovation-intensity of the industry by using integrated circuits (IC) patents filed in the United States. Table 2.6 shows the number of integrated circuits' (ICs) patents filed by the East Asian economies in the United States over the period 1985–2019. The focus on R&D has produced a massive expansion in patents filed by firms and organizations located in South Korea and Taiwan. Besides, national firms dominate patents filed in South Korea and Taiwan. These countries are then followed by Singapore and China. While foreign firms accounted for most of the patents filed from Singapore and China until 2005, national firms have become

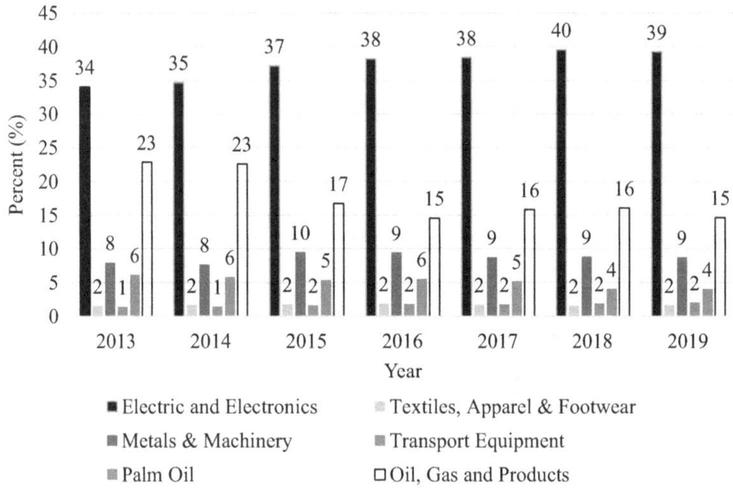

Fig. 2.8 Main exports, Malaysia 2013–2019. *Source* Compiled and plotted from Bank Negara Malaysia (2020) data

Table 2.6 IC patents filed in the united states by selected country firms, 1981–2019

Period	1981–1985		1986–1990		1991–1995		1996–2000		2001–2005		2006–2011		2012–2019	
Country	N	F	N	F	N	F	N	F	N	F	N	F	N	F
China	0	0	0	0	0	3	0	27	11	52	409	265	7816	1100
Indonesia	0	0	0	0	0	0	0	0	0	0	0	20	0	48
Malaysia	0	0	0	0	0	1	0	5	4	39	24	318	34	644
Philippines	0	0	0	0	0	0	0	5	0	40	0	102	37	124
Singapore	0	0	0	1	0	14	0	36	4	216	683	449	1752	995
South Korea	1	0	32	5	529	3	2230	73	4165	222	9430	475	23,843	1339
Taiwan	0	0	12	8	368	41	3361	215	6212	455	6186	418	21,521	1404
Thailand	0	0	0	0	0	0	0	3	0	45	12	9	39	68
Vietnam	0	0	0	0	0	0	0	0	0	0	0	1	0	3

Note *N—national; F—foreign
Source USPTO (2020)

more dominant over the period 2006–19. Although Malaysia holds a strong lead over Thailand, the Philippines, Vietnam, and Indonesia, it lags way behind South Korea, Taiwan, and China.

Taken together, it is clear that Malaysia's leading manufacturing industry has performed better than that of Indonesia, the Philippines, and Thailand. However, its performance is significantly short of South Korea and Taiwan. Indeed, in the IC industry, it is not just that Taiwan's and Korea's firms are at the frontier competing with global firms (Mathews & Cho, 2000; Amsden, 1989; Amsden & Chu, 2003), in Samsung and Taiwan Semiconductor Manufacturing Corporation these countries have the leading global firms in memory and logic chips respectively. Singapore and China have also performed better than Malaysia but the distance is not great. While Korea and Taiwan have enjoyed a significant lead, Malaysia's lead over Indonesia, the Philippines, Thailand, and Vietnam suggests that its policies may be superior to the latter. If production history is an important determinant then Malaysia has clearly outperformed the Philippines as IC Multinational Corporations began relocation operations in these countries at about the same time in the early 1970s. We examine this question in the next section.

Three industrial master plans, launched in 1986, 1996, and 2006 focused on stimulating industrial upgrading in Malaysia. However, it was only after the launching of the Action Plan for Industrial Technology Development (APITD) in 1991 meso organizations were established to promote technology development (Rasiah, 1999). The Human Resource Development Council, Malaysian Technology Development Corporation, Multimedia Development Corporation, Multimedia Super Corridor, and Malaysia Industry, Government High Technology (MIGHT) were launched over the period 1993–95. These organizations were targeted to solve collective action problems to strengthen human resources, provide venture capital funding for innovation, promote multimedia product, offer specialized high tech infrastructure, and encourage strategic high technology collaboration. They were also targeted to coordinate and support incubation in science and technology parks that were created since the 1990s.

Learning by doing was the prime mode of technological upgrading in the 1970s as no effort was made to introduce innovation rents *a* la Schumpeter (1934, 1943). Neither were grants targeted at R&D and incubation nor were they targeted at training and standards acquisition as was pursued in Taiwan through the industrial technical research institutes (ITRIs) of Taiwan. Hence, export-oriented industrialization in Malaysia in the 1970s was dominated by low wage and low value added processing, testing and assembling operations (Rasiah, 1995). At the same time a dual economy in which the principal customs area (the primary, secondary and tertiary sectors) was subjected to restrictions imposed by the NEP while the export-oriented sector was exempted from it (Jomo, 1993).

The emphasis on foreign direct investment, however, as noted earlier, fell in the first half of the 1980s when the government assumed nationalistic efforts to bulwark national capital in heavy industries. Impressed by the successes of Japan, and South Korea, the government launched the Look East Policy in 1981 to spearhead national-ownership based heavy industrialization. Since the examples used were

Japan and Korea, one could claim that the influence came from Abramovitz (1956) and Gershenkron (1962) but specifically Johnson (1982) and Amsden (1989), but the direct influence of Japanese associates of Prime Minister Mahathir. Protection and state ownership targeted at eventually leaving control to *Bumiputeras* became the rallying cry of the government to industrialize. High commodity prices in the late 1970s enabled such a policy, which included massive highway and bridge construction across the Western corridor of Peninsular Malaysia. While restrictions were not imposed on export-oriented foreign capital, incentives to these firms were gradually terminated. Import-substitution policies resembled the type advocated by structural economists. However, these industries failed miserably because they not only lacked the introduction of Schumpeterian innovation rents that Amsden (1989) had argued were critical in South Korea's catch-up, they also lacked the use of the stick to ensure discipline and performance. Although the car-maker Proton is still functioning it does not have a significant presence in the national economy.

Heavy industries were derailed by a combination of sharply falling commodity prices and the appointment of top managers without the requisite tacit knowledge. Supporting the preferred national capital with subsidized credit was similar to what South Korea did. However, unlike South Korea which forced the chaebols to export their way out of the 1975–76 balance of payments and debt crisis, Malaysia imposed no performance standards on these firms. The situation got worse in 1984–1985 when a cyclical trough occurred in the main export product of the electronics industry due to overproduction and an appreciating Yen following the Plaza Accord in 1985 that raised external debt exposure. Rather than following the Korean strategy of imposing export quotas the Malaysian government devalued the ringgit and reissued generous tax holidays to attract FDI, while calls to introduce technological deepening were deferred.

External developments changed the economic environment dramatically from the second half of the 1980s. Following the Plaza Accord of 1985, the Yen, Won, NT dollar, and Singapore dollar began to appreciate. In addition to a devaluation of the Ringgit in 1986 and the withdrawal of the generalized system of preferences from the Asian newly industrialized countries in February 1988 attracted an avalanche of FDI from Japan, South Korea, Taiwan, and Singapore to the whole of developing Southeast Asia's market economies, including Malaysia (Rasiah, 1995). Hence, the share of FDI in gross domestic investment in Malaysia rose from 10.7% in 1980–90 to 24.6% in 1991–93 (UNCTAD, 1996). Korea and Taiwan emerged as major new investors from the second half of the 1980s as a consequence.

Exports were also stimulated through the use of export refinancing schemes, export abatement allowances, and double deduction tax exemptions (Malaysia, 2001). Several industries began to experience export surges primarily due to rising global demand and FDI redeployment. While the export-oriented foreign-led manufacturing sector grew rapidly making Malaysia's economy successful as the annual average GDP growth rate exceeded 8% over the period 1988–96, the inward-oriented IS sector in contrast performed dismally. Despite enjoying huge rents from protection, heavy industries in Malaysia did not enjoy massive profits because of escalating costs of imports and royalties until the early 1990s. The captive domestic market, which grew substantially through growth in employment from export manufacturing and resource-based industries, helped generate demand for domestic ventures in the country. Hence, Proton, Perodua, Kedah Cement, Perak Hanjoong, UEM, Renong, Sime Darby, and PNB reaped enormous rents. A significant share of the rents were mere transfers from domestic consumers whose options were sharply restricted by duties and opaque selection procedures.[12] The domestic economy grew so much that even national textile and garment firms, such as South Island garment began to move in a major way into real estate sector speculation and property development (Rasiah, 1995). With the exception of a few obvious failures such as Perwaja (Jomo, 1990), the microeconomic losses in consumer welfare were not evident during the boom of 1987–95 as strong domestic demand masked such transfers in deadweight losses. Hence, a number of inward-oriented national ventures benefited from demand created from FDI-led export manufacturing growth.

Hence, with the exception of resource-based processed palm oil and oleo-chemicals, most nationally owned manufacturing industries did not experience strong growth in value added. Some inward-oriented manufacturing industries became successful from second round import-substitution. Domestic rents helped create the scale needed for learning in klinker and cement production, and highway construction. Hence, YTL Corporation acquired Perak Hanjoong (a Korean firm) to become a successful cement manufacturer, while United Engineers Malaysia (UEM) acquired the knowledge to build modern highways that enabled its successful forays abroad, including India, China, United States, and Japan (NST, 2017). Where export markets and import competition was stiff as in steel and car manufacturing the firms have either failed or are merely surviving through the help of state-created rents.

However, as argued by Rasiah (1999), these organizations failed to galvanize rapid upgrading in the country. In Korea and Taiwan, these meso organizations were led by managers who not only studied related courses in the best universities in the United States but had also gained tacit knowledge managing high technologies in lead firms.[13] This is a key catch-up route deployed by South Korea and Taiwan (Rasiah & Lin, 2005; Saxenian, 2006). In Malaysia similar experts were bypassed. R&D Grants were offered in Korea, Taiwan, and Singapore but while the former emphasized *ex ante* vetting, monitoring and *ex post* appraisal to limit rent dissipation, such evaluations were loosely carried out in Malaysia. Both Singapore (since 1986) and Malaysia (since 2005) offered R&D grants to foreign firms too. However, Singapore's leveraging strategy ensured that there was human capital and technological development in the country (Rasiah, 2020a, b). Also, while the leading Taiwanese high technology firms were spun out from science parks through coordination by experts who gained tacit and experiential knowledge from abroad, Malaysian incubators did not enjoy such direction and discipline. Hence, without the use of experts carrying

[12] Malaysia had in place not only high duties on imported cars until 2004, it has continued to restrict automobile imports through the mandatory requirement of application permits (APs).

[13] The managers of Malaysia's high technology supporting organizations not only lacked tacit knowledge, but was also colored by ethnic considerations. Jesudason (1989) had long argued that ethnic considerations slowed down Malaysia's economic development.

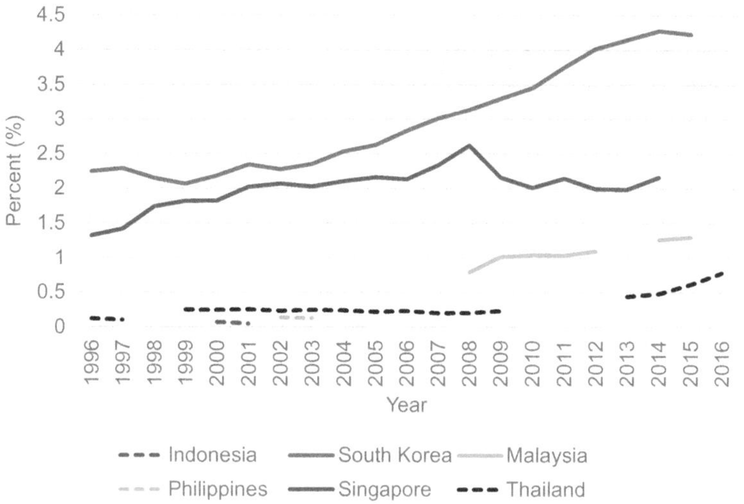

Fig. 2.9 R&D expenditure in GDP, Southeast Asian market economies, 1996–2017. *Source* World Bank (2020) data

tacit (Polanyi, 1966) and experiential (Penrose, 1959) knowledge, the management of Malaysian meso organizations lacked the drive and experience to strategize and appraise to support potential innovators.

Recognizing that Malaysian manufacturing firms have failed to upgrade to move up the value chain, the government began increasing expenditure on R&D so that Gross Expenditure in R&D (GERD) as a share of GDP rose in trend terms over the period 2008–2016 (Fig. 2.9). Grants were not only offered to selected firms but also to universities and public laboratories. However, as can be seen in Fig. 2.9, Malaysia's GERD still fell significantly below that of Korea and Singapore although it was higher than that of Indonesia and Thailand.

However, the trend increase in Malaysia's GERD/GDP since 2008 is little reflected in technological upgrading within manufacturing, which is demonstrated by the low trade balance achieved in intellectual property (IP) payments and receipts. While all countries in Fig. 2.10 recorded a negative IP balance in the period 1981–2017, whereas Malaysia improved slightly since 2015, Singapore and Korea have improved dramatically from higher levels in 2014 and 2015, respectively. Wong and Goh (2010) and Gopi Krishnan et al. (2015) used regression results to show that investments into R&D in Malaysia positively impacted increased scientific publications, but showed no relationship with patent filing in the United States and GDP growth. In contrast, Wong and Goh's (2010) regressions on Korea and Taiwan showed a positive and strong relationship between R&D investment and patent filing in the United States and GDP growth. Central to this anomaly is the lack of effective human capital development policies. We examine this issue in the next section.

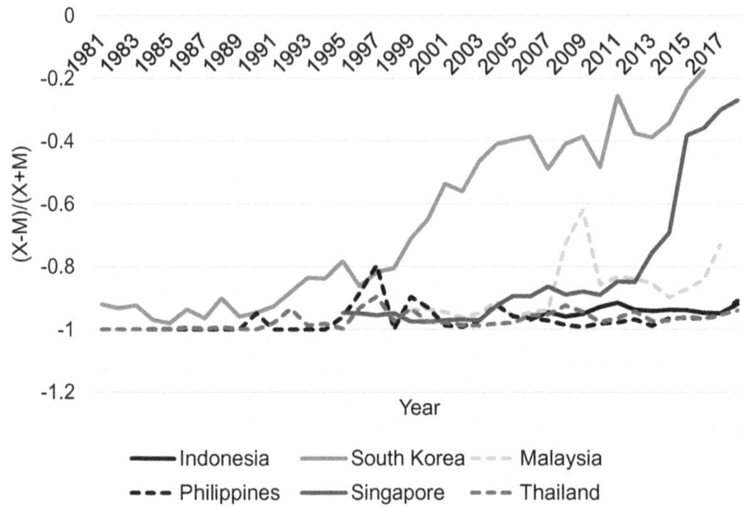

Fig. 2.10 International property trade balance, selected countries, 1981–2018. *Note* M and X—refer to import payments and export receipts, respectively. *Source* World Bank (2020) data

Challenges to the Education System

Underlying Malaysia's limited innovation capacity, as pointed out, has been the lack of sufficient training and experience of the personnel available to industry and other research and development efforts. Efforts to greatly improve physical infrastructure, institutional efficiency, and mass education (particularly in the fields of science and technology) were very successful in Korea, Taiwan, and Singapore, there is evidence to suggest that Malaysia's performance on these three dimensions were considerably less impressive, and that is particularly the case in the area of education. Malaysia has made much progress in expanding access to education but much less progress in upgrading the quality of education. We will examine in this section the quality of the Malaysian education system by looking at two components: high school and universities.

The State of High School Education

For the assessment of the high school component, we use the PISA (Programme for International Student Assessment) scores collected by the OECD every three years, beginning in 2000. PISA tests the scholastic performance of 15-year old students around the world in Mathematics, Reading, and Science. Malaysian participated in the 2009, 2012, and 2015 assessments, but the 2015 Pisa scores of Malaysia were excluded from the final tabulation because they were judged to be insufficiently reliable.

The 2009 PISA scores for Malaysia did not appear in the regular official PISA report of 2009 published in 2010 by the OECD, they appeared instead in a supplement volume, PISA, 2009 "Plus Results: Performance of 15-year olds in reading, mathematics and science for 10 additional participants," published in 2011 by the Australian Council for Educational Research (ACER). Ten countries (including Malaysia and the United Arab Emirates) were added to the original sample of 65 countries in the regular official 2009 PISA report. Since the United Arab Emirates included Dubai as a member, we dropped Dubai from the expanded 2009 sample set we constructed, bringing the consolidated 2009 sample size to 74 countries.

From the official 2012 PISA report of 65 countries we created a comparator group of 6 countries to provide a benchmark to assess the quality of Malaysian education and the change in quality over 2009–2012. These six countries were picked on the basis of two reference points.

First, we chose 2012 as the reference year because we want to assess the performance of Malaysian high schools in the ASEAN context. And the 2012 Pisa Report contains more ASEAN members (Indonesia, Malaysia, Singapore, Thailand, and Vietnam) than 2009 Pisa Report (where Vietnam was absent).

Second, we chose Mathematics as the reference subject area. This is because PISA (2009, pp. 6) stated that, more so than Reading and Science, "Proficiency in mathematics is a strong predictor of positive outcomes for young adults, influencing their ability to participate in post-secondary education and their expected future earnings". In the 2012 sample of 65 countries, Malaysia ranked No. 52 in Mathematics in 2012, Chile was No. 51 and Mexico was No. 53—and we put similar-ranked Chile and Mexico into our comparator group (which already includes Indonesia, Singapore, Thailand, and Vietnam).

Table 2.7 shows that, for every country, the international ranking of its students' performance in each of the three areas (Mathematics, Reading, and Science) are generally quite close. In 2012, the respective ranks for Thailand were 50, 48, and 49, and for Indonesia were 64, 62, and 64. This feature of similar international rank for a country across the three disciplines was also seen in the two Latin American countries: 51, 48, and 47 for Chile, and 53, 51, and 53 for Mexico– a maximum difference of 4 across disciplines.

Table 2.7 also shows that the international rank of a country was relatively stable in 2009–2012. Thailand's respective rank for the three subjects (Mathematics, Reading and Science) in 2009 was 51, 51, and 50; Indonesia's was 63, 59, and 62; Chile was 48, 43, and 43; and Mexico was 50, 49, and 52—a maximum difference of 5 across time for any discipline. Of course, this general stability in ranking over time might be the artifact of the short 3-year period.

For Malaysia in 2012, its respective rank for the three subjects was 52, 59, and 53—a difference of 7 between Reading and Math-Science, which suggests that the reading ability of Malaysian students is unusually low for this level of mastery of Math-Science. What is more worrying is that the general performance of Malaysian students fell in the 2009–2012 period compared with the other six countries in

Table 2.7 Scholastic performance of 15-year old students in selected countries

	Income (GDP per capita, PPP)	International rank			Mean score		
	Constant 2011 International $	Mathematics	Reading	Science	Mathematics	Reading	Science
2012 PISA score (official sample of 65 countries)							
Singapore	75,777.4	2	3	3	573	542	551
Vietnam	4,910.3	17	20	21	511	508	528
Thailand	14,584.7	50	48	49	427	441	444
Chile	21,142.0	51	48	47	423	441	445
Malaysia	22,706.6	52	59	53	421	398	420
Mexico	16,158.3	53	51	55	413	424	415
Indonesia	9,282.7	64	62	64	375	396	382
2009 PISA score (our constructed reference sample of 67 countries)							
Singapore	63,610.8	2	5	4	562	526	542
Vietnam	4,260.0	NA	NA	NA	NA	NA	NA
Thailand	12,663.0	51	51	50	419	421	425
Chile	18,505.6	48	43	43	421	449	447
Malaysia	20,051.8	55	53	51	404	414	422
Mexico	14,843.4	50	49	52	419	425	416
Indonesia	8,074.5	63	59	62	371	402	383

Source Pisa Scores are from Walker (2011) and OECD (2014), and GDP per capita data from World Bank, World Development Indicators, https://databank.worldbank.org/source/world-development-indicators. Accessed 27 March 2017

Table 2.7. The two-place improvement in Mathematics (from 55 in 2009 to 53 in 2012) was very much offset by the 6-place drop in Reading and 1-place drop in Science.

When we look at the mean PISA score in each subject across time, we see two classes of outcome in Table 2.7: definite significant improvement versus mixed performance. Singapore and Thailand showed definite improvement with increases in score in all three subjects, ranging from 8 to 20 points. For Mathematics, Chile, Malaysia, and Indonesia showed improvement but Mexico's score declined. For Reading and Science, retrogression characterized Chile, Malaysia, Mexico, and Indonesia.

Malaysia displayed the most volatile changes in the country sample: a 17-point rise in Mathematics score but a 16-point decline in Reading. Because there was a general improvement in the mastery of Mathematics across the comparator group of countries, the 17-point rise for Malaysia translated only to a 2-place improvement in rank. The 16-point decline in Reading, on the other hand, caused a 6-place drop

Table 2.8 Mastery of different reading skills, 2009

	Overall reading score		Score on the components of the reading test			
		Access and retrieve	Integrate and interpret	Reflect and evaluate	Continuous texts	Non-continuous texts
	(a)	(b)	(c)	(d)	(e)	(f)
OECD average	493	495	493	494	494	493
Singapore	526	526	525	529	522	539
Thailand	421	431	416	420	423	423
Chile	449	444	452	452	453	444
Malaysia	414	408	417	407	414	410
Mexico	425	433	418	432	426	424
Indonesia	402	399	397	409	405	399

Source Walker (2011)

in rank. Overall, Table 2.7 shows that it is easier to argue that the quality of high school education in Malaysia has decreased rather than increased in the international context. It was at best unchanged.

We are able to look further into the nature of the large decline in Malaysia's PISA score on Reading in 2009–2012 because the 2009 Pisa Report contains the breakdown of the Reading score according to the five components of Reading Skill: (1) Access and Retrieve, (2) Integrate and Interpret, (3) Reflect and Evaluate, (4) Comprehension of Continuous Texts, and (5) Comprehension of Non-Continuous Texts. Table 2.8 presents the data for 6 of the 7 countries in our comparison group (Vietnam was not in the 2009 Report). The Overall Reading Score for Malaysia in 2009 (414) was substantially lower than Singapore (526), Thailand (421), Chile (449), and Mexico (425) but substantially higher than Indonesia (402).

Singapore, Chile, and Mexico dominated Malaysia in every component of the Reading Test. Thailand did not dominate Malaysia only because its score for "Integrate and Interpret" was 1 point below that of Malaysia. It is noteworthy that Malaysia could not dominate Indonesia in Reading because its score for "Reflect and Evaluate" was 2 points lower than Indonesia's score (409). Table 2.8 confirms that Malaysian high school students had a particularly difficult time mastering Reading Skills.

The most unexpected aspect in Table 2.7 is that although the income level of Malaysia (22,706.6[14]) in 2012 is higher than those in Vietnam (4,910.3), Thailand (14,584.7), and Chile (21,142.0), the scholastic performance of Malaysian high school students was dominated in all three fields by the performance of students in these three countries. Although Mexico's income (16,158.3) is only 71% of

[14] Measured as GNP per capita in PPP constant 2011 international dollars.

Malaysia's, its Reading score in 2012 (424) was substantially higher than Malaysia's (398).

Since the academic achievements of Malaysian high school students in 2012 were worse than in the lower-income countries of Vietnam, Thailand, and Chile, could this outcome be due to education being inadequately supported by the Malaysian government budget? The education budgets of the seven countries are expressed as a percent of total government expenditure in Table 2.9 and as a percent of GDP in Table 2.10. By expressing the education budget as a percent of the total government budget, we are able to assess the priority that the government gives to education. The 20.1% of budget that the Malaysian government allocates to education is second only to Singapore (24.1%), and is as strongly committed to supporting education as Thailand (20.3%), and Mexico (19.1%).

The normalization of the education budget by GDP in Table 2.10 shows the amount of resources that a country is investing in education relative to its income. The figure of 5.4% of GDP for Malaysia is the highest in the sample, being 2.1% higher than Singapore (3.3%). Only two other countries invested more than 4% of GDP in the economy: Vietnam and Mexico. Given that Malaysia has lower PISA scores than Singapore and Vietnam, and ties with Mexico, it appears that the high investment by Malaysia on education has been either inefficiently implemented or rendered ineffective by something in the system.

Figure 2.11 shows the cross-country relationship between the Mathematics score and the pay of the teacher (measured as a percent of per capita income) in 2012. It is found that a statistically significant positive relationship exists for countries with per capita income of US$20,000. For countries with per capita income of less than US$20,000, this relationship is negative but not statistically significant. Malaysia has a Mathematics score slightly lower than that of Chile, but Malaysian teachers were paid 210% of average income compared to 140% for Chilean teachers. Thailand's Mathematics score was substantially above Malaysia's but its teachers were paid only 125% of the average income. The policy message from Fig. 2.11 is that Malaysia had greatly overpaid its ineffective high school teachers.

It also appears that the high expenditure on education in Malaysia has greatly increased the quantity of educational opportunities but it has not increased the quality of the educational experience. Figure 2.12 reports the categorization of countries into a graph where the Y-axis is performance in Mathematics and the X-axis is accessibility to education. Malaysia is in the southeast quadrant which is characterized by "below-average mathematics performance and above-average equity in education opportunities". Indonesia, Mexico, and Thailand are also in this southeast quadrant. Like Malaysia, these three countries have greatly increased access to high school education but the quality of their high schools is lagging.

The reservation of large proportions of student bodies at Malaysian public universities to Bumiputeras caused two responses by members of the non-Bumputera community: (1) a massive outflow of non-Bumiputera students to foreign universities (especially to Taiwan, Australia, and the United Kingdom); and (2) the growth of private education institutions. There had always been private colleges (e.g. Taylor College) providing training for professional exams like accountancy and law. Two

Table 2.9 Education budget as percentage of GDP

	Malaysia	Indonesia	Singapore	Thailand	Vietnam	Chile	Mexico	China	India
1987	–	–	–	–	–	–	–	9.46	–
1988	–	–	–	–	–	–	–	10.74	–
1989	–	–	–	–	–	–	–	–	–
1990	–	–	–	–	–	–	–	–	–
1991	–	–	–	–	–	–	12.15	–	–
1992	19.11	–	–	–	–	–	15.10	12.29	–
1993	17.31	–	–	–	–	13.52	–	14.77	–
1994	19.92	5.86	–	–	–	14.13	21.56	20.06	–
1995	19.50	6.15	–	18.90	–	15.02	24.12	18.72	–
1996	22.77	7.50	–	20.04	–	15.76	–	19.51	–
1997	20.05	7.71	–	21.20	–	14.50	–	–	13.32
1998	–	–	–	19.48	–	15.17	16.32	14.55	14.16
1999	21.19	–	–	18.98	–	15.65	16.69	12.63	16.96
2000	21.39	–	20.31	28.39	–	16.43	19.65	–	16.73
2001	24.35	11.59	21.56	24.24	–	–	20.62	–	–
2002	25.90	14.37	21.42	16.22	–	17.45	21.46	–	–
2003	24.54	16.28	24.76	20.87	–	17.64	22.47	–	12.41
2004	21.01	14.17	22.74	21.46	–	17.02	22.05	–	11.20
2005	–	15.15	22.28	20.55	–	16.20	21.90	–	11.21
2006	16.75	–	22.54	22.00	–	16.23	20.82	–	11.69
2007	16.12	14.94	23.23	18.48	–	16.75	19.89	–	–
2008	14.04	13.67	30.10	18.16	18.05	17.40	17.38	–	–
2009	18.46	19.31	21.85	18.18	15.24	17.04	18.67	–	11.19
2010	18.41	16.65	18.57	16.22	17.11	17.84	18.64	–	11.83
2011	20.98	18.01	28.86	22.63	17.81	17.75	18.42	–	13.56
2012	19.85	18.09	31.37	21.40	18.78	–	18.09	–	13.99
2013	19.45	17.60	28.84	19.13	18.52	19.65	16.91	–	14.05
2014	19.80	17.67	–	–	–	19.92	18.81	–	–
2015	19.81	20.50	–	–	–	19.59	19.02	–	–
2016	20.94	–	–	–	15.60	21.16	17.94	–	–
2017	21.68	–	–	–	–	21.30	–	–	–
2018	19.74	–	–	–	14.47	–	–	–	–
Average	*20.12*	*14.18*	*24.17*	*20.34*	*16.95*	*17.09*	*19.07*	*14.75*	*13.25*

Source Data are from World Bank, World Development Indicators, https://databank.worldbank.org/source/world-development-indicators. Accessed 15 March 2020

Table 2.10 Education budget as percentage of GDP

	Malaysia	Indonesia	Singapore	Thailand	Vietnam	Chile	Mexico	China	India
1987	6.33	–	–	3.12	–	2.82	–	1.80	–
1988	–	–	3.65	2.75	–	–	–	1.76	–
1989	–	0.87	–	2.50	–	–	2.28	–	–
1990	–	–	–	.	–	2.25	2.32	–	–
1991	–	–	–	3.09	–	–	2.55	–	–
1992	5.11	–	–	3.05	–	–	3.01	1.65	–
1993	4.65	–	–	–	–	2.38	–	1.66	–
1994	4.71	1.00	–	3.41	–	2.51	3.65	1.99	–
1995	4.34	1.00	–	3.14	–	2.56	3.69	1.84	–
1996	4.91	1.08	–	3.50	–	2.80	–	1.85	–
1997	4.62	1.07	.	4.58	–	3.01	–	–	3.36
1998	–	–	–	4.63	–	3.34	3.37	1.84	3.57
1999	5.69	–	–	4.83	–	3.73	3.54	1.89	4.42
2000	5.97	–	3.32	5.25	–	3.78	3.99	–	4.32
2001	7.48	2.46	3.54	4.82	–	–	4.24	–	–
2002	7.66	2.65	3.88	3.86	–	4.08	4.45	–	–
2003	7.50	3.22	3.98	3.73	–	3.96	5.07	–	3.61
2004	5.92	2.75	3.65	4.03	–	3.54	4.73	–	3.35
2005	–	2.87	3.20	3.94	–	3.26	4.85	–	3.19
2006	4.49	–	2.86	4.05	–	3.02	4.70	–	3.14
2007	4.37	3.04	2.95	3.60	–	3.21	4.69	–	–
2008	3.96	2.90	2.76	3.51	4.89	3.79	4.82	–	–
2009	5.97	3.53	3.01	3.86	4.82	4.23	5.19	–	3.28
2010	4.97	2.81	3.08	3.51	5.14	4.16	5.16	–	3.38
2011	5.76	3.19	3.03	4.81	4.81	4.05	5.11	–	3.80
2012	5.74	3.41	3.07	4.54	5.53	–	5.10	–	3.87
2013	5.48	3.36	2.85	4.12	5.65	4.53	4.70	–	3.84
2014	5.21	3.29	–	–	–	4.73	5.26	–	–
2015	4.97	3.58	–	–	–	4.88	5.24	–	–
2016	4.82	–	–	–	4.34	5.34	4.91	–	–
2017	4.74	–	–	–	–	5.40	–	–	–
2018	4.53	–	–	–	4.17	–	–	–	–
Average	*5.38*	*2.53*	*3.26*	*3.85*	*4.92*	*3.66*	*4.26*	*1.81*	*3.63*

Source Data are from World Bank, World Development Indicators, https://databank.worldbank.org/source/world-development-indicators. Accessed 15 September 2017

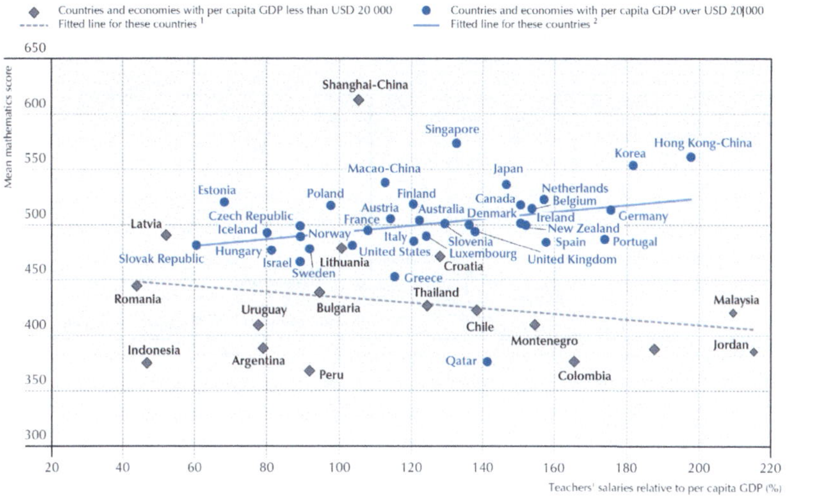

Note: Teachers' salaries relative to per capita GDP refers to the weighted average of upper and lower secondary school teachers' salaries. The average is computed by weighting lower and upper secondary teachers' salaries according to the enrolments of 15-year-old students (for countries and economies with valid information for both upper and lower secondary education).

1. A non-significant relationship ($p > 0.10$) is shown by the dotted line.

2. A significant relationship ($p < 0.10$) is shown by the solid line.

Fig. 2.11 Overpaid but ineffective teachers in Malaysia—Teachers' pay and score on mathematics. *Source* OECD (2014: 27)

private colleges, INTI and HELP, emerged in 1985 offering courses to connect local students to overseas university degrees ("twinning programmes"). HELP started with a South Australian degree programme, and INTI with an American degree programme. They were adopting what MARA College had been doing—credit transfer courses at MARA before sending the students overseas. Both INTI and HELP started with about 30 students.

The Tertiary Education sector expanded rapidly in the 1967–2007 period. The number of public universities increased from 1 in 1967 to 20 in 2007, and the number of private tertiary institutions rose from zero to 33 in the same period. The number of students enrolled in domestic tertiary institutions went from 4,560 to 873,238; and the number of Malaysian students studying abroad was 54,915 in 2007. The outcome was that the ratio of the population in the 18–24 age group attending tertiary education institutions (home and abroad) was 26.7% in 2007 which is very much above the 4% attendance rate in 1967.

However, this almost 30% university attendance rate in Malaysia is too low. The university attendance rate of the 18–24 group is about 80% in South Korea and about 60% in the United States. The access to tertiary education in Malaysia is still too limited to permit knowledge-based growth to be the new norm. In short, Malaysia still has a quantity problem.

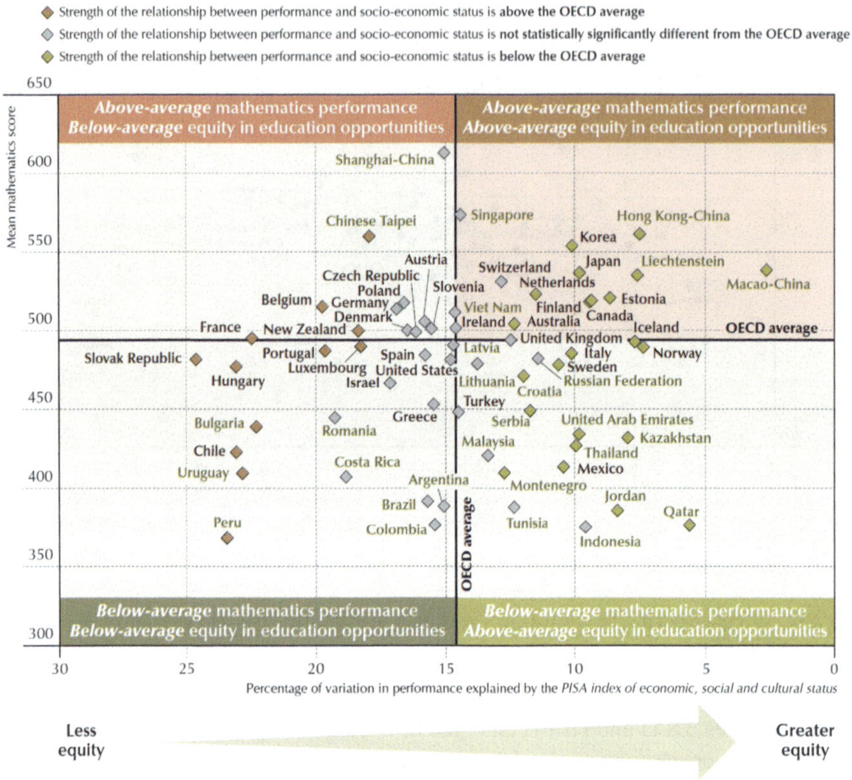

Fig. 2.12 Education in Malaysia is highly accessible but quality is low—score on mathematics and equity in access. *Source* OECD (2014: 13)

Brain Drain from Malaysia

In 2011, the World Bank issued a worrisome report on brain drain from Malaysia (Schellekens, 2010), which is summarized in Fig. 2.13. The Malaysian diaspora was estimated to be about one million people in 2010, compared to about 750 thousand in 2000. When we define "brain drain" as the outward migration of people with tertiary-level education, the brain drain from Malaysia was 335 thousand in 2010, up from 217 thousand in 2000. The proportion of the diaspora that represented brain drain was therefore 29% in 2000 and 33% in 2012, which means that 43% of the outward migration was brain drain. Thus, the trend in outward migration is that it is becoming more and more the preserve of the skilled.

The number of skilled Malaysians living abroad has tripled in the last two decades with two out of every 10 Malaysians with tertiary education opting to leave for either OECD countries or Singapore. This is four times the world average. Malaysia's brain drain is worsened by inadequate compensating inflows. 60% of immigration into

Malaysia has only primary education or less, and the number of skilled expatriates has declined by 25% since 2004.

Given the lower skill base—as proxied by educational attainment—the impact of a person leaving should also be higher in Malaysia than elsewhere, keeping all else constant.

According to the World Bank (2011) report, the top three drivers for brain drain were career prospects, social injustice and compensation. "Social injustice" refers to the non-inclusiveness nature of many Malaysian government policies (e.g. exclusive scholarship programmes for Bumiputras), causing much discontent in the non-Bumiputera community, whose members make up the bulk of the diaspora (88% in 2010). Philip Schellekens, the lead author of the World Bank report, has concluded that brain drain "is likely to intensify, further eroding the country's already narrow skills base in the absence of mitigating actions" (Lee, 2011).

As to the question of what is to be done, we would like to quote at length the frank recommendations of Schellekens (2010)

> [There is the fundamental] need to update Malaysia's inclusiveness strategies so as to realign them with the objective of becoming a high-income economy.

The need to update Malaysia's inclusiveness strategies reflects both new realities and new challenges. The new reality is that poverty is no longer the key issue when

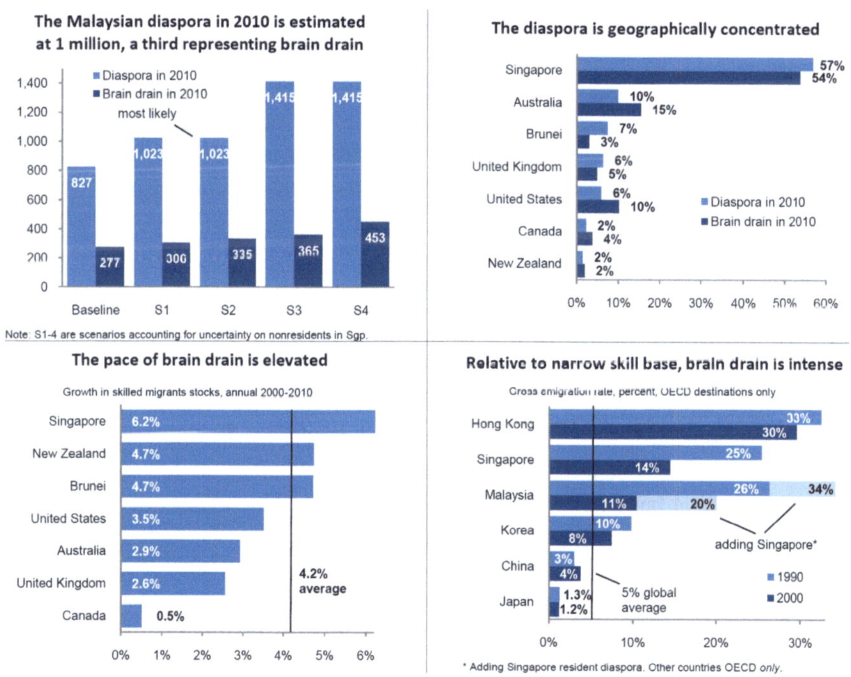

Fig. 2.13 Brain drain in Malaysia, and the benefits of tapping overseas talents

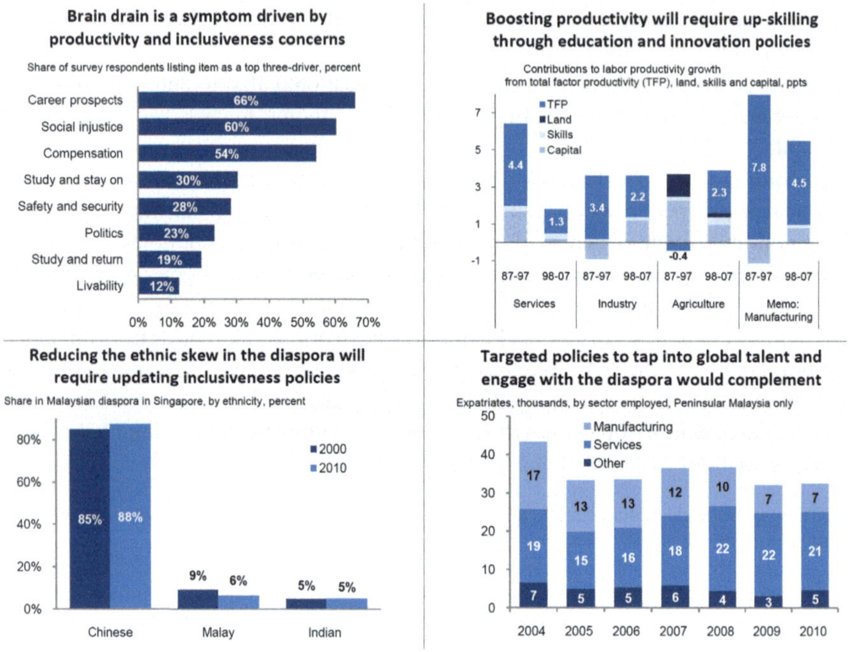

Fig. 2.13 (continued)

thinking about inclusive growth. Poverty still exists—and pockets of poverty remain deep and concentrated. Individual socio-economic characteristics, such as activity status, sector of employment, urban versus rural stratum, and educational attainment are now the capital explanatory factors, no longer ethnicity (Cheong & Lee, 2020; Selvaratnam, 2022; Kuppusamy, 2020).

Conclusions

Since independence in 1957, Malaysia launched policies that both supported economic growth and a major restructuring of society. The restructuring was designed first to eliminate the identification of occupation with race and second to reduce poverty in general but among Bumiputera specifically. The policies that made this growth and transformation possible relied on market forces, macroeconomic stability, and major government investments in infrastructure and education. After 1971, the favoured position of Bumiputera with respect to access to government appointment was reinforced by policies designed to pressure the private sector to hire more Bumiputera and to give Bumiputera a larger share in the ownership and management of the economy. Of particular importance, public education at the university level was reoriented to give the major share of student places to Bumiputera and to support a steadily increasing role for Bumiputera in the faculties and management of public universities.

As this chapter has demonstrated, these policies succeeded in achieving their major goals. GDP since 1960 has averaged a growth rate of 6.3% per year, while GDP per capita averaged 3.8% per year. This growth alone has eliminated much of the poverty that existed in the country at the time of independence. For the poorest Bumiputera, the impact of growth on poverty has been reinforced by a wide range of government efforts to promote Bumiputera education, employment, and income. By the twenty-first century, each of the major ethnic groups in the nation was well represented in professions, in business, and most areas of employment. The major exception was government employment where Bumiputera dominated. Ownership was also widely shared with Bumiputera dominating in economic activities where the government role was central and Chinese-Malaysians dominating in the private sector (35 of the 50 wealthiest Malaysians, for example, were Chinese-Malaysians).

While the policies put in place at independence and substantially revised after 1971 have largely accomplished their objectives to date, there is ample reason to suggest that these same policies carried forward into future decades are likely to be much less successful and may even lead Malaysia into the much-feared "middle-income trap". GDP growth and growth per capita, for example, have held up at 4.8 and 3.0%, respectively, since 2000. While this is a slowdown from the past, it is likely that the slowdown to date mainly reflects the fact that Malaysia has achieved a level of per capita income (US$25,000 in 2011 PPP prices) when all countries that have gone on to high-income status have slowed down.

The problem going forward is first and foremost that at this level of income sustaining economic growth increasingly depends on the ability of a country to innovate at the frontier of knowledge. As our discussion above argued, in the electronics industry, Malaysia does have some capacity to innovate at a level that has kept Malaysian products in this sector internationally competitive as the country has moved up the technology ladder. Malaysia's innovative capacity in this sector is superior to that in other Southeast Asian countries, such as Thailand, Indonesia, and the Philippines, but even in this sector, Malaysian innovating capacity falls far behind that of the economies of Northeast Asia.

Malaysia thus needs a domestic innovating capacity that is based in Malaysian companies and carried out by Malaysian workers and entrepreneurs. There is no secret as to why Malaysia has to date failed to create the human resource base required for an innovating society and economy. The post-1971 New Economic Policies, while once necessary in order to include all of the country's people in development and thus ensure their support for development, have outlived their usefulness. Where once they created stability and broad support for the government, they now are increasingly slowing down the country's capacity to upgrade into higher value added activities. Their impact on the education system has had an even more direct and negative impact on the ability of the country to become an innovation leader.

The real problem with the post-1969 ethnic policies lies with those that primarily benefit the Bumiputera elites. These elites that are already highly educated and have high incomes continue to receive favoured access to a wide range of government favours ranging from finance to government contracts and much else. While many of these favoured positions are legal according to Malaysian law, they are often widely perceived by many (including many well-educated Bumiputera) as corrupt. The alienation of so many of the younger educated elites in all ethnic groups has driven those determined to hold on to their elite privileges to move in an increasingly conservative direction towards policies that are antithetical to continued rapid growth and a rise to high-income status.

The most direct impact of these policies is on the education sector, particularly at the university level. All great universities around the world hire faculty and university leaders strictly on the basis of merit—not on political or ethnic criteria or even on nationality in the very best universities. While there are many very able Malaysian faculty members and deans in the public universities, the quality of Malaysian university education falls far below what one would expect in a country with Malaysia's high per capita income.

The continued pursuit of such a strong ethnic agenda has caused one other problem that inhibits growth to high-income status. In countries such as China and Korea, governments have made major efforts and have offered a wide variety of incentives, and particularly strong elements of nationalism to get their most skilled and highly trained people to return home and stay home. Northeast Asia's success in moving rapidly up the technology ladder has resulted from the hundreds of thousands of people trained in the best institutions abroad, many also with work experience in places such as Silicon Valley, have given up good positions abroad to return home. Malaysia has done the opposite for the large share of its population that is not Bumiputera. Large numbers of non-Bumiputera trained abroad never come home and many of the ablest trained at home leave, notably to Singapore.

References

Abramovitz, M. (1956). Resource and output trends in the United States since 1870. *American Economic Review, 46*, 5–23.

Amsden, A. H., & Chu, W. W. (2003). *Beyond late development: Taiwan's upgrading policies*. MIT Press.

Amsden, A. H. (1989). *Asia's next giant: South Korea and late industrialization*. Oxford University Press.

Bosworth, B. P., & Collins, S. M. (2003). The empirics of growth: An update. *Brookings Papers on Economic Activity, 2*.

Chamhuri, S., Rospidah, G., & Mohamad, I. (2021). Agriculture and food security. In: R. Rasiah, K. Salih, & K.C. Cheong (Eds.), *Malaysia's leap into the future: the building blocks*. New Delhi: Springer.

Chee, P. L. (1986). *Small industry in Malaysia*. Berita Publishing.

Cheong, K. C., & Lee, L. L. T. (2022). Developing Talent: The Role of the State. In R. Rasiah, K. Salih, & K. C. Cheong (Eds.), *Malaysia's leap into the future: The building blocks for balanced development*. Singapore: Springer.

Corden, W. M., & Neary, P. J. (1982). Booming sector and de-industrialization in a small open economy. *Economic Journal, 92*, 825–848.

Feenstra, R. C., Inklaar, R., & Timmer, M. P. (2013). *The next generation of the Penn world table.* Available: www.ggdc.net/pwt
Gershenkron, A. (1962). *Economic backwardness in historical perspective.* Harvard University Press.
Gopi Krishnan, V., Santha, C., & Rasiah, R. (2015). Human capital and innovation output in Malaysia's economic development. In N. P. Tey, K. C. Cheong, & R. Rasiah (Eds.), *Revisiting malaysia's population-development nexus* (pp.101–120). Kuala Lumpur: University of Malaya Press.
Jesudason, J. V. (1989). *Ethnicity and the economy: The state, Chinese business and multinationals in Malaysia.* Singapore: Oxford University Press
Johnson, C. (1982). *MITI and the Japanese miracle.* Stanford University Press.
Jomo, K. S. (1990). *Growth and structural change in the Malaysian economy.* Macmillan.
Jomo, K. S. (1993). Malaysia's industrialization in historical perspective. In Jomo, K. S. (Ed.), *Industrializing Malaysia: Policy, performance and prospects* (pp. 14–39). London: Routledge.
Kuppusamy, S., & Salih, K. (2022). Cities, urbanization and infrastructure. In R. Rasiah, K. Salih, & K. C. Cheong (Eds.), *Malaysia's leap into the future: The building blocks for balanced development.* Singapore: Springer.
Lee, W. L., (2011). Malaysia's brain drain getting worse, says World Bank. The Malaysian Insider.
Lim L. Y. C. (1978). *Multinational firms and manufacturing for export in less-developed countries: The case of the electronics industry in Malaysia and Singapore.* Doctoral thesis submitted to University of Michigan, Ann Arbor.
Malaysia (1971). *Second Malaysia Plan 1971–1975.* Kuala Lumpur: Government Printers.
Malaysia. (2001). *Sixth Malaysia Plan 2001-2005.* Government Printers.
Malaysia. (2020). Malaysia: External trade statistics 2020. Accessed on 20 Dec 2020 from https://www.matrade.gov.my/en/malaysian-exporters/services-for-exporters/trade-market-information/trade-statistics/181-malaysian-exporters/trade-performance-2020
Mathews, J. A., & Cho, D. S. (2000). *Tiger Technology: The creation of a semiconductor industry in East Asia.* Cambridge University Press.
NST. (2017). UEM - connecting people, New Straits Times. August 30, Accessed on 13 Dec 2021 from https://www.nst.com.my/business/2017/08/274545/uem-connecting-people
OECD, Organization for Economic Cooperation and Development (2014). *PISA 2012 results in focus: What 15-year-olds know and what they can do with what they know.* OECD, Paris.
Penrose, E. T. (1959). *The theory of the growth of the firm.* Oxford University Press.
Perkins, D. H., & Woo, W. T. (2000). Malaysia: Adjusting to deep integration with the world economy. In W. T. Woo, J. D. Sachs & K. Schwab (Eds.), *Asian financial crisis: Lessons for a resilient Asia.* Cambridge: MIT Press.
PISA (2009). *Plus results: Performance of 15-year olds in reading, mathematics and science for 10 additional participants.* Published in 2011 by the Australian Council for Educational Research (ACER).
Polanyi, M. (1966). *The tacit dimension.* Chicago University Press.
Rasiah, R. (1989). Competition and restructuring in the semiconductor industry: Implications for technology transfer and absorption in Penang. *Southeast Asian Journal of Social Sciences, 17*(2), 41–57.
Rasiah, R. (1993). Free trade zones and industrial development in Malaysia. In K. S. Jomo (Ed.), *Industrializing Malaysia: Policy, performance and prospects* (pp. 118–146). London: Routledge.
Rasiah, R. (1995). *Foreign capital and industrialization in Malaysia.* Macmillan.
Rasiah, R. (1999). Malaysia's national innovation system. In K. S. Jomo & G. Felker (Eds.), *Technology, competitiveness and the state.* London: Routledge.
Rasiah, R. (1998). The Malaysian financial crisis: Capital expansion, cronyism and contraction. *Journal of Asia Pacific Economy, 3*(3), 358–378.
Rasiah, R. (2011). Is Malaysia facing negative deindustrialization? *Pacific Affairs, 84*(4), 715–736.

Rasiah. (2020a). Malaysia: Trade statistics 2020. Accessed on Dec 2020 from https://www.matrade.gov.my/en/malaysian-exporters/services-for-exporters/trade-market-information/trade-statistics/181-malaysian-exporters/trade-performance-2020

Rasiah, R. (2020b). Industrial policy and industrialization in Southeast Asia. In O. Arkebe, C. Cramer, H. J. Chang, & R. K. Wright (Eds.), *Oxford handbook ofiIndustrial policy*. Oxford: Oxford University Press.

Rasiah, R., & Lin, Y. (2005). Learning and innovation: The role of market, government and trust in the information hardware industry in Taiwan. *International Journal of Technology and Globalization, 1*(3/4), 400–432.

Rasiah, R., Yap, X. S., & Chandran, V. G. R. (2014). Crisis effects on the electronics industry in Southeast Asia. *Journal of Contemporary Asia, 44*(4), 645–663.

Rasiah, R., Norma, M., & Chandran, V. G. R. (2015). Royal professor Ungku Abdul Aziz: A key pillar in Malaysia's development. *Institutions and Economies, 7*(3), 1–19.

Sala-i-Martin, X. (1997). I just ran four million regressions. National Bureau of Economic Research, Working Paper No. 6252.

Salih, K., Young, M.L., & Rasiah, R. (1988). Changing dimensions of the periphery: The case of the Semiconductor Industry in Malaysia. *International Journal of Urban and Regional Research, 12*(3), 375–403.

Saxenian, A. L. (2006). *The new argonauts: Regional advantage in a global economy*. Harvard University Press.

Schellekens, P. (2010). Why updating Malaysia's inclusiveness strategies is key. 8 November http://blogs.worldbank.org/eastasiapacific/print/2926

Schumpeter, J. A. (1934). *The theory of economic development: An inquiry into profits*. Credit, Interest and the Business Cycle (Transaction Press).

Schumpeter, J. A. (1943). *Capitalism*. Harvard University Press.

Selvaratnam, V. (2015). *Education policy in Malaysia: The past, the present and the future*. mimeo.

Selvaratnam, V. (2022). Malaysian education: The past and the future. In R. Rasiah, K. Salih, & K. C. Cheong (Eds.), *Malaysia's leap into the future: The building blocks for balanced development*. Singapore: Springer.

Shah, S. N. (2017). *Charting the economy: Early 20th Century Malaya and contemporary Malaysian contrasts*. Oxford University Press.

Shah, S. N. (2019). *Striving for inclusive development: From Pangkor to a modern Malaysian State*. Oxford University Press.

Solow, R. (1956). A contribution to the theory of economic growth. *Quarterly Journal of Economics, 70*(1), 65–94.

Solow, R. (1957). Technical change and the aggregate production function. *Review of Economics and Statistics, 39*(3), 312–320.

Tan, T. W. (1982). *Income distribution and determination in West Malaysia*. Oxford University Press.

Thoburn, J. (1977). *Primary commodity exports and economic development: Theory*. Wiley.

UNCTAD (1996). *Trade and development*. Geneva: United Nations Conference for Trade and Development.

USPTO (2020). Patent data, semiconductor and solid state devices, compiled from United States Patent Office. Accessed on 25 Aug 2020 from http://patft.uspto.gov/netahtml/PTO/search-adv.htm

Vogel, E. (1991). *The four little dragons: The spread of industrialization in East Asia*. Harvard University Press.

Walker, M. (2011). *PISA 2009 plus results: Performance of 15-year olds in reading, mathematics and science for 10 additional participants*. ACER Press.

Wong, C. Y., & Goh, K. L. (2010). Growth behavior of publications and patents: A comparative study on selected Asian economies. *Journal of Informetrics, 4*(4), 460–474.

Woo, W. T. (2012). China meets the middle-income trap: The large potholes in the road to catching-up. *Journal of Chinese Economic and Business Studies, 10*(4), 313–336.

Woo, W. T. (2011). Understanding the middle-income trap in economic development: The case of Malaysia: Invited World Economy Lecture delivered at the University of Nottingham. *Globalization and Economic Policy Conference.*

World Bank. (2020). *World development indicators.* World Bank Institute.

Dwight Heald Perkins is Professor Emeritus at Harvard University. He was previously the Director of the Harvard Institute of International Development. He specializes on the Economics of East and Southeast Asia.

Rajah Rasiah is Distinguished Professor of Economics at Asia-Europe Institute, Universiti Malaya, and visiting Professor at the Institute of Energy Policy and Research, UNITEN. He received the 2014 Celso Furtado Prize from the World Academy of Sciences for advancing the frontiers of social science (Economics) thought.

Wing-Thye Woo is Distinguished Professor of Economics at the University of California, Davis. He is also Director and Professor at the Jeffrey Sachs Institute on Southeast Asia, Sunway University.

Chapter 3
Population and Demography

Nai Peng Tey

Abstract This chapter on population and demography provides a description of population growth, fertility, mortality, and migration trends that resulted in population outcomes, on the age structural shifts and changes in the ethnic composition over the 1970–2020 period. The second part of this chapter presents the likely changes in population size and structure for the period 2020–2050. The implications of population changes are discussed in relation to the demographic dividend, labour supply, challenges of an ageing population, and the need to prepare the youths to compete globally. The chapter concludes with recommendations to make use of demographic research for planning purposes.

Keywords Population growth · Age structural shift · Demographic dividend · Ethnic composition · Projection · Labour force · Ageing

Introduction

Large numbers of workers from China and India brought in by the British to work in tin mining and rubber plantation in the nineteenth century and early part of the twentieth century contributed to rapid population growth and shaped Malaysia's multi-ethnic composition. With strict immigration policy enforcement after World War II, natural increase has been the predominant determinant of population growth. Malaysia experienced the post-war baby boom, which generated the momentum for population growth in the following decades amidst falling mortality rates. However, the natural increase was inadequate to meet the demand for labour of a rapidly expanding economy in the 1980s, and this led to the influx of a new wave of migrant workers, which continues unabated till today.

Soon after the formation of Malaysia in 1963, concerns over rising unemployment and the economic implications of rapid population growth led to the launching of the National Family Planning Programme in 1966 to reduce the population growth

N. P. Tey (✉)
Faculty of Business and Economics, University of Malaya, 50603 Kuala Lumpur, Malaysia
e-mail: teynp@um.edu.my

R. Rasiah et al. (eds.), *Malaysia's Leap Into the Future*, Dynamics of Asian Development, https://doi.org/10.1007/978-981-16-7045-9_3

from 3% per annum to 2% by 1985. Nevertheless, the emergence of a labour shortage prompted the government to adopt a pro-natalist policy in 1984, when the population grew at 2.5% per annum. The new population policy called for the achievement of a 70 million population by 2100. A larger population was deemed necessary to support industrial development (Economic Planning Unit, 1983). Rapid socio-economic development and the increased contraceptive use resulted in the continuing fertility decline to replacement level by 2012. The rate of population growth dipped below 2% per annum, to a level of 1.9% between 2000 and 2010, and 0.4% in 2020, despite the influx of migrant workers (DOSM, 2011, 2020a).

Policymakers and planners need population projections to plan for the future demand for resources. The future course of population changes depends on past and current demographic dynamics. Hence, this chapter begins with an elucidation of population growth, age-sex composition, fertility, mortality, and migration trends that resulted in population outcomes over the 1970–2020 period. The second part discusses the changes in population size and structure for the period 2020–2050. This chapter concludes with some discussions of the implications of future population changes and the necessary policy interventions.

Data for the exposition of the demographic and labour market dynamics are taken from published reports of the Department of Statistics, Malaysia (DOSM) and the United Nations (UN) Population Division (UN, 2019a, b). The UN projected the population of all countries up to 2100. The projections were revised based on the most recent data. In contrast, population projection by the DOSM covers only up to 2040 (DOSM, 2016).

Population Growth, 1970–2020

Over the 50 years between 1970 and 2020, Malaysia's population grew from 10.9 million to 32.7 million, at a rate of 2.2% per annum. However, due to declining fertility, population growth decelerated in the first decade of the new millennium to 1.9% per annum. The crude rate of natural increase (CRNI) was rather close to the population growth rate in the 1970s and 1980s. However, the population growth rate exceeded the CRNI since the 1990s due to the influx of foreign workers (Table 3.1). Between 2019 and 2020, the population grew at only 0.4%, while the CRNI was at around one percent per annum. The number of non-citizens increased from 63,700 in 1980, 0.7 million in 1990 to 1.4 million in 2000 to 2.3 million in 2010, and an estimated 3.0 million in 2020, making up 0.5%, 4.3%, 6.0%, 8.1%, and 9.2% of the total population (DOSM Population Censuses, various years, and current population estimates, 2020a).

Table 3.1 Total population, citizens and growth, Malaysia, 1970–2020

Year	Total population (million)	Citizen (million)	The annual rate of growth of the total population (%)	The CRNI (%)
1970	10.9	10.9	-	-
1980	13.9	13.8	2.4	2.4
1990	18.1	17.4	2.6	2.4
2000	23.3	21.9	2.5	2.3
2010	28.3	26.0	1.9	1.7
2020	32.7	29.7	1.4	1.3

Sources DOSM, population censuses (1970–2010), *Vital Statistics Reports (various years)*; Current population estimates (2020a)
Note Between 2019–2020, population grew at 0.4%; crude rate of natural increase = 1.0%

Changes in Age-Sex Composition

The age-sex composition of a population is affected by past trends in fertility, mortality, and migration. The sex ratio at birth has remained constant at around 107 males per 100 females. The 2010 population census shows more males than females in all age groups below 70, with a sex ratio ranging from 1.01 for the population aged 65–69 to 1.12 for those aged 30–34. Owing to their longer life expectancy, females outnumbered males at older ages. The sex ratio was estimated at 0.96 and 0.83 for those aged 70–74 and 75 and over, respectively (DOSM, 2011).

Consequent to the continuing fertility decline and rising life expectancy, the population's age structure had changed dramatically between 1970 and 2020, as shown by the population pyramid (Fig. 3.1). There has been a sharp reduction in the population aged below 15 and an increase in the working age 15–64. Between 1970 and 2020, the population aged below five had declined from 15.7 to 8.1%, and those below 15 from 44.8 to 23.4%. There was a corresponding increase in the working age (15–64) from 51.9 to 69.4%, and those aged 65 and older from 3.3 to 7.2% (Fig. 3.2). The increase in the proportion of working-age population represents a demographic dividend and a window of opportunity for economic growth, as relatively more people are in the working-age groups, resulting in a lower dependency burden.

Fertility Transition

In Malaysia, fertility decline began in the early 1960s. The crude birth rate (CBR) fell from 41.8 per thousand in 1961 to 37.3 per thousand in 1966, and the total fertility rate (TFR) fell from 6.2 children per woman to 5.7 during the same period. Economic problems associated with rapid population growth, including rising unemployment rates, led to the launching of the National Family Planning Programme in 1966. One of the programme objectives was to reduce the population growth rate from 3%

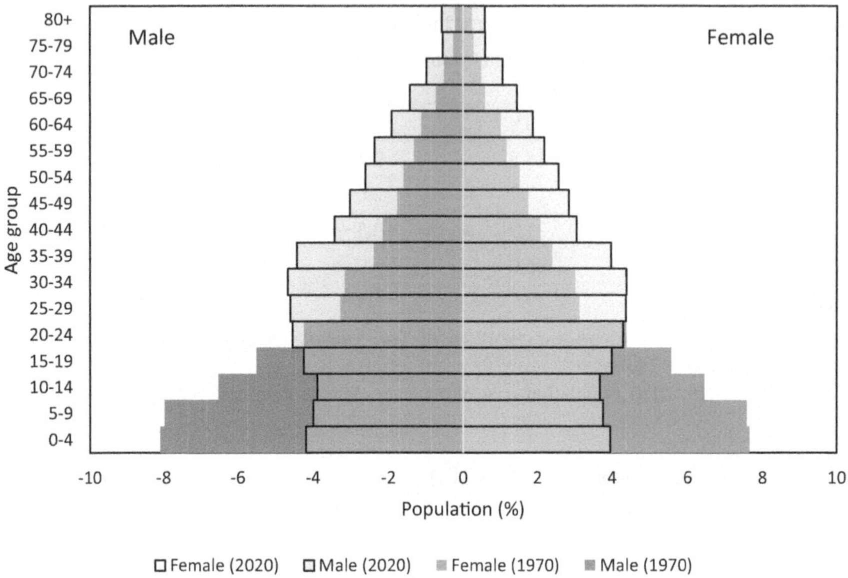

Fig. 3.1 Population pyramid, Malaysia, 1970 and 2020. *Source* UN (2019a)

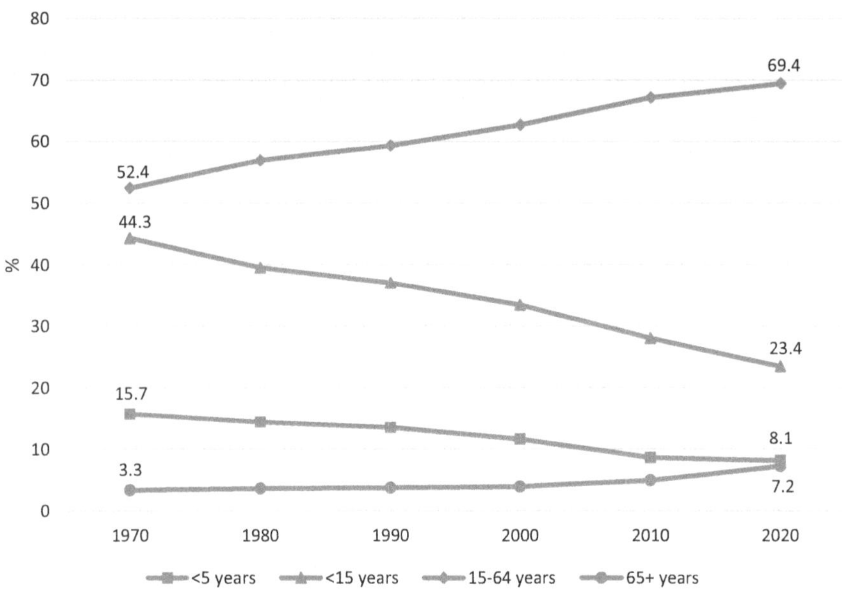

Fig. 3.2 Distribution of population by age group, Malaysia, 1970–2020. *Source* UN (2019a)

Table 3.2 Crude birth rate by ethnicity, Malaysia, 1963–2019

Year	Malaysia	Bumiputera/Malays	Chinese	Indians
1963	38.1	39	36.6	41
1965	36.1	36.6	35	39
1970	32.4	32.8	30.8	31.7
1975	30.7	32.8	27.3	29.8
1980	30.6	33.7	25.6	29.4
1985	31.5	36.2	23.6	27.1
1990	27.9	31.3	21.4	24.2
1995	26.8	30.3	20.5	23.4
2000	22.9	25.4	20	20.8
2005	18.2	20.9	14.5	16.1
2010	17.2	20.5	11.5	14.3
2015	16.7	20.8	10.6	11.7
2016	16.1	20.3	9.9	11.1
2018	15.5	19.8	8.6	10.7
2019	15.0	18.9	8.7	10.3

Sources DOSM, various years, *Vital Statistics*

in 1966 to 2% by 1985 by recruiting new family planning acceptors to reduce the fertility rate. The CBR fell to 31 per thousand, and the TFR also declined to 4.2 by the mid-1970s. However, over the next decade, the TFR declined modestly to 3.6 children per woman in 1985. Also, there was a slight rise in CBR to 31.5 in 1985 before resuming the declining trend to 15.5 in 2018 (Table 3.2). After stalling at 3.3 children per woman in the early 1990s, the TFR declined to 3.0 in 2000 and 1.8 in 2019 (Table 3.3).

The various ethnic groups in Malaysia have undergone a different fertility transition (Leete, 1996). The Chinese and Indians had higher fertility than the Bumiputera/Malays in the 1960s. However, their fertility level declined much more rapidly to fall below that of the Malays by 1970. In 2019, the CBR was highest among the Bumiputera/Malays at 18.9 per thousand population and lowest among the Chinese, at 8.7 (Table 3.2). The Malaysian Chinese and Indians are now having ultra-low fertility globally, at 1.1 and 1.2, respectively, in 2019. However, the fertility rate of the Bumiputera/Malays is still slightly above the replacement level, at 2.3 children per woman (Table 3.3).

The fertility rate has declined for all age groups. The decline was most pronounced among those aged below 25 and above 40. Sharp fertility decline among younger and older women was due to marriage postponement and earlier cessation of childbearing. Between 2005 and 2018, the adolescent fertility rate oscillated between 7 and 14 per thousand women aged 15–19. On the other end of the age spectrum, the birth rate for women aged 45–49 had come down to just 2 per thousand women since the late 1990s (Table 3.4).

Table 3.3 Total fertility rate by ethnic group, Malaysia 1960–2019

Year	Malaysia	Bumiputera/Malays	Chinese	Indian
1960	6.1	5.8	6.3	7.2
1965	5.7	5.7	5.9	6.6
1970	5.0	5.2	4.6	5.0
1975	4.2	4.6	3.7	3.9
1980	3.9	4.9	3.1	3.4
1985	3.6	4.8	2.7	2.9
1990	3.3	4.1	2.3	2.6
1995	3.3	4.0	2.5	2.6
2000	3.0	3.5	2.5	2.4
2005	2.5	2.9	1.8	1.9
2010	2.1	2.7*	1.5	1.7
2015	2.0	2.6	1.4	1.4
2018	1.8	2.4	1.1	1.3
2019	1.8	2.3	1.1	1.2

Sources DOSM, various years, *Vital Statistics*

Table 3.4 Age-specific fertility rate, and total fertility rate (per thousand women), Malaysia, 1960–2019

	Year	15–19	20–24	25–29	30–34	35–39	40–44	45–49	Period TFR
All races	1960	116	306	308	245	159	68	14	6,080
	1965	80	266	308	246	156	69	19	5,720
	1970	56	224	271	228	144	70	16	5,045
	1975	45	188	236	190	124	46	8	4,185
	1980	35	176	233	177	108	42	5	3,880
	1985	21	135	219	176	111	43	5	3,550
	1990	19	124	203	171	106	39	4	3,330
	1995	15	123	215	170	103	33	2	3,305
	2000	12	92	189	164	98	33	3	2,955
	2005	7	74	166	147	84	23	2	2,515
	2010	14	58	128	131	73	21	2	2,136
	2016	10	47	111	120	74	20	2	1,918
	2018	9	44	103	117	72	22	2	1,841

Note TFR—Total fertility rate
Sources DOSM, various years, *Vital Statistics*

The mean age at first marriage for Malaysian men and women had increased from 25.5 years and 22.0 years in 1970 to 28 years and 25.7 years in 2010. More and more young Malaysians are remaining single. Between 1970 and 2010, the proportion of men and women still single at age 30–34 had increased from 12 and 6% to 28% and 18%, respectively (Tey, 2007; DOSM, 2012).

Soon after its launching, the family planning programme increased contraceptive use sharply and accelerated the fertility decline. However, the contraceptive prevalence rate (CPR) has stagnated at around 50% since 1984, following the adoption of the 70 million population policy, which shifted the programme thrust from family planning to family development. Since then, rising age at marriage and non-marriage, and rapid socio-economic development has become the predominant proximate and distal determinants of fertility. The rapid rise in enrolment in tertiary education since the 1990s increased female participation in the urban labour market, the rising cost of living and childcare, the breakdown of the extended system, and the sharp reduction in infant mortality rate provided the necessary conditions for the fertility to dip below the replacement level, as was the case of many low fertility countries (Jejeebhoy, 1995; Martin, 1995; Bongaarts, 2003; Hirschman, 2003; Bollen et al., 2007, Sanjay et al., 2016; Dierk et al., 2012; Teresa, 1995; Arunachalam et al., 2014; Huan, 1997; Renata & Tienda, 1996).

Mortality Rate and Life Expectancy

Fertility decline in Malaysia was preceded by mortality decline. The crude death rate declined from 19.4 per thousand in 1947 to 15.8 in 1950, 9.5 in 1960, 7.0 in 1970, 5.5 in 1980, and 5.3 in 2019. The infant mortality rate declined from about 100 per thousand births in the late 1940s to 68.9 in 1960, 39.4 in 1970, 23.80 in 1980, 13.1 in 1990, and 6.4 in 2019 (DOSM, various years, vital statistics reports).

Mortality decline has resulted in an increase in life expectancy of more than ten years between 1970 and 2020. In 1970, life expectancy was 61.6 years for males and 65.6 years for females, and these increased steadily over the years to reach 72.6 years and 77.6 years, respectively, in 2020 (Table 3.5). The abridged life table for 2020

Table 3.5 Life expectancy by gender, Malaysia, 1970–2020

Year	Males	Females
1970	61.6	65.6
1980	66.4	70.5
1990	68.9	73.5
2000	70.0	74.4
2010	71.9	77.0
2020	72.6	77.6

Sources DOSM, various years, Abridged life tables

shows that males and females at age 60 can expect to live another 18.2 years and 20.9 years, respectively (DOSM, 2020b).

Changes in Ethnic Composition

The ethnic fertility differentials resulted in significant changes in the ethnic composition of the population. In 1970, Malays and other Bumiputera made up 56% of the total population, Chinese 34%, Indians 9.0%, and others 1.0%. In 2010, the proportionate share of the Bumiputera increased to 62% (50% Malays and 12% other Bumiputera), while that of the Chinese, Indians, and others decreased to 23%, 7%, and 0.7%, respectively. The citizen population in Peninsular Malaysia comprised about 64% Malays, 26% Chinese, and 9% Indians. In Sabah, the Kadazan/Dusun was the largest group, making up 24.5% of the citizen population, followed by the Bajau (19.4%), Chinese (12.8%), Malays (7,9%), Murut (4.4%), and all other indigenous groups (28.5%). The Iban was the largest ethnic group in Sarawak, making up 30% of the citizen population, followed by the Chinese (25%), Malays (24%), Bidayu (8%), and Melanau (5%). The changes in the ethnic composition will affect the future course of fertility decline as the Malays' higher fertility level will likely prevent the overall rate from sinking well below the replacement level (Tey et al., 2016).

Non-citizens made up 8.2% of the total population in 2010, and increased to 10% in 2020 (DOSM, 2011, 2020a). In 2020, non-citizens made up 28% of the population in Sabah, in 6.6% in Peninsular Malaysia, and 5.7% in Sarawak.

Urbanization and Population Redistribution

The urbanization level increased from 33.5% in 1970 to 50% in 1990 and 77.2% in 2020, and it is projected to reach 87.3% in 2050 (Fig. 3.3). Malaysia is now the second most urbanized nation in South-east Asia. The 2010 census shows that urbanization level varies widely across states, from 42% in Kelantan, around 50–54% in Pahang, Perlis, Sabah, and Sarawak, to 91% in Pulau Pinang and Selangor, while the Federal Territory of Kuala Lumpur was fully urbanized (table not shown).

The urbanization level also varied widely across ethnic groups, as they have undergone different pace of urbanization. In 1970, 15% of the Malays lived in urban areas, compared to 47% of the Chinese and 35% of the Indians. By 2010, two-thirds of the Malays lived in urban areas, while the urbanization level of the Chinese and Indians had gone up to about 90% each (DOSM, various years, Population Census reports). Rapid urbanization has been brought about by structural changes in the economy and employment. The share of agricultural workers in the labour market declined from 31.2% in 1982 to 10.2% in 2019 (DOSM, 2020c). Urbanization, in turn, affects the demographic processes. Urban couples tended to have a smaller family size than their rural counterparts.

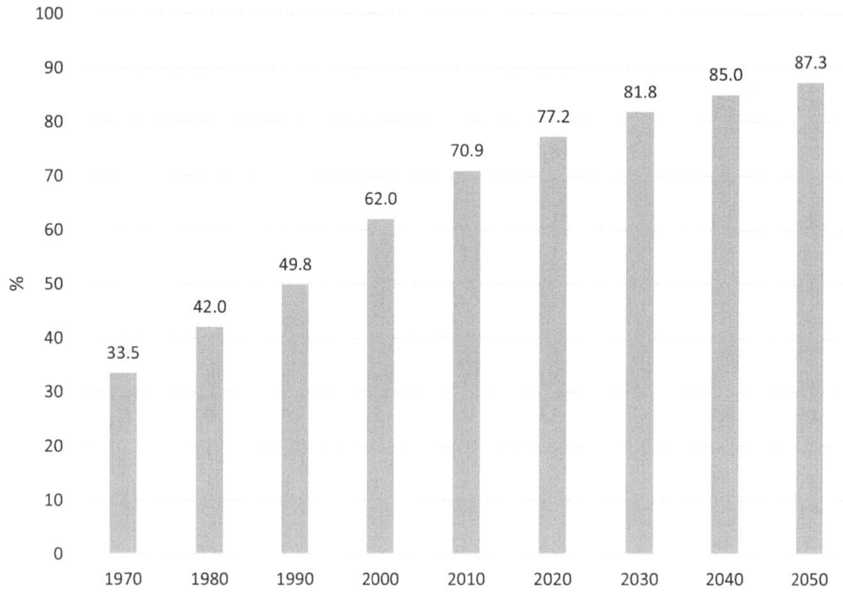

Fig. 3.3 Actual and projected urbanization level, Malaysia, 1970–2050. *Source* UN (2018)

Inter-state migration from the less developed states to the more developed states has contributed to rapid urbanization and population redistribution. Table 3.6 shows that the northern states, namely Perlis, Kedah, Pulau Pinang, and Perak, have been registering a significantly lower population growth rate than states in other regions. Perak was the most populous state in 1970, but it has been experiencing a net loss of population to other states/regions, mainly to the Klang Valley in the central region, such that its proportionate share to the total population has been declining steadily from 15% in 1970 to 7.7% in 2020. Selangor has been registering the most rapid rate of population growth of 3.7% per annum in the 1970s, 4.3% in the 1980s, 6.0% in the 1990s, and 2.2% between 2000 and 2020. Consequently, the proportionate share of Selangor's population had increased from 9.4% in 1970 to 20.0% in 2020. Sabah is another state that registered rapid population growth, primarily due to the influx of migrant workers. The rate of population growth in Sabah reached its peak at 5.7% per annum in the 1980s before tapering off at 3.8% per annum subsequently and 2.0% per annum during the 2000–2020 period. Between 1970 and 2020, Sabah's share of the national population doubled from 6.1 to 12.0%. In contrast, the northern region has a relatively lower rate of population growth due to out-migration. The proportionate share of the population in this region declined from 32.7% in 1970 to 20.6% in 2020.

Table 3.6 Population distribution by state, Malaysia, 1980–2020

State	Population (thousand)/Percent					Average annual rate of growth	
	1980	1990	2000	2010	2020	1980–2020	2010–2020
Total	13,879.3	18,102.4	23,494.9	28,588.6	32,657.3	2.1	1.3
Johor	1,646.2	2,139.6	2,762.5	3,362.9	3,781.1	2.1	1.2
Kedah	1,119.9	1,352.2	1,671.9	1,949.3	2,185.2	1.7	1.1
Kelantan	895.7	1,187.2	1,361.4	1,589.9	1,906.7	1.9	1.8
Melaka	466.9	534.2	646.6	823.6	932.7	1.7	1.2
Negeri Sembilan	576.7	713.4	866.1	1,029.5	1,128.8	1.7	0.9
Pahang	802.1	1,054.3	1,295.8	1,501.9	1,678.6	1.8	1.1
Perak	1,807.4	1,992.9	2,091.7	2,379.0	2,510.3	0.8	0.5
Perlis	148.7	187.0	207.6	235.8	254.9	1.3	0.8
Pulau Pinang	960.7	1,118.5	1,332.7	1,575.9	1,773.6	1.5	1.2
Sabah	1,055.1	1,787.6	2,603.5	3,260.0	3,908.5	3.3	1.8
Sarawak	1,351.1	1,687.8	2,071.5	2,487.1	2,816.5	1.8	1.2
Selangor	1,524.1	2,345.4	4,188.9	5,502.1	6,538.1	3.6	1.7
Terengganu	541.7	784.6	902.6	1,055.4	1,259.2	2.1	1.8
WP KL	982.9	1,217.8	1,416.0	1,674.8	1,773.7	1.5	0.6
WP Labuan	–	–	76.1	88.2	99.6	–	1.2
WP Putrajaya	–	–	–	73.4	110.0	–	4.0
Johor	11.9	11.8	11.8	11.8	11.6		
Kedah	8.1	7.5	7.1	6.8	6.7		
Kelantan	6.5	6.6	5.8	5.6	5.8		
Melaka	3.4	3.0	2.8	2.9	2.9		
Negeri Sembilan	4.2	3.9	3.7	3.6	3.5		
Pahang	5.8	5.8	5.5	5.3	5.1		
Perak	13.0	11.0	8.9	8.3	7.7		
Perlis	1.1	1.0	0.9	0.8	0.8		
Pulau Pinang	6.9	6.2	5.7	5.5	5.4		
Sabah	7.6	9.9	11.1	11.4	12.0		
Sarawak	9.7	9.3	8.8	8.7	8.6		
Selangor	11.0	13.0	17.8	19.2	20.0		
Terengganu	3.9	4.3	3.8	3.7	3.9		
WP KL	7.1	6.7	6.0	5.9	5.4		
WP Labuan	–	–	0.3	0.3	0.3		
WP Putrajaya	–	–	–	0.3	0.3		

Sources DOSM, various years, Population Census reports; (2020a)

Internal and International Migration

The migration surveys conducted annually by DOSM show that migration rates varied widely from year to year (Table 3.7). The number of net migrants for 2010–2018 was pooled to present more meaningful and reliable estimates of recent migration. Between 2011 and 2018 (except 2017), Selangor had a net gain of 153.2 thousand migrants, while Kuala Lumpur had the most substantial net loss of 179.3 thousand, with a net migration rate of −10.1%. Pulau Pinang, Melaka, and Kelantan also registered a significant net in-migration of between 1.3 and 2.4%, while Perak registered a net out-migration rate of −1.8%. The recent migration trend shows that the development corridors in the northern, southern, and eastern regions have failed to attract the migrants, except for Georgetown (state capital for Pulau Pinang) in the north and Johor Bahru (state capital for Johor) in the south. The proportionate share of the population in these regions has continued its declining trend, notwithstanding the launching of the corridor development projects.

In 2018, migrants made up 1.6% of the total population. Of these, 10.7% were international migrants. Of the internal migrants, 32% were inter-state migrants, and 68% were intra-state migrants. Urban-urban migration was the main migration stream, accounting for 66.9% of the total internal migrants, followed by urban–rural migrants, a distant second, at 19.8%, and rural-rural stream at 7%, and rural–urban stream at 6.3%. A sizable proportion of the migrants had moved between adjacent states/regions, especially between Kuala Lumpur and Selangor, involving intra-regional migration. The 2018 Migration Survey report shows that 36% of the migrants to Selangor had come from Kuala Lumpur, while 45% of the out-migrants from Kuala Lumpur had settled in Selangor (DOSM, 2019). The outflow from Kuala Lumpur to Selangor can be attributed to the booming housing development in the suburbs, and many residents find it convenient to commute daily to work.

Over the last two centuries, Malaysia has been a major receiving country of international migrants. Despite growing at a rate of 2.5% per annum since independence in 1957, population growth was insufficient to meet the labour demand in a rapidly expanding economy, which accelerated in the 1980s. The labour shortage has resulted in the influx of foreign workers, which continues unabated till today. The population censuses show that the number of enumerated non-citizens doubled from about 0.7 million in 1991 to 1.4 million in 2000 and then 2.3 million in 2010, and 3.0 million in 2020 (DOSM, various years. Population Census reports, and 2020a). The number of migrants is probably underestimated, as there are many irregulars or illegal migrants who have not been enumerated (Azizah Kassim, 2014). As many as 93% of these recent migrants were low-skilled workers, and they were concentrating in the manufacturing sector (39%), followed by plantation (20%), construction (14%), and agriculture and domestic services, at about 9% each (Azizah Kassim, 2014).

According to the UN's data on international migrant stock, the number of immigrants has increased from 695,920 in 1990 to 3.4 million in 2019 (Table 3.8). Of the migrants in 2019, 35.7% were from Indonesia, 16.9% from Nepal, 12% from Bangladesh, 10% from Myanmar, and between 2 and 6% each from Singapore,

Table 3.7 Net migrants (thousand) by state, Malaysia, 2011–2018

State	2011	2012	2013	2014	2015	2016	2018	Total	Population (thousand), 2015	Net migration rate (%)
Johor	−6.7	−10.7	0.9	−3	3.7	10.7	9.3	4.2	3,610.3	0.1
Kedah	−2.7	2.1	−1.4	−1.2	−2.3	−1.6	−1.7	−8.8	2,096.5	−0.4
Kelantan	3.2	8.1	4.4	3.3	−0.5	1.6	3.2	23.3	1,760.6	1.3
Melaka	−0.2	−1.1	0.7	5.5	3.3	3.1	5.1	16.4	889.0	1.8
Negeri Sembilan	−2	−6.6	−9.2	0.5	−3.4	5.2	2.4	−13.1	1,088.8	−1.2
Pahang	−1.2	−5.2	−1.8	1.8	5.2	−3.2	−8.1	−12.5	1,607.9	−0.8
Perak	−3.3	−7.9	−7.7	−6.1	−6.2	−9.8	−3.3	−44.3	2,466.9	−1.8
Perlis	−2.2	0.5	−0.1	−1.9	−0.6	1	−1.6	−4.9	248.5	−2.0
Pulau Pinang	8.8	5.2	2.5	1	8.4	12	3.3	41.2	1,698.1	2.4
Sabah	−0.1	1.8	6.5	4.5	5.8	−1	−3.3	14.2	3,720.5	0.4
Sarawak	5.5	7.1	4.3	2.4	4.8	−1.9	−0.4	21.8	2,701.5	0.8
Selangor	17.7	22.4	31	30.5	22.7	19.4	9.5	153.2	6,178.0	2.5
Terengganu	−0.4	−3.3	1	−1.3	−2.3	4.4	−0.2	−2.1	1,161.0	−0.2
WP KL	−14.1	−11.2	−26.8	−34.7	−32.3	−37.7	−22.5	−179.3	1,780.4	−10.1

Sources DOSM, various years, Migration Survey reports

Table 3.8 International migrant stock, Malaysia, 1990–2019

Year	Immigrants	Emigrants
1990	695,920	562,762
1995	937,368	863,664
2000	1,463,598	1,203,638
2005	1,918,504	1,380,437
2010	2,417,395	1,598,510
2015	3,280,681	1,795,763
2019	3,430,380	1,689,222

Source UN (2019b)

Vietnam, Philippines, India, and Pakistan. Malaysia also has a substantial emigration of mainly skilled workers. The number of Malaysian diasporas increased from 562,762 in 1990 to about 1.4 million in 2019. Of these, about 69% were in Singapore, 14% in Australia or New Zealand, 8% in Europe, and 7% in North America (UN, 2019b). Many are commuting to work in Singapore daily (Hugo, 2011, 2014).

Population Projection

Population projections indicate the future size of a population and the age and sex distribution if the assumptions of fertility, mortality, and migration hold. The cohort component methods are commonly used to perform long-term population projections based on data from the most recent population census and assumptions about fertility, mortality, and migration.

Experience from European countries and low fertility Asian countries shows that fertility level has remained below replacement level since the 1970s (UN, 2015). As Malaysia has attained a low fertility and mortality level, the scope for further decrease or increase is somewhat limited. Hence, results of different population projections are likely to vary within a narrow range in the short run, barring large-scale international migration.

Under the medium projection by UN (2019a), the overall total fertility rate was assumed to remain at around two children per woman throughout the projection period. Life expectancy, a summary measure of mortality, was assumed to increase by one year every five years. In 2020, life expectancy was 72.6 years for the males and 77.6 years for the females. The number of non-citizens was assumed to remain constant at 2.6 million throughout the projection period. The UN projected the Malaysian population to increase to 36.1 million in 2030, 38.8 million in 2040, and 40.6 million in 2050 (Table 3.9). In comparison, DOSM indicated a projected population of 36.0 million in 2030, and 38.6 million in 2040 (including about 10% of non-Malaysians for each period).

Table 3.9 Population projection, Malaysia, 2015–2050

	2020	2030	2040	2050
Age/Population (thousand)	32,366	36,095	38,755	40,550
	Percentage distribution			
0–4	8.14	7.09	5.91	5.49
5–9	7.75	7.35	6.26	5.51
10–14	7.56	7.32	6.62	5.67
15–19	8.25	7.01	6.91	6.05
20–24	8.85	6.95	6.98	6.49
25–29	8.98	7.61	6.74	6.80
30–34	9.05	8.10	6.63	6.83
35–39	8.41	8.13	7.17	6.53
40–44	6.48	8.10	7.54	6.36
45–49	5.85	7.43	7.48	6.79
50–54	5.17	5.63	7.33	7.03
55–59	4.55	4.98	6.60	6.86
60–64	3.78	4.28	4.88	6.59
65–60	2.87	3.62	4.18	5.75
70–74	2.03	2.79	3.36	4.02
75–79	1.13	1.86	2.53	3.11
80–84	0.71	1.09	1.65	2.16
85+	0.44	0.67	1.22	1.98
Total	100.00	100.00	100.00	100.00
Median age	30.3	34.1	37.8	40.5
<5	8.1	7.1	5.9	5.5
<15	23.4	21.8	18.8	16.7
15–64	69.4	68.2	68.3	66.3
65+	7.2	10.0	12.9	17.0
Young dependency	33.80	31.89	27.53	25.15
Old dependency	10.36	14.70	18.96	25.63
Total dependency	44.16	46.58	46.49	50.78

Source UN (2019a)

As different sub-groups of the population are growing at a different rate, there will be significant changes in the ethnic composition of the citizen population. Population projections by DOSM show that the Bumiputera proportion will continue to rise from 69.1% in 2020 to 72.1% in 2040, with a corresponding decrease of the Chinese and Indian proportion from 22.8% and 7.0% to 20% and 6.4%, respectively (Table 3.10).

The urbanization level will continue to rise from 80.1% in 2025 to 87.3% in 2050 (UN, 2018). The migratory flow from the less developed to the more developed

Table 3.10 Ethnic composition of the citizen population, Malaysia, 2020 and 2040

Ethnic group	2020	2030	2040
Bumiputera	69.1	70.7	72.1
Chinese	22.8	21.3	20.0
Indians	7.0	6.7	6.4
Others	1.1	1.3	1.2
Total	100.0	100.0	100.0

Source DOSM (2016) (Population Projections (revised), Malaysia, 2010–2040

regions will result in further redistribution. The urban population will be gravitating towards the cities. The National Physical Plan of Malaysia estimated the population in the three largest conurbations at 8.46 million in Kuala Lumpur, 2.42 million in Pulau Pinang, and 1.84 million in Johor Bahru in 2020 (cited in Jones, 2014). The development corridors have yet to induce mass migration to these areas, besides to the capital cities.

The age structure of the population will continue to change. The population's median age is projected to rise from 30.3 in 2020 to 40.5 years in 2050. The superimposed population pyramid shows significant age structural shifts between 2020 and 2050, with a substantial reduction in the youngest age population and a sharp increase in the older population (Fig. 3.4). Table 3.9 shows that there will be a shift from youth dependency to old-age dependency, which will have profound implications on the

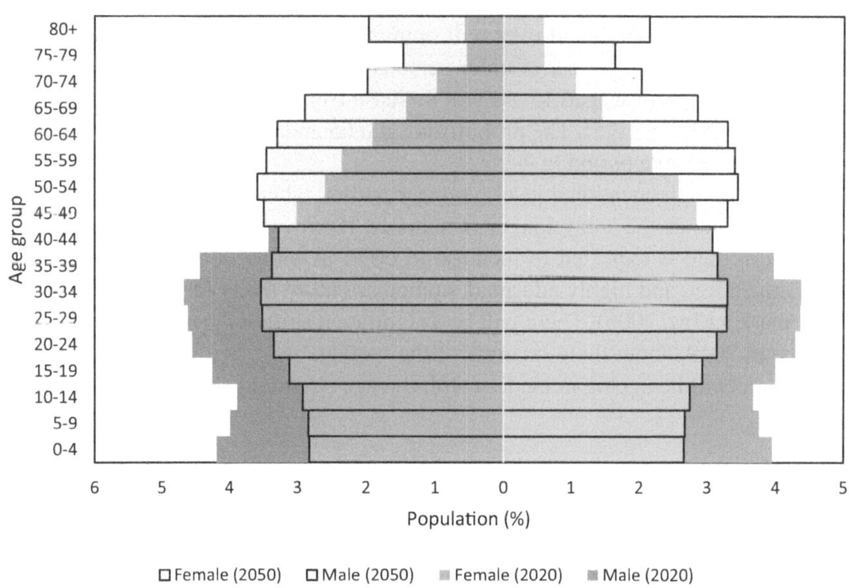

Fig. 3.4 Population pyramid, Malaysia, 2020 and 2050 *Source* Computed based on UN (2019b)

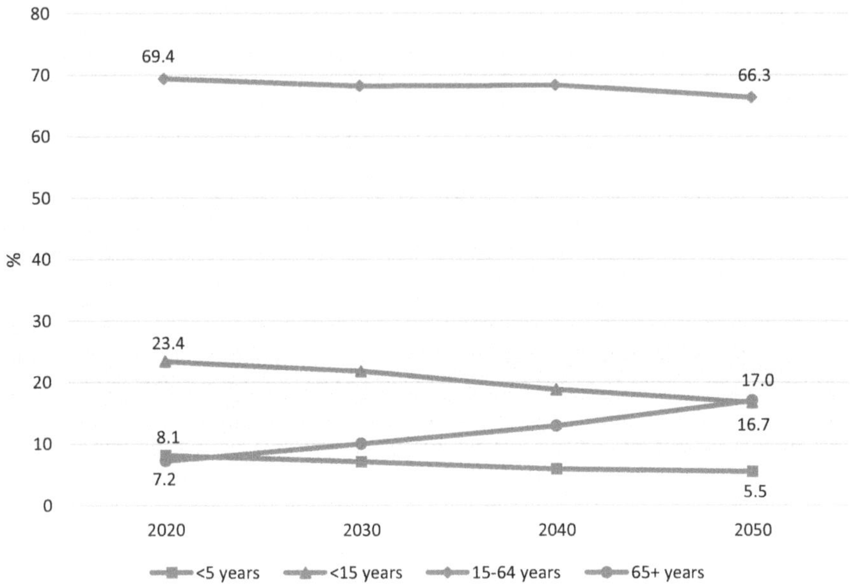

Fig. 3.5 Distribution of population by age group, Malaysia, 2020-2050. *Source* Computed based on Table 3.9

labour market, health care, social protection, domestic consumption, investment, and development planning.

Older persons aged 65 and over will outnumber those below five years around 2020, and by 2050 the number of older persons and those aged below 15 will make up 16–17% each. Those aged 15–64 will increase from 69.4% in 2020 and taper off to 66.3% in 2050 (Fig. 3.5). The proportion aged 65 and over will increase from 7.2 to 17% over the same period.

With the rising educational level, younger adults' labour force participation rate will remain low as they stay longer in schools. However, the female labour force participation rate is expected to increase to 60%, as more women are enrolled in higher education, and highly educated women are more likely to work in the urban labour market (Tey, 2006). There will be a significant shift in the age structure of the workers. In 2019, about three-quarters of the workers were below 45 years, but the labour force will be ageing in tandem with the age structural shift.

Discussions

Trends in mortality and fertility in Malaysia have followed the paths of the Demographic Transition Theory and the demographers' dictum that once fertility has fallen by 10%, it is likely to continue to fall until replacement levels are reached (Kirk,

1996). The mortality rate began to decline as early as the 1940s, followed by fertility decline in the 1960s. The fertility continued to decline, after a brief stalling in the 1990s to reach the replacement level in 2012 and 1.8 in 2019. The demographic transition was not uniform across the various sub-groups of the population, resulting in significant population composition changes. Recent demographic trends show that Malaysia will be entering the phase of low population growth. What will be the likely demographic and social scenarios of Malaysia by 2050? What are the implications of these trends, and what policy measures are needed?

Today's population issues are very different from those in the past. At the formation of Malaysia in 1963, the country was primarily a rural agrarian society. Rapid population growth posed severe problems, such as rising youth unemployment. A slower population growth rate was seen as advantageous as more resources could be devoted to development due to the lower dependency burden. Hence, efforts were made to slow down the population growth rate. However, with economic expansion, the natural increase was insufficient to provide adequate human resources, and Malaysia has been experiencing labour shortage since the 1980s.

Experience of many countries shows that once low fertility is attained, it has remained at a low level for many decades, as in the case of most European countries and Japan (Lutz et al., 2006; Jones et al., 2009; Dudley et al., 2009; McDonald, 2009; UN, 2015). Will Malaysia also be caught in the low fertility trap? With rapid socio-economic development, urbanization, and the rising cost of children, it is unlikely for fertility to rebound substantially. Malaysian Chinese and Indian fertility levels are likely to remain at an ultra low level, as in Singapore, Hong Kong, Mainland China, and Taiwan. Although Malay fertility is still above replacement level, it has also declined rapidly to approach replacement level. Measures taken by low fertility countries to prop up fertility have not been successful (Castles, 2003; Demeny, 1997; Jones, 2012). Some policymakers have already expressed concern over the low fertility. Therefore, there is a need to monitor the fertility trend to prevent it from falling to the problematically low levels reached in many East Asian countries such as Japan, South Korea, and Singapore. Policy measures are needed to support women and men's work-life balance and address the rising age at marriage and non-marriage. Measures to allow work-life balance may include extending maternal/paternity and child care leave (paid and unpaid), flexible working hours; provision of child-minding facilities at the workplace, and providing government subsidies for childcare costs incurred by working mothers; increasing tax concessions for dependent children; and programmes to encourage husbands to be more fully involved in child-rearing and household activities. The 2020 federal budget also provides RM500 monthly incentive for two years for women aged 30–50 who return to work; an RM300 hiring incentive each month for two years for employers; extends income tax exemptions for women returning to work until 2023, and increases maternity leave from 60 to 90 days (National Population and Family Development Board-NPFDB, 2012). The effectiveness of these pilot programmes should be evaluated before up-scaling nationwide.

The mortality level in Malaysia has reached a low level, and as such, the scope for the further decline is somewhat limited. With the ageing of the population, the crude death rate will rise to about 8 per thousand population in 2050. This level is about the same as the current level in the United States and many developed countries. With the improvement in health services and standard of living, life expectancy will rise further, albeit more gradually.

Although Malaysia has attained replacement level fertility, the population will continue to grow due to high fertility in the past, resulting in a young age structure, with momentum for future population growth. Nevertheless, the population growth rate is projected to decelerate to 1.1% between 2020 and 2030 and 0.45% between 2040 and 2050. The UN projected the Malaysian population to stop growing at 44 million in 2065–2070. This demographic reality means that the target population of 70 million in 2100, as envisaged in the New Population Policy adopted in 1984, will not be achieved. The slow population growth will result in a labour shortage after a time lag, implying that Malaysia will continue to rely on foreign labour.

Declines in mortality and fertility have resulted in an age structural shift, and Malaysia will become an aged nation in 2035 when 15% of its population will be aged 60 and over. However, the overall dependency ratio will remain low as the proportion of the population in the working-age group will only decline slightly from 69% in 2015 to 66% in 2050. This demographic dividend provides an opportunity for the country to save and invest in the future. Although population ageing is still at the initial stage, it has received increasing attention from policymakers, as evidenced by the National Policy for the Elderly in 1996 and the revised National Policy for Older Persons in 2011 (Department of Social Welfare, 1995, 2011). There has also been a proliferation of research on ageing in Malaysia. The rise in chronic disease due to population ageing has increased the strain on the existing health care system. Specialized services must be improved to meet older persons' health care needs and reduce disability and deaths among those inflicted with chronic diseases. There is also inadequate social provisioning for older adults. Employee Provident Fund (EPF) or Pension Scheme does not cover about 40% of the labour force. Half of the retirees exhausted their EPF savings within five years of retirement (Holzmann, 2014). With rising life expectancy, a retiree at age 60 can expect to live for 20 more years. Hence, despite the revision of retirement to 60 since 2013, many retirees still lack the financial resources to last their lifespan. Individuals must, therefore, be encouraged to start financial planning in their early working life. A well-developed infrastructure must be put in place to allow older individuals to continue working in a less stressful environment with flexible employment.

As for the younger population, there is a need to prepare them to be competitive in an increasingly borderless world. The government has allocated a lion share of its operating and development budget to the education sector, and Malaysia spends more on education as a share of GDP and as a share of the total government budget than most of its East Asian peers. At the individual level, parents are better positioned to invest in children's education, owing to the smaller family size. Notwithstanding the substantial investment in education, a disturbing trend is the erosion of Malaysian education's standard. A recent study found that Malaysia's absolute scores, not just rankings, in mathematics and science for grade 8-equivalent students fell between 1999 and 2011, below the international average score of 500 by 2007 and far below those of the newly industrialising economies (NIEs) (Cheong et al., 2016). The poor quality of graduates from local universities has become a regular refrain both among employers and in the media (Fernandez-Chung et al., 2014, cited by Cheong et al., 2016). These are issues that warrant urgent attention and remedial actions from all stakeholders. Measures to improve Malaysian education may include recruiting the best graduates into teaching by improving remuneration, fringe benefits, working conditions, and promotion prospects. Technical and vocational skill training programmes should be expanded to those who cannot pursue academic courses (NPFDB, 2012).

The past high fertility means that there will continue to be larger numbers of young Malaysians entering the workforce than older Malaysians retiring for the next two decades. Despite the increasing number of new job seekers, recent media reports point to a severe labour shortage. According to Minter (2016), there is a shortage of 27,000 workers in the furniture industry, farmers are struggling to find local labourers, and 84% of the Federation of Malaysian Manufacturers face human resources shortages. The labour shortage is made worse by Malaysian workers' attitude who shun the 3D (Dirty, Dangerous, and Demeaning) jobs.

The female labour force participation rate (FLFPR) had increased steadily from 44.5% in 1982 to 55.6% in 2019. However, the FLFPR still lagged far behind that of the males (80.8%) and its ASEAN neighbours. The World Bank (2012) estimated that about 2.3 million Malaysian women were absent from the labour market, representing skill and brain "drain" from the workforce.

The economic agenda of the Eleventh Malaysia Plan is to create 1.5 million jobs by 2020, with targetted improvements in labour productivity and reduced dependency on low-skilled foreign workers, both of which are a result of the continuous shift from labour-intensive to knowledge- and innovation-based economic activities that require TVET-related skills (Economic Planning Unit, 2015). The Eleventh Malaysia Plan (2016–2020) has set a much more realistic target than that proposed in the Ninth Malaysia Plan (2006–2010), which targetted the five development corridors to create 11 million new jobs by 2025.

The persistence of labour shortage means that Malaysia will continue to rely heavily on foreign workers. Foreign workers must fill a shortage of 3.0 million workers. The Eleventh Malaysia Plan (2016–2020) stated that "a comprehensive immigration and employment policy for foreign workers will be formulated, taking into account industry requirements and the welfare of foreign workers. Heavy reliance on low-skilled foreign workers, particularly in labour-intensive activities, will be addressed holistically. Greater automation, especially in labour-intensive activities, as well as migration to knowledge intensive activities, will be encouraged in all sectors of the economy, particularly in the agriculture, manufacturing, and construction sectors, which currently employ more than 30% of foreign workers" (Economic Planning Unit, 2015). Innovation and greater use of technology must be pursued urgently for Malaysia to break out from the middle-income trap, move away from labour-intensive production and reduce the dependence on foreign workers. Moreover, with the fertility level declining globally, including the major labour exporting countries such as Indonesia and Bangladesh, Malaysia will face stiff competition from developed and developing countries in attracting the diminishing supply of foreign workers in the long run.

Despite the call for comprehensive immigration and employment policy for foreign workers in the Eleventh Plan (2016–2020), the Malaysian policy on foreign workers continues to be inconsistent, and there is a lack of inter-agency coordination. A clear example is a proposal to allow 1.5 million Bangladeshi workers into the country, as reported in the mass media in February 2016. However, following a widespread backlash, the government quickly backtracked, imposing a moratorium on hiring foreign workers of all kinds (Minter, 2016). There is a need for a more consistent and coherent policy on foreign workers. Instead of working in silos, the various government agencies should work closely and consult the employers to ensure that the policies and programmes are consistent and workable. To strengthen the policy coherence will require the integration of migration policy and other socio-economic policies, with the participation of all the relevant agencies. There is a need to move away from a "policing" model to a "management" model, which facilitates the types of migration needed, regulates it, and protects both the migrants, their employers, and Malaysian society generally. Developing collaboration and cooperation with sending countries will be crucial for effective migration management.

While receiving low-skilled workers, Malaysia has been losing its skilled workers who migrated mainly to Singapore, Australia, Europe, and the United States of America. From 1980 to 1990, the World Bank (2011: 91) estimated that this outflow grew at 4.2% per annum, increasing by 50% the stock of Malaysian migrants overseas. Over the following decade, this stock increased by another 40%, averaging 3.6% a year (cited in Cheong et al., 2016). Efforts to bring back skilled Malaysians have only limited success, and hence there is a need to review such policy to make the necessary changes. The World Bank Economic Monitor (World Bank, 2011) listed "social injustice" as the second most important reason to migrate (60% of those surveyed), after "career prospects" (66%). There is a need for policy changes to arrest the brain drain. Apart from efforts to bring back the expatriates, the diaspora policy may include giving them incentives to invest in Malaysia and using their connection to foster international trade and investment (NPFDB, 2012).

Policymakers and researchers, and the public have paid increasing attention to international migration. However, much less attention has been given to internal migration and population redistribution. Migratory flows from the less developed region to the more developed regions will accentuate regional disparity and affects national integration. The over-concentration of the population in a few cities will pose severe environmental and social issues. As alluded to above, in 2020, almost 40% of the national population will be residing in the conurbation of Kuala Lumpur (8.54 million), Pulau Pinang (2.4 million), and Johor Bahru (1.8 million). There will be many challenges in managing these megacities to meet the needs for essential services and amenities. These services include education and health, water and electricity, recreational parks, public transportation, sanitation, and garbage disposal, creating more jobs for a large number of new job seekers, and tackling social issues such as crime and poverty. There is also a need to improve the infrastructure, such as building more roads and managing traffic congestion and building affordable housing. All of these challenges require sustainable solutions.

Conclusion

As Malaysia is bracing for a slower population growth rate, there is an urgent need to monitor the demographic trend for policy intervention. Population research should be prioritized, and research findings should be effectively utilized to formulate, monitor, and evaluate policies and programmes. Compared with previous plans, The Eleventh Malaysia Plan (2016–2020) has given more prominence to population factors. It has dealt with the various demographic processes such as fertility, mortality and migration, population size and growth, and addressed vital population concerns such as heavy dependence on foreign workers and the need to promote active ageing, urbanization, and urban management. It has even included a sub-section on demographic changes shaping the workforce. Issues relating to the various sub-groups of the population, such as the youth, women, Orang Asli (indigenous people), the disabled, and poor households, were highlighted in the Plan document. The incorporation of population factors in development planning is a move in the right direction, as the ultimate goal of development efforts is to improve individuals' and families' wellbeing.

References

Bollen, K. A., Glanville, J. L., & Stecklov, G. (2007). Socio-economic status, permanent income, and fertility: A latent-variable approach. *Population Studies, 61*(1), 15–34.

Bongaarts, J. (2003). Completing the fertility transition in the developing world: The role of educational differences and fertility preferences. *Population Studies, 57*(3), 321–335.

Castles, F. (2003). The world turned upside down: Below replacement fertility, changing preferences and family-friendly policy in 21 OECD countries. *Journal of European Social Policy, 13*(3), 209–227.

Cheong K. C., Goh, K. L., Kuppusamy, N. A., & Lee, H. (2016). Population, human capital and development—The Malaysian experience. In N. P. Tey, K. C. Cheong & R. Rasiah (Eds.), *Revisiting Malaysia's population-development Nexus—The past in Its future.* (pp. 83–100). Kuala Lumpur: University of Malaya Press.

Demeny, P. (1997). Replacement-level fertility: The implausible endpoint of the demographic transition. In G. W. Jones, R. Douglas, J. C. Caldwell & R. d'Souza (Eds.), *The continuing demographic transition.* Oxford: Claendon Press.

Department of Social Welfare. (1995). *National Policy for the elderly.* Malaysia.

Department of Social Welfare. (2011). *National policy for older persons.* Malaysia.

Department of Statistics, Malaysia. (2011). *2010 population and housing census Malaysia: Population distribution and basic demographic characteristics.* Malaysia.

Department of Statistics, & Malaysia. (2012). *Population and housing census of Malaysia, 2010–education and social characteristics of the population.* Putrajaya.

Department of Statistics, Malaysia. (2016). *Population projections (revised) Malaysia, 2010–2040.*

Department of Statistics, Malaysia. (2019). *Migration survey report, 2018.*

Department of Statistics, Malaysia. (2020a). *Current population estimates.*
Department of Statistics, Malaysia. (2020b). *Abridged life tables, Malaysia, 22018–2020.*
Department of Statistics, Malaysia. (2020c). *Labour Force Survey (LFS) times series statistics by state, 1982–2019.*
Department of Statistics, Malaysia. (various years). *Reports of population censuses of Malaysia.*
Department of Statistics, Malaysia. (various years). *Vital statistics, Malaysia.*
Department of Statistics, Malaysia. (various years). *Abridged life table, Malaysia.*
Department of Statistics, Malaysia. (various years). *Migration survey reports, Malaysia.*
Dharmalingam, A., Rajan, S., & Philip Morgan, S. (2014). The determinants of low fertility in India. *Demography, 51*(4), 1451–1475.
Dudley L., Poston, J.R., Heather, T. K., & Yoon, J. (2009). Socio-economic development and fertility in the People's Republic of China and the Republic of Korea. in G. Jones, P. T. Starughan & A. Chan (Eds.), *Utrra-low fertility in Pacific Asia.* Routledge, London and New York.
Eonomic Planning Unit. (1983). *Mid-term review of fourth Malaysia plan, Malaysia.*
Economic Planning Unit. (2015). *Eleventh Malaysia plan—Anchoring growth on people, Malaysia.*
Fernandez-Chung, R., Cheong, K. C., Leong, Y. C., & Hill, C. (2014). *Employability of graduates in Malaysia: The perceptions of selected employers.* Report to the British Council, Kuala Lumpur
Herzer, D., Strulik, H., & Vollmer, S. (2012). The long-run determinants of fertility: One century of demographic change 1900–1999. *Journal of Economic Growth, 17*(4), 357–385.
Hirschman, C. (2003). Fertility transition, socioeconomic determinants of. In P. Demeny & G. McNicoll (Eds.), *Encyclopedia population* (Vol. 1, pp. 425–431). Macmillan Reference USA.
Hugo, G. (2011). Malaysian migration to Australia. *Malaysian Journal of Economic Studies, 48*(2), 147–174.
Hugo, G. (2014). The changing dynamics of ASEAN international migration. *Malaysian Journal of Economic Studies, 51*(1), 43–67.
Holzmann, R. (2014). *Old-age financial protection in Malaysia: Challenges and options* (SSRC Working Paper Series No. 2014–3).
Jejeebhoy, S. J. (1995). *Women's education, autonomy, and reproductive behaviour: Experience from developing countries.* Clarendon Press.
Jones, G., Straughan, P. T., & Chan, A. (2009). Very low fertility in Pacific Asian countries. In G. Jones, P. T. Starughan & A. Chan (Eds.), *Utrra-low fertility in Pacific Asia.* Routledge, London and New York.
Jones, G. (2012). Population policy in a prosperous city-state: Dilemmas for Singapore. *Population and Development Review, 38*(2), 311–336. Blackwell Publishing Ltd.
Jones, G. (2014). Urbanisation and development in South-east Asia. *Malaysian Journal of Economic Studies, 51*(1), 103–120.
Kassim, A. (2014). Recent trends in transnational population inflows into Malaysia: Policy, issues and challenges. *Malaysian Journal of Economic Studies, 51*(1), 9–28.
Kirk, D. (1996). Demographic transition theory. *Population Studies, 50*(1996), 361–387.
Leete, R. (1996). *Malaysia's demographic transition: Rapid development, culture, and politics.* Oxford University Press.
Lutz, W., Skirbekki, V., & Testa, M. (2006). The low fertility trap hypothesis: forces that may lead to further postponement and fewer births in Europe. in Philipov, A. C. Liefboer, & F. C. Billari (Eds.), *Vienna yearbook of population research.* Vienna: Austrian Academy of Sciences Press.
Martin, T. C. (1995). Women's education and fertility: Results from 26 demographic and health surveys. *Studies in Family Planning, 26*(4), 187–202.
McDonald. P. (2009). Explanations of low fertility in East Asia: a comparative perspective. in G. Jones, P. T. Starughan & A. Chan (Eds), *Utrra-low fertility in Pacific Asia.* London and New York: Routledge, Taylor & Francis Group.
Minter, A. (2016). *Malaysia's immigration mess.* Bloomberg View.
National Population and Family Development Board, NPFDB. (2012). *Second population strategic plan study.* Malaysia.

Nguyen-Dinh, H. (1997). A socio-economic analysis of the determinants of fertility: The case of Vietnam. *Journal of Population Economics, 10*(3), 251–271.
Renata, F., & Tienda, M. (1996). What's behind racial and ethnic fertility differentials? *Population and Development Review, 22*(Suppl.), 109–133.
Sanjay, K. M., Günther, F., Rajesh, K. C., & Canning, D. (2016). Distal determinants of fertility decline: Evidence from 640 Indian districts, *Demographic Research, 34*, 373–406.
Teresa, C. M. (1995). Women's education and fertility: Results from 26 demographic and health surveys. *Studies in Family Planning, 26* (4), 187–202.
Tey, N. P. (2006). Gender differentials in educational attainment. In S. Nagaraj, K. L. Goh & N. P. Tey (Eds.), *Statistics in action*. University of Malaya Press.
Tey, N. P. (2007). Trends in delayed and non-marriage in Peninsular Malaysia. *Asian Population Studies, 3*(3), 243–261.
Tey, N. P., Ng, S. T., & Tan, P. P. (2016). Population projection for development planning in Malaysia. In N. P. Tey, K. C. Cheong, & R. Rasiah (Eds), *Revisiting Malaysia's population-development Nexus—The past in Its future*. Kuala Lumpur: University of Malaya Press.
UN, Population Division. (2015). *World fertility data 2015*. New York, USA.
UN, Population Division. (2018). *World urbanization prospects, 2018 revision*, ST/ESA/SER.A/366.
UN, Population Division. (2019a). *World population prospects: The 2019 revision.*
UN, Population Division. (2019b). *International migrant stock 2019* (United Nations database, POP/DB/MIG/Stock/Rev.2019).
World Bank. (2011). *Malaysia economic monitor April 2011: Brain drain*. Bangkok.
World Bank. (2012). *Malaysia economic monitor: Unlocking women's potential.*

Nai Peng Tey is Associate Professor at the Faculty of Business and Economics, Universiti Malaya. He specializes in population and demographic studies.

Chapter 4
Financing Development

Wee Yeap Lau

Abstract As Malaysia continues its journey to move up the value chain and become a fully developed nation by 2050 after gaining its independence from the British administration, there have been five-year Malaysia Plan implemented in conjunction with the two major development phases namely, New Economic Policy (1970–1990) and Vision 2020. This chapter investigates the issue of financing development for Malaysia. This chapter first reviews the past national development phases, theoretical models on the role of finance for development and national budget performances. This chapter also compares Malaysia with other ASEAN economies in terms of GDP and fiscal deficits and estimates the relationship between economic growth and fiscal deficits in Malaysia. This chapter suggests four areas of focus, seven strategies for future development as well as best practices such as maintaining transparency and accountability, effective use of public expenditure, nurturing human capital, upgrading technology and enhancing value-added initiatives as the long-term goals.

Keywords National budget · Fiscal deficit · Economic growth · Five-year plan · National development

Introduction

In the recent World Bank's regional report on East Asia, Mason and Shetty (2019) review the past success of "East Asia", where six out of ten developing economies in the region have moved from low to middle-upper income countries in the past 25 years. They further highlight the policy reforms needed under the five pillars: boosting economic competitiveness, building skills, promoting inclusion, strengthening state institutions, and financing the transition to high income. This report is very crucial to developing countries like Malaysia, and unless correct policies are put in place to direct the limited resources to its intending outcomes, the nation stands to remain in its current spot as regional competition intensifies in the coming years.

W. Y. Lau (✉)
Faculty of Business and Economics, Universiti Malaya, 50603 Kuala Lumpur, Malaysia
e-mail: wylau@um.edu.my

R. Rasiah et al. (eds.), *Malaysia's Leap Into the Future*, Dynamics of Asian Development, https://doi.org/10.1007/978-981-16-7045-9_4

As revealed in the Parliament on 18 October, 2018 by the Prime Minister Tun Dr Mahathir Mohamad, the Mid-term Review of 11th Malaysia Plan 2016–2020 ("11MP") should serve as the base for further policy reform in building high-tech and capital-intensive industries in innovative and knowledge-based sectors. The ideals of becoming a developed nation will not be achievable if talent retention and economic governance are not addressed with the right policies. The incident of 1MDB and alike further exacerbated the needs to have a stringent check and balance on public finance in order to prevent misuse of public fund. The Government must ensure the tax monies collected are used in the best interest of the people.

At the current stage of development, it is clear that Malaysia still needs external financing from Foreign Direct Investment (FDI) to trailblaze some of the high-tech industries in order to spur its economic growth. Hence, the availability of a skilled workforce and good governance will be the deciding factors in the competition for new FDI among the regional economies. Past studies have shown the need for a skilled workforce in MNC-driven electronics clusters in Malaysia (Rasiah, 2002, 2004). In a recent example, factors such as "supply chains, access to markets and the availability of the expertise" were cited as the basis for British firm Dyson to locate its plant for electric cars in Singapore, a clear testimony that skilled human resources provide an edge in attracting high value added investment.[1]

The emphasis on FDI notwithstanding, local public financing for development is no less critical. In Malaysia, this is often channelled through various ministries and agencies like the Ministry of Science, Technology and Innovation (MOSTI) and Malaysia Digital Economy Corporation (MDEC). These government agencies must learn from the experience of South Korea. Chaebols (Korean conglomerates) are given the below-the-market funding rate to acquire cutting-edge technology, and they are expected to deliver the desired results (Rasiah, Mubarik, & Yap, 2017).

The formula of Korean success in pushing up its technological frontier over the last 30 years is something Malaysia can learn from. One good example is the Korean automobile industry. Hyundai has almost the same beginning with Proton in the early 90 s. Time has proven that with correct policies, the made-in-Korea car can thrive in the global market in the face of world-class brands like Toyota and Honda.

Correct policies are only the beginning. Building competitiveness is long and hard work. The question is whether Malaysian bureaucrats and businesses are ready to learn from the best practice. If Malaysia intends to move up into the export market at the higher end of the value chain, the institutional framework, infrastructure, and workforce must be ready to learn and adapt to new technologies, know-how and best practices. The habit of continuous improvement or "kaizen" must be drilled into the fabric of Malaysian culture.

The triumphant story of Malaysian democracy in choosing a new coalition to form a more transparent government as a result of the May 9th 2018 election provides a new lease of hope for Malaysia to reinforce its strength and undo its past mistakes. Institutional reforms, right policies, best practices, and open dialogues are some of the ingredients the new Government must adapt to empower its citizens to provide critical

[1] The Guardian, 23 October 2018.

ideas without fear to shift Malaysia back to the trajectory of becoming a developed nation—a country based on the rule of law and universally accepted principles that encompass the excellent practice of science, technology, and humanities.

This chapter discusses the challenges in financing development and measures needed to overcome constraints to financing. Section one reviews the past and present national development plans, followed by a theoretical background on the Government's fiscal role in Section two. Section three reviews Malaysia's recent budget performance, followed by empirical work in Section four. Section five outlines the policy imperatives for financing future development. The last section concludes the chapter.

National Development Plan

According to the World Bank database, Malaysia's gross national income per capita after adjusting for inflation grew at 3.9% per annum in the first 50 years of the country's existence. By 2015, the country's per capita income was ranked 60th among 200 countries. Going forward, assuming the average per income growth rate of 3.8% over the last five years is maintained for all countries, Malaysia's ranking is projected to rise to around the 40th position by 2050 (Yeah, 2017).

Looking at the past 60 years, the current state of the economy has been shaped by a few critical policies over three phases, as shown in Table 4.1. Beginning with the launch of the New Economic Policy in 1971, the first phase consisted of poverty reduction, particularly for the disadvantaged *Bumiputera* population. This period also witnessed the shift in strategy from import-substitution to export-orientation industries.

The second phase was characterized by the launch of *Wawasan* 2020 (Vision 2020) by then Prime Minister Tun Dr. Mahathir Mohammad. There is no doubt that the success of the Malaysian economy is the fruition of these past policies. The

Table 4.1 Key development phases in Malaysia's transformation plan

	1971–1990	1991–2020	2021–2030
	New economic policy	Vision 2020	Shared prosperity vision
Malaysia's key Development ERAS	"Eradicate absolute poverty irrespective of race and eliminating identification of race by economic function"	"To become a developed nation, in our mould" **9 Challenges** **3 Phases**: National Development Policy National Vision Policy New Economic Model	"Restructuring the Priorities of Malaysia's Development" The Primary Aim of SPV is to provide a decent standard of living to all Malaysian by 2030 **15 Guiding Principles** **8 Enablers**

Source https://www.epu.gov.my and https://www.pmo.gov.my/2019/10/shared-prosperity-vision-2030-2/

income imbalances among the different ethnic groups during the post-independence era were addressed by the New Economic Policy (NEP) (1971–1990). The switch to export promotion had salutary effects on economic growth.

In hindsight, the NEP had achieved great success with the creation of a middle-class with *Bumiputera* commanding an increasing share within the Malaysian economy. The creation of new institutions such as Permodalan Nasional Berhad (PNB) and Lembaga Tabung Haji (LTH) has contributed significantly to national development. The NEP was succeeded by three new phases from 1991 to 2020, namely the National Development Policy (1991–2000), New Vision Policy (2001–2010), and New Economic Model (2010–2020).

Impressive though Malaysia's growth record has been, alarms are being sounded that Malaysia is in danger of falling into a "middle-income trap". What might this "trap" be? According to Gill and Kharas (2007), The "middle-income country trap" is a development stage that characterizes countries as being squeezed between low-wage producers and highly skilled, fast-moving innovators.

Countries caught in this trap tend to grow more slowly and often fall behind in the growth league, unable to advance to high-income status. Cost advantages in labour-intensive sectors these countries had long enjoyed, especially in manufactured exports which once drove growth, are progressively eroded as lower-wage country producers have become more competitive.

While "the success of Malaysia's structural transformation from low to middle income and as one of the most prominent manufacturing exporters in the world" is recognized by the World Bank, the country is squeezed from below by the competition from low-wage economies on the one hand, and the above by more innovative and advanced economies on the other.

Realizing that Malaysia is facing the middle-income trap, the New Economic Model (NEM)[2] launched on 30 March 2010, is an economic plan intended to double the per capita income by 2020. This plan also aims to shift affirmative action from being ethnically-based to need-based, with the result that the market will become more competitive and investor-friendly.

While it is debatable that Malaysia has already emerged from the middle-income trap as claimed by Idris Jala,[3] there can be no escape from the fact that Malaysia needs to shift its growth strategy from being resource-driven to productivity and innovation-driven, with the focus on both high value-added manufacturing and service industries. As much as this shift is crucial, the financing of development remains vital.

It was first made known to the Malaysian public during the presentation of the Federal Government's annual budget in October 2016 that the Government has initiated the dialogue to plan and shape a new vision from 2020 to 2050 to be known as "National Transformation 2050" or "TN50". The objective of TN50 is to propel Malaysia to become a top 20 nation in economic development, promote citizen wellbeing, social advancement, and innovation. *Given this vision, there is a greater need to examine the financing needs for economic development, its infrastructure,*

[2] https://www.pmo.gov.my/dokumenattached/NEM_Report_I.pdf (Retrieved on 30 January 2018).

[3] The Star, 1 September 2016.

and financial governance to ensure key strategies are implemented and development projects delivered effectively, efficiently, and at a reasonable cost.

For a more immediate goal is to provide a decent standard of living to all Malaysian by 2030, the Shared Prosperity Vision 2030 (SPV2030) was launched on 5 October 2019 by the Federal Government. It is a document that outlines 10-year goals to restructure Malaysia's low-skill labour-intensive economy to a knowledge-based economy.

SPV2030 is a commitment to make Malaysia a nation that achieves sustainable growth along with fair and equitable distribution across income groups, ethnicities, regions, and supply chains. The commitment aims to strengthen political stability, enhance the nation's prosperity, and ensure that the rakyat is united while celebrating ethnic and cultural diversity as the foundation of the nation-state.

SPV2030's underlying principle is economic growth through "equitability of outcome". The vision is supported by eight enablers, namely Fiscal Sustainability, Financial Capital, Effective Institutional Delivery, Governance and Integrity, Education and TVET, Big Data, Sustainability, and Enlightened Society. Together with these 8 SPV enablers, there are 15 Guiding Principles that encompass the ideas of development for all by addressing the wealth and income disparities to achieve a united, prosperous, and dignified nation.

Theoretical Considerations

The role of finance for development is firmly grounded in economic theory. Keynes' theory of aggregate demand argues that a country's GDP comprises consumption, investment, government spending, and the net total trade balance (total exports minus total imports). Government spending plays a vital role in stimulating the economy by allocating resources to different sectors to produce economic output. The allocation of resources is done through the annual government budget that signals how the Government plans to achieve its goals for the year by keeping in view its strategy for the longer term.

A country's longer-term goals are economic growth, stabilization, redistribution, and the provision of public goods and services. The budgetary process must be implemented efficiently and effectively to ensure that the allocated resources reach the targeted sectors and desired economic activities are carried out.

With a sound fiscal system, an inclusive financial sector is key to building shared prosperity, as access to finance is critical to the ability of, especially small entrepreneurs, to grow their businesses and incomes and create jobs. Furthermore, a sound financial system can attract foreign capital and stimulate the country's economic growth. Therefore, the Government should also promote financial liberalization that attracts foreign fund into the domestic economy.

Nonetheless, Malaysia faces a persistent fiscal deficit in its Federal Budget. In this respect, there are two schools of thought on the impact of the fiscal deficit on economic growth. Neoclassical economists state that fiscal deficit will have a negative impact on economic growth (Bernheim, 1989). This is because the fiscal deficit will raise an individual's total lifetime consumption by shifting taxes to subsequent generations. If economic resources are fully employed, the increase in consumption implies a decrease in savings. Therefore, the interest rate must increase to bring the capital market back into equilibrium. Thus, a persistent deficit will eventually "crowd out" private capital accumulation and subsequently deteriorate economic growth.

Conversely, the Keynesian school posits a positive relationship between fiscal deficit and growth (Keynes, 1936). This school of thought argues that there is a significant fraction of the population in the economy that face liquidity constraint. These individuals have very high propensities to consume their disposable income. Hence, a temporary tax reduction will have an immediate and significant impact on aggregate demand. Furthermore, suppose the economy's resources are initially underemployed. In that case, the rise in consumption will increase national income, thereby generating second-round effects through the well-known Keynesian multiplier. Therefore, fiscal deficit stimulates consumption and economic growth.

Various empirical studies have been undertaken to reconcile the two competing views. Using cross-section data from 76 developed and developing countries from 1972 to 1981, Martin and Fardmanesh (1990) find a negative relationship between fiscal deficit and economic growth only in middle-income countries. In contrast, Nelson and Singh (1994) examine the deficit-growth nexus for 70 developing countries and found that there is no significant relationship between fiscal deficit and economic growth.

Through panel data, Adam and Bevan (2005) investigate the relationship between fiscal deficit and economic growth for 45 countries from 1970 to 1999. Results indicate that there exists a threshold effect in the deficit-growth relation. If the fiscal deficit is less than or equal to 1.5% of GDP, the deficits are growth-enhancing. A robustness check by replacing government expenditure for fiscal deficit shows that productive expenditure has a positive impact on economic growth. In contrast, residual expenditure is found to have a negative relationship with growth.

Tan (2006) examines the dynamic linkages between fiscal deficit, inflation, and economic growth in Malaysia from 1966 to 2003 and finds that there is unidirectional causality from fiscal deficit to money supply and from money supply to prices. Therefore, the paper concludes that the fiscal deficit could have an inflationary impact on the economy via the monetization of the deficit.

Subsequently, Taylor et al. (2012) examine the relationship between fiscal deficit, government debt, and economic growth for the U.S. economy. Using quarterly data from 1961 to 2011, their results show that the fiscal deficit has a significant and positive effect on economic growth. Moreover, their paper strongly argues that a higher fiscal deficit stimulates the economy during the recession period. Baldacci et al. (2014) find that fiscal stimulus shortens the length of crisis episodes by facilitating the growth of aggregate demand. Specifically, government spending is found to be more effective in shortening the crisis than income tax cuts. However, an increase in government spending would result immediately in a higher fiscal deficit during the crisis period.

Fiscal spending alone is not the only means to drive economic growth. Human-capital-driven technology is becoming an increasingly influential factor. Advanced technology can stimulate investment and consumption by increasing productivity, higher wage and hence, higher consumption. Hence, financing development also requires immediate attention to finance the growth and adoption of the latest technology by enabling the Internet of Things (IoT) to increase the living standard and convenience of people.

Budget Performance

It is essential to review the economic performance over the past ten years and also how the budget is used to finance the development. In addition to the 1986 Global Economic Recession of which was due to a slowdown in the global electronic industry, Malaysia also faced the Asian Financial Crisis (AFC) 1997/98, where the market capitalization of the stock market and currency value against USD were halved. Before the AFC, Malaysia's growth rate was maintained at 8% annually. However, economic growth has reduced to around 5–7% annually after the crisis. The economic performance has affected the government budget, as discussed below.

Fiscal Deficit and GDP

Looking at Fig. 4.1, while the real GDP has grown steadily over the years, the fiscal deficit as the percentage of GDP has been fluctuating around 3–5% in the last few years. This deficit is large in the aftermath of the AFC and GFC, during which the Government needed to put in additional fiscal stimuli to resuscitate the economy.

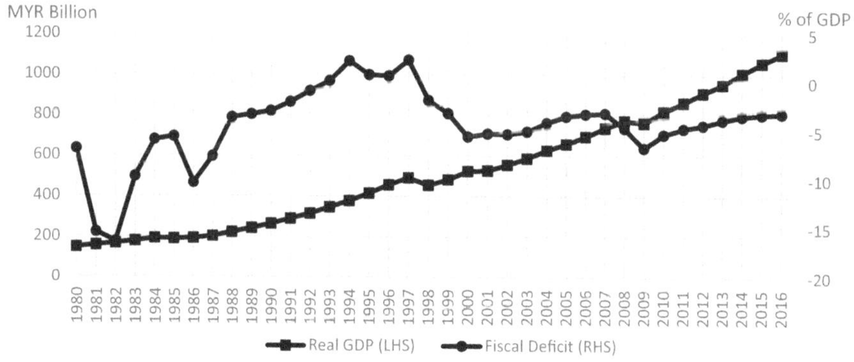

Fig. 4.1 Real GDP and Fiscal deficit, Malaysia, 1980–2016. *Source* WEO April 2017 Database; Ministry of Finance Malaysia

Table 4.2 GDP growth and fiscal balance, ASEAN countries, 2008–2010

ASEAN-10	GDP growth (Annual %)			Fiscal deficit (% of GDP)		
	2008	2009	2010	2008	2009	2010
Brunei	−1.96	−1.78	2.57	27.92	−2.36	15.64
Cambodia	6.48	0.09	5.79	−2.9	−6.2	−8.8
Indonesia	5.84	4.52	6.04	−0.1	−1.6	−0.7
Lao PDR	7.53	7.23	8.18	−2.2	−3.2	−2.2
Malaysia	3.27	−2.56	6.75	−4.6	−6.7	−5.3
Myanmar	9.76	10.03	9.2	−2.38	−4.56	−4.64
Philippines	4.07	1.14	7.36	−0.9	−3.7	−3.5
Singapore	1.77	−0.61	14.18	7.1	7.33	7.57
Thailand	1.71	−0.69	7.24	−0.6	−3.9	−2.9
Vietnam	5.51	5.26	6.23	0.6	−4.2	−2.1

Notes GDP growth is computed based on the GDP at constant USD, 2010 price. *Source* World Bank; Asian Development Bank

A quick comparison among ASEAN countries after the Global Financial Crisis is shown in Table 4.2. The 2008/09 GFC had severely impacted some of the ASEAN member countries, especially their primary engine of growth, i.e. the export sector. Diminished exports led to slower or negative growth in their respective economies. Income and living standard fell, but the impact of the crisis varied from one country to another.

As shown in Table 4.2, Malaysia led the pack of countries experiencing negative growth with a 2.56% decline in 2009, followed by Brunei (-1.78%), Thailand (-0.69%), and Singapore (-0.61%). Furthermore, Cambodia and the Philippines also experienced reduced growth in 2009. In contrast, Myanmar, Lao PDR, Vietnam, and Indonesia were able to maintain their growth momentum, partly due to compensating capital inflow from foreign direct investment to the respective countries.

Moreover, all ASEAN members' policy responses showed a similar pattern—pursuing a fiscal stimulus to support economic growth in the aftermath of the GFC. Table 4.2 also presents the data for fiscal deficit for all ASEAN countries. As observed, Malaysia generated a rather sizeable fiscal deficit, i.e. 6.7% of gross domestic product (GDP) in 2009. The sizeable fiscal deficit enabled Malaysia's economy to recover from the economic stagnation in 2009, as evidenced by the annual GDP growth of 6.75% in 2010.

Fiscal Policy

Sound fiscal policy is vital to economic growth. Arguably the most crucial policy instrument is the Federal Budget. The budget signals the Government's plans to

Table 4.3 Federal government finances, Malaysia, 2014–2017

	2014	2015	2016	2017B
GDP Nominal	1,106	1,157	1,233	1,323
BRENT (USD/pb)	99	52	40	45
Revenue	220.6	219.1	212.6	219.7
Operating Expenditure	219.6	217.0	207.1	214.8
Current Account	1.0	2.1	5.5	4.9
Development Expenditure	39.5	40.8	45.0	46.0
(Loan Recovery)	1.0	1.5	0.8	0.8
Overall Balance	−37.5	−37.2	−38.7	−40.3
% to GDP	−3.4	−3.2	−3.1	−3.0

2017B is the projected number. *Source* Federal Budget 2016, Ministry of Finance (2016)

allocate resources to achieve its goals such as economic growth, redistribution, the provision of public goods and services, and the shift from labour-intensive to technology-driven production. Both the budget process and substance are matters of public concern and need to be discussed and analyzed.

Based on Table 4.3, the Federal Budget in 2017 was designed to strengthen Malaysia's fiscal position to a deficit of 3%, although it is based on Brent crude oil price of USD45 per barrel. With Brent crude averaging $54.15 during 2017, this deficit was achieved (Edge, 2018). The Government has spent considerable effort to reduce the fiscal budget deficit from its 2009 peak deficit of 6.7% despite the need to provide welfare programmes such as Bantuan Rakyat 1Malaysia (BR1M) and affordable housing schemes such as 1Malaysia People's Housing (PR1MA) to lower-middle-income segments of the population.

For the fiscal year 2019, the estimated total expenditure in Table 4.4 consists of Operating Expenditure RM259,850 million and Development Expenditure RM54,044 million. This is financed by an estimated revenue of RM261,814 million and a deficit of RM52,080 million (3.4% of the GDP). The deficit has been reduced from 3.7% to 3.4% of GDP from the 2018 to 2019 Budget.

Revenue

As shown in Table 4.5, Malaysia economy still depends on revenue from petroleum which fluctuates from 15 to 41% from 2009 to 2019. With estimated total revenue of RM 261,814 million collected in 2019, the bulk of fiscal revenue for the Federal budget comes from direct taxes (44.7%), followed by indirect taxes (24.4%) and Petroleum revenue (30.9%). Indirect taxes from GST used to form a bulk of 20% of total revenue in 2016 and 2017. Top on the direct taxes list is the corporate and individual income tax.

Table 4.4 Federal government finances, Malaysia, 2017–2019

	2017		2018[8]		2019[9]	
	RM juta *RM million*	% perubahan *% change*	RM juta *RM million*	% perubahan *% change*	RM juta RM million	% perubahan *% change*
KEWANGAN KERAJAAN PERSEKUTUAN ***FEDERAL GOVERNMENT FINANCE***						
Hasil *Revenue*	220,406	*3.8*	236,460	*7.3*	261,814	*10.7*
Perbelanjaan mengurus *Operating expenditure*	217,695	*3.6*	235,450	*8.2*	259,850	*10.4*
Baki semasa *Current balance*	2,711		1,010		1,964	
Perbelanjaan pembangunan (bersih) *Development expenditure (net)*	43,032	*5.9*	54,337	*26.3*	54,044	*-0.5*
Baki keseluruhan ***Overall balance***	**-40,321**		**-53,327**		**-52,080**	
% KDNK *% of GDP*	*-3.0*		*-3.7*		*-3.4*	
Pinjaman dalam negeri (bersih) *Domestic borrowings (net)*	40,750		51,973[10]		-	
Pinjaman luar pesisir (bersih) *Offshore borrowings (net)*	-342		-293		-	
Perubahan aset *Change in assets*	-87		-353		-	

Note The numbers for 2019 are the projection. The numbers for 2018 are revised figures. *Source* Federal Budget 2019. http://www1.treasury.gov.my/pdf/revenue/carta_malaysia.pdf

Table 4.5 Petroleum and Non-Petroleum Revenue in total revenue, Malaysia, 2010–2019 (%)

Sources	2010	2011	2012	2013	2014	2015	2016	2017	2018	2019
Petroleum related	35.4	35.8	33.7	31.2	30.0	21.5	14.6	15.7	21.7	30.9
Non-Petroleum										
SST/GST	7.6	7.3	7.3	7.5	7.8	**16.1**	**19.4**	**20.1**	9.8	8.4
Direct Taxes	37.8	40.1	39.9	42.6	45.2	45.7	47.6	47.3	**49.3**	44.7
Others	19.2	16.8	19.1	18.7	17.0	16.7	18.4	16.9	19.2	16.0

Source Federal Budget 2019. http://www1.treasury.gov.my/pdf/revenue/section2.pdf

While trying to increase fiscal revenue, the Government also sought to diversify its revenue sources to reduce dependence on oil-related revenue from 21.5% in 2015 to 14.6% in 2016. The special tax unit, the Collection Intelligence Arrangement (CIA), is part of this initiative. However, the Government continues to depend on petroleum-based revenue, as shown in Table 4.5. The dependence has grown over the years, from 15.7% (2017) to 30.9% (2019). There is an urgent need to diversify the sources of revenue for the Government.

Operating Expenditure

In 2019, Federal Government Expenditure comprised mostly operating expenditure of 259.8 billion (82.7%) and a small proportion of development expenditure (54 billion, 17.2%). From the operating expenditure budget in Table 4.6, emoluments continue to be the largest category (26.1%), followed by debt service charges (10.5%), supplies and services (9.2%), subsidies (8.6%), retirement charges (8.4%) and others.

Overall, the 83:17 allocation of operating vs development expenditure and the large share of emoluments speak to the size of a public sector with a considerable workforce but squeezed funds available for development. It also raises the question of the cost of cutting the budget deficit. If more funds are not made available for development initiatives, this will lower the long-term growth.

In the immediate future, the final disclosure by the new Government after the general election of May 2018 of massive fraud under the sovereign fund 1MDB has brought to additional light debt that the outgoing Government had hidden from view (Pooi & Shukry, 2018). This additional debt would pose a major challenge to the new Government in its forthcoming budget. This debt burden proves to be a significant distraction to the Government, preventing it from planning finance for development.

Table 4.6 Federal Government expenditure, Malaysia, 2019

Total Federal government expenditure, Malaysia, 2019	RM 314, 550 million
Development expenditure (% of total expenditure)	**17.4**
Economic	9.3
Social	4.8
Security	2.3
General administration	1.0
Operating expenditure (% of total expenditure)	**82.6**
Emoluments	26.1
Debt service charges	10.5
Supplies and services	9.2
Retirement charges	8.4
Grants and transfers to state government	2.4
Subsidies and social assistance	7.1
Other expenditure	18.9

Note The number shown consists of revenue, borrowings, and use of the Government's assets. The number also excludes contingency reserves. *Source* Ministry of Finance, Malaysiass

As part of an effort to strengthen the oversight process, in May 2016, the Fiscal Policy Committee (FPC) in Bank Negara Malaysia (BNM) has established a Technical Committee on Fiscal Risks and Contingent Liabilities to evaluate and enhance the Federal Government's fiscal risks and contingent liabilities. The committee will monitor and balance the needs between fiscal flexibility and sustainability in the public finances. Thus far, the operating expenditure of the Federal Budget has increased over the years, but the speed of increment in revenue has not. The committee must be more vigilant in their advice to the Government.

Empirical Model—Linking Fiscal Deficit to Growth

What is the actual relationship between the fiscal deficit and growth in Malaysia? To study the impact of the fiscal deficit on GDP, annual data from 1980 to 2016 are used (Table 4.7). The dependent variable is GDP, while the independent variables are fiscal deficit, real exchange rate, real interest rate, and total investment.

Except for the fiscal deficit variable, all series are transformed into natural logarithm. Model 1 is the base model. To enhance the robustness of model 1, the lag of the dependent variable has been added in model 2 to deal with the issue of autocorrelation. Models 3 and 4 include the dummy variable for the Global Financial Crisis and the interaction term with the fiscal deficit.

The models are as follows:

Model 1:$LnGDP_t = B_0 + B_1F.D._t + B_2LnEXR_t + B_3LnINT_t + B_4LnINV_t + \varepsilon_t$

Model 2:$LnGDP_t = B_0 + B_1F.D._t + B_2LnEXR_t + B_3LnINT_t + B_4LnINV_t + B_5LnGDP_{t-1} + \varepsilon_t$

Model 3:$LnGDP_t = B_0 + B_1F.D._t + B_2LnEXR_t + B_3LnINT_t + B_4LnINV_t + B_5LnGDP_{t-1} + B_6GFC + B_7F.D._t * GFC + \varepsilon_t$

Model 4:$LnGDP_t = B_0 + B_1F.D._t + B_2LnEXR_t + B_3LnINT_t + B_4LnINV_t + B_5LnGDP_{t-1} + B_6GFC + B_7F.D._{t-1} * GFC + \varepsilon_t$

where

Table 4.7 List of variables

Variables	Description	Source
GDP	Real GDP (2010 constant price, MYR Billion)	WEO April 2017 Database
F.D	Fiscal deficit (% of GDP)	Ministry of Finance Malaysia
EXR	Real Exchange Rate (local currency per 1 USD)	IMF International Financial Statistics
INT	Real Interest Rate (%)	IMF International Financial Statistics
INT	Total investment (% of GDP)	WEO April 2017 Database

Notes Sample period: 1980–2016

Table 4.8 Descriptive statistics

Variables/Periods	Mean	Std Dev	Skewness	Kurtosis	J-B statistic	Obs
GDP	513.146	289.066	0.456	2.058	2.648 (0.266)	37
F.D	−4.391	3.941	−1.096	5.121	14.344 (0.001)	37
EXR	3.075	0.602	0.207	1.551	3.502 (0.174)	37
INT	3.153	1.873	0.499	2.114	2.746 (0.253)	37
INV	30.704	8.318	0.632	1.969	4.103 (0.129)	37

Notes All statistics are based on the original data. Values in parenthesis are p-values. GDP denotes Real Gross Domestic Product (MYR Billion). F.D. denotes Fiscal Deficit (% of GDP). EXR denotes Real Exchange Rate (Local currency per 1 USD). INT denotes Real Interest Rate (%) INV denotes Total Investment (% of GDP). J-B statistic stands for the Jarque–Bera test for normality. Jarque–Bera test is the goodness-of-fit test of whether the sample data have the skewness and kurtosis matching a normal distribution

Ln = Natural logarithm.
GDP = Real Gross Domestic Product (2010 constant price, MYR Billion).
F.D. = Fiscal deficit (% of GDP).
EXR = Real Exchange Rate (Local currency per 1 USD).
INT = Real Interest Rate (%).
INV = Total Investment (% of GDP).
GFC = 1, Sample period from 2007 to 2009. (During Global Financial Crisis period).
GFC = 0, Sample period from 1980 to 2006 and 2010 to 2016.

As observed in Table 4.8, all variables except for fiscal deficit are normally distributed and positive in value. The mean for Fiscal Deficit is 4.39 for the sample period from 1980 to 2016.

It is clear from the results in Table 4.9 that the fiscal deficit has a positive relationship with GDP. However, the impact is minuscule, as shown by the small coefficient of 0.002. A much more significant impact is through capital formation or investment. Interestingly, the significance of the interaction between the lag of Fiscal Deficit and GFC shows that the stimulus package affects economic recovery only in the following year. For Eqs. (2), (3), and (4), the inclusion of the lagged dependent variable of GDP enables the assumption of no serial correlation to be fulfilled.

Policy Imperatives

While the empirical results do not reveal a significant impact of fiscal deficits on growth, there are nevertheless several policy imperatives that need serious attention if future long-term growth that takes Malaysia to the next level is to be achieved. Several of these are detailed below.

Table 4.9 Results of ordinary least square estimation

Variables	(1)	(2)	(3)	(4)
	$LnGDP_t$			
$F.D._t$	0.016**	0.003*	0.002*	0.002*
	(0.045)	(0.072)	(0.082)	(0.070)
$LnEXR_t$	1.237***	0.038	0.033	0.043
	(0.000)	(0.487)	(0.535)	(0.404)
$LnINT_t$	−0.766***	−0.099***	−0.104***	−0.110***
	(0.000)	(0.000)	(0.000)	(0.000)
$LnINV_t$	0.630***	0.117***	0.113***	0.112***
	(0.001)	(0.003)	(0.004)	(0.002)
$LnGDP_{t-1}$	–	0.903***	0.901***	0.894***
		(0.000)	(0.000)	(0.000)
GFC	–	–	0.105**	0.200**
			(0.047)	(0.014)
$F.D._t * GFC$	–	–	0.024**	–
			(0.026)	
$F.D._{t-1} * GFC$	–	–	–	0.057***
				(0.009)
Constant	3.362***	0.306*	0.346**	0.359**
	(0.000)	(0.088)	(0.046)	(0.034)
Adjusted R^2	0.943	0.998	0.998	0.998
F-statistics	149.953***	3668.492***	2943.519***	3133.365***
Durbin-Watson statistics	0.706	2.351	2.381	2.312
Serial (1)	15.292***	1.281	1.669	1.139
Ramsey RESET Test	6.239**	0.993	1.626	1.723
CUSUM of Squares Test	Stable	Stable	Stable	Stable

Notes *, ** and *** denote statistical significance at 10%, 5%, and 1% level, respectively. Values in parentheses are p-values. Ln denotes that all series have been transformed to the natural logarithm. Serial (1) is the Breusch-Godfrey LM test statistic for the first-order serial relationship. Numbers of the fitted term for Ramsey RESET Test: 2. GFC denotes dummy variable, where 2007 to 2009 are equal to 1

Budgetary Process: A Need for Fiscal Rules

Given global uncertainties, especially those arising from growing anti-globalism, Malaysia must have the resilience to withstand the volatility of shocks in the global economic environment while staying on its desired growth path. A critical source of that resilience has sound fiscal rules, especially after the recent change of Government that has exposed extensive breaches of these rules.

These breaches include allocations and expenditure bypassing ministry oversight. This is made possible by a concentration of power in the hands of the Prime Minister and his control of the Ministry of Finance, itself in control of an enormous number of government-linked corporations (Gomez, 2017). Examples include the award of expenditure contracts without sufficient time for debate in Parliament and the use of the justice system to silence those brave enough to bring these breaches to light.

None of the rules that make for sound fiscal governance is novel. However, the breaches under the previous Government had been so pervasive that the new Government should need to expend considerable energy to redress these problems at the expense of planning for the financing of future development. Moreover, once redressed, good fiscal governance must be maintained over the long term.

Financial Governance: Foundation of Sustainable Economic Growth

Financial governance of fiscal assets sets the stage for sound financial decision-making. Broadly defined, strong financial governance is the sum of many parts, including strong institutions, efficient processes, and practical rules, regulations, and norms. It affects how financial decisions are made, including decisions relating to savings and spending, borrowing and lending, investment and profit distribution, and it is relevant to all economic agents, be they households, businesses, or governments. Effective financial governance has multiple benefits.

Firstly, effective financial governance ensures that financial decisions *take into account all externalities* arising from them. Financial decisions often have consequences that are not entirely borne by the decision-maker. Financial decisions that appear rational at the individual level may be collectively unsustainable. For instance, corrupt practices may be optimal for the individual benefiting from them, but they are detrimental to the welfare of society and the economy. In order to avoid the misallocation of resources, these externalities have to be internalized either by aligning the incentives to the objectives of the decision-maker; introducing a more representative decision-making process; putting in place the appropriate institutional arrangements; and having effectively enforced laws, rules, and regulations; or occasionally, by societal norms.

Secondly, sound financial governance encourages discipline *in adhering to budget constraint*. Inter-temporal budget constraints bound all economic agents, and adherence to them when making financial decisions is key to sustainability. This constraint is particularly relevant when the repercussions of financial decisions fall on parties who are not represented—for example, decisions that shift a massive debt burden onto future generations.

Thirdly, strong financial governance has *robust external checks and balances*. To ensure sound decision-making, especially when externalities are involved, the decision-making process must be subjected to scrutiny by external parties. In this regard, accountability, transparency, and the empowerment of the external party to take consequential action are key to effective financial governance.

All of these principles should be applied thoroughly to the *management of public finances*. Sound public financial governance is the legitimate use of authority in the management of a country's financial resources with integrity to promote sustainable development.

Financial Sector Development

The financial requirement for the Catch-up Model of TN 2050 comes from financial resources such as savings and taxes. There is a need to develop a sound financial system that would be able to mobilize national savings in order to fund the required investment for economic growth and investment and social expenditures for the prosperity and social wellbeing of the Malaysian people.

In order to finance the catch-up to its developed status by 2050, Malaysia should think of the optimal model for fulfilling its financial needs for development as a means to achieve the end. In order to achieve the level of capital deepening to build the capital markets at the desired level towards 2050, Malaysia has several policy choices:

(i) Islamic Finance: Malaysia could continue to be the pioneer of Sukuk bonds and other Islamic financial instruments;
(ii) Conventional Finance: Malaysia could continue to maintain its status as exemplifying the best practices of its conventional banking system inherited from the West;
(iii) Asian initiatives: Malaysia may choose to enhance its ties with the Asian Infrastructure Investment Bank (AIIB) for supporting infrastructure construction.
(iv) The policy of Liberalization: In order to become a financial centre, Malaysia must attract funds from foreign countries to Malaysia. This policy will strengthen the Ringgit and achieve the desired level of capital deepening. At the same time, Malaysia must put in place a policy to curb the excessive flow of funds out of the country.

Towards this end, finance is an enabler for the citizens to accumulate capital and as a means of resource allocation to the productive sectors where the capital is needed. Besides, it should be the enabler for individuals and businesses to obtain financing for productive means. The proliferation of investment funds, REITs, hedge funds, and other avenues of investment also calls for better financial education for her citizens.

However, one worrying trend for the past few years has been closing the savings and investment gap. In Table 4.10, it is observed that the gross savings were reduced to nearly 30% in 2013 compared to 40% in the early years. These reduced savings will affect capital formation in the years to come. Efforts must be made to increase the savings rate and encourage the flow of funds back to Malaysia by the firms to

Table 4.10 The trend of savings-investment gap, Malaysia, 2012–2016

	2012	2013	2014	2015	2016p
	R.M. million				
Public savings	94,383	96,131	85,823	51,134	69,606
Public gross domestic capital formation	104,037	106,908	103,538	104,126	105,609
Deficit/surplus	−9,654	−10,777	−17,715	−52,992	−36,003
Private savings	205,879	203,553	239,206	273,871	275,971
Private gross domestic capital formation	146,048	157,291	172,937	186,221	214,800
Deficit/surplus	59,831	46,262	66,269	87,650	61,171
Gross national savings	300,262	299,684	325,029	325,005	345,578
(as % of GNI)	32.1	30.4	30.4	28.9	28.9
Gross domestic capital formation	250,084	264,198	276,475	290,347	320,409
(as % of GNI)	26.7	26.8	25.8	25.8	26.8
Balance on current account	50,177	35,485	48,554	34,658	25,169
(as % of GNI)	5.4	3.6	4.5	3.1	2.1

Notes p denotes Preliminary. *Source* Department of Statistics, Malaysia and Ministry of Finance, Malaysia

increase domestic investment and avoid hollowing out of industries like in Japan in the 1990s and Taiwan in recent years.

In this respect, efforts must be made to encourage the repatriation of funds by firms and individuals to the domestic market and provide incentives to retain these funds in domestic markets. This will encourage the stability of Ringgit. For this to materialize, the rules of exchange control should not be too tight, or the firms may not have the incentive to bring back the funds to the domestic market.

As early as 2011, the Financial Sector Blueprint (FSBP) had called for the financial sector to:

- evolve the financial sector
- meet growing financial needs of emerging Asia
- emphasize regional integration and
- cement Malaysia's leadership in Islamic finance and further develop Malaysia, as an Islamic Financial Centre.

To achieve these objectives, Malaysian financial institutions are expected to enlarge their regional footprint, diversify their sources of income, tap into the ASEAN Economic Community's (AEC) growth prospects and become its leading regional players. Malaysia needs to become a global financial centre and a leading Islamic Financial Hub in the region by 2050.

At the same time, in supporting economic growth through technological catch-up as set out in Envisioning Malaysia 2050, the lending patterns should have to be adjusted to reflect the higher investment targets in manufacturing and supporting infrastructure for technological development.

Financing the Future

These objectives would require the combined use of macroeconomic fiscal and financial instruments, along with the governance of currency and capital markets (including specially governed portfolios to help the SMEs) consistent with our growth projections to 2050, and integration into the AEC and the global economy. In the area of corporate finance, the integrity of corporate board practices, risk management, accountability, and audit issues are mandatory, especially in the ever-growing Sukuk market in which Malaysia is expected to be dominant by 2050.

For this purpose, the evolving financial system must drive future growth through innovation and exploit to the fullest with current and future financial technology through the adoption of Mobile Trading, Data-Driven Financing, Crypto Currency, Big Data and Analytics, Equity Crowdfunding, and Digital Wallets (e.g. the Suica card in Japan). It should work towards the proliferation of more innovative financial products, e.g. derivatives, insurance, REIT, investment, and enhance its focus on peer-to-peer and small business lending. The system also needs to enhance the regulatory landscape in line with the growth of new products and technology. In this way, the financial system should be an enabler of future inclusive growth (especially with technology and the internet) to achieve the Malaysia 2050 target.

In summary, Malaysia's financial sector development in 2050 should involve:

1. More innovative financial instruments and financial technology
2. Better financing for SME and also capital markets integration into AEC and the global economy
3. Better corporate finance - corporate board practices, risk management, accountability, and audit
4. The proliferation of more innovative financial product—e.g. derivatives, insurance, REIT, investment
5. Achievement of a regulatory landscape able to deal with the growth of new products and technology
6. A continued role for the government-linked companies in mobilizing capital and in investment
7. Active promotion of financial inclusion (closing the urban–rural gap).

Conclusions

Malaysia stands at a very critical juncture in its development history. Its many years of strong performance for which it was given credit by international institutions like the World Bank was brought to an end by the Asian Financial Crisis of 1997/98. Its recovery from that crisis brought back economic growth, but not at the level it experienced in the late 1980s and early 1990s.

While some lessons were learned that reduced the country's financial sector vulnerability, other lessons, especially crony capitalism that led to vested interests capturing the state, were not. The warnings sounded by the authors of the *New Economic Model for Malaysia* (2010) were never seriously heeded. It took a general election that threw out the ruling coalition to uncover massive corruption and fraud. The new Government offers hope of a return to sound economic and institutional governance. The sooner this return occurs, the more rapidly the Government should be able to deal with the issue of finance for development.

There is nothing novel in what this requires. In final analysis, it requires, among others:

1. A judicious balance between recurrent and development expenditure, the latter focusing on areas identified as of high priority;
2. Attention to the high priority areas of industrial restructuring and nurturing human capital deepening receiving not just adequate funding but also in the right mix to maximize the odds of achieving Malaysia's long-term goals;
3. Specific incentives for technological upgrading and value added enhancing initiatives;
4. For recurrent expenditure, ensuring sufficient funds for operations and maintenance of infrastructure and other physical facilities;
5. Effective public expenditure management to ensure such expenditure reach its targets efficiently;
6. Processes that are transparent and accountable.

Malaysia possesses many of the ingredients to escape the middle-income trap, among them a history of strong public institutions, a well-established education system, and a skilled workforce, good infrastructure, many of which had been degraded by politics. In ensuring financing that should serve Malaysia's long-term development, depoliticization of development should be no less important than carrying out the various priorities.

References

Adam, C. S., & Bevan, D. L. (2005). Fiscal deficits and growth in developing countries. *Journal of Public Economics, 89*(4), 571–597.

Baldacci, E., Gupta, S., & Mulas-Granados, C. (2014). How effective is fiscal policy response in financial crises? In *Financial Crises: Causes, Consequences, and Policy Responses* (pp. 431–458). Washington, DC: International Monetary Fund.

Bernheim, B. D. (1989). A Neoclassical perspective on budget deficits. *The Journal of Economic Perspectives, 3*(2), 55–72.

Gill, I.S. and Kharas, H (Eds) (2007). An East Asian Renaissance: Ideas for economic growth. World Bank. Retrieved October 30, 2018, from http://siteresources.worldbank.org/INTEASTASIAPACIFIC/Resources/226262-1158536715202/EA_Renaissance_full.pdf.

Jala, I. (2016). Explaining further why Malaysia is no longer stuck in the middle-income trap, 1 September, 2016. The Star. https://www.thestar.com.my/business/business-news/2016/09/01/gaining-perspective-on-the-road-less-travelled/#hu0LKVeP0rxmADqT.99.

Jolly, J, The Guardian. (2018). Dyson to build electric cars in Singapore—with 2021 launch planned. https://www.theguardian.com/technology/2018/oct/23/dyson-to-build-electric-cars-in-singapore-with-launch-planned-for-2021.

Keynes, J. M. (1936). *The General Theory of Employment, Interest, and Money*. London: Macmillan.
Martin, R., & Fardmanesh, M. (1990). Fiscal variables and growth: A cross-sectional analysis. *Public Choice, 64*(3), 239–251.
Mason, A. D., & Shetty, S. (2019). A resurgent East Asia: Navigating a changing world. World Bank East Asia and Pacific Regional Report. Retrieved January 1, 2019. https://openknowledge.worldbank.org/handle/10986/30858.
Ministry of Economic Affairs, Malaysia. (2018). Mid-Term Review of the Eleventh Malaysia Plan (MTR-11MP), 2016–2020: New priorities and emphases. Percetakan Nasional Malaysia Berhad.
Nelson, M. A., & Singh, R. D. (1994). The deficit—growth connection: Some recent evidence from developing countries. *Economic Development and Cultural Change, 43*(1), 167–191.
Pooi, K.C., & Shukry, A. (2018). Malaysia says government debt is inflated by 1MDB borrowing, *Bloomberg,* 23 May. Retrieved October 30, 2018, from, https://www.bloomberg.com/news/articles/2018-05-23/malaysia-says-government-debt-is-inflated-by-1mdbborrowing.
Rasiah, R. (2002). Systemic coordination and human capital development: knowledge flows in Malaysian's MNC-driven electronics clusters. *Transnational Corporation, 11*(3), 89–130.
Rasiah, R. (2004). Technological capabilities in East and Southeast Asian electronics firms: Does network strength matter? *Oxford Development Studies, 32*(3), 433–454.
Rasiah, R., Mubarik, S., & Yap, X.-S. (2017). Financing technological upgrading in East Asia. *Lahore Journal of Economics, 22*: S.E. (September), 153–182.
The Guardian. (2018). Refer to https://www.theguardian.com/technology/2018/oct/23/dyson-to-build-electric-cars-in-singapore-with-launch-planned-for-2021.
Tan, E. C. (2006). Fiscal deficits, inflation and economic growth in a successful open developing economy. *Review of Applied Economics, 2*(1), 129–139.
Taylor, L., Proano, C. R., Carvalho, L. D., & Barbosa, N. (2012). Fiscal deficits, economic growth and government debt in the USA. *Cambridge Journal of Economics, 36*(11), 189–204.
The Edge. (2018). Malaysia's budget deficit at 3% of GDP as revenue rises. Retrieved August 6, 2018, from http://www.theedgemarkets.com/article/malaysias-2017-budget-deficit-3-gdp-revenue-rises.
Yeah, K. L. (2017). National transformation initiative: shaping of vision and goals for 2010 and beyond under economics for business section, 6 September 2017. New Straits Times. Retrieved December 30, 2017, from https://www.nst.com.my/authors/dr-yeah-kim-leng.

Wee Yeap Lau is Associate Professor at the Faculty of Business and Economics, Universiti Malaya. He specializes in the economics of finance and investment.

Chapter 5
Agriculture and Food Security

Chamhuri Siwar, Rospidah Ghazali, and Mohammed Ibrahim

Abstract This chapter discusses issues and challenges facing agriculture and food security in Malaysia. The evidence amassed shows that the contribution of agriculture to GDP, agricultural employment in total employment, and exports in total exports have decreased in trend terms. Nevertheless, we argue that Malaysia has great potential in increasing agro-industrial exports, enhancing income of rural poor, and ensuring food security. The increasing global demand for agricultural products is a great opportunity to enhance the contribution of the sector to GDP and raise incomes especially for rural population. However, it also shows that Malaysia's dependence on imports of major food items, such as rice, (which is the staple of Malaysians), is worrying largely due to low productivity, high costs, low return to investments and poverty. The way forward requires strategic investments in agricultural R&D and science, technology and innovation (STI) infrastructure, improving agro-ecological systems, cooperation among government agencies, nongovernmental organizations (NGOs) and communities towards sustainable agriculture, agricultural industrialization, the development of *halal* food and food safety measures, as well as strategic policies and programmes to reduce food imports.

Keywords Agriculture · Food security · Food safety · Rice farming · Sustainable agriculture

Introduction

From 1950 to 2020, the world population increased from 2.5 billion to 7.8 billion, which shows that world population more than tripled over the period 1950–2020.

C. Siwar (✉) · R. Ghazali · M. Ibrahim
Institute for Environment and Development (LESTARI), Universiti Kebangsaan Malaysia, 43600 Bangi, Selangor, Malaysia
e-mail: csiwar@ukm.edu.my

R. Ghazali
e-mail: rospidah@ukm.edu.my

R. Rasiah et al. (eds.), *Malaysia's Leap Into the Future*, Dynamics of Asian Development, https://doi.org/10.1007/978-981-16-7045-9_5

Despite rapid technical change and the introduction of greening technologies, population expansion has also been associated with depleting natural resources and arable land for farming.

Meanwhile, a significant share of the world's population, especially those among the least developed countries depend on agriculture for their livelihood. At the turn of the millennium, 80% of the poor among the developing countries still lived in rural areas and directly rely on agriculture for their livelihood (Carvalho, 2006). Regardless of the stage of economic growth, agriculture and forestry plays the greatest role in maintaining biodiversity, conserving natural resources, and enhancing rural livelihood (Kada, 2005).

Meanwhile, food consumption has increased rapidly, while its production has relatively declined due to limited cultivation area, stagnant yield, and low investment (Demeke et al., 2009). There is growing imbalance in food demand supply among several developing countries, whereby growth in food demand is outstripping growth in food supply (Mellor, 1988). Consequently, global prices for major food items have escalated (Trostle, 2008).

Regardless of its potential, however, the ability of agriculture to support the fast-growing population has been central developmental issue globally for decades and continues to be important agenda of development policy. While the growing gap between demand and supply of food has been of concern, some have explored the potential of technological advancement to boost the food supply (Rosegrant & Cline, 2003). Based on common indicators, nevertheless, agriculture's contribution in national economies have tended to fall: the contribution of agriculture in GDP, the proportion of agricultural exports in total exports, and the share of workforce in agriculture in total workforce has progressively decreased (Vyas, 2005). Although "the green revolution" expanded several folds food production, population growth and contracting arable lands has increasingly pushed agriculture into an agribusiness in order to sustain food security for the poor (Sulaiman, 2005).

Similarly, although agriculture plays a significant role in enhancing income of the rural poor and ensuring food security in Malaysia, the contribution of the sector to GDP has fallen in trend terms from 43.7% in 1960 to 7.7% in 2019 (World Bank, 2020). Employment in agriculture in total employment fell from 22.0% in 1991 to 11.1% in 2018. Meanwhile, Malaysia's population is expected to reach 32.7 million in 2020 and 40.6 million in 2050 (Tey, 2020: 2, 14), which will inevitably require expansion in agro-food production to meet expected growth in demand.

This chapter seeks to examine how the agricultural sector has responded to the sectoral shift initially towards manufacturing, and subsequently towards services with a view towards adoption of productivity enhancing technologies and strengthening food security. Malaysia has launched four strategic economic plans, namely the New Economic Policy (1970–1990), Vision Policy 2020 (1991–2020), New Economic Model (NEM, 2010–2020), and in 2018 Share Prosperity Vision (SPV) policy (2019–2030). Along with the four broad policies above, the Government also announced a 30 years National Transformation Plan (T50) over the period 2020–2050 with the aim of transforming Malaysia into developed nation that is at the frontier of sustainable living.

Theoretical Considerations

The agricultural and forestry sector can be grouped into agro-industrial and food sub-sectors. The former includes oil palm, rubber, cocoa, and timber, while the latter includes paddy, fruits and vegetables, livestock and fishery and the miscellaneous group comprising of tobacco, pepper, coconuts, sugar cane, cassava, sweet potato, maize, tea, and coffee. Within the first sub-sector, the newly emerging industries, such as floriculture, sago and aquarium fish and aquatic plants have expanded strongly over the years (Fuad, 2005). Agro-industries have played a major role in generating foreign exchange and employment in Malaysia, especially exports of palm oil and rubber.

While agro-industries have been pivotal in Malaysia's early development, food has always remained a critical focus as it contains essential goods, such as rice. The most acceptable definition of food security, which was framed by the World Food Summit 1996, as a situation "when all people, at all times, have physical, social and economic access to sufficient, safe and nutritious food to meet their dietary needs and food preferences for an active and healthy life" (FAO, 1996). This definition was expanded at the World Food Summit 2009, to include nutritional dimensions as the four pillars of food security. These pillars are availability, access, utilization, and stability. Food insecurity is a serious developmental problem as it will easily translate into poverty.

The definition of food security has evolved over time, following three overlapping paradigm shifts on the framework of food security: "thinking from the global and the national level to the household and the individual level, from a food first perspective to a livelihood perspective, and from objective indicators to subjective perception" (Ecker & Breisinger, 2012). Every country is struggling to provide sustainable supply of food to fulfil the demands and this is a challenging issue for developing nations (Paul, 2013).

Furthermore, poverty is considered a major bottleneck to achieve food security at individual or/and household levels needs far exceed demand. Consequently, the eradication of poverty is fundamental in order to improve access to food (Ecker & Breisinger, 2012). The majority of poor people live in rural areas with small or no access to productive agricultural land. Eighty percent of the hungry live in developing countries with half of them engaged in smallholding farming. Ninety percent of world farmers cultivate and produce on less than two hectares of land, though farmers engaged in intensive agriculture, such as in Taiwan have enjoyed high yields (Rasiah, 2018).

Food insecurity is associated with supply-side and demand-side pressures, caused among others by globalization, population increase, climate change, and urbanization. Most of food security challenges (including socio-economic issues) are rampant in developing nations where environmental pressures are concentrated (Table 5.1). These factors hinder access of the poor to sufficient food (Misselhorn et al., 2012).

Table 5.1 Key supply and demand side pressures on global food security

Pressures	
Supply side	Demand side
Climate change	Population increases
Urbanization	Urbanization
Globalization	Changing demand in food types and levels of processing
Safety and quality—including factors such as environmental pollution and pests and diseases	Disease
Land use change and competition (e.g. biofuels)	Factors linked with under-development, including poverty, gender inequity, low resource access, poor health, and lack of education

Source Misselhorn et al. (2012)

Recent trends show the dropping yields in many regions as a result of declining investment in agricultural research and infrastructure, as well as overcoming problems posed by scarcity of water. One of the main causes of the rise in global and national food insecurity is trade restrictions imposed by major food importers combined with local policy and governance instruments (Ecker & Breisinger, 2012). Another factor that affects agricultural productivity and food security is the socio-cultural variable. Most rice farmers, being Malays, practice the sharia' of inheritance (Fara'idh). The farm is divided up among heirs every generation, which has led to its fragmentation into smaller and smaller sizes. The trend fall in farm size has undermined the capacity of farmers to appropriate scale economies (Lian, 2009). Generally, food security could be significantly improved if agricultural investment increased and food policies are reformed (Rosegrant & Cline, 2003).

In addition, industrialization and urbanization have created new consumers who are wealthy and busy, which influences the supply of agro-food system, which has raised demand for high quality and differentiated products at reasonable prices. The new customers prefer processed easy home-meal substitutes and at the same time are healthy, safe, and fresh (Choe, 2005). Dietary histories do reflect differences arising from cultural variations, which in turn affect the choice of food and their quality (Prescotta et al., 2002). Consumers prefer foods low in fat, less in sugar, and are free from harmful chemicals. The sales for organic foods in the United States and Europe is booming despite the fact that the aggregate food market is significantly low. In short, consumers in developed countries have become more concerned about food safety risk, and thus, demand high standards in product handling. As a result, many high-income countries are revising their food safety regulations to control the safety process to eliminate risks (Unnevehr, 2000).

Rising energy prices have also had a major impact on food security. On the one hand, since energy is one of the factors of production, rising energy prices raises the cost of agricultural production. On the other hand, high energy prices attract the production of biofuel as an alternative energy from agricultural commodities

(Ewing & Msangi, 2009). The rising growth in the bioethanol and biodiesel markets has raised demands for key agricultural products that would otherwise go to the production of food and feeds (Naylor et al., 2007).

In addition, biomass production from either food or energy needs a significant use of natural resources. The conversion of biomass to energy requires a large amount of land and water. Since land and water resources are scarce, the impact of competition from biomass production on the scarce agricultural resources tend to exacerbate pressures on food security and the environment (Müller et al., 2008).

Furthermore, the population of Muslims in the world is projected to grow to 2.2 billion by 2030. While the consumption of *halal* food is not limited to Muslims, the growing Muslim population is a great opportunity for the expansion of the *halal* food industry (Mathew et al., 2014). Muslims consume food that meets the Islamic dietary code, namely, *halal* food. The objective of *halal* is to guarantee that the food produced is safe and hygienic—that is free from contamination and harmful germs. In line with this objective, it is not only religious factors that can influence people to consume *halal* food, but also covers health issues related to food safety. The concept of *Halal* food is not static but dynamic in nature, which has evolved from simply Muslim firms producing halal food to *halal* products, *halal* supply chain, and *halal* value chain (Tieman & Ghazali, 2014).

However, it is pertinent to recognize the following causes of food insecurity, which are critical:

- Distribution: the total global food production is sufficient to feed the world population but not available to the hungry or not accessible by the poor.
- Efficiency: food utilization in many countries is inefficient—one-third of the food produced is wasted, while another third is fed to livestock. Food waste occurred both in developing and industrial countries. In the later, 40% waste occur at retail and consumer outlets, whereas in the developing countries 40% waste occur at post-harvest and processing points. Generally, reducing food waste is one of the major challenges of food security (Tscharntke et al., 2012).
- Land grabbing and speculation on food commodities: Land grabbing by foreign investors has become a problem in developing countries. Land conversion from agricultural to commercial and industrial use has similar implications in Malaysia.

Consequently, this chapter examines the state of the agricultural sector in Malaysia, with a focus on food crop production and food security.

Malaysian Agriculture

Despite the decline in its economic significance over the years, the agricultural sector has always been regarded as an important sector in Malaysia, which is the case with most countries undergoing early stages of economic development. Apart from its contribution to economic growth, the agricultural sector is also strategically important from the social and political perspectives. The sector plays a vital role in partially meeting food requirements of the nation and it is always the policy of the government to encourage domestic food production. The general policy on food is to ensure reasonable returns to producers and to supply affordable food to consumers.

As with rapidly industrializing nations, the contribution of agriculture sector to the economy has declined steadily since the 1960s. As shown in Table 5.2, the share of agriculture in GDP decreased sharply from 37.8% in 1961 to 30.8% in 1970, 19.7% in 1980, 12.8% in 1990, and 5.3% in 2000 before rising to 7.3% in 2010 and 8.1% in 2015. However, the contribution of the sector declined from 8.1% in 2015–2016 to 7.5% in 2018 (see also Fig. 5.1). Nevertheless, real value added of the agricultural sector expanded in trend terms from RM26.2 Billion in 1970 to RM95.5 Billion in 2018 (World Bank, 2020).

The main factors that caused the relative fall in agriculture's contribution to GDP include the conversion of agricultural land to manufacturing, construction, and urbanization. Table 5.3 shows changes in land use pattern in agricultural activities over the period 1960–2010. Land use pattern for industrial crops accounted for almost 90.0% of total land use, while land use for food crops accounted for only 9.2% in 2015 (Department of Statistics, 2020). Among the crops, palm oil recorded the highest land use, which accounted for over 60% of it in 2015.

Another factor that has negatively affected agricultural productivity and food security in Malaysia is the socio-cultural variable. Most rice farmers, being Malays, practice the sharia' of inheritance (Fara'idh). The farm is divided up among heirs every generation, which has led to its fragmentation into smaller and smaller sizes. The trend fall in farm size has undermined the capacity of farmers to appropriate scale

Table 5.2 Contribution of agriculture to the Malaysian economy

Year	GDP (RM billion)	Agriculture (RM billion)	Agriculture/GDP (%)
1961	5.2	2.0	37.8
1965	6.6	2.0	31.5
1970	12.3	3.8	30.8
1975	51.6	4.6	29.8
1980	77.5	10.2	19.7
1985	115.7	11.9	13.3
1990	222.5	14.8	12.8
1995	339.4	17.1	7.7
2000	339.4	18.2	5.3
2005	495.3	21.0	4.2
2010	821.4	82.9	7.3
2015	1,157.7	94.2	8.1
2016	1,107.9	89.5	8.1
2018	1,446.9	99.5	7.5

Source Department of Statistics (2020)

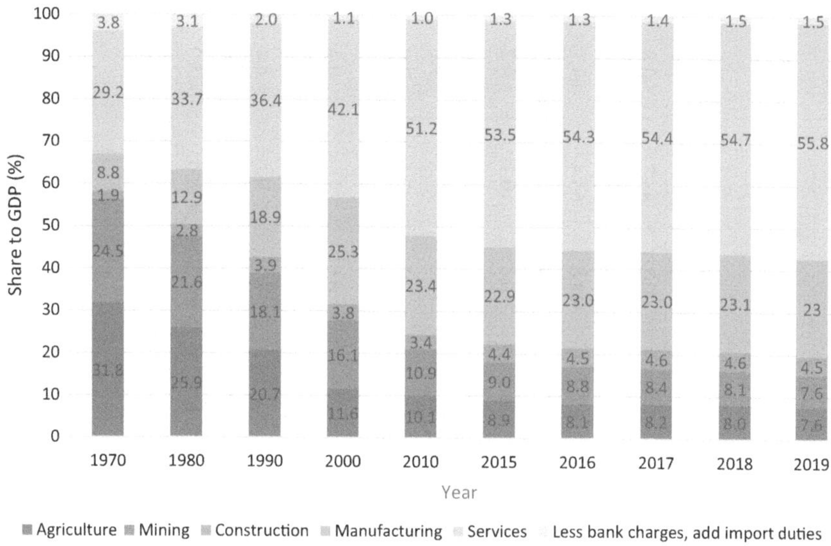

Fig. 5.1 Malaysia gross domestic product GDP by sector, Malaysia, 1970–2019 (%) y sector 1970–2019). *Source* Economic Planning Unit (2019) and Jomo and Wee (2014)

economies (Lian, 2009). Generally, food security could be significantly improved if agricultural investment increased and food policies are reformed (Rosegrant & Cline, 2003).

Figure 5.2 shows employment trends in Malaysia by sector from 1960 to 2017. The employment share of the agricultural sector has declined steadily from 66.2% in 1960 to 55.7% in 1970, 39.7% in 1980, 26.0% in 1990, 15.2% in 2000, and 13.6% in 2010. Nevertheless increased efforts by the government has seen the contribution of the sector to total employment rise to 12.4% in 2015 and 12.8% in 2017.

Government Policies

While several smaller initiatives were launched in the 1960s to promote agriculture, especially those involving the Bumiputeras, which included FELDA, RISDA, and FELCRA, the New Economic Policy (NEP) contained the most incisive blueprint to stimulate the sector with heavy focus on rural development (Ikmal, 2019; Rasiah & Salih, 2019a, b). Despite the lack of strong government supported R&D in the 1970s, the role of MARDI and infrastructure development, which included the construction of irrigation canals, mechanization, and the provision of fertilizer subsidies for farmers and fishing boats for fishers, along with successful inroads to reduce

Table 5.3 Land use, Malaysia, 1960–2010

CROP	1960	1965	1970	1975	1980	1985	1990	1995	2000	2005	2010
Industrial crops	68.5	71.7	68.0	69.3	71.7	76.1	81.3	77	80.2	83.7	90.8
Rubber	65.7	66.9	58.6	51.2	45.1	39.3	44	30.6	26.1	19.6	26.2
Palm oil	2.1	4.0	8.4	16.5	23	29.9	30.4	37.9	48.8	63.4	64.1
Cocoa	0.0	0.1	0.2	0.7	2.8	6.1	6.3	7.9	4.7	0.5	0.2
Pineapple	0.6	0.6	0.6	0.5	0.3	0.2	0.1	0.2	0.3	0.1	0.2
Tobacco	0.1	0.1	0.1	0.3	0.3	0.3	0.2	0.2	0.2	0.2	0.1
Food crops	31.5	28.3	32.0	30.7	26.8	22.6	17.9	21.7	18.8	16.3	9.2
Paddy	17.5	16.8	20.8	19.5	16.5	13.1	10	11.3	7.5	7.1	7.0
Coconut	9.2	8.1	8.7	7.4	7.9	6.7	4.7	5.7	4.1	2.8	1.5
Vegetables	1.3	0.7	0.5	0.3	0.3	0.3	0.5	0.3	0.8	1	0.4
Fruits	1.5	1.6	1.6	1.7	2.1	2.4	2.7	4.3	6.4	5.2	0.3
Others	1.9	1.1	0.4	1.9	1.5	1.4	0.9	1.3	1	0.3	n.a
Total (%)	100.0	100.0	100.0	100.0	100.0	100.0	100.0	100.0	100.0	100.0	100.0
Total (hectares)	2667.0	3066.0	3445.0	3887.0	4446.6	4952.4	6636.3	5716.3	5367.3	638.0	4693.0

Source Malaysia (1986, 1991, 2000, 2006); MoA (2010)

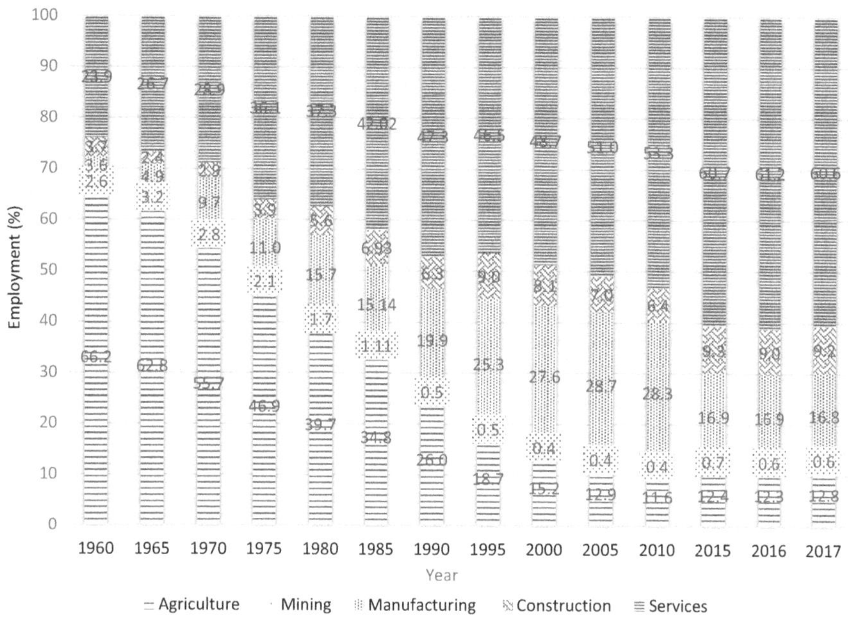

Fig. 5.2 Employment by sectors, Malaysia, 1960–2017 (%). *Source* Department of Statistics of Malaysia (various years)

middlemen exploitation through the formation of parastatals helped raise productivity in food production (Rasiah & Salih, 2019b). The large plantations enjoyed in-house R&D, while smallholders enjoyed such support from the Malaysian Rubber Board (MRB) (Jeyaraj, 2013).

However, government support for small farmer-based food production gradually fell since 1981, which began to undermine self-sufficiency in a number of items. Consequently, the government launched the First National Agricultural Policy (NAP) in 1984 to address the problem. The NAP was designed to ensure a balanced and sustained rate of growth of the agricultural sector vis-a-vis other sectors in the economy. However, the 1980s saw increasing emphasis on industrial crops, which was aimed at producing more oil palm, to create employment, to promote foreign exchange earnings, and reduce rural poverty through investing on infrastructure and new land development schemes (Rasiah & Salih, 2019a). The policy also aimed to enhance efficiency, competitiveness, and productivity of the agricultural sector through modernization of agricultural activities. During 1984–1991, Malaysia witnessed a significant transformation of its economic structure where manufacturing and services overtook the agricultural sector as the leading engine of economic growth (Harron et al., 2001).

The Second National Agricultural Policy (NAP2 1992–2010) and the overlapping Third National Agricultural Policy (NAP3) (1998–2010) attempted to balance development between the agricultural sector and manufacturing sector, while promoting linkages between the sector and other sectors, and emphasizing sustainability (Malaysia, 1996b). Furthermore, NAP2 also aimed to enhance the participation of the private sector in the agriculture, especially in increase food production. However, over the period 1990–1995, the agricultural sector grew at only 2% per annum, which reduced its contribution to GDP from 12.8% in 1990 to 7.7% in 1995 (Table 5.2). Meanwhile, the food trade balance account recorded a deficit in 1989 and has since stayed negative (Rasiah, 2018, 2020).

The gradual fall in the contribution of agriculture in GDP is normal when rapid industrialization takes place, but the fall became exceptionally too quick for a resource rich country. Apart from plantation agriculture, the focus on agriculture in general fell. In doing so, food crops were given little support as the main concentration in the agriculture was industrial crops, such as palm oil and rubber (Rasiah, 2018). Indeed, the self-sufficiency in rice fell to 65% in 1998 (Vijian, 2001). Although the NAP2 and NAP3 recommended an import-substitution strategy for food crops, import of food commodities continued to rise as commercial cash crops took precedence (Harron et al., 2001). In fact, rising food imports have coincided with declining acreage allocated to paddy cultivation (Alam et al., 2011).

The performance of Malaysia's agro-food sector is low compared to the neighbouring counterparts. Using comparable figures from a common year, it can be seen that rice yield in Malaysia in 2008 fell significantly lower than Bangladesh, Vietnam, Myanmar, Indonesia, China, and Australia (see Fig. 5.3). Although yields in Malaysia are higher than in Thailand and India, both the latter countries enjoy positive food trade balance.

One of the challenges facing rice farming is high cost of production associated with low return. As well as rice farmers are smallholders those produce at small farm size and lack economies of scale as the farming methods are associated with moderately extensive farming. To make matters worse, the removal of price subsidies enforced by the World Trade Organization (WTO) has aggravated the problem (Lian, 2009).

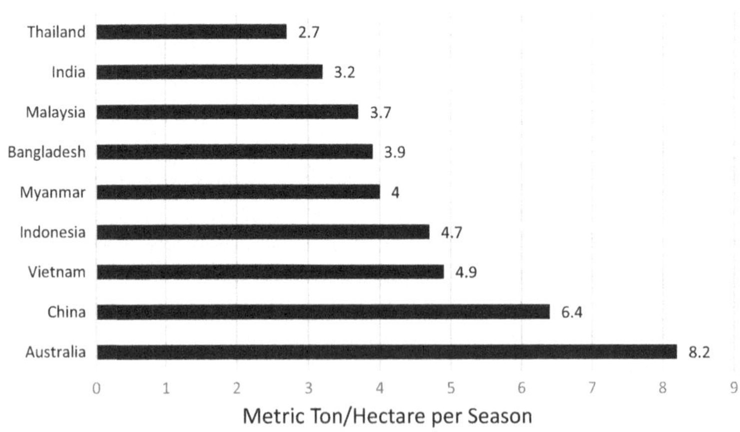

Fig. 5.3 Average paddy yield, selected countries, 2008. *Source* Malaysia (2012)

Scarcity of water has emerged as a critical problem in paddy farming in Peninsular Malaysia, which specializes on wet paddy. The per capita available water resource is declining everywhere and several countries already relied on "fossil" waters for use in irrigation (Carvalho, 2006).

In addition, the trade-off between food security and biofuel energy production is another challenge facing the agricultural sector (Ewing & Msangi, 2009). In Malaysia, this problem is primarily observed in the cultivation of oil palm, which among others, is used in the production of biodiesel. Although oil palm lands do not compete with wet paddy, they could be used to produce other food crops.

Moreover, the low return from investment and low productivity of agriculture are challenges for investors in the sector. The primary motive of investors is maximizing their return. Thus, as the Malaysian economy moved towards industrialization and services, investors in agricultural sectors have continued to shift their resources and investment into more productive sectors. In fact, new developments in the energy sector, industrial, commercial and residential centres are fast attracting resources from agricultural sector (Vijian, 2001).

Although initiatives have been taken to improve the situation, food safety standards compliance measures has discouraged the export of food products from Malaysia to the global market. Food safety is mainly the issue of fresh food product trade than other kinds of agricultural product trade. The development of fresh food export from developing to developed countries is a challenge. Food safety hazards are many kinds and their importance depends on products. Pesticide residues, use of hazardous feedstocks in fishery and poultry, and microbial contamination in fruits and vegetables have switched a number of exporters to focus on the domestic market (Unnevehr, 2000).

The growing deficits in food trade along with its deleterious impact on the incomes of the poor farmers drove the government to introduce the National Agro-Food Policy (2011–2020) and the National Commodity Policy (2011–2020) as important policy roadmaps to guide the development of agriculture sector. These policies aim to enhance food production and export of industrial commodities. However, the actual food trade balance excluding vegetable oils and fats, has been negative over the period 1989–2018 (Rasiah, 2020). Exports only exceed imports when vegetable oil and fat items are included, especially from oil palm (see Fig. 5.4).

Unfortunately, until 2019 Malaysia has yet to formulate an explicit food security policy, though the food security agenda has been discussed in the context of self-sufficiency targets. Since rice is the main staple food in Malaysia, special attention and treatment has been given to the sector along the supply chain of the sector. Meanwhile, in order to assess the progress of the sector in achieving food security's objective, the government used self-sufficiency level as the proxy (see Table 5.4), deploying two strategies in the process, i.e. establishing self-efficiency level and maintaining rice stocks (Alam et al., 2011).

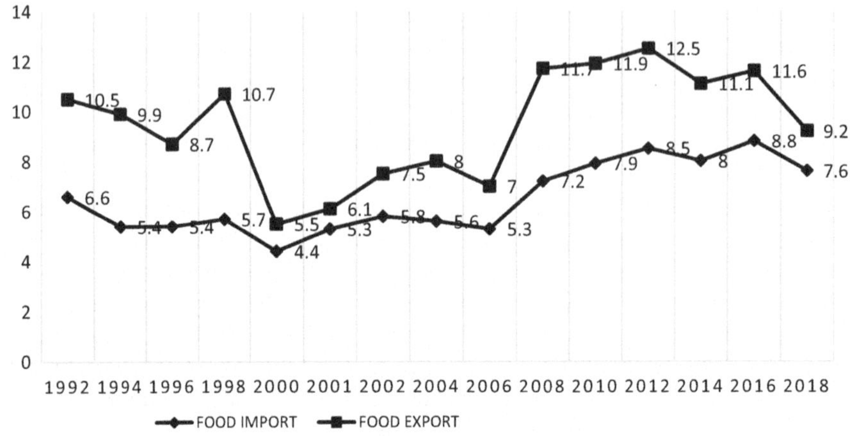

Fig. 5.4 Import and export of food products (%). Note: The figures include vegetable oils and fats. *Source* Department of Statistics Malaysia, Annual Statistics (various years)

Table 5.4 Self sufficiency level of food commodities, Malaysia, 1995–2018 (%)

Commodities	1995	2000	2005	2010	2015	2018
Rice	76.3	70	72	72	64.8	68.7
Fruits	88.9	94	117	138	80.6	78.4
Vegetables	71.6	95	74	108	52.4	44.6
Fishery products	92.2	86	91	104	93.1	92.1
Beef	19.2	15	23	28	23.1	22.9
Mutton	6.0	6.0	8	10	11.3	10.9
Pork	104.0	100	107	132	93.6	90.1
Poultry	110.7	113	121	122	104.2	104.0
Eggs	110.3	116	113	115	114.0	116.8
Milk	3.5	3	5	5	1.8	1.9

Sources Malaysia (2001) and MoA (2020)

Self-sufficiency in Rice

Malaysia has relied on rice imports to meet domestic demand rely on rice imports since colonial rule (Rospidah & Aminah, 2019). Grist (1950), recorded that Malaya imported 453,000 metric tonnes of rice to feed the people prior to independence. Statistics recorded that the area of paddy cultivation in Malaya in 1934 was about 765,000 acres, of which 691,000 acres were cultivated as a wet land paddy using irrigation or inundation by water, and 74,000 acres with dry land paddy. Dryland paddy is produced mainly in Sabah and Sarawak where farmers commonly farmed using traditional methods.

Rice is a strategic good and is highly protected for the following three reasons (Selvadurai, 1972): one, it is a staple food of Malaysians; two, to meet the self-sufficiency level (SSL); and three, the sector is a home of the poorest people in the country with the majority of them being Malays. Therefore, poverty eradication, which is one of the two objectives of the New Economic Policy (NEP), has attracted a strong focus by the government to not only address their livelihood, but also to avert any possible social and political upheaval from them.

Malaysia recorded its highest self-sufficiency rate of 87% in rice in 1975 (Rasiah & Salih, 2019b: 129). However, rice self-sufficiency gradually fell to 64.8% in 2015 before rising to 68.7% in 2018 (Table 5.4). Malaysia's main sources of rice imports have been Vietnam, Thailand, Myanmar, India, and Pakistan. High reliance on rice imports has made Malaysia vulnerable to food insecurity, particularly during global food crises. For instance, during the global financial crisis of 2007–2008, Malaysia faced severe shortage of rice supply. Prices of several species of rice rose in this period. As a controlled item, prices of only the basic national rice were capped.

Table 5.5 provides selected important indicators for paddy and rice production in the country. Granary areas are the main contributors of paddy and rice production in Malaysia. Almost 80% of the products derived from granary areas, which include the Muda Irrigation Scheme. As per capita consumption of rice has varied between 71 and 94 kgs a year, domestic production is not sufficient to supply the demanded amount (Fig. 5.5). Malaysia has to import the rice to fulfil the gap in demand (Paul, 2013) (see Fig. 5.6).

In short, it can be argued that the NAP1, NAP2, and NAP3 were not successful largely because they were organized to complement manufacturing and services, and plantation agriculture. Furthermore, instead of creating competitive advantage, the government reduced emphasis on the agricultural sector by accepting the mainstream arguments that Malaysia no longer enjoyed the comparative advantage to produce food crops. Also, while Taiwan targeted and achieved 97% self-sufficiency in rice production in 2011 (Lee, 2011), the Malaysian government only targeted an 80% self-sufficiency level, and given the losing focus, only managed a 65% self-sufficiency level in 2015 (Table 5.3).

Following the failure of the three NAPs, *Pemandu* launched National Key Economic Area (NKEA) with the target of raising domestic rice production in Malaysia to 85% of domestic consumption by 2020. However, mismatch between farming methods and scale of operations, weak linkages with domestic suppliers, and lack deployment of frontier technologies, (such as the use of robots and drones), has reduced the competitiveness of local farmers (Malaysia, 2012).

Along with the production of food crops, the complementarity between animals and crops is a robust strategy to attain the desired self-sufficiency level in food production. However, such mixed farming operations are rarely deployed in food production in Malaysia (Devendra, 2009). The presence of animals enhances crop growth and sustainability of the system.

Table 5.5 Selected indicators, paddy and rice, Malaysia, 1986–2018

Item	Year								
	1986	1990	1995	2000	2005	2006	2011	2014	2018
1. Area (Hectare)									
a. Paddy Parcel[1]	np	np	–	478,187	461,205	461,224	428,605	289,882	284,047
Peninsular Malaysia	np	np	37,5821	361,564	342,003	341,627	284,441	289,882	284,047
Granary areas	np	np	216,483	212,156	205,270	205,276	200,103	210,842[3]	214,281
Sabah	np	np	np	58,529	58,259	58,259	46,826	na	na
Sarawak	np	np	np	58,364	60,943	61,338	60,848	na	na
b. Planted area[2]	650,875	680,647	672,787	698,702	676,169	676,803	683,677	689,732	699,980
Peninsular Malaysia	452,294	493,986	496,542	518,927	508,833	508,505	517,555	516,444	522,122
Granary areas	334,082	373,588	383,201	391,012	380,468	379,863	389,861	396,080[3]	426,046
Sabah	41,694	54,815	53,095	48,894	40,118	41,557	42,526	44,921	42,442
Sarawak	156,887	131,864	123,150	130,881	127,218	126,741	123,596	128,367	135,426
c. Harvested area	np	np	np	688,741	660,962	658,181	680,572	678,132	699,860
Peninsular Malaysia	np	np	np	515,261	498,560	496,568	514,450	503,776	521,992
Granary areas	np	np	380,773	388,951	379,456	378,731	387,522	377,909	425,932
Sabah	np	np	np	48,894	40,118	41,557	42,526	na	42,442
Sarawak	np	np	np	124,586	122,284	120,056	123,596	na	135,426
2. Average yield[2] (kg/Hectare)	2,640	2,769	3,162	3,064	3,226	3,254	3,898	3,835	3,770
Peninsular Malaysia	3,149	3,289	3,702	3,564	3,547	3,559	4,467	4,392	4,312
Granary areas	3,298	3,474	3,987	3,749	4,021	4,060	4,720	4,808	4,682
Sabah	1,877	1,730	2,703	3,171	3,714	3,658	3,414	2,676	2,884

(continued)

Table 5.5 (continued)

Item	Year								
	1986	1990	1995	2000	2005	2006	2011	2014	2018
Sarawak	1,403	1,298	1,191	1,043	1,784	1,891	1,682	1,999	1,959
3. Production estimates ('000 TONNES)[2]	1,718	1,885	2,127	2,141	2,181	2,202	2,665	2,645	2,640
Peninsular Malaysia	1,424	1,625	1,838	1,849	1,805	1,810	2,311	2,268	2,251
Granary areas	1,102	1,298	1,528	1,466	1,530	1,542	1,196	1,904	1,995
Sabah	78	94	144	155	149	152	91	120	122
Sarawak	215	165	145	136	227	240	124	256	265
4. Most popular varieties in Peninsular Malaysia									
Most popular	np	np	MR 84	MR 84	MR 219	MR 219	MR219	MR 219	MR 220 CL2
Second popular	np	np	IR 42	MR 185	MR 220	MR 220	MR220	MR 220	MR 297
Third popular	np	np	SEMARAK	MR 167	MR 84	MR 84	MR232	MR 220 CL2	MR 219

Source Ministry of Agriculture and Agro based Industry (2006), Jabatan Pertanian Semenanjung Malaysia (2014), MOA (2018), Rospidah and Aminah (2019)
Note [1] A paddy parcel is a piece of land which usually used for paddy planting
[2] Consists wetland paddy and dryland paddy
[3] An additional data for new granary areas namely IADA Pekan and IADA Rompin
np: Not provided
na: Not available

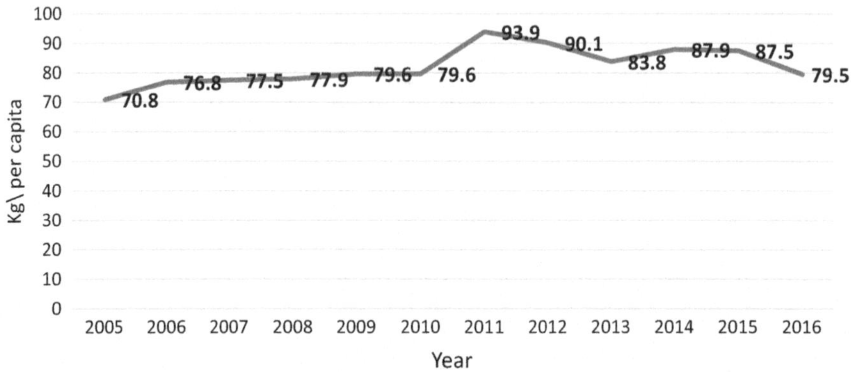

Fig. 5.5 Rice consumption per capita, Malaysia, 2005–2016 (kgs). *Source* MoA (2018)

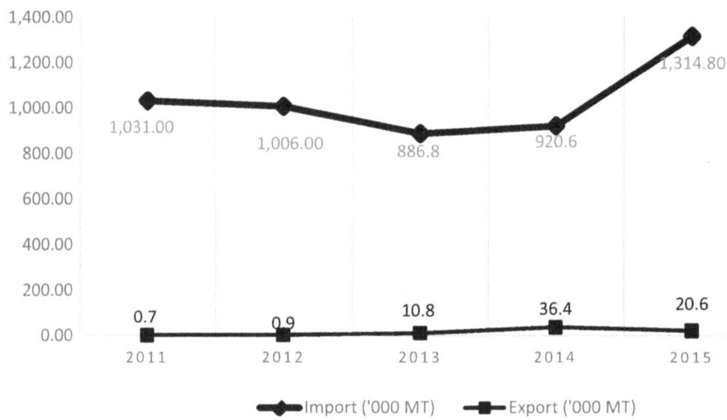

Fig. 5.6 Rice trade, Malaysia, 2011–2015 (Metric Tonnes). *Source* MOA (various years)

Building Blocks for the Future

Achieving substantial level in improving food security is difficult. However, innovations in agro-ecological combined with investment in research and agricultural infrastructure can make significant improvement to food security (Rosegrant & Cline, 2003). In assessing prospects for the future of agriculture, there are many uncertainties and concerning issues such as: global economic growth, energy prices, biofuel production, as well as there is an issue of supply response capacity of the global agricultural production system such as cost of inputs, additional cropland (quantity and quality), water shortages and biophysical response to climate change (Trostle, 2008).

All of these issues require investment in research, system development, and knowledge sharing. To implement agricultural innovation, we need collective action at the local level, as well as the participation of government and non-governmental organizations that work at the community level.

(a) **Intensive-Farming Methods**

The transformation of the agricultural sector in Malaysia will result in the structural change in rural employment and its modernization will support value added upgrading in the supply chain of agro-business in the rural areas (Malaysia, 2012). Given the scarcity of arable land, the government's target for the agricultural sector to grow at 3.5% per annum can only be achieved through emphasis on enhancing productivity, as well as raising self-sufficiency levels in the agro-food sub-sector (Malaysia, 2015).

The NKEA has targeted to boost the contribution of agriculture to GNI to reach RM49.1 billion by the end of 2020 and in the process to create bulk job opportunities, overcome food trade account deficits, and double the income of farmers in which the lion's share of government expenditure is aimed at rural areas (Paul, 2013). In order to achieve the objective of self-sufficiency, the NKEA targeted to boost domestic food production generally, and specifically to achieve 85% domestic consumption of rice by 2020 (Malaysia, 2012).

To achieve the objectives set in Malaysia (2012), the successful initiatives of the 1970s when the government introduced marketing support to offer reasonable prices to farmers should be adapted to absorb the changing environment from 2020 (Rasiah, 2018). It is critical to identify essential food items, such as rice, chillies, and tubers to raise their self-sufficiency levels. Since the focus is on small farmers a minimum guaranteed price should be offered to farmers while subsidy support for fertilizers, joint use of machinery, robots, and drones be encouraged for farmers to appropriate scale economies—aggregating scope economies of small farmers in the process. Small farms should be connected with incubators and farm-support service to address problems. Taiwan has managed to generate 90% self-sufficiency in rice that way (Rasiah, 2018). These changes are essential to reinvigorate Malaysia's parastatal led farming, such as FELDA, FELCRA, and RISDA.

Efforts must be increased to modernize small-scale agriculture in Malaysia to raise productivity and handle crop spoilage and wastage. Intensive-farming methods must be targeted at them so that the use of robots and drones in farming along with disease resistant species can be handled collectively by requiring small-scale farms to cooperate so as to enjoy collective efficiency. Such practices are widespread in Europe, which has a historical tradition for the promotion of farm cooperatives (Gijselinckx & Bussels, 2014; Rasiah, 2021).

(b) **Organic Farming**

A number of definitions have been provided for sustainable agriculture, ranging from the concept of productivity to inclusion of culture and philosophy. The definition that incorporates the diverse dimensions and elements is that "sustainable agriculture is ecologically sound, economically viable, socially just and humane" (Kada, 2005).

In response to climate change and environmental degradation, governments in high-income countries, such as those in the European Union, are forcing retailers and producers to be more accountable for ensuring environmental sustainability (Malaysia, 2012). There is a high level of fertilizer and manure application in the agricultural practices in Malaysia that lead to environmental pollution. To maintain the sustainable environment, government has been promoting sustainable agriculture and organic farming. This is because, despite the increased production, excessive use of hazardous fertilizers can cause serious contamination of food production. Organic farming significantly benefits farmers and environment, which should be promoted in the country. Hence, sustainable agriculture should be made the nucleus of organic agriculture. This agricultural approach is not relevant only for developed nations but it also applicable for developing countries like Malaysia (Tiraieyari et al., 2017), including to support rural development programmes targeted at generating employment and income (Shamsudin et al., 2010).

The adaptation of organic farming could help solve demand–supply food deficits as it can raise yields while strengthening the environment. Because of increasing awareness regarding health and nature the demand of consumers for organic products is rising (Terano et al., 2016). Consequently, the market for organic products in Malaysia has been growing fast since the turn of the millennium. The government anticipated this development when it promoted organic agriculture in the NAP3, but much more have to be done to see that the policy is executed effectively on the ground.

(c) **Agro-food Industry**

Government efforts to initiate industrialization in Malaysia began with the Pioneer industry Ordinance of 1958, which emphasized import-substitution, which was accompanied by export-oriented industrialization since 1972 following the opening of Free Trade Zones and Licensed Manufacturing Warehouses (Rasiah, 1995). Food processing enjoyed strong focus during the import-substitution phase. Although export-orientation saw Malaysia's manufacturing sector dominated by electric and electronics exports since the 1970s, emphasis on food crop cultivation, especially those that formed a major platform of livelihood of the Bumiputeras continued to enjoy massive government support (Rasiah & Salih, 2019a). As a result of the policy, a number of agro-based industries emerged and the international trade for consumer products and processed foods expanded. Agro-industrial goods production has been promoted aggressively over the first, second, and third industrial master plans, which were launched in 1986, 1996, and 2006, respectively (Malaysia, 1986, 1996, 2006).

In light of its importance, the Eleventh Malaysia Plan targeted agro-food production to grow by 3.5% per annum so as to raise the agricultural and forestry sector to reach 7.8% of GDP by 2020. Meanwhile, the contribution of the agro-food in total agricultural value added has been targeted to reach 42.4%

in 2020. (EPU, 2015). The following strategies were earmarked to achieve the above targets:

- Increasing productivity and improving farmers' income through the adoption of ICT, farming technology and intensive R&D.
- Building capacity of agricultural cooperatives along vertical integration of supply chain for selected crops and promoting export to achieve international competitiveness.
- Improving access to domestic and international markets.

(d) **Food safety**

As argued earlier, the issue of food safety has become critical in international trade. Food safety indicators are measures of compliance regulations to protect safety of the citizens and the environment, which have increasingly become important in global food trade (FAO & WTO, 2017). Food industries have increased the adoption of quality management practices that aim at preventing the spread of hazardous food (Unnevehr, 2000).

International standards compliance is important to export domestic products to the world market. Standards such as Global Good Agriculture Practices (GAP) require that pesticide free farming undertaken without the use of harmful chemicals whereas Good Manufacturing Practices (GMP) ensure the adoption of safety processes in food manufacturing (Malaysia, 2012).

Safety standard uses as one of the indicators help consumers to evaluate alternative products to meet their quality expectations. Safety is increasingly considered as an important part of quality, and it determines the purchasing intentions and choice. The provision of information on quality and safety can be categorized as risk information that aims at minimizing consumers uncertainity in purchasing decisions (Verbeke, 2005).

(e) **Halal food**

The *Halal* food industry is growing at alarming rate and it is one of the fastest-growing food industries in the world, which is among the reasons why the Malaysian government has prioritized (Khalek, 2014; Malaysia, 2010). Thomson Reuters reported that the food industry is estimated to be worth USD 1.3 billion in 2013, globally, and was projected to grow to USD 2.5 billion by 2019 (Zailani et al., 2015). The growing market demand in the *halal* food offers comparative advantage for countries that have competency and excellence in producing and exporting *halal* food. According to (Zailani et al., 2015), Malaysia must implement an operational strategy called *halal* orientation strategy (HOS), which is the best instrument to help *halal* firms to comply with the requirements.

Despite heavy promotion of halal food production by the government, the results have not been encouraging owing to issues that should be addressed to appropriate more economic synergies from the industry. One such problem facing the *halal* food industry in Malaysia is that most of the food supply chain members and retail outlets are controlled by non-Muslim countries and businesses. Thus, to examine and ensure the *halalness* of halal food, including its manufacturing process, logistics, and distribution, *halal* certification body is needed. A study by (Rezai et al., 2012) states that consumers are so sensitive towards *halalness* of food products and *halal* logo. In Malaysia, according to their findings " halal food consumers react more positively toward food products with the Department of Islamic Development (JAKIM) *halal* logo, but are less confident with other *halal* logos on food products". JAKIM is the official authority responsible for *halal* certification in Malaysia and the sole body for *halal* regulatory affairs. In light of the controversies associated with *halalness*, the government must rationalize its use so that consumers can enjoy sufficient confidence over its certification.

Conclusions

While large-scale plantation agriculture in Malaysia, especially in oil palm cultivation, enjoys international competitiveness, small-scale farming, especially in food production has been hampered by low technological progress. Farming has become increasingly intensive in the use of science and technology, but one that focuses on organic elements that are in harmony with nature. Given the public goods characteristics of knowledge and innovation, the appropriation of economic synergies from the development of new productive and sustainable species of fauna and flora and farming methods will require strong integration with science and technology parks. Malaysia already has several science and technology parks. Efforts to integrate R&D, especially development in incubators with small and large farmers will go a long way to raise productivity. The future facing Malaysian agriculture should incorporate the dominant deployment of robots and drones, which would require the expansion of the digital infrastructure, internet of things, big data analytics, and cloud computing. Such a development will also help the government ease reliance on foreign low-skilled labour imports.

While the technologies deployed so far have denied small-scale food producers in Malaysia the competitive advantage to compete on costs and quality, external factors, such as food safety standard compliance and stringent standards set by the WTO have had an adverse effect on the export of agricultural products from Malaysia. Food security is highly linked with smallholders and rural areas, which calls for a shift in focus from extensive-farming to intensive-farming *a la* Taiwan. Small-scale farmers can realize collective efficiency at the level of the locality so that they shall specialize on the basis of scope economies, while appropriating scale economies at the regional and national level. Agricultural policies and self-sufficiency strategies in Malaysia, hence, should centralize smallholders at micro level, which should offer rural farmers the institutional support to evolve their farming methods to compete effectively with imports. Such a shift should help the government's T50 initiative plan to address technological progress requirements to meet growing urbanization and rising megacities in the country.

Furthermore, the transformation of the agro-food sub-sector into a sustainable and high-income sub-sector is essential to enhancing self-sufficiency levels to meet national food security objectives. Some of the key directions that the government should take have already been determined in Malaysia (2012). However, much needs to be done to take the instruments related to food security, food safety, the halal food industry, and organic farming to much higher levels to stimulate stronger economic synergies. Also, to achieve the objectives of national food security it requires holistic policies that integrate various relevant sectors, such as agriculture, energy, and infrastructure.

Acknowledgements The authors acknowledge funding from research projects GUP 2015-015, from Universiti Kebangsaan Malaysia.

References

Alam, M. M., Siwar, C., Murad, M. W., & Toriman, M. E. (2011). Farm level assessment of climate change, agriculture and food security issues in Malaysia. *World Applied Sciences Journal, 14*(3), 431–442.

Carvalho, F. P. (2006). Agriculture, pesticides, food security and food safety. *Environmental Science & Policy, 9*(7–8), 685–692. https://doi.org/10.1016/j.envsci.2006.08.002

Choe, Y. B. (2005). New agriculture, new paradigm and new challenges facing Asian Agricultural Economists. In *New Challenges Facing Asian Agriculture under Globalisation*. Malaysian Agricultural Economics Association.

Demeke, M., Pangrazio, G., & Maetz, M. (2009). Country responses to the food security crisis: Nature and preliminary implications of the policies pursued. FAO Initiative on Soaring Food Prices.

Ecker, O., & Breisinger, C. (2012). The food security system: A new conceptual framework. International Food Policy Research Institute (IFPRI).

Ewing, M., & Msangi, S. (2009). Biofuels production in developing countries: Assessing tradeoffs in welfare and food security. *Environmental Science & Policy, 12*(4), 520–528. https://doi.org/10.1016/j.envsci.2008.10.002

Harron, M. H., Shamsudin, M. N., & Latif, I. A. (2001). *Challenges for agribusiness: A case for Malaysia.* Paper presented at the International Symposium Agribusiness Management towards Strengthening Agricultural Development and Trade, Chiang Mai University.

Prescotta, J. O. Y., O'Neill, L., Yau, N. J. N., & Stevens, R. (2002). Motives for food choice: A comparison of consumers from Japan, Taiwan, Malaysia and New Zealand. *Food Quality and Preference, 13*, 489–495.

Jeyaraj, R. (2013). *The legacy of Mardec: Origin.* University of Malaya Press.

Kada, R. (2005). Balancing agricultural growth and environment under globalization: Focusing on sustainable agriculture and food security in Asia. In *New challenges facing Asian agriculture under globalisation*. Malaysian Agricultural Economics Association.

Lian, T. S. (2009). Rice and other main staple food crops in Malaysia. *Food Security Malaysia.* Akademi Sains Malaysia.

Lee, W. C. (2011). Promoting self-suffiency in food. *Taipei Times*, p. 8. Retrieved Sep 15, 2020, from https://www.taipeitimes.com/News/editorials/archives/2011/03/04/2003497297#:~:text=Currently%2C%20Taiwan's%20general%20food%20self,it%20is%20above%2080%20percent.

Mellor, J. W. (1988). Global food balances and food security. *World Development, 16*(9), 997–1011.

Misselhorn, A., Aggarwal, P., Ericksen, P., Gregory, P., Horn-Phathanothai, L., Ingram, J., & Wiebe, K. (2012). A vision for attaining food security. *Current Opinion in Environmental Sustainability, 4*(1), 7–17. https://doi.org/10.1016/j.cosust.2012.01.008

Müller, A., Schmidhuber, J., Hoogeveen, J., & Steduto, P. (2008). Some insights in the effect of growing bio-energy demand on global food security and natural resources. *Water Policy, 10*(S1), 83. https://doi.org/10.2166/wp.2008.053

Naylor, R. L., Liska, A. J., Burke, M. B., Falcon, W. P., Gaskell, J. C., Rozelle, S. D., & Cassman, K. G. (2007). The Ripple effect: Biofuels, food security, and the environment. *Environment: Science and Policy for Sustainable Development, 49*(9), 30–43. https://doi.org/10.3200/envt.49.9.30-43.

Paul, B. (2013). *Food security in Malaysia: Challenges and opportunities for Malaysia of present and in 2050 for maintaining foods security.* University of Alberta.

Rasiah, R. (1995). *Foreign capital and industrialization in Malaysia.* Macmillan.

Rasiah, R. (2018.) *Developmental states: Land schemes, parastatals and poverty alleviation in Malaysia.* Universiti Kebangsaan Malaysia Press.

Rasiah, R., & Salih, K. (2019a). Poverty reduction. In Rasiah & Salih (Eds.), *Driving development: Revisiting Razak's role in Malaysia's economic progress.* University of Malaya Press, pp. 75–94.

Rasiah, R., & Salih, K. (2019b). Connecting farmers and fishermen with markets. In Rasiah & Salih (Eds.), *Driving development: Revisiting Razak's role in Malaysia's economic progress.* University of Malaya Press, pp. 123–140.

Rasiah, R. (2020). Industrial policy and industrialization in Southeast Asia. In O. Arkebe, C. Cramer, H. J. Chang, & R. K. Wright (Eds.), *Oxford handbook of industrial policy.* Oxford University Press.

Rasiah, R. (2021). Poverty and inequality. In R. Rasiah, K. Salih, & K. C. Cheong (Eds.), *Malaysia's leap into the future: the building blocks.* Springer.

Rezai, G., Mohamed, Z. A., & Shamsudin, M. N. (2012). Assessment of consumers' confidence on halal labelled manufactured food in Malaysia. *Pertanika Journal of Social Sciences & Humanities, 20*(1), 33–42.

Rosegrant, M. W., & Cline, S. A. (2003). Global food security: Challenges and policies. *Science, 302*(5652), 1917–1919.

Rospidah, G., & Aminah, A. (2019). Food security and sustainable rice production. In S. Norela, I. Anizan, & M. Anni (Eds.), *Agroecological-based integrated pest management for sustainable rice production in Malaysia.* Penerbit UKM

Sulaiman, J. (2005). Future challenges facing Asian agriculture under globalization. In *New Challenges Facing Asian Agriculture under Globalisation.* Malaysian Agricultural Economics Association.

Trostle, R. (2008). *Global agricultural supply and demand: factors contributing to the recent increase in food commodity prices*: US Department of Agriculture, Economic Research Service Washington, DC.

Tscharntke, T., Clough, Y., Wanger, T. C., Jackson, L., Motzke, I., Perfecto, I., et al. (2012). Global food security, biodiversity conservation and the future of agricultural intensification. *Biological Conservation, 151*(1), 53–59. https://doi.org/10.1016/j.biocon.2012.01.068

Unnevehr, L. J. (2000). Food safety issues and fresh food product exports from LDCs. *Agricultural Economics, 23*(23), 21–240.

Verbeke, W. (2005). Agriculture and the food industry in the information age. *European Review of Agricultural Economics, 32*(3), 347–368. https://doi.org/10.1093/eurrag/jbi017

Chamhuri Siwar is Professor Emeritus at Institute for Environment and Development (LESTARI), Universiti Kebangsaan Malaysia.

Rospidah Ghazali is a fellow at LESTARI, Universiti Kebangsaan Malaysia. Her research focuses on agriculture and sustainable development.

Mohammed Ibrahim former Graduate Research Assistant (GRA), LESTARI, Universiti Kebangsaan Malaysia.

Chapter 6
Manufacturing Transformation

Rajah Rasiah

Abstract This chapter seeks to identify the lead industries expected to perform as the engine of growth and development until 2050. Unlike the growth path taken by the Western economies when they industrialized, the new latecomers will have to ensure that they are environmentally sustainable. It starts of with reviewing the critical theoretical issues relevant on industrialization and deindustrialization to develop a stylized framework for examining existing industrial strategies in Malaysia, as well as what needs to be done to achieve developed status with firms' substantive participation at the global technology frontier using two critical industries of the country, i.e. electronics and palm oil. Unlike the dichotomous treatment of industrialization in most works, (which address either government policy or firm strategies, this chapter addresses both in a novel way, including using the three key strategies that the industrial firms have pursued to catch up technologically to support industrial upgrading. It finishes by highlighting the critical issues of financing growth and structural change, as well as the need for switching from fossil to non-fossil fuels to ensure sustainability as the country seeks to transform its manufacturing sector.

Keywords Industrialization · Deindustrialization · Science, Technology, and Innovation (STI) infrastructure · Catching up and leapfrogging · Malaysia

Introduction

Perhaps the single most important economic target the government of Malaysia have pursued since 1991 is to lead Malaysia to a developed country by 2020 (Malaysia, 1991, 2006, 2010). While political stability, harmony, and social balance are also integral components for such an achievement, the expansion in GDP to reach USD15,000 in 2010 prices by 2020 was singled out as the key quantitative target of Vision 2020 (Malaysia, 2010).

R. Rasiah (✉)
Asia-Europe Institute, 50603 Kuala Lumpur, Malaysia
e-mail: rajah@um.edu.my

R. Rasiah et al. (eds.), *Malaysia's Leap Into the Future*, Dynamics of Asian Development, https://doi.org/10.1007/978-981-16-7045-9_6

The roadmap for transforming Malaysia to developed status is through structural transformation from low to high value added activities. The catalyst to drive the transformation is technology, and come 2030 the focus will not only be on just getting to developed status but also to sustain Malaysia's position as a developed country in the years to come. While technology and its propellant, innovation, are complex and encompass a wide range of use, including in consumption and investment rather than just in production and research, we focus here on industrial catch up.

The focus on manufacturing is important here as Malaysia is a typical developing economy, which in per capita terms is not endowed with infinite reserves of natural resources. Also, the economy has not matured sufficiently to have services as the sole engine of growth. Hence, it is important for the government to target manufacturing for further structural change from low to high value added activities. Consistent with the arguments of Young (1928) and Kaldor (1967) growth in manufacturing can be expected to drive GDP growth not only from its own expansion but also from its linkages with the other sectors.

While some economies have developed without massive emphasis on industrialization (e.g. Australia and New Zealand), industrialization has dominated the history of technological progress of most economies. Britain was the first to achieve modern industrialization but it was achieved over the long period of 1487–1750, i.e. from the initial manufacturing of woolen textiles to become the clothing capital of the world (Reinert, 2007). The latecomers have since shortened the period as Germany, the United States, France, Italy, and Japan industrialized over a shorter period. The latest countries to join the ranks of developed and industrialized countries are South Korea and Taiwan both of which achieved this in one generation from the late 1960s to the 1990s (Rasiah & Nazeer, 2016).

The economic argument that latecomers have an advantage over first movers to develop was first advanced by Gerschenkron (1952) and Abramovitz (1956). Latecomers can look at countries ahead of them to avoid errors, skip unnecessary steps and learn by looking and studying as they negotiate the paths taken by countries ahead of them. Such learning is often not linear and does not require direct copying. Such learning is built on adapting knowledge, or integrating different forms of knowledge for different uses, including solving problems and enhancing products (Kim, 1997; Schumpeter, 1934). Much of such knowledge in the early phase of technological catch up remain a public good, i.e. international property right regimes generally do not constrain latecomers from appropriating them by free riding on their non-excludable and non-rivalrous properties (Rasiah, 2014).

Even more important is the innovation capabilities of entrepreneurs who specialize on incremental engineering activities (Schumpeter, 1934), though Schumpeter (1942) glorified the radical innovator as the initiator of new cycles of innovation. What is critical here is how entrepreneurs and technical personnel can appropriate existing stocks of knowledge to incrementally adapt them for solving problems and using them to creatively upgrade technology to raise efficiency levels and produce new products (Kim, 1997; Rasiah, 2014). The prime innovation focus of entrepreneurs is on problem solving. The broad mass of Malaysian individuals, firms, and organizations should be exposed to such innovation activities as it is not only helpful in supporting the economic interests of profiteering firms, but also the general public in solving problems.

Hence, this chapter seeks to identify the lead industries expected to function as the engine of growth and development until 2050. Unlike the growth path taken by the Western economies when they industrialized, the new latecomers will have to ensure that it is also environmentally sustainable. In addressing sustainability the technological focus of countries regardless of their developmental status, will have to not only see that financing growth and structural change can be sustained but also increasingly to power it through switching from fossil to non-fossil fuels.

The rest of the chapter is organized as follows. The next section analyzes industrial structural change in Malaysia to identify the sectors that should be targeted to propel Malaysia into developed status, as well as to sustain growth and structural change until 2050. This is then followed by a section that locates these sectors in the global technology trajectory. The subsequent section examines the pathways to stimulate technological catch up in these industries. The chapter finally finishes with conclusions.

Industrial Pillars

From simple consumer goods, such as food processing in the 1950s and 1960s, Malaysia's manufacturing sector experienced massive growth following the relocation of clothing, textiles, electrical, and electronics firms from abroad, especially from the 1970s. Rapid expansion in these export-oriented industries helped reduce unemployment particularly in Western West Malaysia. Free Trade Zones anchored much of these development as massive numbers of low-skilled workers migrated from rural locations to seek employment.

Government emphasis on the export-oriented manufacturing industries was also driven by volatile fluctuations in prices of tin and rubber, which were the main exports of Malaysia until the 1970s. Along with diversification in agriculture, (which included the introduction of oil palm as a commercial crop), manufacturing provided the fillip for shielding the Malaysia economy from the vicissitudes of export demand swings. Whereas textiles and clothing has remained an important manufactured export of Malaysia, it is increasingly driven by imported low-skilled foreign labour. Clearly the sector will diminish in importance if a successful thrust takes place in value addition. Given that little upgrading has been achieved, the electronics industry should be reinvigorated to support technological upgrading. Not only is the industry characterized by knowledge-based high value added activities, it also acts as a propellant of upgrading in other industries. Thus, electronics should be a major industrial pillar of Malaysia until 2050.

The next set of manufacturing industries that have become important is non-metal minerals processing, which include petroleum and coal, and glass. It is largely dominated by downstream processing of petroleum and gas. However, given the Paris Declaration where 195 countries pledged to participate in the UNFCCC exercise to

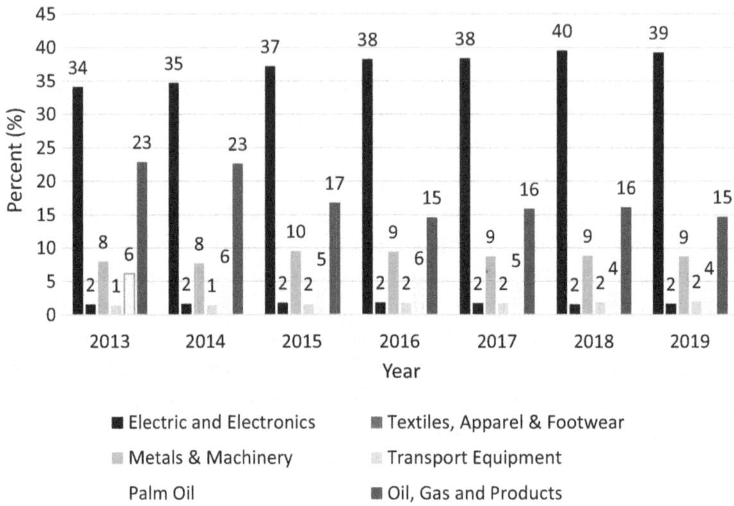

Fig. 6.1 Major exports in total exports, Malaysia, 2013–2019 (%). *Source* Malaysia (2020)

cap temperature rise to 1.5 C as the world is seeking to switch from fossil to renewable sources of energy to check climate change and global warming. Hence, the focus of this industry should be on not just technological upgrading from low to high value added activities but also on rapid substitution of energy source from fossil to green energy. In so doing, Malaysia's oil palm industry could be reinvigorated through extensive support for new product development and the use of environment-friendly technologies in its production, including the conversion of biomass waste into energy. These two sub-sectors can forge a powerful base to make Malaysia a major platform for production of high technology materials.

Figure 6.1 shows the composition of major exports in total exports from Malaysia. Electric and electronics is the main export from the country since the 1980s (Rasiah, 1995), which in the period 2013–2019 accounted for 34–40% of total exports. Oil, gas, and downstream products were the second most important export followed by metals and machinery, and crude and processed palm oil. Among manufactured exports, electric and electronics, metals and machinery, transport equipment, and textiles and garments were the most important exports. Given the structure of industry in mature economies where inward-oriented industries regardless of tariffs, such as food processing and beverages, have remained important, it is pertinent that there is strong emphasis on food processing.

While the key sub-sectors above ought to be targeted for expansion, the regulatory framework of industrial policy should also see upgrading in all existing and potentially new emerging manufacturing industries as comparative advantages change over time. However, the establishment of specific milestones for catching up cannot be established for these industries. Nevertheless, all industries can still be subjected to stringent performance appraisal against incentives enjoyed by firms.

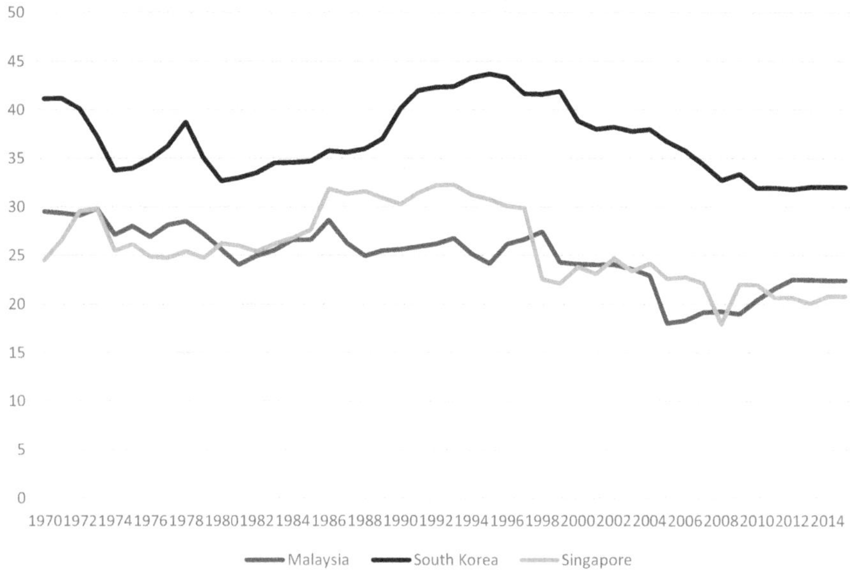

Fig. 6.2 Value added in manufacturing gross output, selected countries, 1970–2015 (%). *Source* Computed from UNIDO (2017a) data

More importantly, the value added share of gross output of the manufacturing sector has not caught up with the commensurate of South Korea, though it overtook Singapore and improved significantly in 2009–12 from its trough of 2008 (Fig. 6.2). The share fell slightly from 2012–15. It is for these reasons Rasiah (2011) classified Malaysia's deindustrialization process as premature. While the share of manufacturing in GDP has fallen, its share in gross output has continued to grow or remain high (over 40%) as countries become developed.

While several industries can be identified for targeting, we demonstrate in this section how the two strongest pillars for promotion can be promoted. Also, while Malaysia has performed better than Singapore it has remained significantly below South Korea and Japan in the electric-electronics industry.

Electric-Electronics

While exports have remained important (Fig. 6.1), the value added share in gross output in the industry shows a trend fall over the period 1970–2005 before rising strongly in 2005–2015 (Fig. 6.3). While any effort to reinvigorate the industry would be daunting, its history and production experience suggests that it should be one of Malaysia's spearheads for rapid growth and structural change.

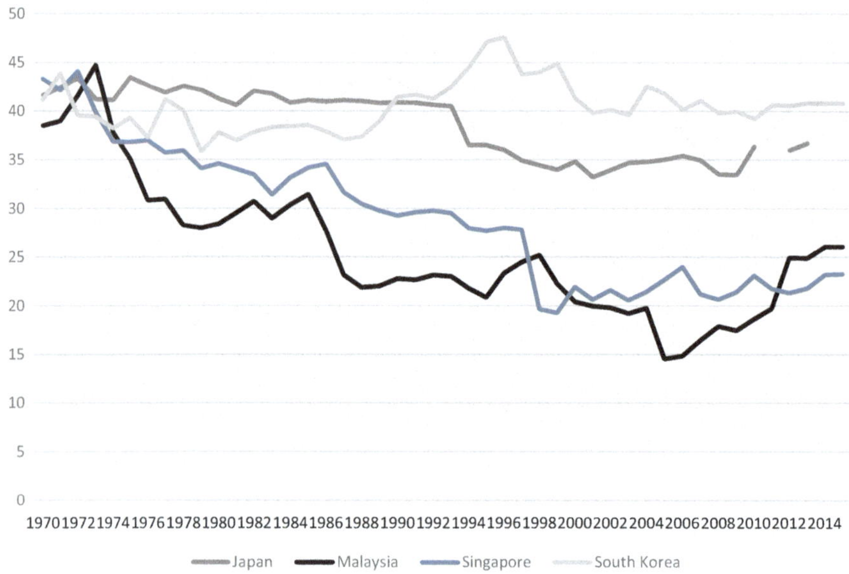

Fig. 6.3 Value added in gross of output, electric-electronics, selected countries, 1970–2015. *Source* Plotted from UNIDO (2018)

Table 6.1 presents the key broad products in the electronics industry. The IC constitutes the core of the electronics industry as it provides the coordination and control through active command. Hence, ICs vary from the simple Read Only Memory (ROM) chips that act as starters, (including a wide range of instructions) and Random Access Memories (RAM) to microprocessors that function as computers. The industry branches into computers, office equipment, consumer appliances, telecommunication devices, server and storage devices, automotive electronics, medical electronics, industrial electronics, and military and aerospace electronics.

Trade Balance

After a slight fall over the period 2014–16, nominal electric and electronics exports rose strongly from USD58.3 Billion in 2016 to USD83.0 Billion in 2018 (Fig. 6.4). Consequently the trade balance, (which had fallen from 53.4% in 2014 to 46.2% in 2016), rose to 60.7% in 2018.[1] In this regard, several commentators have argued that significant improvements in innovation capability will be critical to sustain expansion in manufactured exports over the next few decades (e.g. Rasiah, 2010, 2019; Yusof & Evenett, 2002; Yusof & Nabeshima, 2009).

[1] Trade balance was measure using the formula—[(Exports-Imports)/(Exports + Imports)100]%.

Table 6.1 Main electronics product categories, products, and lead firms

Product category	Examples of products	Lead firms
1. Integrated circuits	Microprocessors, microcontrollers, memories, logic chips	Intel, Samsung, TSMC, Texas Instruments, Toshiba
2. Computers	Desktop, notebook, and netbook	Fujitsu, Siemens, Hewlett-Packard, Dell, Apple, Acer, Lenovo, Asus
3. Office equipment	Printers, fax machines, copiers, scanners	Hewlett-Packard, Xerox, Epson, Kodak, Cannon, Lexmark, Acer, Fujitsu, Sharp
4. Consumer appliances	Game consoles, television, home audio and video, portable audio and video, mobile phone handsets, musical equipment, toys	Toshiba, NEC, Vizio, Sony, Sharp Apple, Nintendo, Microsoft, Samsung, LG, NEC, Matsushita, Hitachi, Microsoft, HTC, Philips
5. Telecommunications	Public telecommunications, private communications networks, Internet, mobile phones	Samsung, Apple, Alcatel, Nortel, Cisco, Motorola, Juniper, Huawei, LG, Ericsson, Nokia, Tellabs
6. Server and storage devices	Portable, internal, external, backup systems, storage services	Toshiba, Western Digital, EMC, NetApp, Hewlett-Packard, Hitachi, Seagate, Maxtor, LeCie, Quantum
7. Automotive electronics	Entertainment, communication, vehicle control (braking, acceleration, traction, suspension), command navigation	TomTom, Garmin, Clarion, Toyota, General Motors, Renault, Bosch, Siemens
8. Medical electronics	Consumer medical, diagnostics and testing, imaging, telemedicine, meters and monitoring, implants, fitness	General Electric, Philips, Medtronic, Varian
9. Industrial electronics	Security and surveillance, factory automation, building automation, military systems, aircraft, aerospace, banking and ATM, transportation	Diebold, Siemens, Rockwell, Philips, Omron, Dover
10. Military and aerospace electronics	Ground combat systems, aircraft, sea-based systems, eavesdropping and surveillance, satellites, missile guidance and intercept	L-3 Communications, Lockheed Martin, Boeing, BAE Systems, Northrop Grumman, General Dynamics, EADS, L-3 Communications, Finmeccanica, United Technologies

Source Adapted and expanded from Sturgeon and Kawakami (2011)

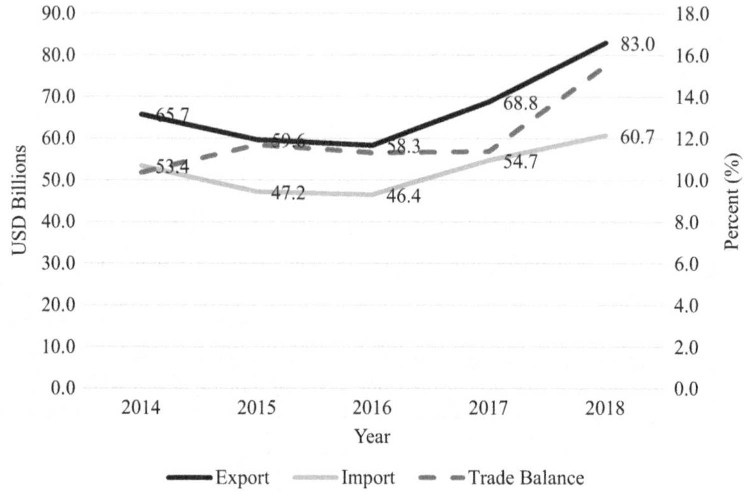

Fig. 6.4 Electric and electronics trade, Malaysia, 2014–2018. *Source* World Bank (2020)

In addition, despite strong positive trade balances, much of the exports is dominated by foreign firms, which repatriate a significant amount of their profits. In addition, the industry in Malaysia is dominated by the manufacture of electronics components, electronic data processing, office machinery and telecommunications equipment office equipment and equipment and parts. The country does not have a strong presence in computers, household appliances, and military and aerospace electronics. Meanwhile, electronics components have fallen in relative significance since 1990 owing to weak human capital support to sustain technological upgrading in the sub-industry.

While some firms have progressed to undertake R&D none are at the forefront shaping the product technology frontier in their respective industries. Foreign flagship firms, such as Intel, Samsung, Texas Instruments, and Omron operate in Malaysia but their main specialization is in assembly and test in addition to undertaking supportive R&D and chip design (Rasiah, 2011).

Palm Oil

Unlike the electric and electronics industry, Malaysia is the market leader in oil palm and oil palm-related products in general, but particularly in low value added items, such as edible oil. A strong focus on R&D by the Malaysian Palm Oil Board (MPOB) has given oil palm farming and the extraction of crude palm oil a big lead over competitors. However, the advantage Malaysia enjoys, which is largely in the primary endowment of crude palm oil is unlikely to last long as Indonesia has not only a larger acreage planted with oil palm trees but also has the latent capacity

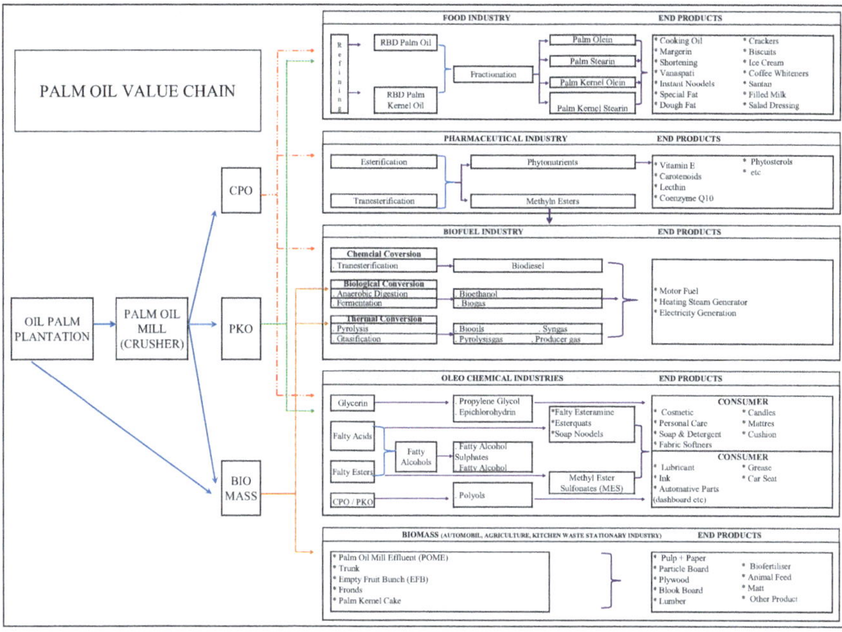

Fig. 6.5 Palm oil value chain. *Source* Reproduced from Malaysia (2016)

to more than double Malaysia's production capacity. Figure 6.5 shows the palm oil value chain—upstream and downstream. Firms in Malaysia are engaged in all of the activities shown in the figure.

Exports and supply of palm oil grew in trend terms from 10.6 and 13.4 metric tonnes respectively in 2000 to 18.0 and 22.9 tonnes respectively in 2014 (Fig. 6.6). Its continued success in generating innovative process improvements and sustainable production capability has benefited enormously from innovations oil palm and related companies organized under the Malaysian Palm Oil Board (MPOB) by the government of Malaysia. Although much of the R&D undertaken by the large oil palm firms are carried out in-house, the cess collected from exports have also financed process improvements and other problem solving activities in the industry. The strategic collaboration between oil palm firms has successfully led to the allocation of taxes collected from members of MPOB, which is a major source of oil-palm related R&D activities. Over the years, MPOB was able to add value to the palm oil industry by creating new technologies and new products.

Value Added Intensity of Output

Technological advancement in such an industry has to be based on one, reducing cost and increasing yield in the upstream industry as the acreage under oil palm

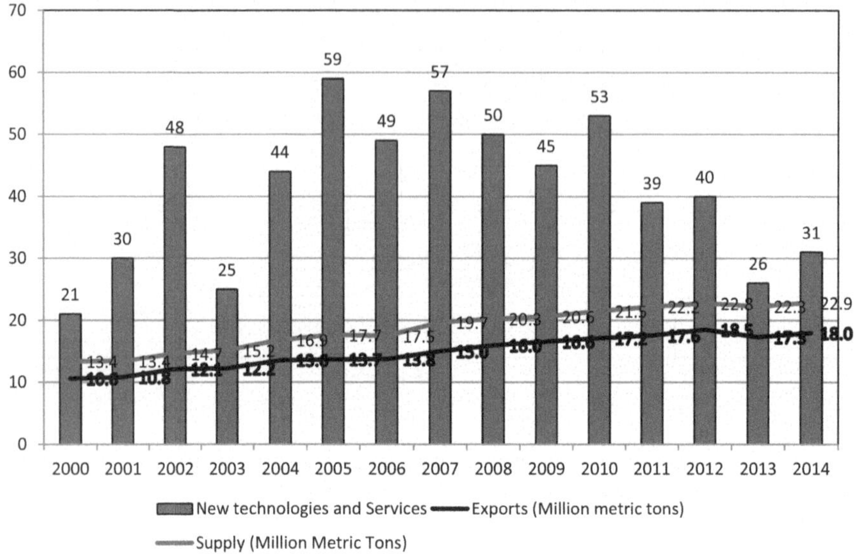

Fig. 6.6 Key indicators, oil palm, Malaysia, 2000–2014. *Source* MPOB (2015) and Comtrade website

cultivation in Malaysia have faced capacity limitations. Upgrading into higher value added activities is critical for the industry to continue to play an important role in stimulating economic growth in the country.

In the absence of comparable industries among the more developed East Asian nations, we used the broader classification of food and beverages industry in which edible oils (including palm oil) is a component. It can be seen that Malaysia's share is extremely low when compared to Japan, South Korea, and Singapore (Fig. 6.7). Specialization in low value added activities has undermined the value added intensity of output of Malaysia's food and beverages industry. Indeed, food and beverages is one of the industries that has faced a trend decline in its trade balance deficit over the period 1989–2016 (Rasiah & Salih, 2018).

Theoretical Considerations

Industrial policy has a long history with the first considered to have originated accidentally in Britain in the fifteenth century (Reinert, 2007). The early efforts to define industrial policy saw the term referred to as a policy or a set of policies targeted at expanding industry in general, and manufacturing in particular, with the focus on value added and employment shares in the economy (Kaldor, 1967). Given the rapid expansion of automation in all manufacturing industries and its consequent impact on reducing employment, we focused in this paper on value added shares rather than

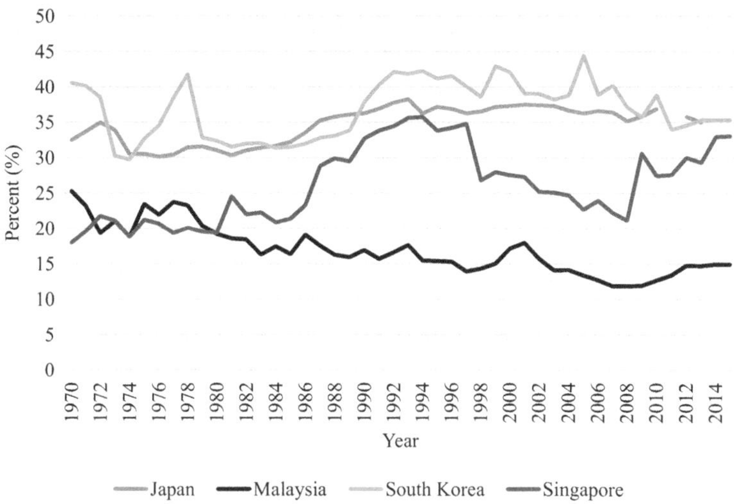

Fig. 6.7 Value added in gross output, food and beverages, selected countries, 1970–2015

employment as a measure of industrialization and deindustrialization (Rasiah et al., 2015a).

While structural economists, such as Young (1928) and Kaldor (1957) focused on the differentiating characteristics of industrialization and its impact on the division of labour and economic expansion they did not analyse specifically technological deepening issues. Chenery et al. (1986) attempted to do this but confined analysis to the categorizations by capital goods, consumer durables, intermediate goods, and raw materials. Lall (2003) subsequently used the classifications of high tech, medium tech, and low tech industries to address the sophistication of countries' economic structures, which became the basis eventually of UNIDO's (2017b) competitiveness of industrial production (CIP) index. However, these classifications did not address innovation and technology directly.

Marx (1957), Veblen (1915), and Schumpeter (1934, 1943) created the foundations for the real assessment of technology, which was further unbundled from the black box by Rosenberg (1976, 1982), opening the path to a plethora of works on technological capabilities (Dahlman, 1984; Lall, 1992; Pavitt, 1984). The catch-up literature, which has its historical origins in Marx's (1957) notion of capitalist integration and accumulation, was expounded further through the work of Gerschenkron (1952), and Abramovitz (1956). These works gave rise to the developmental functions of the state, which goes beyond the regulatory role of the state. The empirical foundations of the developmental state articulating the role of government in stimulating industrial structural change can be found in works explaining industrial catch-up by Japan (Johnson, 1982), Korea (Amsden, 1989), and Taiwan (Wade, 1990). However, while Amsden (1989) and Amsden and Chu (2003) provided explicit accounts of catching up in particular industries, Johnson (1982) and Wade (1990) did not present the empirical evidence on innovation and technology against the particular industrial policy pursued in Japan and Taiwan respectively. Hence, the work of Rosenberg (1982), Dahlman (1984), Lall (1992), and Rasiah (2004) becomes important in attempting to examine the evolution of technological capabilities in the developing economies. It is also important to see how government-initiated institutional change affected firm-level technological upgrading in particular countries. While technology and technological capabilities were the prime focus of these scholars, manufacturing became a major platform for the stimulation productivity through learning and innovation in process, product, and organizational technologies (Rasiah, 2003, 2004).

Past accounts show that a wide range of industrial policies, both explicit and implicit, were introduced to stimulate economic growth in the East Asian economies. China, Korea, Malaysia, and the Philippines enjoyed explicit industrial policies targeted at stimulating particular manufacturing industries. Korea and Malaysia even targeted champions selected for state-led promotion, such as Korea's Samsung, Hyundai, Daewoo and POSCO (Amsden, 1989), and Malaysia's Proton and Perwaja (Jomo, 1990). The Philippines had the People's car launched in the 1960s (Ofreneo, 2016). Thailand and Indonesia enjoyed trade and investment policies targeted at stimulating manufacturing but without any handpicked firms for specific support (Rasiah, 2010). The differential outcomes of industrial policy experiences of the East Asian economies suggest that specificities are important and particular strategies are key as to when industrial policy will work. All the more so when South Korea has grown faster than the Philippines over the 1960–2014. Hence, we examine the extant literature in the next section to identify the key signposts to look for when analysing industrial policy against its impact on economic and manufacturing growth.

The transformation of production into different stages and the evolution of embodied knowledge in which innovation depth has transcended product and service boundaries means that it no longer matters whether countries experience structural transformation from a specialization in consumer and intermediate goods to capital goods. For example, Taiwan and Singapore show greater specialization in components and intermediate goods than Malaysia, while Taiwan's manufacturing industry is technologically superior to that of Malaysia and Singapore, which is reflected in their respective value added activities (Rasiah, 2019). Hence, a successful industrial policy should be viewed as an exercise in which it successfully stimulates sustainable economic transformation from low to high value added activities of targeted, as well as other industries in the economy. Technological change should be viewed as the fuel that powers upgrading in value added.

The catch up literature, which has its historical origins in Marx (1957) and Luxembourg (1913), the concepts of capitalist integration and accumulation was expounded further through the work of Veblen (1915), Gerschenkron (1952), and Abramovitz (1956). These works gave rise to the developmental function of the state, which goes beyond a regulatory role. The empirical foundations of the developmental state articulating the active role of government in stimulating industrial structural change can be found in works explaining industrial catch up by Japan (Johnson, 1982), Korea (Amsden, 1989), and Wade (1990). However, while Amsden (1989) and Amsden and Chu (2003), Chang (1994) and Kim (1997) provided explicit accounts of catching up in particular industries, Johnson (1982) and Wade (1990) did not present the empirical evidence on innovation and technology against the particular industrial policy pursued in Japan and Taiwan, respectively. Hence, there is a need to investigate this topic again. In doing so, we attempt to compare a range of countries with Korea being clearly successful, while Pakistan, and the Philippines being the least successful.

Since the purposive promotion of particular industrial sectors is very much in the hands of the government in power, we identify the two leading manufacturing industries in Malaysia to offer pathways that can help transform these industries from low to high value added activities, and that can be eventually led by national firms at the technology frontier. Hence, we use the electric and electronics, and oil palm industries as some of the industries that can be targeted to spearhead Malaysia's transformation into a technological leader.

While Malaysia will inevitably promote industries new to the country owing to the emergence of a wide range of complementary technologies, such as nanotechnology and futuristic health and transport technologies, the history of technological catch up is characterized by transforming markets to outwit the competition. The blue ocean strategy is the most extreme in such an orientation as successful firms innovate products or services that transform markets so as to leave the old competition out (Kim & Mauborgne, 2005). Just as supermarkets have taken control over the horticultural value chain, so has specialized wafer foundry houses have increasingly dominated wafer fabrication. Hence, the pursuit of catching up and leapfrogging requires a profound strategy of not only learning and innovating in particular technologies (Kim, 1997; Rasiah, 1995), it also requires the organizational transformation of the markets to propel consumer demand.

Catching up and Leapfrogging

The catch up literature has focused on government promotion of industries to stimulate potentially the biggest economic synergies. Schumpeter's (1943) accounts emphasize lead technologies that initiate new business cycles through the advancement of cycles of innovation. South Korea drove successful catch up of national firms in the industries of shipbuilding, electronics, steel, and automobiles from nothing when these industries were launched from the late 1960s. Hence, the distance from the lead firm at the beginning does not necessarily disadvantage the latecomer as argued by Gerschenkron (1952). Nevertheless, for brevity we analyze the location of Malaysia's leading manufacturing industries to put in perspective how technological catch can be driven in electric and electronics, and oil-palm industries. Hence, we discuss in this section how such strategies can form the building blocks for the development of a world class electric and electronics, and oil palm industries.

The government blueprint on technology listed all these broad products as strategic—not only on their own but also in propelling other industries—for promotion (Malaysia, 1991). Efforts to catch up will obviously require learning from the paths taken by the lead firms in the industry.

Attempts to learn from the leaders would require a profound understanding not only of their technological location, but also the entire ecosystem that supports their activities. In doing so there is a need to capture the whole value chain, the complimentary supplier and buyer firms, technological links through university-industry links, human capital movements, and the institutions that stimulate their activities. While it is not helpful to reinvent the wheel, imitation must focus on creative transformation of knowledge acquired through watching, doing (using), and experimentations.

Fortunately, significant institutional development has evolved in Malaysia. Both the electronics and palm oil clusters have experienced the introduction of incentives and grants, and formation of organizations to solve collective action problems, especially in supporting export expansion, stimulation of training, research support (through the Malaysian Institute of Microelectronics Systems (MIMOS), and the Malaysian Palm Oil Board (MPOB). In addition, major organizations have been setup following the Action Plan for Industrial Technology Development (APITD) in 1991. The Multimedia Super Corridor, the Malaysia Technology Development Corporation, Malaysia Industry Government High Technology, the Human Resource Development Council, and the Multimedia Corporation were set up in the 1990s to spearhead technological upgrading in firms.

However, these organizations have not fulfilled their roles effectively. Nevertheless, because these organizations are already there it is pertinent that the government revamps their management so as to ensure that there is effective evaluation of their activities, which includes vetting at selection for support, monitoring, and *ex post* appraisal. This framework was widely used in Japan just after the second world war (Johnson, 1982), and South Korea (Amsden, 1989) and Taiwan (Wade, 1990) since the early 1970s.

Electric and Electronics

MIMOS should be the cornerstone propelling technological catch up in the electronics industry as microchips are the drivers of its global value chains. It is pertinent that proven captains of industry carrying the tacit knowledge spearheading R&D and buyer–supplier relationships, and links with the knowledge nodes of the industry, such as Morris Chang of the Taiwan Semiconductor Manufacturing Corporation (TSMC) should lead MIMOS. An equivalent Malaysian that could be considered is Loh Kin Wah who helmed Qimonda before its sale in 2009, which arose from the global financial crisis that erupted in 2007 when DRAM prices crashed. The leadership of other organizations created to stimulate catch up, such as MTDC), as well as strategic firms, such as Silterra must be headed by Malaysians endowed with strong tacit and experiential knowledge.[2] These leaders must not only show engineering and marketing knowledge of the products produced by the lead firms but also must be

[2] See Rasiah (1988), Mathew and Cho (2000) and Brown and Linden (2009) for empirical evidence on how crises have shaped the global electronics industry.

key players in the knowledge network of R&D labs, and buyers and suppliers. This is what Morris Chang and Wu Tai Yuan brought to strategize technological catch up in Taiwanese firms (Saxenian, 2006; Rasiah et al., 2015b).

The initial pathway in electronics should target read only memory (ROM) related to application specific integrated circuits (ASIC) chips to stimulate the proliferation of chip controlled automation in the whole Malaysian economy. This path should remain the prime focus of learning and adaptation as it is not only less expensive and risky but offers synergies to the entire national economy. While the ultimate objective of taking leadership of a particular value chain is desirable it is not necessary to achieve technological catch up as the lower order chips are adapted continuously to stimulate incremental innovation in national firms and organizations. The specific firm strategy dealing with this approach is discussed in the next section.

The institutional framework to spur technological catch up in the electronics industry should include the provision of R&D grants but with stringent performance criteria attached to them. The role of MIMOS must be expended to cover all electronics research and commercialization with strong links between it, and science parks and universities to spin out winning start-up companies.

The most recent examples of latecomers that have taken leadership among electronics products, i.e. South Korea and Taiwan, have very different institutional structures. Whereas giant firms with internalized R&D operations characterize South Korean electronics firms, a de-verticalized structure has dominated Taiwanese electronics firms. Indeed, Taiwanese firms tend to specialize in particular segments of key products, while South Korean firms are either vertically integrated or operate as conglomerates (Rasiah, 2014). Also, significant amounts of research, and commercialization in Taiwan takes place in universities and science parks, respectively.

Given the presence of over 10 science and technology parks in Malaysia, and government emphasis on supporting business R&D, Malaysia should attempt to keep the decentralized institutional structure, such as in Taiwan, but should seek to stimulate firms in vertically integrated product lines. Whatever the choices made there should be government-industry coordination to calibrate incentives to stimulate technological catch up in these industries. Indeed, the technological upgrading strategy of other industries should be identified by a consortium comprising government, firms, and universities, which should then follow the technological catch up framework as paths of lead firms leave behind trails that guide the route of new latecomers.

The current route of Silterra to use foreign technology should be retained. However, for Silterra to move forward it is necessary to acquire firms with strategic technology. This is the route Samsung Semiconductor (with Zenith, Schlumberger, and Micro Technology), and TSMC (merger and subsequent acquisition of Philips' semiconductor division) took. All these acquisitions took place during moments of crisis when incumbent firms were priced cheaply. Old firms not only offer newcomers strategic technology but also markets to sell their products. The acquisition of Siemens semiconductor by Infineon and Qimonda, and Advanced Micro Devices by Mubadalla Corporation offered these firms catching up opportunities but the lack of heavy investment into R&D has restricted their capacity to leapfrog incumbents.

Palm Oil

Whereas electronics firms in Malaysia can look at the global leaders to orchestrate catch up strategies, palm oil firms will have to look at other industries to broaden value added through both deepening and widening of product use, improvements in productivity through innovations to best practices and products, and to raise farm yields in the face of saturating farm acreage.

The most promising route is to focus on biotechnology. The grants drawn from cess collected from palm oil exports should be extended to support R&D targeted at intensive farming, digital control of smart robots in both farming and processing. Oil palm generates massive biomass waste that is currently used to generate power. However, its appropriation is sporadic and not integrated. Also, technological upgrading can raise its efficiency, and the development of multi-capable machinery can utilize a wide range of renewable energy sources so as to ensure endless supply of green power. Other renewable sources include solar, wind, and currents.

Having established the electronics and oil palm industries as the engine of growth among existing manufacturing industries, successful technological catch up would require also emphasis on the complimentary industries that support their operations. Hence, ultimately industry-based strategic focus should also include the complimentary industries of information communication technology, (which is part of the electronics industry), machine tools, biotechnology, and clean energy.

Firm Strategies

While several routes of focus can be identified to spearhead catch up in the electronics industry, the historical rooting that Malaysia has had suggests that the microchip industry should be the target for the electronics industry. Indeed, microchips are the drivers of the electronics global value chain. Two broad Schumpeterian innovation focus are essential here, viz., first on incremental innovations in the fabrication of old generation chips targeted at automating production and service operations in the whole economy (Fig. 6.6); and second on radical innovations that require catching up and leapfrogging in a particular semiconductor domain (Fig. 6.7). The third is to adopt the blue ocean strategy so as to multi-task products to perform multiple functions (Fig. 6.8). The first is much simpler and cheaper than the other two, while the second is the most expensive as it requires enormous investments against low margins enjoyed by latecomers until leapfrogging is achieved.

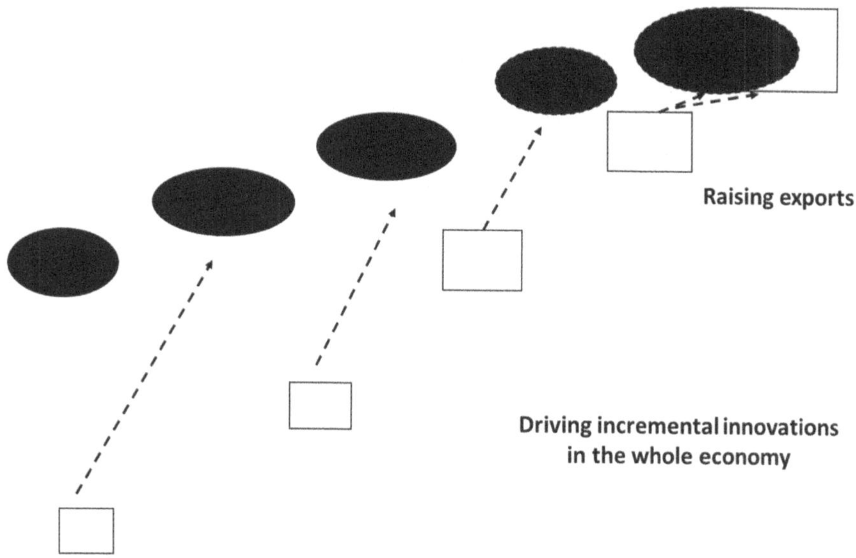

Fig. 6.8 Innovation proliferation. *Source* Author

Incremental Innovation

Innovation strategies that focus on adaptive learning to enhance or create new products in existing and other industries is the key mode that drives economic progress (Fig. 6.8). It is not only the cheapest form of innovation to appropriate economic synergies, it is also amenable to small entrepreneurs, though its reach is widest when they connect with the knowledge nodes offered by universities and science parks. Rasiah (1994), Kim (1997), and Ernst et al. (1998) had focused on minor improvements a la Schumpeterian explication of learning as an adaptive process as the basis of incremental innovation. Rasiah (2014) transformed the logic of incremental innovation to power massive forward thrusts in economic savings and accumulation. Indeed, as Rasiah (2019) has argued, a number of them radicalize economic transformation of different industries. The return on investment is high as existing technologies—e.g. Read Only Memory (ROM) chips, Radio Frequency Identification (RFID), and opto-electronics lenses—are revolutionizing anti-theft support in libraries, fishing, manufacturing, and farming.

These simple technologies that are associated with the adaptation of mature products that not only have become cheap but with matured IPRs that offer economic agents—individuals, firms, and organizations—the opportunity to earn high return on investment. Vernon (1966) was the first to discuss the importance of customer-producer interactions when determining location factors. This was extended later by Lundvall (1992), Rasiah (1994), and Best (2001) through discussion of user-producer interactions. Rasiah (1994) focused on how the movement of experienced human capital from MNCs to start local firms were driven by self-expansion motive of the former to source dissimilar but complementary inputs. The diffusion of Industry 4.0 technologies that is led by digitalization and robotization is one classic example of the new wave of technological transformation that have become the key pillar of economic development since the 1990s. Taiwan-owned United Microelectronics Company is one company that fabricates application specific integrated circuits that have migrated into all sectors.

Catching up and Leapfrogging

Economic transformation is also supported by national firms catching up and leapfrogging global incumbents to shape the technology frontier. This is the route latecomer firms, such as Mitsubishi Nagasaki Shipyard and later Daewoo took to lead in the construction of super tankers, and Samsung Semiconductors and Taiwan Semiconductor Manufacturing Company (TSMC) took leadership of memory and logic chip production (Fig. 6.9).

Economically, this strategy requires firms to grow big with massive investment into R&D targeted at catching up and overtaking incumbents. Licensing initially, acquisition later and a massive focus on R&D drove Samsung and TSMC to the technology frontier. In doing so, TSMC even pioneered an entirely new business model by specializing in brand-less wafer fabrication (Rasiah & Lin, 2005).

Efforts must be taken by the Malaysian government to assist national firms, such as Silterra to acquire technologically strong firms but rendered weak by financial crises and cashflow problems. In doing so, proven national experts, such as Loh Kin Wah

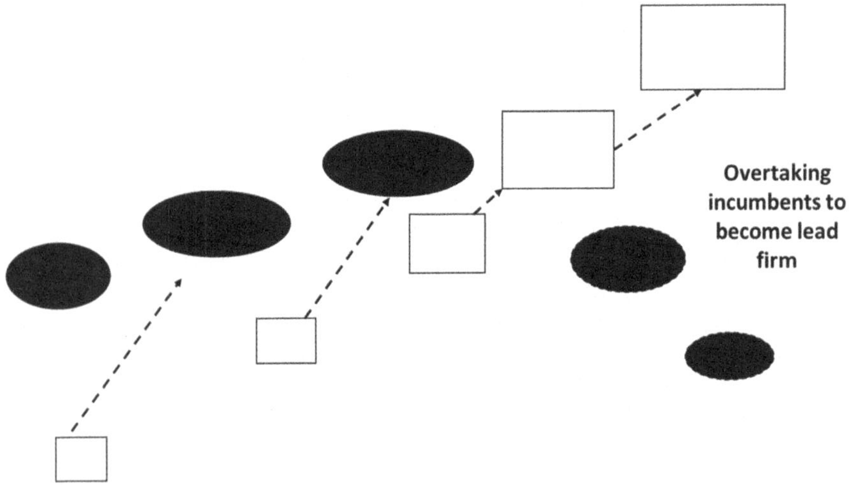

Fig. 6.9 Catching Up and Leapfrogging. *Source* Author

who had successfully led Qimonda before to lead the acquisition and transformation of such firms. AMD is no longer available now but future opportunities should be taken.

Integrating Markets

This third innovation strategy largely relies on incremental innovations, but focuses on integrating markets. The economic synergy through multiplying uses and the amalgamation of several technologies to successfully stimulate innovation of new products and services offers firms the opportunity to radically take control of markets. Kim and Mauborgne (2005) refer to this as the blue ocean strategy (Fig. 6.10).

A Malaysian example that goes well with the blue ocean strategy is Air Asia, though it is not part of manufacturing. While old management strategies to improve employee and customer satisfaction and cheapening costs have been important, Air Asia's transformation of budget airlines is very much pivoted by a strategy to widen the market to low-income groups. The economic focus to achieve this came through pricing differently along the ticket price cycle, removing items that not many customers seek, making consumables, such as food and beverages directly priced,

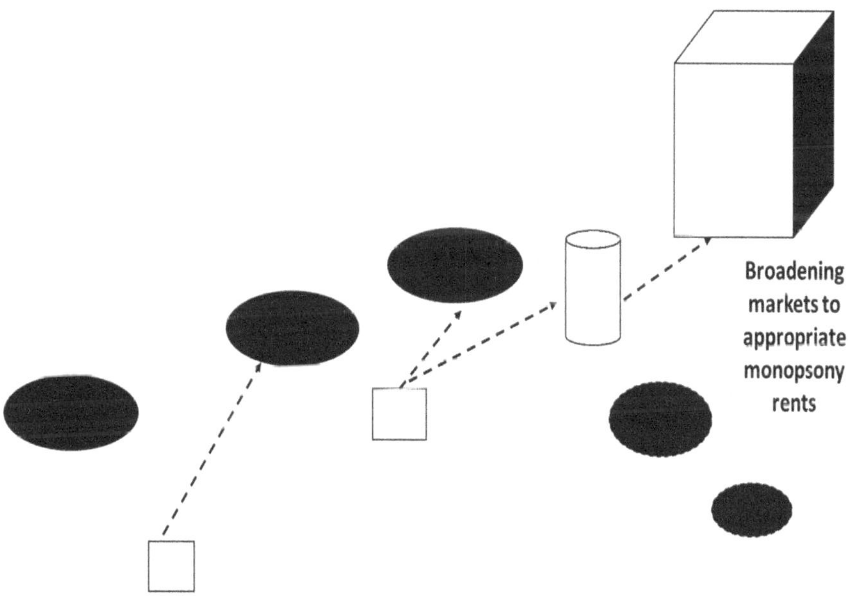

Fig. 6.10 Integrating markets. *Source* Author

and leaving airport taxes to customers. The prime technological strategy focused on flying the plane longer hours by ensuring that its maintenance is not compromised.[3]

With the proliferation of robotization and digitalization (both communication and storage), innovation strategies in Malaysia must focus on cross adaptation technologies to exponentially raise economic synergies. Several examples can be experimented in the two major industries discussed in the paper. One, oil palm estates should transform innovation strategies to expand the use of palm estates from just production of edible oils and oleo-chemicals, to use biomass to generate power for their own use and sales to residential homes. Plantations should also focus on animal husbandry, especially cattle and goats. Farming methods should use both digital control and robots for farming, weeding, and harvesting. Two, integrated circuit chips should be adapted to stimulate radio frequency identification device (RFID) applications in the electronics industry, as well as in other industries.

Strategies can include acquisition when opportunities arise, especially during times of crisis, which is how Samsung took its initial steps in memories (Edquist & Jacobbsen, 1987), and Taiwan Semiconductor Manufacturing Corporation (TSMC) in logic chips (Rasiah & Lin, 2005). Silterra in Malaysia took that route but has not been as successful because of a lack of a clear roadmap to strategize catch up and to complement it with strong networking with buyers and suppliers. Malaysia lost an opportunity when Advanced Micro Devices (AMD) was available for sale at a much reduced price during the 2007–08 global financial crisis. However, AMD is no longer available as it was acquired by Mubadalla Corporation of Dubai.

If branding is not a key option, then the focus must be on brand-less new product development that is geared towards supporting buyers' products. However, such original design manufacturers are leveraged strongly to share leadership or lead value chains only when their technology is the key driver of the chains, e.g. microchips. Otherwise, they remain entrenched with modular capabilities with control held by brand holders. This is the case with Foxconn, Flextronics, and Celestica, which supply key components to giant computer firms.

Firms in the electronics industry seeking to catch up will have to position themselves strategically to acquire technology through licensing, firm-acquisition, and other strategies to close the gap with leaders. Also, the attempt to catch up will require creative learning through tangible changes in the technology acquired (see Kim, 1997). Mistakes should be skipped and new and simpler processes should be evolved in the adaptive learning process. Product proliferation is also a key component of such incremental innovation routes.

Attempts to align government policy in the country with firm strategies to drive increasing returns economic activities should ensure that economic growth will guarantee material prosperity to Malaysians over the next few decades. However, emphasis must be placed on sustainability so that a balance in socioeconomic equity and environmental stability is achieved over the decades. This would require that innovation strategies should embrace distribution to the broad masses of the country and are cognizant of the need to support sustainable development.

[3] Interview with a senior manager conducted in 2009 in Petaling Jaya on 15th May.

Conclusions

The successful per capita income catching up trajectory to reach South Korea's GDP per capita in US Dollars of 2019 (in 2010 prices) requires a profound set of innovation strategies (see Rasiah et al., 2021). A combination of government policy and firm strategies are pertinent to support economic growth raising innovative activity. This chapter discussed the steps needed to strengthen a major pillar of stimulating a shift in focus from low to high valued added economic activities in the country. Given the trend slowdown in upgrading experienced in the country, it is pertinent to revive value added upgrading in the whole economy with manufacturing as a key sector until when services can take over once it matures.

Along with oil and gas, the electric/electronics and palm oil industries have been the major propellants of economic growth in Malaysia over the last few decades. This chapter focused on the electric and electronics and the palm oil industries as oil and gas is not only a non-renewable resource it is increasingly targeted for displacement to mitigate climate change and global warming (Rasiah et al., 2016; Stern, 2007; Nordhaus, 2008). Although the industry is still competitive, electronics manufacturing has undergone significant relative downgrading since the 1990s. While Malaysia has remained the leader in downstream oil palm products, Indonesia is well positioned to challenge its leadership. Hence, there is an urgent need to stimulate upgrading in palm oil and electric-electronics industry.

Three firm-based strategies were discussed in this chapter on how the creation and establishment of strong coordination between government policy and firm strategies can stimulate value added upgrading. Incremental, catching up and leapfrogging, and integrating markets routes should be promoted with strong selection, evaluation, monitoring, and appraisal to ensure that all implicit subsidies are translated into productive rents. The rationale used from the two leading industries should be extended to power upgrading in all sectors of the Malaysian economy.

References

Abramovitz, M. (1956). Resource and output trends in the United States since 1870. *American Economic Review, 46*(2), 5–23.

Amsden, A. (1989). *Asia's next giant: South Korea and late industrialization*. Oxford University Press.

Amsden, A. H., & Chu, W. W. (2003). *Beyond late development: Taiwan's upgrading policies*. MIT Press.

Bank Negara Malaysia. (2015). *Annual report*. Bank Negara Malaysia.

Best, M. H. (2001). *The new competitive advantage: The renewal of American Industry*. Oxford University Press.

Brown, C., & Linden, G. (2009). *Chips and change: How crisis reshapes the semiconductor industry*. MIT Press.

Chang, H. J. (1994). *The political economy of industrial policy*. Macmillan.

Chenery, H., Robinson, S., & Syrquin, M. (1986). *Industrialization and growth: A comparative study*. Oxford University Press.

Dahlman C. (1984). Foreign technology and indigenous technological capability in Brazil. In M. Fransman & K. King (Eds.), *Technological capability in the third world* (pp. 317–334). Springer International Publishing.

Department of Statistics, Malaysia. (Unpublished statistical data).

Edquist, C., & Jacobbsen, S. (1987). The integrated circuit industries in India and South Korea in an international techno-economic context'. *Industry and Development, 21*, 1–62.

Ernst, D., Ganiatsos, T., & Mytelka, L. (Eds.). (1998). *Technological capabilities and export success in East Asia*. Routledge.

Gerschenkron, A. (1952). Economic backwardness in historical perspective. In B. F. Hoselitz (Ed.), *The progress of underdeveloped areas* (pp. 3–29). University of Chicago Press.

Johnson, C. (1982). *MITI and the Japanese miracle: The growth of industrial policy*. Stanford University Press.

Jomo, K. S. (1990). *Growth and structural change in Malaysia*. Macmillan.

Kaldor, N. (1957). A model of economic growth. *Economic Journal, 67*(268), 591–624.

Kaldor, N. (1967). *Strategic factors in economic growth*. Cornell University Press.

Kim, L. S. (1997). *Imitation to innovation: The dynamics of Korea's technological learning*. Harvard Business School Press.

Kim, W. C., & Mauborgne, R. (2005). *Blue Ocean strategy: How to create uncontested market space and make competition irrelevant*. Harvard Business School Press.

Lall, S. (1992). Technological capabilities and industrialization. *World Development, 20*(2), 165–186.

Lall, S. (2003). Indicators of the relative importance of IPRs in developing countries. *Research Policy, 32*(9), 1657–1680.

Lundvall, B. A. (1992). *National systems of innovation: Towards a theory of innovation and interactive learning*. Pinter.

Luxembourg, R. (1913). *The accumulation of capital*. Routledge and Kegan.

Malaysia. (1991). *Action plan for industrial technology development*. Ministry of Science, Technology and Innovation (MOSTI).

Malaysia. (2006). *Ninth Malaysia plan 2006–2010*. Government Printers.

Malaysia. (2010). *The new economic model*. Government Printers.

Malaysia. (2016). *Eleventh Malaysia plan 2016–2020*. Government Printers.

Malaysia. (2020). *Malaysia external trade statistics*, April 2020. Accessed on October 20, 2020 from Department of Statistics Malaysia Official Portal (dosm.gov.my).

Marx, K. (1957). *Capital: A critical analysis of capitalist production*. Swan Sonnenschein.

Mathew, J. A., & Cho, D. S. (2000). *Tiger technology: The creation of a semiconductor industry in East Asia*. Cambridge University Press.

MPOB. (2015). Unpublished information supplied by Malaysia Palm Oil Board (MPOB).

Nordhaus, W. D. (2008). *A question of balance—Weighing the options on global warming policies*. Yale University Press.

Ofreneo, R. (2016). Auto and car parts production: Can the Philippines catch up with Asia? *Asia Pacific Business Review, 22*(1), 48–64.

Pavitt, K. (1984). Sectoral patterns of technical change: Towards a taxonomy and a theory. *Research Policy, 13*(6), 343–373.

Rasiah, R. (1988). The semiconductor industry in Penang: Implications for the new international division of labour theories. *Journal of Contemporary Asia, 18*(1), 24–46.

Rasiah, R. (1994). Flexible production systems and local machine tool subcontracting: Electronics components transnationals in Malaysia. *Cambridge Journal of Economics, 18*(3), 279–298.

Rasiah, R. (1995). *Foreign capital and industrialization in Malaysia*. Macmillan.

Rasiah, R. (2003). How important is process and product technology capability in Malaysia and Thailand's FDI-driven electronics industry. *Journal of Asian Economics, 14*(5), 785–811.

Rasiah, R. (2004). *Foreign firms, technological capabilities and economic performance: Evidence from Africa*. Edward Elgar.

Rasiah, R. (2010). Industrialization in the second tier NIEs. In R. Rasiah & J. D. Smidt (Eds.), *The new political economy of Southeast Asia.* Edward Elgar.

Rasiah, R. (2011). Is Malaysia facing negative deindustrialization. Pacific Affairs.

Rasiah, R. (2014). *Technological capabilities and economic development.* Celso Furtado Prize Lecture, World Academy of Sciences, Vienna, 20 November.

Rasiah, R. (2019) Building Networks to Harness Innovation Synergies: Towards an Open Systems Approach to Sustainable Development, *Journal of Open Innovation: Technology, Market, and Complexity,* MDPI, Open Access Journal, vol. 5(3): 1–20

Rasiah, R., Al-Amin, A. Q., Ahmed, A., Filho, W. L., & Calvo, E. (2016). Climate mitigation roadmap: Assessing low carbon scenarios for Malaysia. *Journal of Cleaner Production, 133,* 272–283.

Rasiah, R., Crinis, V., & Lee, H. A. (2015a). Industrialisation and labour in Malaysia. *Journal of Asia Pacific Economy, 20*(1), 77–99.

Rasiah, R., & Lin, Y. (2005). Learning and Innovation: The role of market, government and trust in the information hardware industry in Taiwan. *International Journal of Technology and Globalization, 1*(3/4), 400–432.

Rasiah, R., & Nazeer, N. (2016). Comparing Industrialization in Pakistan and the East Asian Economies. *Lahore Journal of Economics, 21,* 167–192.

Rasiah, R., & Salih, K. (2018). Connecting farmers and fishermen with markets. In R. Rasiah & K. Salih (Eds.), *Driving development: Revisiting Razak's role in Malaysia's economic progress.* University of Malaya Press.

Rasiah, R., Salih, K., & Cheong, K. C. (2021). Introduction: Problematizing the building blocks. In R. Rasiah, K. Salih, & K. C. Cheong (Eds.), *Malaysia's leap into the future: The building blocks.* Springer.

Rasiah, R., Yap, S. F., & Yap, X. S. (2015b). Sticky spots on slippery slopes: The development of the integrated circuit industry in emerging East Asia. *Institutions and Economies, 7*(1), 52–79.

Reinert, E. (2007). *How the rich nations became rich ..... and why the poor nations stay poor.* Anthem Press.

Rosenberg, N. (1976). *Perspectives on technology.* Cambridge University Press.

Rosenberg, N. (1982). *Inside the black box.* Cambridge University Press.

Saxenian. (2006). *The new argonauts: Regional advantage in a global economy.* Harvard University Press.

Schumpeter, J. A. (1934). *Theory of economic development.* Harvard University Press.

Schumpeter, J. A. (1943). *Capitalism, socialism, and democracy.* Harvard University Press.

Schumpeter, J. A. (1943). *Capitalism.* Harvard University Press.

Stern, N. (2007). *The economics of climate change.* Cambridge University Press.

Sturgeon, T., & Kawakami, M. (2011). Global value chains in the electronics industry: Characteristics, crisis, and upgrading opportunities for firms from developing countries. *International Journal of Technological Learning, Innovation and Development, 4,* 120–147.

UNIDO. (2017a). *Industrial statistics data.* United Nations Industrial Development Organization.

UNIDO. (2017b). Competitive industrial performance report. United nations Industrial Development Organization. Retrieved January 20, 2018, from http://stat.unido.org/content/publications/volume-i%252c-competitive-industrial-performance-report-2016

UNIDO. (2018). *Industrial statistics.* United Nations Industrial Development Organization.

Veblen, T. (1915). *Imperial Germany and the industrial revolution.* Batoche Books.

Vernon, R. (1966). International investment and international trade in the product cycle. *Quarterly Journal of Economics, 80*(2), 190–207.

Wade, R. (1990). *Governing the market: Economic theory and the role of government in East Asian industrialization.* Princeton University Press.

World Bank. (2020). *World development indicators.* World Bank.

Young, A. (1928). Increasing returns and economic progress. *Economic Journal, 38*, 527–542.
Yusof, S., & Evenett, S. J. (2002). *Can East Asia compete?: Innovation for global markets*. World Bank.
Yusof, S., & Nabeshima, K. (2009). *Tiger economies under threat*. World Bank.

Rajah Rasiah Ph.D., is Distinguished Professor of Economics at the Asia-Europe Institute, University of Malaya. His research interests include technology and international development, foreign investment, human capital, public health, and environment. He holds external positions at UNU-MERIT, Oxford University, Cambridge University, and Universiti Tenaga Nasional. He is the 2014 recipient of the Celso Furtado Prize awarded by the World Academy of Sciences for advancing the frontiers of social science thought.

Chapter 7
Knowledge Intensive Services

V. G. R. Chandran

Abstract This chapter assesses the Malaysian knowledge intensive services industry. It tracks the contribution and progress of the industry and assesses the prospects of knowledge intensive services in Malaysia. The findings show that the knowledge intensive services industry in Malaysia is progressive, but its contribution to value-added activities as well as services exports remain relatively low. Despite Malaysia's agenda for a knowledge-based economy, the said contributions have not yet developed to the levels seen in other emerging countries. Given the important role of the knowledge intensive services sector in catalysing productive transformation – especially in the real sectors (i.e. manufacturing)—efforts within industrial policy should be focused on building inter-industry knowledge spillover. This is especially important in transforming production and process capabilities that would support the next wave of industrial revolution, i.e. Industry 4.0. This chapter further explores the policy implications of current developments.

Keywords Knowledge intensive services · Trade in services · Commercial services · Malaysia · Value added in services

Introduction

Structurally, Malaysia's services sector accounted for a substantial share of Malaysian output, contributing nearly 55% of GDP in 2019. Indeed, this structural change—where services accounts for a higher share of GDP is taken as an indicator that Malaysia is moving into specialization into the tertiary sector. Accordingly, government policies and plans have identified services as the potential future driver of overall economic growth (Malaysia, 2011). However, it is pertinent to note that the shift to services ought to translate into upward economic movement for it to become the engine of economic development, which inevitably requires an expansion into knowledge intensive services. Such a transformation will also act as a

V. G. R. Chandran (✉)
Faculty of Business and Economics, University of Malaya, Kuala Lumpur, Malaysia
e-mail: vgrchandran@um.edu.my

R. Rasiah et al. (eds.), *Malaysia's Leap Into the Future*, Dynamics of Asian Development, https://doi.org/10.1007/978-981-16-7045-9_7

complement to raising the competitiveness of all other sectors—agriculture, mining, and manufacturing, in particular, knowledge intensive services (KIS) sectors.[1] Information communication technologies (ICT)[2] are an important component of KIS that is essential to realize the full potential of Industry 4.0 initiatives (Rasiah, 2019; Chandran, 2020). As Shearmur and Doloreux (2013) highlighted that knowledge intensive business services had significantly contributed to manufacturing innovation activities. The key to unleash the potential of the knowledge-based economy is human talent and skills. Embedding technology within the production of services and leveraging its technological advancement are critical. In contrast to manufacturing, services require less capital, but depend highly on entrepreneurship and culture, for example, in software development. Importantly, trade in services plays a critical role and Malaysia, being a net services importer, is positioning itself to promote services trade. The Ministry of International Trade and Industry aims to strengthen the trade in services via local capacity building by promoting domestic and foreign investments, imposing local sourcing and targeting certain services sectors, for instance, the architecture and engineering services. Targets in establishing regional hubs, expanding the healthcare services and services related to green technology, logistics, and tourism are among the new initiatives.

Malaysia's journey to attaining a knowledge-based economy started with the launch of Vision 2020 in 1991 under the blueprint of the *Way Forward*, which is a commitment the government made to become a scientific and progressive society focused on innovation, creativity, and technological progress (Malaysia, 1991). The knowledge economy development plan (which started in 2001) was instrumental as a useful compliment but was not diligently pursued thereafter (Rasiah, 2019, 2020a). In order for Malaysia to accelerate technological upgrading in the country, it is important to pursue some key developments, including, the knowledge intensive services sectors that offer growth opportunities; services that have the potential to catalyse other sectors; and what is needed to aid the knowledge intensive sectors in growing and contributing to Malaysia's aspirations for developed nation status. Consequently, this chapter analyses the progress of KIS industries in Malaysia. It focuses on documenting the contributions of KIS, and further assesses its competitiveness in the region. It then explores policy interventions and options available for Malaysia to improve KIS in the country. Human capital remains a challenge for Malaysia to move towards knowledge intensive services. Importantly, the limitations of its labour market have made it hard for Malaysia to progress towards a knowledge-based economy. Malaysia's manufacturing is largely trapped in low value-added activities; a situation partly caused by a weak services sector that has

[1] KIS is classified as a sector that highly depends on professional knowledge. Due to data limitations, we confine KIS as follows: financial services (banking, insurance, securities, stock market, etc.); business services (engineering, consulting, and R&D services); and information services (computer programming and IT services).

[2] Refer to Chan-Yuan, W., Chandran, V. G. R., & Boon-Kwee, N. G. (2016) for the development of the telecommunication industry in Malaysia.

not given the push for upgrading in the manufacturing sector.[3] Lessons from the experience of the manufacturing sector could provide insights into designing better policies for the services sector to avoid such a trap (see Rasiah, 2020c). Promoting services require bundling its links to the real sectors and other services sectors—e.g. forward and backward linkages—apart from policies that target productivity, efficiency, technology, and innovation of the specific service sectors. It involves new thinking, taking into consideration horizontal and vertical policy design. Indeed, Chandran and Devadason (2017) vividly argued that MNCs in manufacturing are also capturing more value by moving into manufacturing services activities in which Malaysia is lagging. Likewise, the industrial upgrading in the manufacturing sectors depends on the facilitation and support of the services sectors to minimize transaction costs in the manufacturing sectors as well as maximize investment returns. Positioning KIS and policy coordination across sectors are essential because establishing such services is crucial for Malaysia moving forward to 2050 and sustaining its competitiveness.

Theoretical Considerations

It is important to briefly define the KIS sector. In this chapter, we classify KIS as industries that incorporate science, engineering, and technology into their services or the delivery of their services, which consist of business, information, education, financial, and health care services.

Growth theories have emphasized the importance of knowledge as the main driver in sustaining long-term economic growth. More specifically, the endogenous growth theory highlights the importance of investing in human capital, innovation, and knowledge (Romer, 1994). The emphasis of endogenous growth theory is on knowledge accumulation that is endogenous in nature, i.e. multiple factors affect the accumulation of knowledge. The focus of the theory is also on positive externalities and spill-over effects of the knowledge-based economy that sustain long-term economic growth. After witnessing how KIS contributes to knowledge accumulation, one should understand that KIS on its own does not create the needed knowledge (e.g. that is needed by the manufacturing sector in particular). Rather, KIS acts as a critical enabler that catalyses knowledge accumulation in other sectors—particularly in ICT, engineering, and other related services. Given that the knowledge content of these services sectors is high, one can then leverage these sectors to transmit knowledge effectively to other sectors (Rasiah, 2006). Likewise, it is also important to note that—similar to Kaldor's (1967) argument that the industrial sector is the key growth driver—the KIS sector would also allow productivity gains, as it can also catalyse manufacturing sector's productivity.

---

[3] See Rasiah (2020b) in this book for strategies on how manufacturing can be transformed to a higher value added specialization.

Given the importance of knowledge, countries around the world began emphasizing the so-called "knowledge-based economy", with many policies and programmes launched to promote its attainment (World Bank, 2007). The idea was to bring about the positive externalities of driving the knowledge-based economy, which could possibly result in increasing returns—given that knowledge is not restricted by diminishing returns. While there are various definitions of knowledge-based economy in the literature, one common feature is that it is considered synonymous with knowledge intensive industry for several reasons as follows.

Scholars have argued incisively that the KIS sector is an enabler of knowledge accumulation, given its complementary and supporting role to other sectors (e.g. Rasiah, 2006). Investments in this sector would potentially create knowledge spillover—as learning by doing within this sector would benefit not only the sector itself but also other industries through improving production technologies. In other words, the growing significance of knowledge intensive industry would play an important role in inter-industry knowledge diffusion. In addition, with the growing interest in vertical disintegration and outsourcing activities, knowledge intensive industry can make an even greater impact. However, this is not to say that promoting knowledge intensive industry would automatically lead to growth—rather, the industry should be connected with the various processes of other industries, as well as with the national innovation system as a whole. The evidence seems strong that KIS is growing and has been contributing to various sectors. For instance, the ICT industry has not only catalysed other sectors in the economy but it has also transformed society as a whole—particularly through the faster rate of dissemination of information, as a crucial source of knowledge for all (whether firms or farmers). As Foray and Lundvall (1996) rightly argued, knowledge-based economy requires moving towards learning economy and therefore KIS plays an important new role as a catalyst of knowledge production and distribution. In this sense, KIS can contribute when there is technical interrelatedness, i.e. if technical complementariness exists between KIS and the manufacturing sectors. In addition, KIS can also help the manufacturing sectors achieve increasing returns through the technical changes that KIS sectors can offer. For instance, knowledge reach can be expanded with the support of ICT service industries. As manufacturing prematurely declines (e.g. as in the case of Malaysia), KIS can offer opportunities for future growth strategies to propel manufacturing ahead. Indeed, productivity in KIS is higher than in manufacturing. For instance, labour productivity in the information and communication sectors in Malaysia is three times higher than in manufacturing.[4] Given the declining performance of manufacturing, sustaining growth may require structural change that promotes growth (e.g. shifting from manufacturing to KIS) as well as labour productivity growth within the services sector. KIS is in the position to offer both.

Secondly, KIS sectors also act as a driver for the knowledge-based economy, in the sense that knowledge can be translated into innovation which in turn leads to

[4] Author's calculation based on value added and employment of the respective sectors in 2016. Labour productivity is measured as value added per worker.

creative destruction. There is also "the conscious application of science" within these sectors that provides new opportunities in the way that products are produced and delivered. One good example is the so-called Industry 4.0 which is driven by artificial intelligence as well other information technology related services sectors. In both cases, the so-called "technological spillovers" can possibly improve productivity transformation, specifically in real sectors and the economy as a whole. Malaysia's lack of productivity growth—a condition which stalls the progress of manufacturing sectors—would benefit from the development of knowledge intensive sectors, particularly those related to business and professional services. Likewise, there is also an opportunity for knowledge to be reused at zero marginal cost, which encourages the firms that use knowledge in production to earn quasi-monopoly profits. The proliferation of knowledge in this sense—widely available due to the progress in knowledge intensive services—can improve Small Medium Enterprises (SMEs) to better prepare themselves to compete. For instance, farmers as a unit of micro-enterprise can proliferate price information, more efficiently market their crops and earn better gains by shortening the supply chain through eliminating the middleman. This will only be possible when the role of KIS is further promoted.

Thirdly, the growing tradability of services enables countries to place services as one of the crucial sectors that contribute to national development. Indeed, services are seen as a new source of growth that enables countries to diversify their economy and improve their competitiveness. In particular, KIS is crucial within the services sector, given that it may have a higher content of value-added activities, productivity gains, and learning spillovers.

Contribution of Services Sector in Malaysia

In Malaysia, there is a clear indication that the post-industrial phase is coming into effect. Premature industrialization (Chandran & Devadason, 2017; Rasiah, 2011) has also been a concern, given the declining contribution of the manufacturing sector and the rise in the services sector's share of value added and employment. The contribution share of services to GDP increased from 32% in 1974 to 58% in 2019 (Table 7.1). In 2019, services contributed nearly RM 1,405 billion in value-added output. Employment wise (Fig. 7.1), it rose from 47% in 1991 to 63% in 2019. The growing contribution in terms of value-added output and employment warrants further investigation. Within the services sector, wholesale and retail trade, accommodation, and food and beverage services account for the highest contribution (36% of the total contribution of the services sector. Within the commercial business services, other subsectors, such as financial, real estate, and business (20%) and transport, storage, and information and communication services (17%) are among the highest contributors to the total services sector. As a whole, in 2019 commercial business services accounted for nearly 85.5% of the total services sector contribution, while government services accounted for 14.5%. While the service sector's contribution has been significantly growing, its share of contribution should evolve

Table 7.1 GDP by Sectors, Malaysia, RM Million (2015 Prices)

Year	2010	2011	2012	2013	2014	2015	2016	2017	2018	2019	CAGR
Agriculture, Livestock, Forestry, and Fishing	85,642	91,504	92,383	94,217	96,146	97,539	93,977	99,509	99,579	101,549	1.91
Mining and Quarrying	96,892	92,123	93,610	94,730	97,878	103,059	105,368	105,838	103,512	101,438	0.51
Manufacturing	207,238	218,507	228,154	235,939	250,339	262,379	273,899	290,464	304,843	316,320	4.81
Construction	33,444	34,998	41,347	45,745	51,109	55,382	59,508	63,522	66,194	66,266	7.89
Services (Total)	475,455	508,538	541,368	573,493	611,570	643,883	680,561	723,361	772,685	820,069	6.24
GDP (RM Million)	898,670	945,669	996,862	1,044,124	1,107,041	1,162,242	1,213,313	1,282,693	1,346,813	1,405,642	5.10
Sub-Sectors (Services)											
Utilities	25,887	26,908	28,217	29,463	30,586	31,710	33,412	34,396	36,079	38,254	4.43
Wholesale and Retail Trade, Accommodation, Food and Beverage	160,056	170,738	178,807	189,896	206,062	220,241	234,539	251,633	272,660	292,221	6.92
Transport, Storage, Information, and Communication	72,911	77,744	83,301	89,349	96,604	104,360	111,764	120,326	129,429	138,077	7.35
Finance, Insurance, Real Estate, and Business Services	102,331	108,966	117,337	122,119	127,417	130,064	135,687	143,663	152,690	161,776	5.22
Other Services	45,372	47,635	49,779	52,565	55,099	57,725	60,539	63,649	67,145	70,870	5.08
Government Services	68,899	76,547	83,927	90,101	95,803	99,783	104,620	109,694	114,682	118,871	6.25

Source Author's calculation based on Department of Statistics Malaysia

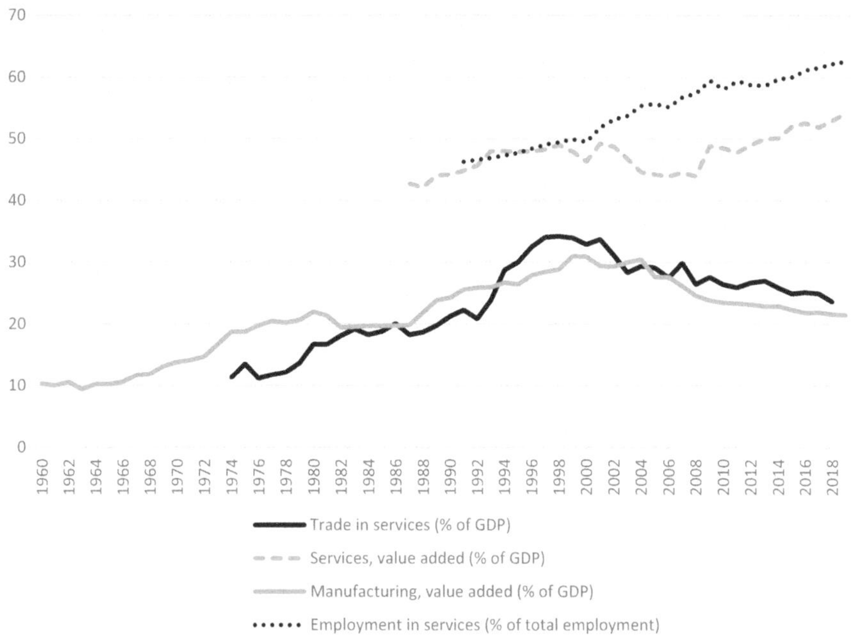

Fig. 7.1 Value Added, Trade, and Employment, Malaysia, 1960–2019. *Source* World Development Indicators

from traditional services to more knowledge-based services—as structural domination in traditional services will not be able to progress Malaysia farther into the future. For instance, the business services should be driven by the emergence of new services sectors based on innovation and technology. In terms of average annual growth, only selected services sectors have grown more than six percent. Among these: wholesale, retail, food and beverages, and real estate grew seven percent per annum; while transport, storage, information, and communication recorded a growth rate of 7.3%. Although financial services are among the largest contributors to GDP, its average annual growth is only 2.7%[5]—indicating that the domestic market has become saturated, thus providing few growth opportunities. Due to this, it seems that the sector has expanded into ASEAN markets, with domestic firms venturing into markets such as Indonesia, Thailand, Vietnam and others. The services sector structure also indicates that Malaysia is still largely concentrated in the low-knowledge content sectors. For instance, the services diversity into complex services providing more R&D, technical, and knowledge-related services is missing. Indeed, recently many manufacturing firms are shifting towards services merging their product and expanding services that align to customer knowledge, logistic options for various destination and increasing service sophistication.

[5] Based on 2015 data which provides information specifically for financial sector.

Globally, trade in services has grown from six percent of world GDP in 1975 to 12.9% in 2015. The share of services in export of total goods and services doubled from 17% in 1970, to 32% in 2014 (Loungani et al., 2017). The trend shows that trade in services is growing faster, and developing countries are also accounting for higher shares of services trade—not only in traditional services but also in KIS. From 1990 to 2014, developing countries progressively increased their KIS exports to almost 30% of global exports (Loungani et al, 2017). In Malaysia, trade in services increased from 11% share of GDP in 1974 to 24% in 2018. Trade-in services was highest in 1997 at 34%. The trend seems to follow the manufacturing activities measured by the value-added activities. This may suggest that the current trade in services is predominately related to services that support manufacturing activities; namely finance, logistics, transportation, and insurance. The declining trend of manufacturing activities may further affect trade-related services. In general, Malaysia's services exports also remained mainly in tourism, education, and health care. For instance, international tourism receipts accounts for ten percent of total exports in 2019.

Knowledge Intensive Services

Within the services sector, KIS is seen to be an important sector for reasons established in the theoretical section of this chapter. Strengthening KIS contribution is one of the key strategies which can enable Malaysia to not only revive its manufacturing sectors, but also to find new sources of growth. In this section, we analyse the progress of KIS sectors and make inferences on their contribution to the Malaysian economy.

Value-Added Contribution

In terms of value added and globally, within the knowledge intensive services (KIS) it is business, financial, and information which have the largest share (15% of GDP); while public knowledge intensive services such as education and health care have the second-largest share (nine percent of GDP). In Malaysia, the KIS sectors which includes financial, business, health care, education, and information services have steadily grown in value-added output over the years—from USD 15,450 million in 2000 to USD 46,596 million in 2016 (Table 7.2). Among the services, financial services contributed the largest value-added output comprising nearly half (45%) of the total value-added outputs of KIS. The large contribution of the sector may reflect its diverse activities, namely banking, insurance, leasing, and others. On an annual average basis, from 2010 to 2016, KIS grew at a rate of three percent.

As for the financial sector, the Financial Master Plan (2001–2010) recognized the lagging performance of domestic banks as compared to foreign-owned banks (BNM, 2001). Foreign banks with better global networks, experience, and access

Table 7.2 Knowledge Intensive Service Value Added, Malaysia, 2001–2016 (USD Million)

Industry	2001	2010	2011	2012	2013	2014	2015	2016
Financial Services [1]	8,486	19,117	21,029	22,677	22,975	23,032	20,919	20,951
Information Services [2]	4,005	12,267	13,945	15,107	16,217	17,220	14,510	15,169
Business Services [3]	1,399	4,787	5,447	6,003	6,519	6,871	5,706	5,803
Health Care	707	1,634	1,865	2,007	2,133	2,228	2,144	2,185
Education Services	853	1,834	2,110	2,281	2,419	2,526	2,447	2,488
Total KI Services [4]	15,450	39,639	44,396	48,075	50,263	51,877	45,726	46,596
Total Commercial Services [5]	13,890	36,172	40,421	43,787	45,710	47,122	41,136	41,923

Note [1]Financial services include finance and insurance, and rental and leasing; [2]Information services include computer programming and IT services; [3]Business services include professional and technical services, and management of companies and enterprises; [4]KIS includes financial, business, health care, education services, and information services; [5]Commercial Services includes financial, business, and information services only. *Source* US Science and Engineering Indicators 2018

to talent and high value corporate clients had shown significantly better performance. The situation is similar for the insurance industry. The implementation of the various recommendations and measures highlighted in the plan has contributed to the progress of the domestic financial sector. However, it has not reached a level that significantly contributes to value-added activities. The missing element seems to be consistency in the financial sector's development plans. While the master plan rightly highlighted the need to create a more vibrant financial industry, the financial blueprint (2011–2020) seems not to continue the aims of the master plan. The emphasis shifted to the need for the financial sector to catalyse economic transformation. This is the direct result of the government's focus on the Economic Transformation Program which focused the financial sector blueprint (2011–2020) on the need to catalyse value-added activities of other sectors—specifically, to support economic transformation and structural change (BNM, 2011). Although the blueprint indirectly discussed the need for the financial sector to venture into new forms of financing markets (interpretable, perhaps, as the financial sector attempting to improve its value-added activities) to support the transformation of the manufacturing and other services sectors, implicitly less attention was paid to improving the sector's contribution. Neither there was any review of the achievements of the financial sector as the result of implementation of the financial master plan. Without such a review, it will be difficult for policy makers to plan or improve the sector's contributions through intervention. The effort to improve capability and capacity is vital, including identifying the efforts to internationalize the financial sector. This is a much neglected aspect of the policies. Additionally, old stocks of knowledge may not be enough to accelerate the progress of the financial services sector. Increasing proliferation of ICT use in financial services has been instrumental to the development of the sector. Also, production in the financial services sector is largely driven by various network properties, e.g. information network, distribution, and externalities of stock exchange, and agglomeration effect in liquidity. Marriage between financial services and ICT is crucial, especially in software solutions and hardware. Linkages should be promoted, and policies that direct those linkages should be a priority. More so, the links between financial and real sectors are crucial, both domestically and in the global markets. The new role of the financial sector in supporting R&D activities and technological development should be further encouraged. Within the financial sector, product diversification is crucial to attain higher value-added activities. Likewise, the insurance industry in Malaysia is relatively small by global standards. The industry is also encountering various challenges, notably: lack of economies of scale among local insurers; lack of skill development in management, information technology, and underwriting; and lack of competitiveness. For instance, Nourani et al. (2018, 2020) found that the insurance industry is largely inefficient. More crucially, the efficiency level of local firms is below that of foreign firms. This is mainly attributable to deficiencies in human, intellectual capital, and managerial capability.

Information services contributed USD 15,619 million in 2016. This sector is cross-cutting, where the sector is strongly linked to many other sectors such as manufacturing and other services sectors, and also including the knowledge intensive services sector. As such, there should be better policy coordination from various organizations to promote the sectors in a more holistic way. In other words, horizontal policymaking processes should be more efficient. Nonetheless, vertical policymaking should also be enhanced to ensure that policies are implemented as required. The contribution by business services, health care, and education sectors seems to be relatively low compared to finance and information services. Malaysia seems to fail to capture business services—which is highly globalized, as these services can be contracted globally. Similarly, despite the effort to promote Malaysia as an education hub, the value-added output contribution of the sector is still low. Bringing more foreign currency into the education sector requires strengthening the quality of education, a parameter where Malaysia is lagging behind. Procedural delays, e.g. issuing of student visas and granting of permits to skilled teaching staff, is a probable disadvantage that public universities face currently. The liberalization of the education sector is seen as the result of active participation by the private sector. Nevertheless, several factors need consideration. First, private sector ventures are largely in business-related education programmes, not technical and science-based programmes, and this may limit generation of adequate value-added activities given its internal competition. Second, Malaysia can be more competitive and attract more students from developed countries only if the quality of education (from both private and public sectors) is improved. In this regard, brand building is crucial. New future demand requires the education sector to revamp its curriculum—not only to support the creation of new forms of labour force, but also for its own survival.

Likewise, healthcare services have undergone various challenges. In this sector Malaysia is less competitive—for instance, the neighbouring countries of Thailand and Singapore have grown better due to improved quality of care and better price leveraging. The health tourism sector in Malaysia also seems to suffer from exogenous shocks. The pharmaceutical sector is less competitive internationally, hence unable to support the healthcare services sectors including generic drug discoveries. In these sectors, Malaysia is more of a consumer than a producer; production remains relatively low as shown by the import–export deficits. To make the sector more competitive, Malaysia should strengthen diagnostic services, clinical research, and healthcare travel services. The Economic Transformation Program (ETP)[6] targeted and gave priority to several sectors in healthcare services, including clinical research, generics exports, health travel, diagnostic services, and health metropolis. Despite ETP generally gaining increased legitimacy, this shift has not translated into significant improvements in value-added contribution of the healthcare services sectors. The sector is very skilled, knowledgeable, and R&D intensive. The limits posed by Malaysia—in human capital, R&D infrastructure and collaborative partnership between academia, industry, and government—limits the progress of the sector. This can also be the result of the lack of state capacity to carry intervention programmes successfully, mainly in coordinating the drivers of the sector.

Malaysia's share of commercial KIS of Asia including telecommunications in Asia remained the same, hovering in the range of 1.2%-1.6% with an average of 1.42% in total value added (Table 7.2). Meanwhile, Malaysia's average share of the world is 0.38%. In terms of value, Malaysia is far below many of the "tigers" of East Asia such as Taiwan, South Korea, and Singapore. Indeed, Malaysia's total value-added activities are far below that of even the Philippines and Thailand. It also seems to be difficult for Malaysia to converge in terms of catching up with other emerging markets in commercial KIS. The average compounded annual average growth (CAGR) of Asia stands at 6.6%, while the CAGR of Malaysia is only 2.49%—again, lower than even the Philippines (8.6%) and Thailand (6.5%) (Table 7.3).

Trade in Knowledge Intensive Services

Table 7.4 shows the exports of commercial KIS, its growth, and its global share for selected economies. A notable trend emerging from the data shows the export value of commercial KIS increasing in all the selected countries. India emerged as the top exporter within Asia, surpassing even the other developed countries in Asia like Singapore, Japan, South Korea, and Taiwan. India has a strong presence in providing IT, accounting, legal, and other services to the developed countries. Singapore has been the top exporter within ASEAN. Nevertheless, commercial KIS contribution to GDP for Singapore is much higher than for India. Malaysia's commercial KIS exports increased (albeit slowly), with an annual average growth of three percent from USD 7,517 million in 2010 to USD 9,001 million in 2016. Notably, Malaysia's exports are low, recording only 0.6% share of global exports. Although given that Malaysia is a small open economy, without expanding these services to the world

[6] The ETP was initiated to transform the Malaysian economy.

Table 7.3 Commercial Knowledge Intensive Service Value Added, Selected Countries, 2001–2016 (USD Million)

Country	2001	2010	2011	2012	2013	2014	2015	2016	CAGR (2010–2016)
Bangladesh	3,300	10,036	10,696	11,737	14,196	16,359	18,673	21,202	13.28
China	167,829	786,622	977,192	1,154,128	1,373,911	1,560,919	1,806,011	1,934,749	16.18
India	52,109	192,932	217,684	220,407	240,528	261,406	264,736	294,010	7.27
Indonesia	12,865	62,793	72,776	77,632	78,451	76,038	75,769	84,928	5.16
Japan	700,671	922,903	993,828	989,156	800,278	736,199	674,732	751,222	-3.37
Malaysia	13,890	36,172	40,421	43,787	45,710	47,122	41,136	41,923	2.49
Pakistan	4,511	16,963	19,520	20,737	20,026	23,161	24,482	26,903	7.99
Philippines	8,676	26,082	29,520	33,727	37,543	39,231	41,135	42,858	8.63
Singapore	14,826	39,303	46,038	49,760	54,165	57,453	55,904	55,557	5.94
South Korea	62,933	129,351	142,909	148,560	154,490	168,734	166,445	169,833	4.64
Sri Lanka	883	4,126	3,898	4,301	4,639	5,041	5,216	5,450	4.75
Taiwan	43,257	53,267	58,870	59,676	61,227	63,373	62,011	63,264	2.91
Thailand	11,448	33,889	38,081	42,143	47,463	47,608	46,512	49,313	6.45
Vietnam	1,502	9,211	10,437	11,756	13,270	14,047	14,745	15,874	9.50
Total (Asia)	1,100,701	2,325,660	2,663,881	2,869,519	2,947,910	3,118,705	3,299,522	3,559,102	Average (6.56%)
Malaysia's Share of Asia	1.26	1.56	1.52	1.53	1.55	1.51	1.25	1.18	Average (1.42%)
Malaysia's Share of World	0.27	0.38	0.39	0.41	0.41	0.41	0.37	0.36	Average (0.38%)

Note Commercial KIS includes financial, business, health care, education, and communication services. *Source*: US Science and Engineering Indicators 2018

Table 7.4 Key global exporters of knowledge intensive services, 2010–2016

Country/Region	Exports (USD Million)							Share of world (%)
	2010	2011	2012	2013	2014	2015	2016	2016
World	1,131,790	1,289,883	1,349,566	1,463,289	1,602,508	1,536,916	1,568,398	–
United States	207,015	228,951	240,052	262,582	283,802	284,529	287,805	18.35
EU	382,135	432,402	452,962	499,459	548,938	503,002	520,048	33.16
China	13,534	74,141	72,485	81,514	98,179	90,345	90,635	5.78
Japan	38,335	44,462	32,014	35,703	49,442	49,208	55,804	3.56
South Korea	14,847	17,230	20,141	21,753	26,195	24,937	26,606	1.70
Taiwan	6,999	8,246	9,610	10,589	11,745	12,246	13,207	0.84
Brazil	16,499	20,363	22,329	21,385	24,642	20,792	19,750	1.26
Singapore	38,836	47,293	52,346	59,985	68,403	70,808	68,846	4.39
India	82,652	94,495	103,501	108,976	110,922	112,472	115,748	7.38
Malaysia	7,517	9,708	11,451	11,829	10,587	8,940	9,001	0.57
Philippines	13,506	14,060	14,484	16,729	18,264	21,544	23,885	1.52

Source US Science and Engineering Indicators 2018

the progress of its KIS will be limited. Malaysia remained a net importer of KIS. External markets are important to further improve and drive the value-added activities of these sectors, especially for the most tradeable services. Hence, tradeable services diversification should be the top priority of policy makers, i.e. moving away from traditional services to KIS. These services are highly dependent on knowledge and skills embedded in human capital. Preparing the labour force for work in these sectors could be an important policy direction of policy makers. In fact, promoting business start-ups (e.g. by SME Corporation Malaysia) would be a viable policy choice—especially in promoting Small and Medium Enterprises, where constraints are low in terms of capital requirements, and the scale does not matter. Services trade facilitation can be better promoted by the export promoting agency, Malaysia External Trade Development Corporation.

Dissecting the trade of services in more detail indicates the following (Table 7.5). In most cases, trade deficit is evident in KIS. Only computer and information services show a trade surplus, although the gap is not that large. Malaysia's narrowing of the current account surplus reflects the lower trade surplus in goods, but more importantly, it reflects the persistent structural deficits in KIS. In other words, Malaysia has been a net importer of knowledge intensive services, which is also very much reflected in royalties and fees payments. Indeed, government officials are also highly dependent on imports of business services, lacking in-house capability for development in those services.

Table 7.5 Knowledge intensive service trade by sub-sector, Malaysia, 2010–2016 (USD Million)

KIS sectors	2010	2011	2012	2013	2014	2015	2016
Exports							
Computer and information services	1,983	2,366	2,768	3,192	3,136	3,211	3,079
Financial services	527	794	861	766	808	710	850
Royalties and fees	101	149	136	110	76	92	115
Other business services	4,861	6,492	7,666	8,205	7,019	5,568	5,766
Commercial KI services*	7,517	9,708	11,451	11,829	10,587	8,940	9,001
Imports							
Computer and information services	2,129	2,421	2,924	2,858	2,760	2,662	2,384
Financial services	2,668	3,025	3,402	3,220	3,178	2,798	2,829
Royalties and fees	1,318	1,634	1,543	1,395	1,424	1,257	1,319
Other business services	6,233	7,533	8,329	8,860	8,253	7,439	8,499
Commercial KI services*	10,884	12,924	14,499	15,272	14,567	13,448	14,406

Note *Includes business, financial, communications, education, and health. *Source* US Science and Engineering Indicators 2018

Conclusions

The evidence shows that Malaysia's catching up in the KIS sectors requires significant reform to move the sectors forward. At least four broader policy focus areas are critical in moving the sectors to be more competitive, as well as in preparing the sectors to enhance their value-added activities.

Firstly, building more resilient KIS sectors requires improvement of the current systems of education and preparing a more skilled workforce. This has been one of the fundamental pillars of creating a knowledge-based economy. Malaysia's education system requires comprehensive reform, as it also lacks the critical mass of educated professionals and blue-collar workers to support the KIS sectors. While numerous efforts and reforms have resulted in improvements in several key education performance indicators, the challenges of the education system remain—particularly concerning skills and quality of teaching staff and students. These two factors should be the primary concern of policy instruments. Placing emphasis on quality rather than quantity is important. As for learning outcomes, instilling logic, creative, and reasoning skills will determine Malaysia's success in transforming not only the KIS sectors but also the economy as a whole. Indeed, institutional reforms—e.g. supporting institutions like training institutions, and incentives governing those reforms—should be further revamped. For instance, in supporting financial sectors, Malaysia lacks qualified institutions that can retrain financial officers in risk management, forecasting, and the like. In this aspect, university and industry collaboration is critical—instead, the state of collaboration is low by any global standard. Likewise, the KIS sectors need to establish strategic alliances with universities and actively participate in the global knowledge system. This may also include learning the best practices within the sectors. Bridging an effective informational infrastructure and having more effective human resource management would clearly benefit the KIS sectors.

Secondly, improving the performance of the KIS sectors requires setting and reviving new and existing regulatory environments. For instance, governing the progress of ICT and e-commerce requires the government to facilitate the market with new legal and regulatory frameworks so that more competitive markets as well as conductive business development are created. The risks of digital development as well as moving the industry to a more borderless world requires the government's role in facilitating legal and regulatory reforms to encourage enterprises to move towards embracing digital revolution. The intellectual property rights legal framework—that predominantly caters for the industrial sectors—should be further looked at so that the intangibility of the service sectors can also be protected. Examples include creating awareness on the forms of informal protections that do not require official registration (e.g. secrecy, restricted access to information, customer relationship management, and the like) as well as semi-formal protection such as contracts (e.g. employee inventions). These types of protections decrease the risk of losing core knowledge, prevent leaking of knowledge, limit the risk of imitations, and encourage business investments and business efficiency and innovativeness.

Thirdly, policy choice should focus on promoting innovation and technology adoption in the KIS sectors. The sectors need to be more innovative to compete globally—specifically, they should engage more aggressively in service, process, and organizational innovation. These types of innovation involve internal and external knowledge acquisition and are characterized by customer-specific solutions, where delivery of the services is improved. Similarly, it requires the KIS sectors to align technology, human resource management, and firm-level strategy. Given that KIS is based more on professional knowledge and is driven by network-based services, project management becomes a critical element within the KIS sectors. Indeed, many small services firms which are still supplier-driven should be encouraged to become more customer-driven. The sector is also highly information-intensive and requires having good communication flows between suppliers, clients, and data and information management. As a result, process innovation and leveraging technology are crucial. Therefore, encouraging service innovation within KIS by using the current policy instruments (e.g. STI policy) requires policy makers to go beyond the narrowly defined terms of innovation. Similarly, incentives and reward mechanisms to support service innovation should focus on the processes of particular KIS sectors. While promoting innovation and technology adoption is important, making KIS able to contribute to the national innovation system is equally critical.

Lastly, policies need to address a complex system of agents/stakeholders and their linkages and interactions. Improving sectoral linkages and interactions within the KIS as well as other real sectors is critical. For instance, linkages within KIS information and communication services ought to support the other KIS sectors such as finance, health care, and education. Similarly, KIS sectors should have strong linkages with the other real sectors like manufacturing so that mutual productivity gains can occur. For instance, the banking sectors are undergoing substantial automation—linking ICT services together with manufacturing capabilities would allow the services sector to significantly improve its productivity. Other options include prioritizing policies that would encourage the real sectors (e.g. manufacturing and agriculture) to venture into KIS on their own—this means encouraging vertical integration within specific manufacturing or agricultural sectors. In this way, more synergy can be achieved that can perfectly substitute their current operations. Reciprocally, the policy should also address how the knowledge content of KIS can be exploited by other economic sectors, as well as how the knowledge and activities of other sectors can be used by KIS. Studies show that manufacturing sectors greatly benefit from the progress of the non-financial KIS sectors, and as such, supportive policies should be in place to connect these sectoral linkages. This entails revamping the current industrial policy—where possible, KIS interaction and linkages must be specifically highlighted by taking the systemic and network interaction approach, rather than a standalone approach. Likewise, similar efforts are needed in improving the KIS-related trade. Improving KIS trade would encourage the sector to build its economies of scale and improve productivity. Market expansion requires facilitations from the meso-institutions such as Malaysia External Trade Development Corporation in promoting services trade—who could strategically bundle KIS services with the export promotion of other sectors. Similarly, policy instruments should support the knowledge flow—generation, accumulation, dissemination, and spillovers—through connectivity and coordination among the firms.

References

BNM. (2001) Financial Sector Masterplan 2001–2010, Retrieved from, http://www.bnm.gov.my/index.php?ch=en_publication&pg=en_fsmp&ac=7&en.

BNM. (2011) Financial Sector Blueprint 2011–2020, Retrieved from, http://www.bnm.gov.my/index.php?ch=en_publication&pg=en_fsmp&ac=8&en.

Chandran, V. G. R. (2020) Embracing industry 4.0: Policy and progress in Malaysia, presented at regional economic studies programme Webinar, Yusof Ishak Institute, Singapore, Retrieved from, http://www.vgrchandran.com/I4.pdf.

Chandran, V. G. R., & Devadason, E. S. (2017). Energizing the manufacturing sector: Can Malaysia move forward? *Journal of Southeast Asian Economies, 34*(3), 523–551.

Chan-Yuan, W., Chandran, V. G. R., & Boon-Kwee, N. G. (2016). Technology diffusion in the telecommunications services industry of Malaysia. *Information Technology for Development, 22*(4), 562–583.

Foray, D., & Lundvall, B.-A. (1996). The knowledge-based economy: from the economics of knowledge to the learning economy. In *OECD Documents: Employment and Growth in the Knowledge-Based Economy* (pp. 11–32). Paris: OECD.

Kaldor, N. (1967). *Strategic Factors in Economic Growth*. Ithaca: Cornell University Press.

Loungani, R, Mishra, S, Papageorgiou, C., & Wang, K. (2017). World trade in services: Evidence from a new dataset. IMF Working Paper No. 17/77. Retrieved from, https://www.imf.org/en/Publications/WP/Issues/2017/03/29/World-Trade-in-Services-Evidence-from-A-New-Dataset-44776.

Malaysia (1991) *Sixth Malaysia Plan 1991–1996*. Kuala Lumpur: Government Printers.

Nourani, M., Kweh, Q. L., Devadason, E. S., & Chandran, V. G. R. (2020). A decomposition analysis of managerial efficiency for the insurance companies: A data envelopment analysis approach. *Managerial and Decision Economics, 41*(6), 885–901.

Nourani, M., Chandran, V. G. R., Kweh, Q. L., & Lu, W.-M. (2018). Measuring human, physical and structural capital efficiency performance of insurance companies. *Social Indicators Research, 137*, 281–315.

Rasiah, R. (2011). Is Malaysia facing negative deindustrialization? *Pacific Affairs, 84*(4), 714–735.

Rasiah, R. (2006). ICT and GDP per capita growth. *International Journal of Internet and Enterprise Management, 4*(3), 202–214.

Rasiah, R. (2019). Building networks to harness innovation synergies: Towards an open systems approach to sustainable development. *Journal of Open Innovation: Technology Markets and Complexity, 5*, 70.

Rasiah, R. (2020a) Manufacturing transformation. In R. Rasiah, K. Salih & K. C. Cheong (Eds), *Malaysia's Leap Into the Future*, Dynamics of Asian Development.

Rasiah, R. (2020b) Industrial policy and industrialization in Southeast Asia. In O. Arkebe, C. Cramer, H. J. Chang, & R. K. Wright (Eds), *Oxford Handbook of Industrial Policy*.Oxford: Oxford University Press.

Rasiah, R., & Gopi, K. (2020c) Industrialization and industrial hubs in Malaysia. In O. Arkebe & J. Lin (Eds), *Oxford Handbook of Industrial Hubs and Economic Development*. Oxford: Oxford University Press.

Romer, P. (1994). The origins of endogenous growth. *Journal of Economic Perspectives, 8*(1), 3–22.

Shermur, R., & Doloreux, D. (2013). (2013) Innovation and knowledge-intensive business service: The contribution of knowledge-intensive business service to innovation in manufacturing establishments. *Economics of Innovation and New Technology, 22*(8), 751–774.

World Bank. (2007). *Building Knowledge Economies: Advanced Strategies for Development*. Washington D.C.: World Bank Institute.

Chapter 8
Education: The Past and the Future

Viswanathan Selvaratnam

Abstract Malaysia since independence in 1957, has underpinned and sustained the capacity and capability of its human resource development as a national priority. The nation's leadership till 1996 prioritised a state-driven national education system at all levels as the chief enabler of the country's human resource development strategy. Its aim was to drive economic growth, reduce income and wealth disparities between the races and boost national unity, political stability, and social change. This chapter attempts to dissect the country's past and present education policies, strategies and provisions and tease out the education system's positive achievements as well as any unintended consequences; in particular, the negative impact the Malaysian education system has had on issues of equity versus excellence, quantity versus quality and inclusivity versus diversity. The weaknesses are attributed, since 1971, to the New Economic Policy's (NEP's) race-based affirmative action policies and its near-term, politically driven strategies to meet the challenges and demand targets of the majoritarian Bumiputera community. The consequential fault-lines comprised racial polarisation, inequalities, brain-drain, mismatches, talent and skills shortages, and graduate unemployability. For Malaysia to leap-forward into an increasingly technologically-driven and highly competitive global economic system, the country has to move away from the NEP's opaque and obstructive race-based policies towards an inclusive and affordable education system that effectively and efficiently moves the country in the direction of a high-skill, high-income and a developed nation.

Keywords Education · Affirmative action · New economic policy · Skills and talent · Malaysia

V. Selvaratnam (✉)
8, Jalan Batai Barat, Bukit Damansara, 50490 Kuala Lumpur, Malaysia

R. Rasiah et al. (eds.), *Malaysia's Leap Into the Future*, Dynamics of Asian Development, https://doi.org/10.1007/978-981-16-7045-9_8

Introduction

The country's multiracial leadership has, from the inception of self-rule in 1955 and independence in 1957, prioritized and strategized, concerted policies and actions to implement a national system of education as the main driver of human capital development and the chief enabler of economic development, national prosperity, and social justice. The leadership's primary contention was the closely entwined relationship between human capital and economic development will reduce the nascent nation's prevailing economic and social disparities between the races and promote national unity, racial harmony, political stability, and social change.

The country's leadership, thus, prioritized the development of a principally public-funded school to tertiary level education system both as a public and private good. Nevertheless, with the continuing operation of vernacular Chinese and Tamil medium as well as Islamic religious schools, a legacy of the colonial era, the nation's education provision since its independence can be characterized as a fractured one. Accordingly, the system has implicitly prearranged credibility to inequality in resource allocation, racial and religious polarization, as well as continued with the colonial policy of unequal access to employment opportunities and in the distribution of wage income.

Since 1996, to free-up the government's scarce resources for more urgent development projects and on grounds of market competitiveness, efficiency, and cost-saving, the provision of higher education was partly "commodified". Therefore, higher education once provided to eligible candidates without profit motive, has in the last three decades, in part, driven by for-profit providers as commodified skills to be traded. The policy has led to a surge in both private institutions and student numbers and transformed the country's higher education system from one which was predominantly a public provision towards a mixed public/private funded system. It is envisaged that the present public/private balance is to shift towards the for-profit private sector, with the state acting as an incentivizer, facilitator, and regulator.

This chapter seeks to dissect Malaysia's past education policies and the positive and negative impacts it has had on its provision till now with a view towards generating recommendations for building competent, innovative, and highly skilled human capital for the future. In doing so, the study focuses on the main policy instruments, institutions, and organizations that have shaped and driven the country's politically resolute "quantity versus quality" education system which has contributed towards its lag behind the high-tech East Asian economies.

Looking towards the future, the study will outline the sustainable and inclusive building blocks that have to be incorporated into the education system, to nurture a critical mass of diverse creative and innovative talents critical both to initiate a knowledge-driven economy as well as offer an array of opportunities to every well-rounded Malaysian student who could benefit from higher education. A strategy of this nature could meet the formidable challenges the country faces both to achieve a technology-savvy, export-driven, and high-income developed nation status as well as to successfully navigate the Fourth Industrial Revolution (4th IR) to leap forward.

The Role of Education in Development

There is no quantitative measurement to ascertain the causal relationship between human capital development and economic development (Lucas, 1988; Romer, 1986). More often than not, this is achieved by government investments into the sector to synergize knowledge externalities as a public good. Hence, the rapid development of South Korea and Taiwan was driven by an educational focus on science and technology (Vogel, 1991; Perkins, 2013). Since the 1960s Malaysia took this key concept into its development plans to promote and accelerate science-based higher education through the setting-up of the University of Science Malaysia or Universiti Sains Malaysia (USM) to train more doctors, dentists, engineers, scientists, innovators, and teachers for the benefit of society as a whole.

The catalysts that shaped the growth of the country's national school education system was the ground-breaking Razak and Rahman-Talib Reports of 1956 and 1960, respectively, followed by the National Education Act of 1961 (Razak Report 1956; Rahman-Talib, 1960; FOM, Education Act 1961). The policy initiatives formulated by the two reports and their legitimization by the National Education Act, spurred a visionary, vibrant, and expansionary national education system. The high-point of the policy was the initiation of a free place for every Malaysian child irrespective of class or race in the country's public-school system. The policy accelerated the near universalization and democratization of primary education within a mere decade and aided the country's rapid expansion of lower- and upper-secondary schooling. Malaysia's public education system by 2019 could be credited to its large provision of 6,152 preschools with an enrolment of 205,200 pupils, while the 7,772 primary and 2,436 secondary schools had 2,726,761 and 2,007,496 students enrolled, respectively, with an all-level teacher strength of 419,782 (MOE, Quick Facts, 2019). In numerical terms, this is indeed a stellar achievement for any country in the South.

The examination-centred curriculum was primarily aimed towards moulding students to fit into the workforce and become good citizens (Razak Report 1956; Rahman-Talib Report 1960 and FOM-National Education Act, 1961). Yet, while flexibility was advocated in the teaching and learning process, teachers largely adhered to the "tried-and-tested methods outlined in guidebooks". This methodology was distinctly paternalistic, emphasizing rote learning and regurgitation to achieve high test scores and grades. Naively, it is assumed that the achievement of high test scores on standardized tests is equated with quality education. This has obviously impeded the development of creative thinking and independent initiative among students to this day, skills that are increasingly demanded by employers.

In 1979, the Report of the Cabinet Committee to Review the Implementation of Education Policy (known as the Cabinet Committee or Mahathir Report) implemented reforms with the aim of developing intellectual, spiritual, and emotionally healthy students for the future. However, the system did not nurture and endow students with the capability of being innovative as well as in critical thinking. Instead, the system has stifled creative thinking and has largely catered to the manpower requirements of the public sector and low-tech industrial and service sectors. This posed a dilemma as most employers needed workers who could think outside the box.

New Economic Policy

With independence, the contention of the majoritarian Bumiputera's community's ruling elites was that as sons of the soil they had the legitimate right to a larger share of the country's growing wealth and distributive income. Due to the beginning neglect of the British colonial state, education and, in particular, Bumiputera access to higher education and their opportunities to higher-wage employment were truncated. The Malay leadership also attributed the May 13, 1969 race-riots to the "ridiculously insignificant" (Mahathir, 1970: 51) *Bumiputer*a achievements to the laissez-faire development policies promoted by the post-Colonial state. To address the economic malaise of the *Bumiputera* community, the government introduced the landmark New Economic Policy (NEP) in 1971. The NEP's primary goal was to reshape the economic, social, cultural, and political life of Malaysia through a state-engineered top-down socio-economic transformation strategy. The aim was to rectify the country's extensive economic inequalities and racial divide, in particular, the identification of race with occupation. Thus, the NEP's politically motivated policy was to eradicate the stark under-representation of Bumiputeras students in the country's higher education system, one of the main causes for inequality between Bumiputera and non-Bumiputers. The contention being the rectification between the prevailing stark divide between bumiputra and non-Bumiputera graduate numbers would produce more Bumiputera graduates, which will redress the inequalities in employment between the races as well as eliminate the predominancy of race with economic function.

The NEP's race-based affirmative action policy radically reshaped the character and composition of the country's public education system, bolstering a rapid rise in Bumiputera student access into primary, secondary, and tertiary education institutions and their upward social mobility into middle-class status through high-wage employment. Nevertheless, the ideological message of raising the prosperity of students via higher education has in turn produced a ritualized process of qualification-earning, the "diploma disease", rather than broad-based educational enrichment (Dore, 1997). The funnelling of mainly Bumiputera students into university places, their "graduation" into premium waged employment and upward social mobility became the UMNO-led BN government's primary policy engine.

With schooling leading to university degrees singled out as a key tool to produce equitable economic development the government became firmly wedded to restructuring of the education system in order to provide free and greater access to academically eligible Bumiputera students. To this end the Majid Report, Constitutional (Amendment) Act, and the Universities and University Colleges Act (UUCA) of

1971 were passed to bring into line the primary function of the universities to meet the objectives of the NEP. The constitutional amendments and UUCA gave wide-ranging powers to the government and its politically aligned bureaucracy to determine the universities' core policy ethos, its leadership and its management. This change politicized the role of Vice-Chancellors who were appointees of the Minister of Education, primarily on the grounds of their "suitability and acceptability" to the UMNO dominated government. In turn this impinged on academic freedom and on the teaching, research, and publications of academic staff, stifling the long-established balance between the academic mission of universities and their socio-economic role (Collini, 2012).

The NEP's most potent policy initiative was the mandatory race-based quotas, reserving 55% of university places for Bumiputera students and administered in a measure of secrecy. The secrecy in the implementation quota policy changed the ethos of the country's higher education provision. Apart from being anti-elitist, it was a challenge to the established university tradition of achieving an equitable merit-based, colour-blind, and diverse student body as well as a well-endowed high-quality human capital critical for the country's economic development. The exclusive race bias quota admission policy gave a relentless push to a quantity driven Bumiputera student enrolment, primarily as a precursor to their employment and social mobility, rather than a quantity-cum-quality driven higher education agenda without an "understanding that meritocracy and the free exchange of ideas form the core of the university" (Wildavsky, 2010: 195). Meritocracy and the free exchange of ideas are indispensable requirements for any university to be world-class as well as to help their students grow intellectually with prospects for competitive employment and be civic partners in the nation's development (Economist, 2016a).

To effectively implement, administer, and achieve the NEP's mandatory race based quotas, a Central Admission Unit (Unit Pusat Universiti, UPU) for student intake into public universities was established within the Ministry of Education. The UPU administered the selection of candidates, their course assignments and their enrolments into the respective university faculties. The universities were not allowed to compete for the best students, while the best students were not allowed to enrol in programmes and universities of their choice. Thus, many students were shoehorned into courses they were not suited for.

Once the quota admission system was institutionalized, it widened the higher education opportunities for Bumiputera candidates, in particular, those from disadvantaged rural backgrounds with lower academic qualifications. The majority of these students were clustered into "soft-option" programmes. The policy galvanized the access of a large number of Bumiputera students into higher education institutions and has boosted their graduate numbers. However, it has negated the development of the country's critically needed science and technology human capital. Thus, while it transformed the economic and social lives of a huge number of Bumiputera students and their families from disadvantaged backgrounds, it has also created a set of unintended consequences and challenges. A basic unintended consequence that has underpinned the system is the question of education and equality. In other words, does the Malaysian education system offer the real possibility of equal educational opportunity for every Malaysian student to achieve his or her full potential to contribute to the nation to leap forward.

Massive Government Investment

During this period the country's public sector educational expenditure as a percentage of GDP grew steadily. It was 3.7% in 1961, 4.3% in 1965, and 4.5% in 1970 (Leete, 2007: 181). To expand the provision of public education, Malaysia's capital investment and recurrent expenditure on education since 1970 until 2016 has been increasing to assume a larger share of the GDP. At near 6.3% of the GDP in 2016 (MOE, Quick Facts, 2017), the country's expenditure on education was 1.5 times the corresponding proportion in Thailand and China, and nearly twice those in India, Singapore, and South Korea (Cheong et al, 2011: 163). The unprecedented huge investments and growth in public educational provision pushed the rapid growth in student numbers at all levels of the school system. The increasing student numbers and their growing aspirations gave the upward push for the rapid expansion of community colleges, polytechnics, and public universities with varied quality to meet the rising aspirations of the increasing numbers of school-leavers. However, in 2019 due to the country's economic downturn, the education budget was trimmed to 4.5% of the GDP (MOE, Quick Facts, 2019).

Between the years 2013 to 2017, the share of expenditure on education has risen from 18.61% in 2013 to 20.67% in 2014 but declined sharply to 15.62% in 2015 and in 2017 and 2018 it again increased to 16.92 and 21.25%, respectively. In 2019, the expenditure declined to 19.03% (MOE, Quick Facts, 2015, 2019). Capital expenditure declined progressively from RM 2,100 million in 2013 to RM 1,521 million, RM 1,216 million, RM 1,393, and RM 1,097 in 2014, 2015, 2016, and 2017, respectively, while the government's austerity drive, drove the recurrent expenditure marginally down from RM 39, 944 million in 2013 to RM 39, 042 million in 2014. It was marginally increased to RM 39,336 million, RM 39, 614 million, and RM 42, 892 million in 2015, 2016, and 2017, respectively. As a share of overall education expenditure, capital expenditure sharply declined over the years 2013 to 2017 from 8.68 to 2.49%, a drastic reduction, while recurrent expenditure rose from 91.32 to 97.51% (MOE, Quick Facts, 2014, 2015, 2017). However, the years 2018 and 2019 saw a steep rise in both capital and recurrent expenditure in monetary terms. For capital expenditure from RM 1,096 million in 2017 to RM 4,412 million and RM 5,111 million for the years 2018 and 2019, respectively, while recurrent expenditure increased from RM 43,783 million in 2017 to RM 55,553 million and RM 60,238 million for the years 2018 and 2019, respectively (MOE, Quick Facts, 2019).

Impact on Growth and Education Investment

Yet, has Malaysia's sustained expansionary education policy with its concomitant huge capital investments and recurrent expenditures support ensured the best value for the taxpayers' money in terms of quality-enhancement of its human capital to meet the country's aspiration to achieve developed nation status as well as Malaysia's leap into the future? The government's continuous expansionary drive to meet the mounting youth aspirations has contributed to notable quantitative growth trends in provisions and they stand out when compared to other middle-income countries and, in some instances, even to developed country tendencies. The youth (15–24 years) literacy rate is at 99%, which is nearly universal, while the adult population (aged 25 and above) with no schooling declined from 60% in 1950 to 5.8% by 2018. The proportion of people 25 years and above who have completed at least secondary education rose from around seven percent in 1950 to more than 51% by 2018 (MOE, Quick Facts, 2019). Malaysia currently enjoys a near-universal literacy and numeracy rate among its population.

Student Enrolment Trends

The government initiated and funded preschool education achieved an impressive enrolment of 84.5% by 2015. The democratization of school education has led to a near-universal primary (96%) and lower secondary (91%) school participation rates. At the upper-secondary school level, the gross enrolment rate in 2017 was a high 86% and by the year 2025 the country is envisaged to achieve a 100% enrolment at all levels (Malaysia Education Blueprint 2013–2025). At the tertiary level the participation rate is at a high of 48%. The country has within four decades, from 1971, transformed itself from an elitist to a mass higher education system and is projected by 2025 to provide universal access. In addition, Malaysia has the distinction of achieving a respectable gender balance from preschool to school education (MOE, Quick Facts, 2019) and this has enabled them to make a significant contribution to the nation's workforce and development. At the tertiary level the country has achieved a 52.37% female participation rate (MOE, Quick Facts, 2015, 2019), with 381,315 out of 617,617 enrolled being females. Female students also have a higher graduation rate than their male counterparts. Malaysia's achievements in female participant rates are comparable to that of advanced industrial countries of Finland (53.28%), Japan (47.46%), and Germany (48.25%) (MOE, Quick Facts, 2019).

Wider education provision has contributed to a large number of people being drawn into premium wage employment. In particular, the expansion of highly subsidized public higher education over the years has given opportunities to a large number of first-generation Malaysians particularly from disadvantaged rural backgrounds to seek university degrees and professional qualifications. This has led to the growth of a sizeable urban middle-class with rising disposable incomes producing a growing consumer society and drastically reducing the rural–urban income divide, hardcore poverty, and income disparities between the races. Yet the benefits have not been accrued equally and the Malaysian Education Blueprint 2013–2025 (Preschool to Post-Secondary Education) (MEB), a major reform policy initiative recognizing some of the earlier shortcomings, has targeted to achieve full enrolment from preschool to upper-secondary school, as well as the implementation of compulsory schooling for pupils from ages six to 11 (MOE, Education Blueprint, 2013: 7–6).

Student Transition Rates

Malaysia's educational achievements have been rooted in the notable student transition rates at all levels of the education system. The MEB highlights the impressive quantitative achievements in student transition rates in schools since the country's independence in 1957 (MOE, Education Blueprint, 2013: 3–1). The success is credited to Malaysia's robust quantitative education push backed by sustained budgetary provision. Though the current gross enrolment ratio at secondary level is 86%, the country has yet to reach the 100% participation rate that developed countries such as Finland, Japan, Germany, and Australia have achieved (MOE, Quick Facts, 2015), though, the country has had the infrastructural, teaching, and administrative capacity to achieve this benchmark since 2013 (MOE, Quick Facts, 2013).

By the end of 2015, at the national preschool level around 84.26% of those aged 4+ to 5+ were enrolled in some form of either public or private run preschools, a dramatic increase from 67% in 2009 (MOE, Quick Facts, 2015). There was a remarkable increase in the transition rate of pupils from primary to lower secondary (Form 1) as well as from lower to upper secondary. The transitional rate from primary to lower secondary almost doubled from 45% in the 1980s to 81% in 2010 and in 2019 to 96.81%, while from the lower to the upper-secondary level the rate in 2018 was 96.76% (MOE, Quick Facts, 2019). The persistent upward enrolment push facilitated the majority of children to complete 11 years of schooling.

At the upper-secondary school level, Malaysia has made significant gains in enrolment numbers and remains nearly on par with developed Asian economies of Japan, Singapore, South Korea, and Taiwan, where enrolment levels have consistently exceeded over 95%. While the overall educational attainment rate of the Malaysian population still lags behind, 19.7% of those above the age of 25 have achieved only primary education (Japan had none and South Korea only 9.8%) and while the rates of lower and upper secondary attainment was respectable, Malaysia's attainment of level of tertiary education was only 16.7% (16.7% for Japan and 15.9% for South Korea) (MOE, Quick Facts, 2019).

Expansion in Higher Education

On independence the country had just one flagship university, the University of Malaya, a bastion of elitist education that combined access with excellence and meritocracy, and limited student enrolment to less than one percent of the age cohort. With the introduction of the NEP in 1971 and the liberalization of higher education in 1996, the growth from an "elite" to a "mass" system with huge student numbers was quite simply staggering. The dramatic rise of student numbers saw by 2016 a proliferation of higher education institutions. The country now has a significant number of public and for-profit private universities, foreign-affiliated university branch campuses, university colleges, and colleges as well as several public sector polytechnics and community colleges. The Klang Valley has a high concentration of these institutions, while the rest are unevenly spread across the country. Parked outside the university system are 14 specialized publicly funded Higher Education Centres of Excellence. At the second and third-tier levels there are 33 polytechnics and 91 community colleges (MOE, Education Blueprint (HE), 2015: Chapter B). In the private sector there is a proliferation of institutions and by the latest figures of the Malaysian Qualification Agency (MQA) there are 76 universities, 36 university colleges, and 386 colleges spread throughout the country.

Though all the 20 public universities are characterized as "research, comprehensive, and focused institutions of higher learning', only five of them have been accorded Research University (RU) status. USM was awarded in 2008 the rank of Accelerated Programme for Excellence (APEX) University. The APEX University is part of the government's agenda to propel at least one of the nation's universities to "world-class" status. After more than a decade USM has not been able to achieve a rank within the top 100 of world-class universities.

Formal student entry into public higher education is based on two pathways, the highly competitive STPM programme, either in the arts or the sciences, or the less competitive one or two-year fully subsidized pre-university preparatory Matriculation Programme in science, accountancy, and technical education, administered by the Ministry of Education exclusively for Bumiputera candidates. From 2012, ten percent of the intake was open to non-Bumiputera candidates, mainly Indians, from disadvantaged backgrounds. By 2014, the Matriculation Programme was offered by 15 Matriculation Colleges with an enrolment of 26,262 students and 71.21% of them were female students (MOE, Quick Facts, 2015). The government in 2019 increased the number of colleges by two and the intake to 40,000 while retaining the 90% to ten percent quota between Bumiputera and non-Bumiputera students. In addition, MARA Colleges also provide these programmes exclusively to Bumiputera students.

In 2002 the quota system was officially abolished and was replaced by a "merit system". Under this new selective "merit system" a candidate has to achieve not only a good academic GPA (Grade Point Average) but also be a well-rounded and "holistic" candidate, indicated by extra-curricular activities. In spite of this modification, many non-Bumiputera students with GPA scores of 4.0 (perfect score) who applied for admission into high demand programmes, such as medicine, pharmacy, and dentistry to public universities were denied places. The justification was that they were not well-rounded candidates (Tan & Yojana, 2013). The quota system, the race-based matriculation institutions, and the new selective "merit system" do play a significant role in shaping the life chances of Bumiputera versus the non-Bumiputera students and act as a detriment to the development of an inclusive high-quality national higher education system.

The for-profit private higher education institutions are allowed to operate an open-access system and permitted to admit candidates with the minimum required entry qualification for programmes as stipulated by the MQA. There appears to be a lack of data to verify whether the job-related programmes students are enrolled for in the for-profit institutions may disappear soon with the rapidly advancing technology-dependent economy. For the majority of academically qualified non-Bumiputera students, apart from the overseas route for the brightest and the rich, the for-profit private tertiary institutions are the main pathway to higher education and the possibility of employment. For students from low-income families their entry into these institutions is through a means-tested student loans system provided by the state-backed National Higher Education Fund Corporation (PTPTN). Though the PTPTN loan system has over the last two decades diversified the undergraduate student body both in terms of socio-economic and ethnic composition but it has saddled many of them in steep debts upon their graduation. Though there is a moral obligation to repay loans, student loans, indebtedness, and defaults have proved to be toxic as many unemployed or underemployed graduates have not been able to service their loans. The for-profit institutions to boost their revenue stream have embarked on a proactive and intensive competition to increase their student numbers and this has resulted in a huge diversion of resources from academic teaching to marketing budgets. The Ministry of Higher Education has instituted Malaysian Quality Evaluation System for Private Colleges (MyQuest) to help students and their sponsors gauge the quality of colleges and universities (Azura & Aina, 2017).

Decline in Quality

The country's declining quality of education is a grave and recurrent concern to the government, employers', parents, students, and the public at large. The fear is that apart from driving an overall poor-quality human capital for the country's development needs, it will hold back students from disadvantaged backgrounds with substandard educational qualifications from good-paying jobs in a highly saturated graduate employment market and impede their social advancement as well as exacerbate further class divisions. The national examination results indicate that over time there is an absolute improvement in grades in the core subjects of Bahasa Malaysia, English, Mathematics, and Science (MOE, Education Blueprint, 2013: 3–5). However, when compared against regional and international benchmarks, the quality appears to be low. Indeed, the rapid quantitative expansion in education has been accompanied by a diminution in educational quality, which has become a central concern, as well as a policy polemic and prickly political issue. The former Deputy Prime Minister and Minister of Education and current Prime Minister, Muhyiddin Yassin, acknowledged this when noting that the amount invested in education from preschool right up to university "is the same or even more than some foreign countries like the United States" but "our students' performance isn't as good as those in the developed nations" (The Star, 2015).

From English to Bahasa Malaysia

There is a "dramatic and drastic" decline in the proficiency of the English language among younger Malaysia (Azman, 2017a, b). Schools are being staffed with English teachers who are even regarded by the Ministry of Education as not being proficient enough to teach the subject (Ibid. 2017). This has contributed to a weakening of academic standards in schools and tertiary institutions as a large number of students who lacked proficiency in both written and spoken English language faced serious learning handicaps in some of their course work. English has become the world's pre-eminent language of communication, the *lingua franca* of global business, a gateway to knowledge and employment opportunities. Good English is a critical tool as most essential text and reference books, as well as journals and research papers, particularly in Science, Technology, Engineering, and Mathematics (STEM) disciplines at the tertiary level. Teaching and research in medicine, dentistry, pharmacy, engineering and technology, and computer science are overwhelmingly in English. Apart from this, global business, the internet, and diplomacy are pre-eminently in English. If Malaysia wants to take its place in the world marketplace and move forward as a developed nation, then its education system has to keep abreast with, if not be ahead of, global trends and global knowledge growth. For this a mastery of English is a prerequisite (Selvaratnam, 2019).

The relegation of English to a second language has not been matched by a corresponding effort to translate scholarly articles and reference books into Bahasa Malaysia. Language deficiency is a handicap to their access to the main sources of advancing global knowledge, particularly in science and technology education. This is a barrier to nurturing the requisite science-based human capital to meet the needs of a scientific anchored knowledge economy. In contrast, Japan, South Korea, and Taiwan using their national language have not only strengthened nationalism but have also evolved strongly a world-class indigenous language-based scientific culture to support education in science and technology and innovation-driven R&D (Ibid).

To mitigate this shortcoming, Malaysian schools are allowed to opt for a Dual Language Programme (DLP) from 2017. Under the DLP, schools will be granted the option to teach Science, Mathematics, Information Technology, and Communication and Design and Technology in English or Bahasa Malaysia (The Star, 2016b). Research shows there is a direct correlation between English skills and the economic performance of a country and job seekers with exceptional English proficiency earned 30% to 40% higher salaries (McCormic, 2017).

Lack of Cognitive Skills

The weakness in nurturing and embedding students with cognitive skills has undermined the country's education system. Rote learning and regurgitating at tests have failed to stimulate and challenge the students. This has contributed to the general lack of critical thinking and reasoning, decision-making, problem solving, communication abilities, interpersonal and leadership skills, and innovation skills which continues to be a major problem plaguing the nation's pool of human capital (MOE, Education Blueprint, 2013). The poor quality of Malaysia's education outcome is indicated in its Trends in International Maths and Science Study (TIMMS) and Programme for International Student Assessment (PISA) scores.

TIMSS Scores Trend

When Malaysia first participated in TIMSS in 1999, its eighth grade student score was above the international average for Mathematics with 519 points and was ranked 16th out of 38 countries. The Science score of 492 was also above the international average, although the country was ranked lower at 22nd position. However, Malaysia's grading in the 2007 and 2011 results, respectively, fell sharply to below the international average in both subjects. The Mathematics score fell from 474 points in 2007 to 440 points in 2011 (26th position out of 42 countries). The Science score dropped from 471 in 2007 to 426 points in 2011 (32nd out of 42 countries). In the latest TIMSS assessments Malaysia's average scale score was 461 for mathematics and 460 for science.

Furthermore, 38% of students in Malaysia did not meet the minimum benchmark in Mathematics and Science in 2011 and only one percent to two percent of Malaysian students performed at the highest benchmark level. In contrast, over 40% of students in Singapore scored at a very much higher level in Mathematics and Science. The report noted that Malaysian students generally understood basic Mathematics and Science concepts but struggled in the application of knowledge. However, in the 2015 report, the performance of Malaysian students was 465 in mathematics and 471 in science showing an improvement from 440 and 426, respectively, as graded in 2011 and is now ranked at the mid-table in the list of participating countries. The average scores for 2019 do not indicate Malaysian students on the average have not shown any significant improvement and even reached the intermediate score of 475 points. Singapore's students both in 2015 and 2019 were the highest scorers with 621 for mathematics and 597 points for science and 625 in mathematics and 595 in science, respectively, among the participating countries.

PISA Scores Trend

In 2009 Malaysia participated for the first time in the Organisation for Economic Co-operation and Development's (OECD) triennial PISA. The programme tests the core in maths, literacy, and science of 15-year-olds from randomly selected schools. Out of 74 countries that participated in 2009, Malaysia was placed in the bottom third for Reading, Mathematics, and Science, well below both the international and OECD average in all three areas as shown in the results published in 2010.

In the 2012 assessment, Malaysia's performance faltered further. Malaysian students scored 421, 398, and 420 in mathematics, reading, and science, respectively, and were ranked 52 out of the 65 countries that took part. It was at least 100 points below that of the fast developing of East Asian Economies of Singapore, Japan, South Korea, and Hong Kong on all three subjects. With PISA a 38 points difference is equivalent to one year of learning. The 2015 PISA scores announced by the Ministry of Education were 446 in mathematics, 431in reading, and 443 in science. In 2018 the Malaysian scores were 440 in mathematics, 415 in reading, and 438 in science. These scores lag well behind the global average of 490 for mathematics and 493 both for reading and science.

Almost 60% of Malaysian students failed to meet the minimum benchmark in Mathematics, which is the baseline proficiency required for students to participate effectively and productively in life. Similarly, 44 and 43% of the students did not meet the minimum proficiency levels in Reading and Science, respectively.

Widening Gap in STEM Achievements

High-quality STEM education is widely regarded as an essential ingredient for a "knowledge economy" and for the Fourth Industrial Revolution. An education system with STEM at its core will be able to consistently prepare a critical mass of scientifically based and technologically savvy knowledge workers. Such a workforce is a vital prerequisite for the country to drive a knowledge and innovation-based society. An innovative society can push Malaysia towards a high-tech and income growth trajectory.

The latest survey indicates that less than 30% of the students in schools elected to join the science stream, though the country had as early as 1967 targeted student uptake in science and technology programmes to be 60% by 1987 (Ahmad, 2015; HEPC, 1967: 186). In 2016 the 20 Malaysian public universities combined graduated a total of 102,279 graduates and out of this large graduate pool the number with STEM-based subjects was 38,726 or 38% (MOE, Quick Facts, 2017), far short of the 60% targeted in 1967. According to the OECD *Reviews of Innovation Policy: Malaysia 2016*, the business sector is facing a shortfall in the quality and supply of science and technology graduates to meet the growing skill needs. The country continues to face a declining number of students opting for the science stream (Sunday Star, September 6, 2020). For the country to achieve developed nation status by 2020 the projection is that it needs 500,000 graduates in science and technology (S&T) or 60% of the country's workforce, while currently there is a stock of only 85,000 S&T graduates (Dzulkifli, 2016).

To achieve this, it must make science an interesting and creative subject by moving its teaching towards an enquiry-based learning method in all schools (NST, September 7, 2016b). In particular, underrepresented young people should be encouraged to pursue STEM subjects and careers. This has to be further bolstered by a national science policy that inspires and incentivizes the aspirations of the career pathway as well as with better monetary rewards for young scientists and researchers (The Sun, September 9, 2016).

ICT Education

With the rapid global advancement of ICT (Information Communication Technology) and its accelerating global connectivity, it is imperative that technology-based teaching and learning tools and facilities are integrated into all levels of the country's education system. More importantly, Malaysia's vision to be a high income and developed nation too warrants a critical and talented stock of technologically literate workers to productively participate in the fast changing and advancing global technology-driven knowledge economy. "However, the intensive penetration of ICT education in Malaysian schools still remains elusive and school teachers in the country have been slow to embrace the technology" (Hazlina, 2017). This is because of poor teacher training and a lack of good computer labs and technical support (Ghavifekr & Ibrahim, 2015). The shortfall prevails despite the investment of RM 663 million into the Bestarinet project which has connected over 10,000 government schools across Malaysia to a single learning programme through the internet (Hazlina, 2017).

Under the MEB leveraging the ICT is identified as one of the key components to shift the national education system to world-class standards. Hopefully this will equip students in schools and fortify them with the skills for the Fourth Industrial Revolution (IR4.0) and the digital economy, an economy that will be rapidly underpinned by artificial intelligence (AI), robotics, the Internet of Things, autonomous vehicles, and 3-D printers.

Paradoxically, the country's higher education institutions have made significant progress and are fast-moving forward in ICT education. Both the public and private higher education sectors provide a wide range of ICT programmes and have expanded online course offerings from 64 in 2015 to 300 in 2016 (Hazlina, 2017). Lifelong learning is critical to the development of an inclusive knowledge society that will lead to greater efficiency, productivity, and higher quality of life.

Teacher Quality

With the exception of a few elite residential and urban schools, a sizable number of students come from schools that lack quality teaching and adequate infrastructure. Poor-quality teaching and learning skills as well as teacher absenteeism in schools are handicapping students both from coping with the rigorous demands of high-quality tertiary education, and benefiting from it. The World Bank attributed this malaise to the high degree of centralization of the school system. Further, the country continues to maintain 27 Teacher Training Institutes and just over 3,000 academic personnel despite the drastic fall in the enrolments of teacher trainees from 30,650 in 2015 to 13,576 in 2017 (MOE, Quick Facts, 2017). The World Bank points out that apart from the lack of ethnic and gender diversity in the teaching profession, there is an inherent weakness in the quality of teacher trainee recruitment and training in the teacher education institutes (World Bank, December, 2013: 76). In a sample of 125 lessons observed in 41 schools across the country by researchers, it was found that 50% of the lessons delivered by teachers were unsatisfactory and did not sufficiently engage students (MOE, Education Blueprint, 2013: 5–2). The Economist (December 10, 2016b) says that "... what matters most is what happens in the classroom ... successful children are those who are exposed to good teaching more often".

Dismissing incompetent teachers is almost impossible and the system is saddled with a "rising tide of mediocrity". Recognizing the role of educators to ensure the progress of students, steps have been taken to improve the quality of teachers by recruiting only the top 30% of applicants, as well as to use more stringent measures to select principals. In Finland's world-class education system, only the ablest, highly trained, and talented individuals are channelled into the teaching profession. This strategy is pursued to ensure that every child is taught by the best minds in the nation and to make every Finnish school a good school (Sahlberg, 2011). Some teachers are being trained to apply Higher Order Thinking Skills (HOTS) to enhance their skills (MOE, Education Blueprint-Schools, 2013: 5–30), and policies are being implemented to rebrand Teacher Training Institutes under the Malaysian Education Blueprint.

Technical and Vocational Education and Training

High-quality Technical and Vocation Education and Training (TVET) are critical in supporting minor innovations that entrepreneurs in the small and medium industries (SMEs) require. Rasiah and Osman (1996) reported that there is not only a mismatch in skills demanded and supplied but also the training provided by the existing Malaysian TVET organizations as they are both fragmented and dated. This is compounded by a lack of recognition of TVET graduates and poor-quality instructors. TVET graduates have to be in tune with ICT and digital proficiency to meet the latest market demands.

TVET is provided by seven ministries—Education, Higher Education, Human Resources, Public Works, Agriculture, Rural and Regional Development, and Youth and Sports, and there is a lack of coordination that contributes to programme overlap. There is a stigma attached to vocational qualifications as they do not enjoy the same parity of prestige and status as a university degree. The vocational-academic divide has led to both low enrolment and a declining number of graduates produced by the combined vocational technical institutions (NEAC, Part 1, 2010: 56).

The education system is currently not producing the skills demanded by employers (NEAC Part 1, 2010: 6). The former Chief Minister of the State of Sarawak, Adenan Satem had reiterated that the state is "facing a shortage of graduates from vocational and technical schools because it was not given priority before" (Mail-on-line, September 10, 2016). Neither are many firms willing to spend money and time to train their employees. According to the World Bank's December 2016 "Quest for Productivity Growth" report only 19% of Malaysian firms provide formal worker training and this provision is less than the ASEAN average (World Bank, December 2016).

To address the need to up-skill the workforce and enhance their employability, the government is targeting all levels of tertiary education. The aim according to the 11th Malaysia Plan is to have 35% of its workforce in the highly skilled category by 2020. The goal is to identify technology-related skills that are in high demand and low in supply and in line with the demand, to identify and increase industry-led training programmes. The strategy is anticipated to produce more skilled graduates to meet both the growing demand, particularly from the predominantly small-scale industries for their various levels of skilled workers as well as improve the public perception of TVET as a viable pathway to greater opportunities of employability (MOE, Education Blueprint, 2015: 4–8).

The shift in policies has improved the growth in the intake from 113,000 in 2010 to 164,000 in 2013 (EPU, 2015). To further boost student TVET uptake, a Task Force steered by the MQA and the Department of Skills Development (DSD) of the Ministry of Human Resources, was established in 2012 to coordinate the delivery and improve efficiency among the institutions (EPU, 2015) to ensure that supply matches demand (MOE, Education Blueprint, 2015). Since 2017, the My Apprenticeship programme was initiated by the government through 18 different agencies to offer on-the-job industry-based training and thus minimize skill-gaps to diploma or bachelor's degree holders entering the workforce to kick-start their career.

Liberalization of Higher Education

The government's rationale for the introduction of the Private Higher Education Institution (PHEI) Act 1996 (Act 555) was attributed primarily to its fiscal and debt constraints. The liberalization of higher education was also in line with the recommendations and support of the World Bank and the International Monetary Fund, the sanctums of neoliberal economic orthodoxy. The liberalization policy was a significant paradigm shift in the country's higher education provision. The logic was that, apart from reducing public expenditure for the provision of higher education to private providers, it would continue to generate public benefit through the transfer of its cost from the taxpayer to the individual consumer—the student, the rationale being that since the individual student is the primary beneficiary of higher education, he should bear the cost burden. The policy has given rise to the proliferation of for-profit diploma and degree-awarding institutions in English medium that offer fairly narrow courses of varying quality, that are supposedly tailored to meet the needs of the job market, thus placing emphasis on the rarely guaranteed employment opportunities in a worsening graduate employment market over intellectual development.

For-Profit Higher Education

With the introduction of the PHEI Act, there was a proliferation of new and untested for-profit, open-access, and market-oriented higher education institutions providing wider programme choices mainly to non-bumiputera students. However, the majority of the for-profit institutions are focussed on cheaper-to-provide narrow professional, business, and finance programmes and refrain from providing high-cost STEM subjects (except for medicine, which till recently has been in high demand). Laboratories and equipment including computer suites involve huge investments and have to be replenished with continuous technology changes. The employment market for Arts and humanities graduates has drastically declined.

On the contrary, the needs of the knowledge economy of today and the future is a combination of both science and humanities. The majority of the for-profit institutions provide predominantly a variety of low-cost programmes that are purported to be market-driven and do not require expensive overheads and are cost-effective. From time-to-time serious issues have been raised in the media on the weak governance, slack admission policy with the sole aim to boost their student numbers and revenue stream, and the poor quality and academic standards in the private institutions. This is largely because there is no yearly rigorously assessed and authenticated league table in the public domain of their governance, academic quality, and the employability of their graduates. However, since 2007 to 2013, there was a two-yearly rating system known as SETARA (Rating System for Malaysian Higher Education) which was developed and implemented by the MQA. Since 2017, a new and improved SETARA instrument comprising three core functions, namely, teaching, research, and services has been rolled out (Ishak, 2020). There is an absence of a countrywide league table that focuses on pertinent issues such as spending per student, student/staff ratio, the quality of teaching, student satisfaction, and their employability. These are vital information for students and parents, when choosing where to study and whether they are getting a value-for-money education.

Impact

Market-based and for-profit-driven higher education provision has a corrosive and corrupting effect on the teaching and learning process weakening the idea of higher education as a public good and its impact on the economy and society. Markets with their distorted imperfections and asymmetries of information can be counter-productive and may therefore not be the best way to deliver the desired public good (Sen, 2009; Surowiecki, 2015).

In spite of this caveat, Malaysia has abdicated its historically entrenched role as the sole provider of higher education. With liberalization the government has taken the additional role of policy formulator, incentivizer, facilitator, and regulator of free-market higher education for the provision to be mainly driven by a mix-bag of profit-motivated entrepreneurs. They range from housing developers, political parties, individuals, and 11 international university branch campuses, mainly from the United Kingdom, Australia, India, and China. The government's policy is to turn Malaysia into a Global education hub and the EduCity @ Iskandar initiative, Asia's first multi-varsity educational complex in the Southern state of Johor is in line with this strategy. A total of 136,293 international students from more than 150 countries are enrolled at the country's higher education institutions (NST, Higher Ed, June 27, 2018).

The current proliferation and overcapacity in the private institutions of higher learning have caused many of them to take desperate measures to survive, including granting heavy discounts to students upon enrolment (New Strait Times, December 19, 2017). According to the former president of the Malaysian Association of Private Colleges and Universities, Parmjit Singh, this unethical policy has compromized their long-term financial viability (New Strait Times, December 19, 2017) and perhaps the quality of their academic standards.

MyQUEST evaluates private colleges twice a year to ascertain their quality, course cluster, and their student services. With the newly amended Private Higher Education Act (Act 555) for-profit colleges come under greater scrutiny and it is compulsory for them to provide information and data on the number of students they have, where they are from, the number of lecturers they have as well as the number classrooms, equipment and other relevant details (Aina, 2017). On the recommendation of MyQuest since 2012, the Ministry of Higher Education has ordered 46 colleges to be closed as they had failed to fulfil the conditions and requirements set by the ministry (Aina, 2017).

PTPTN (Malaysian National Higher Education Fund Corporation) a need-based and means-tested loan scheme at one percent interest was established in 1997 and has facilitated more and more aspiring and eligible first-generation Malaysian candidates below the age of 45 years. The PTPTN government-backed loan scheme has acted as a catalysts for low income and educationally disadvantaged particularly Bumiputera families to seek higher education and social mobility. Graduates have to repay their study loans, regardless of family background or earnings. However, with the growing job insecurity and varied incomes many graduates are unable to service their loans. Many women graduates who are struggling to balance work with family responsibilities are also adversely affected because of career breaks.

The former Minister of Higher Education, Idris Jusoh stated in Parliament that as of August 31, 2016, a total of 753,058 graduates who took PTPTN loans for their studies have not repaid a single cent. In 2019 only 49% of the loan recipients were actively repaying their loans, while 51% were not and 19% of them had not paid a cent. Thus, the gap between the cumulative amount of loans disbursed and those that have been repaid continues to widen every year. To date (December 2019), the PTPTN government-guaranteed debt stood at RM 40 billion in principal plus RM 13 billion in interest and is expected to balloon to RM 76 billion in 20 years (Jaafar, 2019; Jan, 2020). The large outstanding sum owed by graduates is resulting in PTPTN's inability to ensure the continuation of loans to future students from low-income families as well as threaten the viability of the for-profit institutions that have proliferated since the 2000s within the country's educational landscape.

University Rankings

The benchmarking and ranking of Malaysian public universities against the top world-class universities have become the preoccupation of both the government and university administrations. Malaysia's research universities, to cement their reputation as world-class universities, have been in the last decade clamouring to be ranked among the top 100 of the ranking system of world-class universities with a focus on research, teaching quality, publication in high-impact journals, and international outlook. Yet no Malaysian university is on the list of the top 100 in the two most objective and prominent world ranking systems, the Shanghai Jiao Tong University "Academic Ranking of the World Universities" (ARWU), and the Times Higher Education Supplement "World University Ranking" (THE). However, in the Quacquarelli Symonds (QS) "World University Ranking" which places an overwhelming emphasis of 40% on its overall score on peer reviews and thus considered highly subjective and widely criticized both for its methodology and volatility (Margison, 2012) only the University of Malaya was ranked 70 in the world in 2020. Malaysia's other universities were ranked as follows: the Universiti Putra Malaysia (159), Universiti Kebangsaan Malaysia (160), Universiti Sains Malaysia (165), Universiti Technology Malaysia (217), and University Technology Petronas (482).

In the 2020 Times Higher Education's World University Ranking only one university achieved a slot in the 301–350 band, while three others were banded in the lower 501–800 category (THE, 2020). In the 2020 ARWU World University Ranking, University of Malaya was ranked in the 301–400 band, while two of the nation's universities were slotted in the 501–600 grouping. Malaysia's goal to be within the list of 100 world-class universities appears to be elusive.

No Malaysian university is a world leader in research and scholarship in any of the sub-fields in science, engineering, and medicine. The NEAC (2010, Part I: 52) report highlighted that "the number of scientific and technical articles published in internationally recognized journals by Malaysians is also below comparable countries".

Although overall Malaysia is second among the ASEAN countries, the publication records of Malaysian universities fall well below that of those countries particularly in terms of publication in high-impact journals (Thiruchelvam et al., 2014: xxiii). The recent OECD report notes that although there is an unprecedented surge in the number of publications, their impact measured by citation has been very low (OECD, 2016) and more distressingly there is a low level of interaction between industry and university research alongside a poor commercialization rate of R&D output from universities in Malaysia (Mastic, 2016; OECD, 2016; Rasiah et al., 2015). According to the OECD report the attractiveness of university patents to industry, especially in their practical applicability appears weak (OECD, 2016).

Under the NEP the marginalization of qualified and talented non-Bumiputera students and academics has led to a brain drain from the country. With rare exceptions, the majority of bright students from affluent backgrounds seek world-class education at world-ranked universities in the United States, United Kingdom, Australia, and Canada. This trend in recent years has marginally shifted to selected European and Asian universities as well. An increasing number of Malaysian students graduating from Western universities have chosen to remain in the country of their study upon graduation. The World Bank (2014) reported that in 2013 over 300,000 Malaysian graduates decided to work overseas. It is estimated that the number of skilled Malaysians living abroad has risen in the last two decades by 300%, with roughly 20% of them holding tertiary qualifications. Since 2011, the Talent Corporation Malaysia (Talent Corp) under its Returning Expert Programme (REP) has brought home an average of 450 professionals per year (Focus, September 9–15, 2017b). However, for every Malaysian the Talent Corp brings home, 17 leave the country for overseas in search of greener pastures (Ibid). The brain drain continues to deprive Malaysia of its valuable talents unabated.

Mismatch in Demand–Supply and Graduate Employability

Despite making higher education central to the nation's development strategy as well as individual social and occupational mobility, the policy has come up against an increasingly crowded graduate labour market and the problem of unemployment and underemployment among the approximately 300,000 graduates produced by the various public–private higher education institutions annually. The country's 20 public and 38 private universities alone churns out yearly 51,000 graduates. Malaysia has one of the highest graduate joblessness rates in ASEAN (Sunday Star, September 6, 2020). According to the Malaysian Department of Statistics the number of unemployed graduates in 2019 was 170,300 thousand persons. This was an increase of 5.5 percent from the total of 161,300 unemployed graduates in 2018. The yearly decline in graduate employability can be attributed to the rapidly changing trajectory of the labour market forces, mainly due to the elimination of many jobs with rapid technological change and a shift in social norms and attitudes. Therefore, for many graduates finding a job can be depressing and a long-drawn out journey.

Employers persistently complain that the country's graduates leave the universities with the wrong skills. Therefore, there is a significant gap between the country's education system and the skill sets employers seek. Thus, they continue to face difficulty in acquiring the appropriate talents to raise their value-added production. The National Graduate Employability Blueprint (2012–2017) also highlights that the mismatch between the demand and supply of talents is a key reason why graduates are unemployed.

The Graduate Employability Blueprint notes that more than 50% of the graduates are below par in the critical soft skills. They lack the requisite knowledge, communication, and writing skills and the appropriate work attitude. Similarly, in the jobstreet.com survey conducted in late 2013, Malaysian employers' have pointed out that there is a gap between expectations and quality of graduates seeking employment in the country. Nearly 70% of employers think that the country's fresh graduates are just of average quality, while 24% believe they are "bad"; a very small percentage, i.e. six percent, state that they are "good". Employers reported the need for Malaysia's universities to shift their focus and train students in analytic and cognitive skills that are necessary for success in the professional world (Focus week, May 30, 2015). According to jobstreet.com, rapid technological change has forced employers to hire job seekers who not only possess specialist skills but also have the flexibility and creativity and be adaptive to fit into other job roles (NST, January 9, 2016a). In other words, in a crowded graduate labour market, employers are beginning to demand graduates with better all-round intellectual and social skills who can adapt to new technologies in order to be more productive.

Are our universities producing the wrong type of graduates? In most cases the traditional public university system will find it difficult to respond to the varied and changing needs of the vast array of employers. The question is should the industry take the responsibility to bridge this immediate gap by retraining and reskilling their employees? To bridge the disconnect and facilitate workable synergies between employers and graduates, the government has launched the Graduan Aspire fair in 2011 as a strategic platform to bring together prominent employers and quality talents to meet and connect them to develop successful careers (The Star, May 23, 2015).

The progressive decline of English language competency among students both at the school and tertiary levels has markedly affected their quality and employability in the highly competitive and crowded private sector graduate labour market (Selvaratnam, 2016). This was highlighted by an UMNO-BN lawmaker in the State Assembly of Johor when he said that thousands of graduates could not get a job in the private sector because of their poor command of English. These ill-fitted graduates for the private sector had no choice but to join the already bloated public sector civil service upon graduating (The Sun, May 11, 2015). This concern over the failure of large number of graduates to secure employment has been again reiterated by the former Chief Minister of Sarawak, Adenan Satem during his convocation address at the Universiti Malaysia Sarawak (UNIMAS) (NST, November 16, 2015).

Although Malaysia achieved an increase in the graduate employability rate from 70 to 75% over the period 2006–2014,[1] the degree of underemployment in the system (namely graduates who are employed in a role below their level of qualification, or who are working in low paying or vulnerable jobs) has remained high. In a rapidly changing world of work and employment market, graduates are increasingly finding for themselves their education does not open the door to their sought-after career expectations, while they also find themselves saddled with a high level of debt. Both the government's various educational policies and their implementation have not squarely addressed and transformed the system to keep pace with the accelerating changes in the nature of work. If the country's education provision fails to keep pace with technology, it will contribute to greater inequality (Economist, January 14, 2017a).

One potential indicator of high underemployment rates can be seen in the starting salary of 45% of recent graduates who earned below RM 1,500 per month in 2013, which is below the targeted liveable salary range for entry graduates (MOE, Education Blueprint (HE), 2015). Realizing that the higher education institutions are not preparing graduates for good jobs and the political ramifications of this, the government's Economic Planning Unit (EPU) in 2011 established a nation-wide Skim Latihan 1Malaysia (1Malaysia Training Scheme, SL1M) in collaboration with government-linked companies (GLCs) and private companies to bridge the gap between the graduate and the employer's work requirements. Basically, the SL1M programme is meant to provide unemployed graduates soft skill training and exposure to real work experience that will prepare them to secure employment (New Strait Times, March 20, 2018a). At a higher level, since 2012 Ekuiti Nasional Bhd (Ekuinas) through its 12-month long structured management Iltizam Professional Development Programme (PDP), nurtures graduate from public universities to boost their employability as well as develop in them the right attitude to progress in their chosen professional path (New Strait Times, December 2017). The former Prime Minister, Najib Razak at the "Varsity Entrepreneurship Skills and Talent" (VEST) 2017 wanted university graduates to change their mentality from "wage earner" to be entrepreneurs as this could promise a more meaningful future (Malaysiakini, October 15, 2017).

Quantity Versus Quality Dilemma

Since 1971, the country has pursued a politically resolute "quantity versus quality" supply driven education system and this has resulted in a huge increase in the number of school-leavers, graduates, and postgraduates. However, the system has failed to keep pace with the overall quality of its school-leavers and graduates. Therefore, not all school-leavers and graduates are able to secure jobs commensurate with

[1] This measure counts the number of graduates who are employed, self-employed, or in further education at the time of convocation, which is three to six months after they have completed their studies.

their qualification profile, nor fit into the requirements of the employment market. The skill mismatch has led Malaysia to lag behind other more talented and innovative knowledge-driven East Asian economies like, South Korea, Taiwan, Japan, and neighbouring Singapore.

Notwithstanding the glaring underperformance of the country's public schools and the tertiary institutions to meet the country's talent needs, the government, the schools, and the universities are in a denial mode. To abate the perennial issue of poor-quality education and in particular graduate unemployment and underemployment, the Government and the Ministry of Higher Education have taken measures to overcome the problem of surplus graduates and the mismatch between output of graduates and market needs. Ministry of Higher Education has committed itself to a ten-shift transformation programme to transform both the public and private higher education system to spur excellence. The thrust of the shifts are underscored to transform the system to achieve: (1) holistic, entrepreneurial, and balanced graduates; (2) talent excellence; (3) national lifelong learners; (4) quality TVET graduates; (5) financial stability; (6) empowered governance; (7) innovation ecosystems; (8) global prominence; (9) globalized online learning; and (10) transformed higher education delivery. The Ministry of Higher Education has frozen irrelevant and non-viable courses to overcome the glut of graduates in the job market. In addition, new industry-oriented courses and dual-degree programmes have been identified (The Sun, March 17, 2017).

The Malaysian Ministry of Higher Education has taken steps to redesign its curriculum to produce "holistic, entrepreneurial, and balanced" graduates in line with the National Education Philosophy. It directed some of the country's public universities from the new semester in 2016 to implement an Integrated Cumulative Grade Point Average (iCGPA) system. Through this mandatory iCGPA system the anticipation is that the public universities are expected to produce academically excellent as well as "holistic, balanced, and entrepreneurial" graduates. Under the system, students will graduate with "a complete report card" that evaluates and details both their performance and academic achievements as well as in their students' professional capability in entrepreneurship, management, social and communication, and knowledge skills. All these attributes will be displayed in a "spider web" format (The Star, September 2, 2016a). Will this "subjective" and "nebulous" iCGPA evaluative system drive the country's tertiary institutions to achieve the "mythical pot of gold at the end of the rainbow?".

Building Blocks

If Malaysia wants to successfully compete in the world marketplace and achieve high-income status and leap into the future, then the country has to be underpinned by a vibrant and robust knowledge-driven economy to face the challenges of the Fourth Industrial Revolution (defined by economies driven by robotics and artificial intelligence). This requires the country to put in place a strong broad-based world-class educational architecture that enables the workforce to acquire updated and new skills throughout their careers. A flexible and affordable market-driven lifelong education provision that enables workers to earn, learn, and adapt to their continuously changing work environment as a viable option is critical (Economist, January 14, 2017a).

Malaysia has "a colossal mismatch for a country ramping up towards Industry 4.0 requirements and the type of companies that we attract as investors into the country" says Sharala Axryd, the Chief Executive Officer of The Centre for Applied Data Science (Sunday Star, September 6, 2020). The nation faces a huge talent and skill deficit in spite of the fact that Malaysia's successive five-year development plans since independence have recognized and emphasized human resource development as one of the key drivers to its overall growth and economic prosperity. Therefore, the basic questions to ask are: Why is the country's public/private and to a high degree the centralized education system including the universities not producing the critical mass of high quality, creative, and innovative human capital? Skills mismatch is still a major and persistent issue of concern to the nation's employers (Sunday Star, September 6, 2020). What steps have to be taken to prepare students to meet the country's industrial requirements as well as to face the Fourth Industrial Revolution and to fulfil the country's ambitious vision to be a vibrant technologically driven, high-productive, export-oriented, and competitive high-income developed nation as well as lay the foundation to leap into the future? For Malaysia to be a creative and innovative society the government has to urgently launch radical structural changes to the education system to meet the challenge.

As pointed out earlier in this chapter, the quantitative achievement of the Malaysian education system at all levels is remarkable. However, there are many paradoxes and asymmetries that are impeding the system from realizing its full potential. Principally Malaysia's phenomenally expanded public education system is racially polarized, with 97% Bumiputera pupils in national schools, while 96% of students in Chinese schools are ethnic Chinese and Tamil schools have an equal percentage of ethnic Tamils (Rahman, 2020). The ethnic drift combined with the politically resolute highly skewed race-based affirmative action policy has been a major factor hindering the opportunity gap of every Malaysian pupil irrespective of race. It has impeded the vital issues of access, equity, quality, human capacity, efficiency, and unity, the critical enabling ingredients to drive an inclusive and fully participatory, creative, and innovative education system to drive growth and prosperity.

The country now with a sense of urgency needs a precise, sustainable, and inclusive education provision. Firstly, it has to unite the country's children, from diverse economic, racial, and ethnic backgrounds, in order to create social cohesion, a common Malaysian citizenship and political stability. Secondly, it needs to support a common education system to mould students coming from diverse racial, religious, and economic background into a skilled and talented pool of human capital to meet the challenges of the accelerating technological and managerial changes a prerequisite to drive economic development and growth. Thirdly, education at all levels must be properly funded and in particular the country must provide the universities sufficient resources for quality teaching, research, and innovation, while ensuring that all bright students from disadvantaged backgrounds who can benefit from higher education are given access with financial aid. Finally, it needs to rigorously monitor and implement the MEB the MOE has established an independent unit called the Performance and Delivery Unit (PADU). Time will only tell the effectiveness of this machinery.

Malaysia fundamentally requires a much broader, longer-term structural solution to its education system. The country's policy pundits have to rethink the competitive world of work within a technologically advancing high-income country and the purpose of education within it. The race-based affirmative action policy barrier has prevented a large number of talented non-Bumiputera from entering the public education system and this has been both counter-productive as well as unjust. In a diverse educational environment, the interlocking aspects of student's experience can reinforce one another and benefit society. The education system must take cognizance of a more inclusive approach and must be closely interlocked with the labour market to bridge the gap between the talent needs of employers and the education provision. An inclusive high-quality education provision with learning in Bahasa Malaysia, English, and the mother tongue of non-Malay students (a policy initiative that was incorporated in the Education Enactment of Act, 1952) in school will promote among students a culture of critical thinking, reasoning, problem-solving, decision-making, and communication ability with a global outlook. Inclusivity and diversity from school to tertiary level education will give rise to a critical mass of human capital that is creative, innovative, and productivity-driven. Though there is a concerted effort in the Education Blueprint to shift the school education from "rote learning" to "creative and critical thinking" this has to be further reinforced and fully implemented. The aim must be to redesign the Malaysian education system towards a comprehensive and integrated provision that is well funded, efficiently executed by a diverse and competent teaching and administrative staff buttressed by a variety of academic as well as a vocational and technical (TVET) and ICT provision, valued by all Malaysian parents and students.

STEM education has to be a national priority and a core part of the country's education system at all levels. Science (including medicine), technology, engineering, mathematics, and medicine permeate every aspect of today's world. In a knowledge intensive scientific world Malaysia needs to build its capacity in global science to be competitive. Therefore, STEM education is important to transform the country into a knowledge and innovative intensive-based society (NST, July 19, 2017). The aim must be to demystify science and scientific culture with its spread and penetration both within all levels of the school and tertiary systems and make it simple and understandable. The focus has to be a national policy strategy to encompass all the country's educational institutions and the population at large. The aim must be to enhance the scientific capacity and quality of the country by incentivizing and recruiting the country's best science talents with incentivized career paths. The top priority of country's STEM education system must be to inspire and encourage a pool of talented scientist with a diversity of perspectives both at school and tertiary levels and merge them with the fast globally advancing diverse science and technology knowledge platform. The country has to priorities STEM subjects in areas of economic and societal importance which deliver strong graduate employment outcomes. The quality of teaching and research staff with English proficiency is a critical ingredient to achieve this. Through this policy strategy the country will be able to domestically mentor, nurture, and incubate a diverse pool of more rounded and innovation-

driven scientific community. One way to incubate more rounded graduates is to get the university departments to work closer together and not in silos. In other words, universities should become more interdisciplinary. For example, engineering departments should work closely with faculty members of art and design and medicine should work closely with sociologists, psychologists, and economists.

Further, it is crucial that Malaysia must seek to end the brain drain and promote international outlook of student enrolment and academic staff in the country, if it is to produce a premium quality workforce and reach output capable of propelling the country to leap forward into a developed nation status.

For this to be realized, Malaysia must revisit the key planks of its policy blueprints and turn its focus towards inclusivity and full participation over selectivity and restrictive access to all levels of its education provision. To upgrade the quality of education the system must be governed by merit in the selection and grading of students and teachers at every level. Values of academic freedom and autonomy that leading universities of the world take for granted in order to attract the best and brightest students, teachers, and academics from all segments of society has to be instituted. The development of lifelong learning and its credentials has become an economic and social necessity and it can be facilitated through flexible digital education. The system will be able to create people with flexible skills that will enable them to adapt to different jobs. This is critical as increasingly in the economy jobs are no more lifelong and graduates with flexible skills can find new jobs in economic downturns.

This system must be embedded and made a critical component of the country's education system. This can act as a catalyst for the transformation of the national education system with a stronger link with society and reduce the prevailing marked digital as well as the prevailing knowledge divide in the country. The tertiary institutions are the nerve centres of the country's education and as such they have to create more flexible programmes. In particular, provide to the working population more lifelong learning and periodic retraining throughout their multiple careers. A sustained lifelong education and retraining programme has to be a new normal of the country's tertiary education system. This will enable Malaysia to consistently create and upgrade a holistic, innovative, entrepreneurial, and talented human capital base to fuel its social, economic, and cultural transformation.

There is an urgent need to help students make more informed choices about where and what to study and ensure they are getting value for money. In addition, students should be protected from miss-selling institutions and inexperienced young people should be provided the advice they need when making one of the biggest financial decisions of their life.

Teacher quality is central to achieve excellence in any education system. Malaysia is in dire need of high quality and racially diverse teaching profession at all levels of its education system. The recruitment of academically qualified teachers and academics from the country's diverse communities is vital. This has to be reinforced with regular in service professional development for teachers, school heads, and other educational professionals. As technology is today the main medium of connectivity and knowledge transfer highway, it is critical that teachers should be well prepared in ICT competencies. Technology-based teaching and learning both in school and home could provide students the opportunity to improve their academic outcomes. Teachers' professional competency has to be assessed on a regular basis and linked to student performance. Both their professional development and performance assessment has to be linked to their salaries and other professional incentives.

While there is no need to organize new committees, existing national committees should vet, monitor, and appraise all existing programmes with stringent performance standards. The committee should be required to screen best practices across the world that can be adapted to match Malaysia's education objectives and structure.

Conclusion

The government since independence has launched several limited and anodyne ad hoc policy initiatives with massive investments to reform the education system but mainly to create many new institutions as well as reimage the system and its provision to meet the near-term politically driven challenges. The many policy initiatives that have shaped the country's education system have yet to explicitly recognize the root structural causes of the country's education malaise and redesign its architect to empower all Malaysians to participate in it to produce high-quality human capital to meet today's as well as the future competitive global economy. Thus, Malaysia to leap forward has to initiate a robust and vibrant education system that is inclusive and innovative that produces motivated and creative workforce for a globally competitive economic system. The NEP's race-based affirmative action policy, has, apart from impeding an inclusive, diversified, skills-based, and scientifically oriented education system, had created deep-rooted inequalities, quality glitches, mismatches, and employability problems. This has driven the country to persistently face an acute shortage of a skilled and talented workforce, a problem that has become more serious as Malaysia seeks to strengthen its technological capability in pursuit of an advanced country status and leap forwards towards a high-income country. The shortage is further compounded by the out migration of whatever talent the country is left with.

However, in a rapidly globalizing and technologically driven world, to meet the long-term challenges Malaysia's policies have to be forward-looking and drive high-quality talent and skillsets to be responsive to rapid technological changes. To achieve this Malaysia has to consciously move away from the opaque, race-based exclusive and socially unjust policies that has dominated the county's public education provision and employment for the last five decades. The government must have the political will to jettison this debilitating policy and instead, enact and articulate through a widespread consultative process with a range of stakeholders to chart-out an inclusive, common, and sustainable long-term national education vision and agenda underpinned by a need-based affirmative action policy. The national education system has to be reinforced by STEM fields and at the same time nature and imbibe students with the critical "soft skills" that gives them the ability to collaborate, interact, and navigate in the global economy.

Only a policy of inclusivity and implemented effectively and efficiently can move the country towards a high skill, high income, and developed-nation status as envisioned. This entails the designing of a new optimistic road map as well as the setting-up benchmarks and measurements to move towards a futuristic and engaged inclusive education system. These measurements have to be accompanied by clear and transparent targets based on key benchmarks and high academic standards. Building blocks and the targets to be achieved are the proposals, but the real solution is ultimately political.

Acknowledgements I wish to acknowledge the contribution of Professor Rajah Rasiah and Mr. Sarraf Rajesh Kumar.

References

Achariam, Timothy. (2016). *English has deteriorated since the 60s*. The Sun, March 9, 2016.

Ahmad Ibrahim. (2015). *Science Education in Malaysia needs Urgent Overhaul*. New Strait Times, July 27, 2015.

Aina Nasa. (2017). *33 Colleges Ordered to Close: Move to ensure quality of education, says minister*. New Strait Times December 19, 2017.

Azman Ujang. (2017a). *Being English savvy, a must*. The Sun, Friday May 5.

Azman Ujang. (2017b). *Reverse decline in English*. The Sun, Friday, October 6.

Azura, & Aina Nasa. (2017). Students will be placed in other higher learning institutions New Straits Times, December 22, 2017.

Bok, Derek. (2013). Higher Education in America. Princeton: Princeton University Press.

Cheong, K. C., Selvaratnam, V., & Goh, K. L. (2011). Education and human capital formation. In R. Rasiah, (Ed.), *Malaysian economy: Unfolding growth and change*. Kuala Lumpur: Oxford University Press (pp.159–184).

Collini, Stefan. (2012). *What Are Universities For*. London: Penguin Books.

Dore, Ronald. (1997). *The Diploma Disease: Education, qualification and development*. London: Institute of Education (2nd edition).

Douglas, John Aubrey. (Ed.) (2016). *The New Flagship University; Changing the Paradigm from Global Ranking to National Relevancy*. New York: Palgrave Macmillan.

Dzulkifli Abdul Razak. (2016). *Bridging gaps in science education*. New Sunday Times, April 17, 2016.

Economist, April 5, (2014). Is the college worth? p. 22.

Economist, May 30, (2015). Men Adrift. p. 16.

Economist, June 4, (2016). *Under Attack: Curbs on free speech are growing tighter. It is time to speak out*. pp. 9–10.

Economist, December 10, (2016). *Global Education: Homework for all*. p. 16.

Economist, January 14, (2017). *Lifelong Learning*. p. 9.

Economist, March 27, (2017). *Breaking Free: Scientific publishing*. pp. 10–11.

EPU, (2015). Transforming Technical and Vocational Education and Training to Meet Industry Demand, Economic Planning Unit, Malaysia, downloaded from http://www.epu.gov.my/sites/default/files/Strategy%20Paper%2009.pdf.

Focus week, May 30, 2015.

Focus week, January 15, 2017.

Focus week, September 9–15, 2017.

FOM (Federation of Malaya), Education Act 1961, Act of Parliament, No. 45 Kuala Lumpur: Government Printers, 1961.

Ghavifekr Simin & Ibrahim Mohammed Sani. (2015). Effectiveness of ICT Integration in Malaysian Schools: A Quantitative Analysis. International Research Journal for Quality Education Vol. 2(8), August 2015. pp. 1–12.

Goodall, Amanda H., (2009). Socrates in the Boardroom: Why Research Universities Should be led by Top Scholars. Princeton: Princeton University Press.

Government of India. (2009). Recommendations of the National Knowledge Commission. New Delhi: Government of India.

Hazlina Aziz (2017). Digital education still ambigious in schools. NST, December 21, 2017.

HEPC-Higher Education Planning Committee. (1967). Report of the Higher Education Planning Committee. Kuala Lumpur: Government Printers.

Kang Soon Chen (2016). *Poor Show in PISA Ranking*. The Star, February 12, 2016.

Kee-Cheok Cheong, Viswanathan Selvaratnam, & Kim-leng Goh, (2011). Education and Human Capital Formation in Rajah Rasiah (ed.) Malaysian Economy: Unfolding Growth and Change. Kuala Lumpur: Oxford University Press. pp. 159–184.

Jaafar, S. S. (2019). *Special report: PTPTN in search of a Sustainable model*. The Edge.

Jan, W. S. W. (2020). Malaysia's student loan company: Tackling the PTPTN time bomb. ISEAS: Yusof Ishak Institute.

Koh See Hoh. (2016). *Jobless rate among grads worsening*. Sun, December 14, 2016.

Krishna Iyer, Bhavani. (2016). *Doing it right the first time*. The Sun, April 5, 2016.

Lee, M. N. N. (2004). Restructuring Higher Education in Malaysia. Monograph Series: No. 4/2002. School of Education Studies. Pulau Pinang: Universiti Sains Malaysia.

Leete, Richard. (2007). Malaysia from Kampong to Twin Towers: 50 Years of Economic and Social Development. Shah Alam, Malaysia: Oxford Fajar Sdn Bhd.

Lucas, R. (1988). On the mechanics of economic development. *Journal of Monetary Economics, 22*(1), 3–42.

Mahathir Mohamad. (1970). *The Malay Dilemma*. Kuala Lumpur: Times Book International.

Mail-on-line, September 10, 2016.

Malaysiakini, October 15, 2017 (Be a boss not a worker, Najib tells undergraduate).

Marginson, Simon. (2012). Review of Ranking and the reshaping of higher education: The battle for world-class excellence by Ellen Hazelkorn, Houndmillan UK, Palgrave Macmillan, 2011 in Journal of Higher Education Policy and Management, Vol. 34, No 5 October, 2012, pp. 557–560.

Marginson, Simon. (2016). Higher Education and the Common Good. Melbourne: University Publishing Limited.

McCormick, Christopher. (2017). *The link between English and economics*. World Economic Forum in collaboration with Harvard Business Review.

Ministry of Education (MOE). (1980). *Cabinet Committee Report (Mahathir Report)*. Kuala Lumpur: Ministry of Education.

Ministry of Education (MOE). (1980). *Ageneral Review of Major Trends in Higher Education in Malaysia: A Country Paper*. Presented to the UNESCO Study Group on Regional Cooperation in Higher Education in Asia and Oceania, Bangkok 19–25 February. (Mimeograph).

Ministry of Education (MOE). (2013). Malaysian Education Blueprint-2013–2025 (Preschool to Post-Secondary Education). Putrajaya: Ministry of Education.
Ministry of Education (MOE). (2013–2019). Malaysian Education Statistics: Quick Facts. Putrajaya: Education and Planning Research Division.
Ministry of Education (MOE). (2015). Malaysian Education Blueprint-2015–2025 (Higher Education-HE). Putrajaya: Ministry of Education.
Ministry of Higher Education Malaysia (MOHE). (2012). The National Graduate Employability Blueprint 2012–2017. Serdang: Universiti Putra Malaysia Press.
Mohamed Mustafa Ishak. (2020). Setara rating system must be continually enhanced NST, September 7, 2020.
Musa Hitam. (2016). Frankly Speaking. Petaling Jaya: Pelanduk Publications (M) SDN BHD.
National Economic Advisory Council (NEAC). (2010). New Economic Model for Malaysia, Part 1&11. Kuala Lumpur: Percetaken Nasional Malaysia Berhad.
Noor Ashimah Abdul Rahman. (2020). What our education system needs in The Edge Malaysia, September 14, 2020.
NST (New Strait Times), August 4, 2015.
NST (New Strait Times), November 16, 2015.
NST (New Strait Times), January 9, 2016.
NST (New Strait Times), September 7, 2016.
NST (New Strait Times), November 13, 2016.
NST (New Strait Times), November 17, 2016.
NST (New Strait Times). *Ekuinas' Iltizam programme boosts graduates' employability*. December 27, 2017.
NST (New Strait Times). *Malaysia Training Scheme: Matching graduates with jobs*. March 20, 2018.
NST (New Strait Times). Raising the Bar: NTP Boosts Education System. March 31, 2018.
OECD (Organization of European Economic Development). (2016). *Review of Innovation Policy: Malaysia*. Paris: OECD
Rahman Talib Education Committee Report. (1960). Kuala Lumpur: Government Printers.
Rajendram, Rebecca. (2016). Roadmap to continue enhancing English levels. Star, August 31, 2016.
Rasiah, R., Mansor, N., & Chandran, V. G. R. (2015). Royal Professor Ungku Abdul Aziz: A key pillar in Malaysia's development. *Institutions and Economies, 7*(3), 1–19.
Rasiah, R., & Osman, R. H. (1996). Training and Productivity in Malaysian Manufacturing. *IKMAS Working Paper* No. 12.
Razak Education Committee Report. (1956). Kuala Lumpur: Government Printers.
Romer, P. (1986). Increasing returns and Long run growth. *Journal of Political Economy, 94*, 1002–1037.
Sahlberg, Pasi. (2011). Finish Lessons: What can the world learn from educational change in Finland? Teacher's College, Columbia University.
Salmi, Jamil. (2009). *The Challenge of Establishing World-Class Universities*. Washington, DC: The World Bank.
Schumpeter, Joseph. (1934). Depressions. In Economics of Recovery Programme, ed. D. Brown et al. New York: MacGraw-Hill.
Schumpeter, Joseph. (1942). *Capitalism, Socialism and Democracy*. New York: Harper & Sons.
Selvaratnam, Viswanathan. (2016). Malaysia's Higher Education and Quest for Developed Nation Status by 2020 in Southeast Asian Affairs, 2016 (Ed.) Cook, Malcim and Daljit Singh. Singapore: Aziz Ishak Institute of Southeast Asian Studies (ISEAS), pp. 199–224.
Selvaratnam, V. (2019). Malaysia's national language policy and graduate employability, International higher education, No. 96, pp. 16–18.
Sen, Amartiya. (2009). Capitalism beyond Crisis in New York Review of Books, 9 March 2009.
Star, May 23, 2015.
Star, September 2, 2016.
Star, October 6, 2016.

Star, Sunday 8, September, 2020.
Sun, May 23, 2015.
Sun, September 9, 2016.
Sun, March 17, 2017.
Surowiecki, James. (2015). Why the rich are so Much Richer in New York Review of Books, 24 September 2015.
Syahirah Syed Jaafar. (2019). Special Report: PTPTN in search of a Sustainable model. The Edge, December 7, 2019.
Tan, Emilia, & Yojana Sharma. (2013). Uproar over 'race bias' in public university places in University World News, July 17 Issue No. 281.
Thiruchelvam, K., VGR Chandran, Ng Boon-Kwee, & Wong Chan-Yuan. (2004). Malaysia's Quest for Innovation: Progress and Lessons Learned. Petaling Jaya: SIRD.
Times Higher Education (THE) Asia. (2016). World University Rankings 2016–2017, June 23, 2016.
Welsh, Bridget, & Chin Ung-Ho (Eds.) (2013). Awakening: Abdullah Badawi Years in Malaysia. Kuala Lumpur: Strategic Information and Research Development Centre.
Wildavsky, Ben. (2010). The Great Brain Race: How Global Universities Are Reshaping the World. Princeton: Princeton University Press.
World Bank. (1993). The East Asian Miracle: Economic Growth and Public Policy. Washington DC, International Bank for Reconstruction and World Bank.
World Bank. (2013, December). Malaysian Economic Monitor: High-Performing Education. Bangkok: World Bank Office.
World Bank. (2014, June). Malaysian Economic Monitor: Boosting Trade Competitiveness. Bangkok: World Bank Office.
World Bank. (2016, December). Quest for Productivity Growth. Kuala Lumpur: World Bank Office.
Young, K., Bussink, W., & Hasan, P. (1980). *Malaysia: Growth and Equity in a Multiracial Society*. New York: Oxford University Press.
Yuen Meikeng. (2016). Towards a better tomorrow (Science, Technology and Innovation Minister Datuk Seri Madius Tangu spells out the need to look beyond 2020 to gear Malaysia up for what lies ahead, stating that a lot of work needs to be done to prepare the nation for the future) Sunday Star, April 24, 2016.

Viswanathan Selvaratnam is a third-generation Malaysian and a World Bank retiree. He had previously taught at the University of Malaya and the National University of Singapore.

Chapter 9
Talent and Human Capital

Cheong Kee Cheok and Than Lee Lee

Abstract Two global trends that shape, and will likely continue to shape, the fortunes of economies in the decades ahead, are growth through technology and globalization. Both trends speak strongly to the need to develop "human capital". Developing "talent" in the sense of nurturing the deepening of human capital has to be a vital part of any country's development agenda. Malaysia has a vision of advancing from its current status as an upper-middle-income country to become an advanced country by 2050. But its global standing shows a quality deficit. Education, the primary indicator of talent, shows this deficit. Additionally, Malaysia's technical and vocational education training (TVET) system suffers from major weaknesses of its own. A major source of talent, international students, has not been effectively tapped. Nor has tacit knowledge been leveraged from the workforce. Talent development is maximized when all major components contribute to building up the country's talent base. Examples exist of other countries and/or institutions that have been successful in each of the areas. Lessons should be drawn from their experience. For instance, Singapore's education and TVE systems are world-class and worthy of emulation. For attracting talent, the economic work environment, the promise of a bright future, sustained government and institutional support, and a regulatory framework that recognizes meritocracy are important drivers. These same policies serve to retain talent. Finally, match between the expertise of diasporic talent and the technological capability of industries in the home country is needed to facilitate skill transfer to and technological catch-up by the latter.

Keywords Human capital · Talent development · Meritocracy · Technical and vocational education and training

C. K. Cheok (✉)
Asia-Europe Institute, University of Malaya, 50603 Kuala Lumpur, Malaysia

T. L. Lee
Faculty of Business and Economics and Administration, University of Malaya, 50603 Kuala Lumpur, Malaysia

R. Rasiah et al. (eds.), *Malaysia's Leap Into the Future*, Dynamics of Asian Development, https://doi.org/10.1007/978-981-16-7045-9_9

Introduction

There are two global trends today that shape, and will likely continue to shape the fortunes of economies in the decades ahead. These are growth through technology and globalization. Technology as a source of growth has captured the attention of a growing group of scholars ever since Schumpeter surfaced his notion of "creative destruction" and is firmly embedded in neoclassical theories of economic growth. These theories have been given substance not only by early innovators like the US and Europe but by latecomers Japan, and most recently Korea, Taiwan, and a rapidly rising China. With many countries adopting an export-driven growth strategy and many more opening to trade, globalization has proceeded at a pace that is hard to reverse.[1] This pace is driven increasingly less by the volume of trade than by changes in its nature, such as the growth of production networks and by technology both as an enabler of globalization and its substance. Globalization has therefore intensified competition for a country's products. But the process has moved beyond products; ideas have also been globalized, enabled by the rapid development of information and communications technology (ICT).

Both trends speak strongly to the need to develop "human capital", a term popularized by Mincer (1958), Schultz (1961), and Becker (1964), the resources—knowledge, skills, experience, training, and wisdom possessed individually and collectively by individuals in a population. Developing countries have a scarcity of human capital; for some of these, this scarcity, combined with the lack of institutional capacity, will not permit them to reap the benefits of globalization (see, for instance, Polaski, 2006). The lack of human capital also becomes a binding constraint as countries, having reached middle-income, fail to move up the income ladder, falling instead into the "middle-income trap" (Gill & Kharas, 2007).

Developing "talent" in the sense of nurturing the deepening of human capital therefore has to be a vital part of any country's development agenda. Globalization plays a role here too. What has emerged is a "global talent war" which is manifesting itself through individual countries' competing to bring talent to their shores and through talented individuals taking full advantage of what the globalization of talent has to offer. In this "war", developing countries are at a disadvantage. Even as human capital is built up through education, it is being lost through skilled labour outmigration—the so-called "brain drain". For these countries, then, the challenge is not only to develop talent but to retain it. Doing both is referred to collectively as "talent management". What are the ingredients needed to achieve success and what lessons can be learned from experience in the context of the role of the state are the themes of this chapter.

The discussion is framed in terms of Malaysia in the year 2050. Malaysia has a vision of advancing from its current status as an upper-middle-income country to become an advanced country. Mahathir's 1991-announced Vision 2020 wants this to occur by year 2020. Achieving higher-income represents but the means to

[1] This is despite the protectionist stance adopted in the early days of the Trump presidency in the US, the advent of the UK's exit from the European Union, and talk of "peak globalization".

an end. That end is to upgrade the economy to a "knowledge economy" through technological advance that translates into high value-added production. By then, Malaysia will become a country where talent is appreciated and valued; have an intelligent society that embraces thought leadership of individuals and institutions to advance itself; count many technologists driving innovation, is characterized by intense competition for talent, sees the replacement of brain drain by brain circulation, and flexible and adaptable organizations that effectively manage and reward talent. This Vision, unlikely to be achieved in 2020, now just a few years away, for reasons elaborated upon below, nevertheless serves as an appropriate template for the desired scenario for 2050. The key questions this chapter seeks answers to are (1) what is Malaysia's talent situation today, (2) what must be done to achieve these objectives, and (3) what lessons of experience can be drawn from other countries?

Before framing the context of present-day Malaysia as the starting point for initiatives needed to realize the vision for 2050, the concept of talent development needs to be clarified. This is undertaken in the next section through a brief literature review. Section 9.3 describes where Malaysia is today in terms of talent. Section 9.4 examines approaches to talent management. These approaches draw on the experiences of many countries which have been successful in attracting talent including returning diaspora and retaining them. The conditions needed to achieve success are also highlighted, in assessing whether Malaysia can fulfil these conditions.

Theoretical Considerations

The link between the accumulation of human capital and economic growth has been extensively documented. This link is manifested through early work by, among others, Becker (1964) and Mincer (1974) that estimated the returns to education. Macroeconomic growth models have also incorporated human capital as a driver of growth. These models range from neoclassical models (for example, Solow, 1957) to endogenous growth models to which evolutionary growth theory contributes (Aghion & Howitt, 1998; Romer, 1986; Lucas, 1988, Barro, 1991, Barro & Sala-I-Martin, 1995; Schumpeter, 1942 and others). The contribution of human capital to growth is also estimated through growth accounting (Griliches, 1997; Jorgenson & Fraumeni, 1992). It is supported by an even larger body of evidence, for which literature reviews readily exist (for instance, Blundell et al., 1999; Hanushek, 2013; Psacharopoulos & Patrinos, 2004; Sianesi, 2003). Full review of theories and evidence appears in Chap. 6 and need not be repeated here.

While the above arguments and evidence would also lend support to grooming talent, with its large conceptual overlap with human capital,[2] considerably less has been written about the impact of talent on growth. This is changing, thanks to the rise of the "talent economy" (Martin, 2014). Klaus Schwab (2015), convener of the World

[2] It has been argued that the two concepts are distinct. Taylor (2007) argues that talent refers more to the individual while human capital refers to the collective value of humans as an asset.

Economic Forum, wrote about unlocking latent talent as the new key to economic growth. Bianchi (2009) argued for the importance of matching entrepreneurial talent to production technologies, with the extent of financial development affecting this match. Cubas et al. (2015) posited that countries at different levels of economic development differed in two key dimensions—talent and total factor productivity, with talent in rich countries much higher than in developing ones. Mellander and Florida (2012) surveyed literature that contributed to what they termed "the skills revolution", attributable to human capital and "the creative class" (talent), noting the importance of place in attracting talent which explains differences in regional access to talent. In a similar vein, talent has also been recognized as essential for city development (Cortright, 2016).

Recognition of the importance of talent has sparked a "talent war". Globalization has intensified this not only in the sense that movement of people seeking education and training as well as employment in sought-after occupations across borders have become much easier but also production processes have become mobile, with employment to follow. Chambers et al. (1998) were among the first to highlight this growing trend, warning that US talent-building strategies were inadequate. Others also believed technological advances embedded into production processes and growing skill deficits will see these talent wars intensify (Docquier & Machado, 2016), while the avenues for mobility have also increased (Kuputsch & Pang, 2006).

In this "war", advanced countries have an advantage both in terms of the remuneration package they can offer migrants seeking work, a better living environment, superior education, and training facilities for aspiring students, as well as increasing incentives to attract skilled migrants and to encourage students to stay on. Little wonder an increasing body of research on "brain drain" has emerged (for instance, Gaillard & Gaillard, 1997; Gibson & McKenzie, 2011). This literature is punctuated by sentiments of alarm well-expressed in Malaysia's New Economic Model Report (2010: 54): "We are not developing talent and what we do have is leaving".

Recent research has tempered this pessimism. Instead of "brain drain", reference is increasingly made to "brain circulation" in which emigrants return or transfer their skills to their countries of origin (Dodani & LaPorte, 2005; Gaillard & Gaillard, 1997; Saxenian, 2005). It has also been argued (Hanushek, 2013) that the focus on school attainment has obscured the need to assess cognitive skills and other dimensions of human capital. As a result, innovative policies to orchestrate brain circulation have hardly been explored. Indeed, the role of the state in talent management is likewise in short supply (Khilji et al., 2015). Further, as Tyson (2017) argues, the war for talent is "shaped by political considerations that go beyond talent building and retention philosophies designed to improve employee value propositions and managerial performances". Finally, cases of brain drain reversal (see below) are arguably the most convincing argument that such reversals can occur given the right circumstances (see also Perkins et al., forthcoming).

These considerations suggest that brain drain is not an irreversible process or even one where conventional economic sources of brain drain need to be fully addressed. This should lead to optimism that Malaysia's situation today, however deficient, can ultimately be reformed and strengthened to approach its long-term ideal.

Malaysian Context

Any projection into an ideal future must be cognizant of the present, because the gap between the latter and the former represents the ground that must be made up to reach the ideal. It also reveals the areas of strengths that can be leveraged and weaknesses that must be remedied.

The Macro View

Where does Malaysia stand in the international talent war? Two sources provide scores and rankings for the existence of talent in a group of countries, including Malaysia. The first is the IMD World Talent Ranking produced by the IMD World Competitiveness Center (IMD, 2014). The ranking is structured according to three factors: (1) "investment and development", with indicators like public expenditure on education, pupil-teacher ratio, and female labour force, (2) "appeal", with indicators like cost of living, quality of life, and brain drain, and (3) "readiness", with indicators like labour force growth, skilled labor, university education, and language skills (IMD, 2014: 3–4).

By this ranking, Malaysia has done very well despite falling 14 places between 2014 and 2016 (Table 9.1). In 2016, it is ranked 19th in the world, still besting such talent powerhouses as Korea (38th in 2016) and Taiwan (24). The IMD figures also show Malaysia's ranking to have risen rapidly from 20 to sixth by 2010, but declining sharply between 2014 and 2016, whereas for the two comparator countries mentioned above, rankings have all fallen during the period. Until 2014, IMD credited Malaysia's gains to advances in all three factors, citing especially improvements in

Table 9.1 Benchmarked talent ranking Among Asian Countries, 2005–2016

Country	World talent ranking			
	2005	2010	2014	2016
China	48	46	43	43
India	29	34	48	60
Indonesia	49	37	25	44
Hong Kong	13	21	21	10
Korea	35	35	40	38
Malaysia	*20*	*6*	*5*	*19*
Philippines	38	45	41	51
Singapore	10	8	16	15
Taiwan	18	19	27	24
Thailand	25	24	34	37

Source IMD (2014: 12; 2016: 57)

the availability of skilled labour and in the "ability of the country's educational institutions to meet the talent requirement of the market" (IMD, 2014: 10). However, its fall in 2016 has been attributed to falls in all the three factors cited above (IMD, 2016: 57).

There is however another ranking produced by the Economist Intelligence Unit, and called the Global Talent Index (GTI). In contrast to the indicators used by IMD, the GTI is estimated using qualitative indicators—the quality of compulsory education, of universities and business schools, and of the environment to nurture talent, the mobility and openness of the labour market, the stock and flow of FDI, and the proclivity for attracting talent. Data have been collected through a combination of a global survey and selected in-depth interview (Heidrik & Struggles, 2015: 1). In 2015, the GTI was expanded to over 60 countries and a backward estimate for 2011 was made for comparison with 2015.

As Table 9.2 shows, the picture changes significantly when quality indices are used. The findings of IMD studies are not only contradicted but also reversed. Not only is Malaysia no longer a star performer—it's ranking in 2011 was in the bottom half of countries surveyed—but also it's ranking has also fallen in the last four years to almost the bottom one-third. The newly industrialized economies (NIEs) Hong Kong, Korea, Singapore, and Taiwan are well above Malaysia in ranking and so are China's and India's.

While, based on other criteria of capability (see, for instance, Chap. 2, __), the EIU Index appears more plausible than the IMD ranking that shows Malaysia's talent base being superior to the NIEs', indices of this kind suffer two major deficiencies. First, they are aggregated from subjectively chosen indicators, no matter how reasonable

Table 9.2 Benchmarked talent index among selected Asian countries, 2007–2015

Country	Global talent index			
	2007	2012	2011	2015
China	8	6	33	31
India	10	10	35	35
Indonesia	29	29	58	56
Hong Kong	n.a	n.a	8	10
Korea (South)	15	13	22	21
Malaysia	*12*	*12*	*36*	*39*
Philippines	n.a	n.a	44	44
Singapore	n.a	n.a	5	6
Taiwan	n.a	n.a	20	19
Thailand	22	22	46	45
Total # countries	30	30	60	60

n.a. = not available.
Sources For 2011 and 2015 (Heidrick & Struggles, 2015: 4–5); for 2007 and 2012, Heidrick and Struggles website http://weknowglobaltalent.com/gti/window/gti.

these indicators may be in reflecting talent. Second, they assume these indicators can be compared across countries. For instance, the IMD ranking uses as an indicator the unemployment rate. But does Malaysia's low unemployment rate for its low-technology cheap labour model score higher than a higher unemployment rate for South Korea's heavy industry model? Thus, while some indicators, such as the quality of university education (EIU Index) are clearly germane to the availability of talent, these aggregate indices cannot provide much insight into key elements of talent development and their evolution. This insight must come from examining the key components of talent development themselves in some detail. Yet, dimensions that go to make up these indices can prove to be useful, as described next.

Talent Development Components

The first component is education. Malaysia's education is the subject of another Chap. 6. For reasons cited in that chapter, Malaysia's education system is well funded but suffers from a malaise that has seen it losing ground in international comparison, as shown in Table 11.4 in Chap. 11. In both tests for the Trends in International Mathematics and Science Study (TIMSS), conducted every four years[3] and the OECD study Program for International Student Assessment (PISA) conducted in 2009, 2012, and 2015, Malaysia's absolute scores, not just rankings, in mathematics and science for grade eight-equivalent students have fallen between 1999 and 2011, although reviving somewhat in 2015, and dipping below the international average score of 500 by 2007. This stands in sharp contrast to the performance of the NIEs which consistently top all other countries. The results from PISA are similar.

Beyond academic education, technical and vocational education and training (TVET) should be an important component of the nation's education system. Unfortunately, beyond just small numbers enrolled and despite major improvement over the years, Malaysia's TVET system suffers from major weaknesses of its own. In a recently completed study for the World Bank, Cheong et al. (2013) concluded that several major challenges emanate from the government's supervision and delivery of TVET programmes, the lack of coordination among major stakeholders, especially public and private providers, and from the public's attitude towards TVET. Despite significant improvement over the past decade, the numbers enrolled in TVET are small compared to the enrollment in academic education.

The government is aware of these challenges. The NEM1 (2009: 54–55) recognized that "the human capital situation in Malaysia is not improving. Education policies saddled with socio-political goals have stymied the national objective of producing the best talent to meet the country's needs". The Malaysian Education Blueprint 2015–2025 (MEB) (2015a, b: 1–12) has laid out its objective of (1) parity

[3] TIMSS is an international assessment of mathematics and science achievement of students in the fourth and eighth grades (or their equivalents) in participating countries. It was developed by the International Association for the Evaluation of Educational Achievement (www.oecd.org/pisa).

Table 9.3 Malaysia's brain drain and Diaspora, distribution by countries of destination, 2010

Destination	Diaspora (%)[1]	Brain drain (%)[2]	Brain drain as percentage of diaspora[3]
Singapore	57	54	31.5
Australia	10	15	50.8
Brunei	7	3	13.3
United Kingdom	6	5	25.4
United States	6	10	55.7
Canada	2	4	53.2
New Zealand	2	2	41.9
Total destinations	100	100	34.2
Total numbers ('000)	1,023	335	

[1]Refers to all migrants
[2]Migrants aged 25 and above with tertiary education
[3]Diaspora aged 25 and above only. For Singapore, residents only
Source World Bank, 2011, Table 3.7, Figs. 3.17 and 3.18

between academic education and TVET, (2) "earned" autonomy for institutions, and (3) technology-enabled teaching and learning to be accomplished through ten "shifts" two of which are talent excellence and quality TVET graduates. Over the decade, enrollment growth in TVET is expected to be most rapid (7.8% annually), followed by private higher education institutions (5.1%) and public higher education institutions (MEB, 2015a, b: 1–13).[4]

An arguably faster and more cost-efficient way to develop talent is to recruit from overseas. Unfortunately, attracting talent is also not Malaysia's forte. Indeed, brain drain has been a feature of the country's human resource landscape. The World Bank, in its country report, the *Malaysia Economic Monitor*, dated April 2011 (World Bank, 2011), estimated that one million Malaysian diaspora are overseas of whom over half were in Singapore (Table 9.3). A third of this diasporic stock was considered brain drain, of whom, again, over half were in Singapore. Malaysia stands out not only in the numbers but also in the high-skill intensity of this brain drain. High-skill intensity is measured by the World Bank as the ratio of those with high skills overseas to those with these skills at home. Malaysia's intensity of 10.5% (20% if Malaysian non-residents in Singapore were included) in 2000 compares with 3.7% for China and 7.5% in Korea (World Bank, 2011: 106). Efforts to lure some of them back via Talent Corp and other schemes[5] have had limited success for reasons ranging from the overall inability to provide an attractive long-term environment to unattractive

[4] Rather than making explicit the education sector's weaknesses, the MEB talked about the country's education system have grown from strength to strength (MEB, 2014). The issue raised by the NEM was therefore not addressed.

[5] These include a scheme to attract back Malaysian scientists living abroad, launched in 1994, which was managed by the Ministry of Science, Technology, and the Environment, but suspended briefly during the Asian Financial Crisis, a similar programme launched in 2002 under the management of the Ministry of Human Resources, and the Brain Gain programme launched in 2006.

salaries, tedious processes, and an insufficiently hospitable research environment (Thiruchelvam & Kamarul, 2008: 130).[6]

To be fair, although Malaysia's brain drain has been motivated by income differentials and by what migrants refer to as "social injustice" (referring specifically to the discriminatory New Economic Policy) (World Bank, 2011: 118) and policies to attract return and foreign experts have been found wanting, several contextual factors render the country more susceptible to brain drain. The most important of these is the proximity to high-income Singapore which has lowered considerably both the physical and social costs of migration. A second contextual factor is Malaysia's highly internationalized tertiary education system. Malaysia has a tradition of sending students overseas, with both private funding and public scholarships. For year 2010, data from Project Atlas show 79,000 Malaysian students overseas.[7] Given that a significant number of those who are part of the brain drain are those educated overseas who never returned (World Bank, 2011: 112), this overseas study would surely have increased the likelihood of brain drain. To these can be added students in Malaysia enrolled in transnational education programmes, now a major phenomenon in the country's private education system.

As testimony of its success in becoming an international education hub, Malaysia is currently host to about 150,000 international students attracted to the country's relatively modest education cost and innovative higher education programmes. These programmes are offered by local higher education institutions in collaboration with foreign universities and by branches of foreign universities. These students have the advantage of already being in the country and are generally familiar with local conditions. Since they are locally educated, there is also no problem of recognition of degrees.

However, this source of talent remains largely untapped. First, despite assurances to the contrary, Malaysia's current system of tedious processes for visa application and renewal as well as processing of work permits for students that has led to numerous complaints by them stands in sharp contrast to the official rhetoric of brain gain, and is inimical to capturing these talents.[8] This is a good example of the government's policy schizophrenia. Second, even if they are able to acquire visas, the HEIs where they study are of little help in employment placement, having few links with industry. Third, the needs of international students are not well understood not only by their interlocutors and employers but also by society at large. Both the government and HEIs see international students as a source of revenue and little else (Embong, 2012: 126).

---

[6] TalentCorp only managed to bring back 2,500 Malaysians working abroad. Barely one percent of the diaspora was attracted to return by Talent Corp (Merican, 2014). Of those who did, some were planning to return anyway, while others were accused of taking advantage of short-term benefits with no regard for national development (Malaymail, 2015).

[7] http://www.iie.org/en/Services/Project-Atlas/Malaysia/Malaysias-Students-Overseas.

[8] For examples of complaints, see Lavendran (2013). The Complaints Board of Universiti Putra Malaysia has also seen numerous complaints by international students. See http://www.complaintsboard.com/complaints/upm-universiti-putra-malaysia-horrible-visa-processing-for-international-students-c675655.html.

There is finally talent embedded in the existing workforce, both local and foreign, that has not really been tapped. It is the pool of "tacit knowledge", defined as "non-codified, disembodied knowledge that is acquired via the informal take-up of learned behavior and procedures" (Howells, 1996: 92), that the workforce possesses. Although the ease with which such knowledge can be transferred varies, it is generally believed to be difficult, there being no market mechanism to facilitate this transfer. Yet enabling such transfers is important because tacit knowledge is key to technological innovation and firm competitiveness (Howells, 1996: 93).

Malaysian firms have not done a great deal to facilitate tacit knowledge transfer. While Rasiah (2002: 3) lauded the performance of Penang, he also noted that weak network cohesion limited the transfer of tacit knowledge in clusters like the Klang Valley and compounded the "ineffective systematic coordination throughout the country from federal institutions". Similarly, Lee and Gomez (2014) showcased examples of success but stressed the importance of codifying tacit knowledge among family SMEs as they transit from one generation to the next. A number of studies have also found the transfer of tacit knowledge by various stakeholders wanting. Fariza (2006) found Malaysian firms' ability to acquire knowledge, codified or tacit, from their foreign partners to be very limited. Rohana and Kamarulzaman (2009), however, found tacit knowledge sharing among SMEs to be limited. Likewise, Siti Khatizah and Mohd Anuar (2014) found limited impact of tacit knowledge on school innovation, suggesting little knowledge transfer had taken place.

This survey of the current status of Malaysia's talent development shows the country has a long way to go before its goal of grooming talent effectively can be reached. How to reach this goal then becomes the next important question.

Towards Effective Talent Development

What would an ideal scenario for talent development be? It would be one in which all the major components are effective in building up the country's talent base. The components are, as already indicated, education, including TVET, attracting talent, reversing the brain drain, and more effective use of existing talent. How do we get there? Examples exist of other countries and/or institutions that have been successful in each of the areas of focus here. Lessons should be drawn from their experience.

Education

How can Malaysia's academic education be moved out of the current malaise to a situation in which it is competitive internationally by whatever benchmark is used and quantity (coverage) is matched by quality (academic excellence)? As the experience of successful countries show, it requires scholastic merit to be the primary basis for assessment regardless of residence, ethnicity, and group, so that the best talent is nurtured. At the same time, those in need of special assistance, academic or economic, should not be neglected. Helping the disadvantaged is an important role for the state. It also requires complementarity between public and private sector HEIs both functioning on a level playing field. An exemplary TVET system should also be part of this ideal education system. TVET must be an integral part of the education system in which clear pathways exist between it an academic education, and in which all major stakeholders have a voice. The substance of education must encourage critical thinking and enabled by strong English language competency.

For several of these components, one needs to look no further than Singapore which, in the process of becoming a developed economy, had experienced, some, but not all, of Malaysia's challenges. Singapore's education experience, compared to Malaysia, fits the phrase "common roots but different paths" which Mukherjee and Wong (2011) used to describe the differential development of the National University of Singapore and the University of Malaya.

Singapore's education system has been rated the top performer in the world for many years. Singapore also ranks near the top in the Global Competitive Index. What distinguishes Singapore from other countries? Compared with Malaysia's education system, there is much that is common—the primacy given to the transfer of knowledge and the focus on judging excellence through examination performance (Hogan, 2014). Also familiar to Malaysians is Hogan's (2014) comment on Singapore's system: "Classroom talk is teacher-dominated and generally avoids extended discussions". This is hardly surprising given the shared roots of both countries' education systems. What then makes Singapore's system superior to most others?

Hogan (2014) suggested several factors. They include "a broad commitment to a nation-building narrative of meritocratic achievement and social stratification, ethnic pluralism, collective values and social cohesion, a strong, activist state and economic growth", commitment to a long-term perspective, one that increasingly emphasizes quality of learning over quantity, "the quality of leadership across all levels of the system, and Singapore's willingness to grant considerable pedagogical authority to teachers while providing clear guidance as to priorities". Pathak and Pathak (2015) listed six pedagogical traits that made for educational success. First was the focus on student collaborative learning in the classroom. Second, teaching and learning emphasized the application of learning, with "repetitive and mindful practice" (Pathak & Pathak, 2015: 21) in most activities. The third is the integrated use of multimedia and interactive technologies. The fourth is the explicit recognition of context in enhancing teaching of the application of knowledge. The fifth is to achieve, complementary to the emphasis on application, also the proper understanding of concepts. And the sixth is learning from failures as well as success, which requires open admission of errors made.

This high-performing education system has been complemented by an equally impressive TVET system. This system is an integral part of the education system with its clear vision of the importance of human capital in development (Raddon, 2012). Singapore's TVET, from policy formulation to implementation, benefitted from stakeholder engagement through the Tripartite Alliance, made up of the unions representing labour as the beneficiaries of TVET, employers as consumers of TVET output and the government, set up as early as the 1970s (see also Cheong & Lee, 2016). The funding of TVET is also closely tied to achieving Singapore's national economic and educational objectives, though initially less focused on efficiency. At the same time, the fact that programmes were demand-driven ensures that overlaps in programme offerings and wastage are minimized.

In comparing the Singapore model to the Malaysian, several lessons can be drawn. These are the need to give primacy to meritocracy to achieve academic excellence, commitment to a long-term strategy with respect to policy and implementation, with adjustments as the needs change, a degree of autonomy at the institutional level and below, active engagement of all key stakeholders, the integration of technology, including pedagogical, into teaching, and, no less important, the willingness to admit to and learn from failures as much as from success.

Attracting Talent

The alternative to developing home-grown talent is to attract talent that already exists internationally. Such talent can be classified into three groups. First, there is talent from outside the country, i.e. foreign citizens who are resident outside the country. Second, there are those from the country who have moved abroad—for studies and did not return, or for other, mostly economic, reasons. A third group of talent would already be in the country, and the challenge would be to dissuade them from leaving.[9] This group would include international students studying in the country.

To be able to attract these groups to come and/or stay requires understanding of what would motivate them to do so. Some differences exist between these groups as to this motivation. With the first group, the motivation is likely to be primarily economic—a good work environment, strong career prospects, and high income. For the second group, the existence of socio-cultural ties is likely also to figure in any decision to return. However, with the advent of the Internet and almost instantaneous news allowing the diasporic population to stay in close touch with developments in the home country, the power of socio-cultural ties may no longer be that strong. For those who left for other reasons, such as, in the Malaysian case, subjective perceptions of social injustice, these concerns need to be assuaged. With the third group, those who have been in the country must have become familiar with local conditions in terms of living conditions, work environment, and socialization. The social capital that this group has built up can be a factor that can be capitalized.

These different motivations aside, there are also commonalities. The first commonality is that direct measures to attract talent, such as offering incentives and preferences, in the absence of other enabling factors, have had only limited impact on their own (see Rasiah, Lin & Muniratha, 2015). This has been the case with

[9] Ready et al. (2008) taking the perspectives of companies rather the state, distinguished between "promises made" in attracting talent and "promises kept" in retaining talent.

Malaysia's Talent Corporation.[10] But Talent Corp is hardly alone. It is reported that initiatives by the Central European governments of the Czech Republic, Hungary, and Poland have had only modest success (Bottcher, 2014). This is largely because the incentives offered are insufficient to compensate for the perceived sacrifices these talented individuals have to make in relocating. In a nutshell, "return is only an option if the political, economic and social situation in the home country is stable and attractive" (Dumont & Spielvogel, 2008).

International successes and failures in attracting talent offer major lessons of experience. First, the most important drivers of talent relocation are economic conditions of the countries to which talent relocates. The attraction of Singapore for highly skilled Malaysians clearly illustrates this factor, although the fact that Singapore is practically next door and there exists no social distance between the nationals of the two countries is an additional pull factor (Cheong et al., 2017). In this sense, the gravitation of talent to the advanced countries of Western Europe and the US is a better illustration of the attraction of higher financial and intellectual returns for talent migration. This has been undoubtedly the case for Malaysian emigrants—better economic prospects are the most important reason for them to migrate (World Bank, 2011: 121). Korea's experience also confirms the importance of economics. In the 1960s and 1970s, despite its government's best efforts, few Korean scientists and engineers returned. They did, however, as the economy boomed from the 1980s (Song, 1997: 317). For Malaysia, then, achievement of technological catch-up as elaborated in Chap. 2 represents a necessary condition for attracting talent, both foreign and local citizens overseas.

Second, it is not just the presence of existing differentials that attract talent. The potential for these returns to materialize after the talent arrives can be an equally strong magnet. This is especially true of diasporic migrants most of whom have social and/or emotional ties with their countries of origin. The case of Taiwan speaks to the power of promise. Taiwan in the 1970s and early 1980s was "a classic case of brain drain … an estimated 20% of Taiwanese college graduates went abroad for advanced study, and few of them returned. At the peak of the brain drain in 1979, only eight percent of students who studied abroad returned to Taiwan upon completing their studies" (O'Neill, 2003). Yet, as Taiwan's economy grew, migrants began to return in the late 1980s, even before Taiwan had become a developed economy. These returnees were clearly motivated by the potential of a rising Taiwan. A similar logic drives return migration to China (Wang, 2013). This message is both good and bad news for government seeking talent from abroad. The good news is that a well-managed growing economy will automatically attract talent. The bad news is that driving growth is a daunting challenge.

Third, high incomes represent a necessary but not sufficient condition for attracting talent. This is again demonstrated by the experience of Singapore. With a per capita

[10] Talent Corp was reported to have brought back 2,105 Malaysians at a cost of RM 65 million between 2011 and 2013 (Boo, 2013). Whether or not the per capita cost of nearly RM 31,000 was "money well spent", the fact remains that these numbers are very small and are just a fraction of those leaving.

income higher than that of the US, Singapore has experienced a significant flow of highly skilled residents to the US and other Western countries. Ziguras and Gribble (2015) estimated that around one in ten Singapore higher education students are studying outside the country. These students are undoubtedly attracted to the world-class higher education institutions in these countries as well as the opportunities to work in knowledge intensive and innovative industries there. Strategies Singapore adopted to reduce this outflow upgrade the quality of its higher education institutions,[11] promote the return of graduates after their studies, engagement with the Singaporean diaspora, and recruitment of incoming international students into the workforce—have met with some success (Ziguras & Gribble, 2015).

Fourth, the above Singapore initiatives show that while talent programmes have only a modest impact, government support in the form of a package of policies can be a powerful complement to the attraction of rising prosperity. In Taiwan, the government's efforts to build up a critical mass of returnees through the creation of the Hinschu Science-based Industrial Park, combined with supporting diaspora networking and recruitment not only created this critical mass but also facilitated knowledge transfer from those who did not return physically. In China, the National Medium- and Long-term Talent Development Plan (2010–2020), combined with nearly 3,000 local talent plans, are playing a similarly complementary role (Wang, 2013). Two features of the Taiwan and China programmes stand out. They are firstly the importance of a coordinated package of initiatives that go well beyond the talent return programmes upon which many governments pin their hopes. Secondly, the government must view migrants who do not return not as "brain drain" but as "brain reserve", constituting part of a knowledge network and who are valuable assets to the country. For Malaysia, this means reversal of a government and leadership mindset that had for long been at best indifferent and at worst hostile to those who left or never returned (Schellekens, 2011).[12] Further, even with belated recognition by government of the need to attract return migrants, periodic tirades by groups like Perkasa against "immigrants" (ethnic Chinese and Indians) and non-Muslims, unchecked by the government, reflects policy schizophrenia that needs to be addressed.

Fifth, it must be remembered that attracting talent is only a means to acquire benefits from such talent. Unless the government or the private economy is able to capture effectively these intellectual resources, the effort expended to attract talent will have been wasted. Given that arriving or returning talent are more likely in a dynamic environment of growth and innovation, their contribution will likely be to spur this growth

[11] In the 2015/2016 Quacquarelli Symonds (QS) World University Rankings, the National University of Singapore moved up to 12th place, while the Nanyang Technological University moved up to 13th (http://www.topuniversities.com/university-rankings/world-university-rankings/2015#sorting=rank+region=+country=+faculty=+stars=false+search=).

[12] When the World Bank report on Malaysia's brain drain (World Bank, 2011) was released, it was dismissed by former prime minister as politically motivated and inaccurate (Koon, 2010). More guarded, however, was the response of prime minister Najib, who, while asserting that the report's contents was "not quite correct", nevertheless established the National Economic Action Council that authored the report *A New Economic Model for Malaysia* in which brain drain was acknowledged as a problem.

and dynamism rather than bring it about (Dumont & Spielvogel, 2008). Government should not expect them to be the elixir to spark economic vitality to an industry or economy that is moribund. At the same time, the role of the corporate sector is vital because it is mainly this sector that will be using the resources these talented individuals bring with them. Of course, as already indicated, to the extent that some higher education institutions are state-run, the state has a role in talent management too. There is no dearth of material on how to manage talent once acquired. This includes aligning talent with corporate strategies, training, and development tailored to specific roles, and career-pathing (e.g. Miller, 2013; Stahl et al, 2012). In this area where private sector and state roles intersect, an effective public–private partnership will maximize the capture of attracted talent. This partnership should include that between HEIs and industry, since it represents an important institutional channel for the transfer of tacit knowledge.

Retaining Talent

The focus on developing and attracting talent has to an extent obscured the equally important role of retaining talent. The talent to be retained consists of local talent, foreign talent already in the country, as well as those overseas who contribute to knowledge and ideas in the home country—participants of "brain circulation". Fortunately many of the factors that are effective in attracting talent also help to retain them.[13] As indicated above, these include improving economic conditions in the host country, the promise of a brighter future, sustained government support in the form of policies that offer incentives for skills and expertize on demand, institutional infrastructure such as technology clusters and parks ("talent magnets"), and a facilitative regulatory framework that recognizes meritocracy rather than pose bureaucratic burdens that discourage talent.[14] Working in close partnership with the private sector which plays the primary role in talent retention, the state should be fully on board in identifying emerging areas for talent, providing training and retraining of labour to meet these new demand for skills, and thus ensure flexibility and diversity in a dynamic labour market. All these make for clear career paths for talent that enable them to plan for a good future in the country. The point to remember with talent retention is the need for a holistic approach reflected in a package of complementary policies that extend well beyond short-term bureaucratic incentives.[15]

Institutions established to attract international talent or diaspora overseas typically do not have as their terms of reference talent retention. Yet, Singapore and

[13] Documents typically deal with common strategies that attract, develop and retain talent. See, for example, EU (2016).

[14] In the 2014 PWC Annual Global CEO Survey (PWC, 2014: 16), 52% of respondent CEOs felt that regulation was hampering their ability to attract and retain talent.

[15] An example of this is the Malaysian government's relaxation of residency rules as a measure to encourage talent to stay (TalentCorp, 2010).

Malaysia have attracted a large number of international students to their shores. These represent important sources of talent that these countries can tap into. Hawthorne (2012) noted that international students "confront few of the barriers experienced by foreign-trained professionals, in terms of host country language ability, qualification recognition, or acculturation ... Their productive lives will be longer, given their youth at point of enrolment". Increasing the "stay rate" of these students has therefore become the strategy for Singapore (Ziguras & Gribble, 2015) and OECD countries. In the OECD countries, post-study job-search schemes have been put in place, international students are allowed to stay in the country after graduation for job-seeking, and restrictions on work during and after studies and on visa and residence have been reduced and procedures simplified (de Wit & Ripmeester, 2013).

The pool of diasporic talent resident overseas has been shown, in the outstanding example of Taiwan, to be accessible to the home country with the right mix of policies. These policies have already been discussed. At the same time, a degree of match between the expertize of diasporic talent and the technological capability of industries in the home country is needed to facilitate skill transfer to and technological catch-up by the latter. The substance of Chap. 2 again speaks to how the potential for brain circulation can be realized in Malaysia.

Viewed in its entirety, strengthening education, attracting and retaining talent are related activities under the fabric of talent management. As an example of retaining education to the attraction of talent, Altbach and Salmi (2011) noted that one of the most powerful levers for universities to achieve academic excellence has been the ability to count on the services of foreign talent as well as foreign diaspora. In the National University of Singapore, half of the teaching staff and close to 80% of researchers are foreign nationals (Mukherjee and Wong, 2011). The Pohang University of Science and Technology (POSTECH) in South Korea and Hong Kong University of Science and Technology (HKUST) hired overseas Korean and Chinese overseas scholars to rapidly build up the academic strength of these institutions (Altbach & Salmi, 2011; Salmi, 2012). As a second example that links education with tacit knowledge transfer, universities can play a major role in promoting not only awareness but also expertize in different models of such knowledge transfer. Finally, as already elaborated, there exists commonality of policies and measures that attract and retain talent.

Conclusion

Talent management, broadly defined to encompass development of local talent, attraction of talent from overseas (foreigners as well as diaspora), and retaining talent already in the country, requires a confluence of a number of factors to be successful. The role of the state figures prominently among these factors. A conducive political framework, far-sighted science policy and guaranteed funding are major prerequisites for a country to be attractive for scientists. But these must be combined with labour market policies that facilitate productive use of skills and good career prospects, especially for young talent. Talent return programmes are therefore just a part of an entire package of programmes to attract talent. Even with all these in place, the overall economic environment matters a great deal. All successful cases of talent arrival and return in Asia—Korea, Singapore, Taiwan, China, and India—have seen robust economic growth combined with bright prospects for talent, factors that are not necessarily fully under state control.

Moving forward, changes to the Malaysian demographic scene may affect the supply of talent and hence the need for talent development. For instance, as the Malaysian population ages, the propensity to migrate away may be reduced. This may, however, be offset by a reduced number of people of working age, and by greater job mobility among millennials as familial ties loosen. Arguably, the need to enhance value-addition in production as Malaysia loses whatever comparative advantage it has in low-labour cost production will underpin an even greater demand for talent development.

Thus, the need for talent development and management is likely to increase over the medium term. This makes for even greater relevance of learning from successful experiences. The good news is that these success factors, together with how to leverage them to achieve beneficial impact, have been extensively studied and recounted. Hence, in the pursuit of its talent goals for Foresight 2050, Malaysia already has fairly concrete guides as to what needs to be done. Admittedly, the challenges faced by the country to achieve the ideal situation, partly the result of context but no less important also of perverse or inconsistent policies, are considerable. But the fact that countries much less endowed with physical and human resources than Malaysia when they began their journeys have been successful shows that significant progress can be made with the requisite commitment. The key question for Malaysia is therefore not whether the ideal is achievable—it is—but whether such commitment exists and/or can be sustained.

References

Aghion, P., & Howitt, P. (1998). *Endogenous growth theory*. MIT Press.

Altbach, P. G., & Salmi, J. (2011). *The road to academic excellence: The making of world-class research universities*. World Bank.

Barro, R. J. (1991). Economic growth in a cross section of countries. *Quarterly Journal of Economics, 106*(2), 407–445.

Barro, R. J., & Sala-I-Martin, X. (1995). *Economic growth*. McGraw Hill.

Becker, G. (1994). *Human capital: A theoretical and empirical analysis with special reference to education*. University of Chicago Press.

Bianchi, M. (2009). Credit constraints, entrepreneurial talent and economic development. Research paper 2009/20, United Nations University, World Institute for Development Economic Research

Boo, S. L. (2013). Returning Malaysians: 2,105. Price: RM65 m. Minister: money well spent. Malaymail online, July 18. Retrieved December 16, 2015, from http://www.themalaymailonline.com/malaysia/article/returning-malaysians-2105.-price-rm65-million

Bottcher, C. (2014). "What does it take for brain drain reversal to be effective?". EuroScientist Nov. 24. At http://www.euroscientist.com/what-does-it-takes-for-brain-drain-reversal-to=be-,effective.

Blundell, R., Dearden, L., Meghir, C., & Sianesi, B. (1999). Human capital investment: The returns from education and training to the individual, the firm and the economy. *Fiscal Studies, 20*(1), 1–23.

Chambers, E. G., Fouldon, M., Handfield-Jones, H., Hankin, S. M., & Michaels III, E. G. (1998). The war for talent. *The McKinsey Quarterly, 1*(3), 44–57.

Cheong, K. C., Goh, K. L., & Li, R. (2017). The brain drain: Balancing the narrative. In A. Tyson (Ed.), *Talent war in Southeast Asia: The political economy of talent and ethnic hierarchies*. Singapore: Institute of Southeast Asian Studies, forthcoming.

Cheong, K. C., & Lee, K. H. (2016). Malaysia's education crisis—Can TVET help? *Malaysian Journal of Economic Studies, 53*(1), 115–134.

Cheong, K. C., Abdillah, N., Kuppusamy, S., & Lee, H. A. (2013). *Malaysia workforce development*. SABER Country Report. Washington DC: World Bank.

Cortright, J. (2016) How should cities approach economic development? *City Observatory*, September 3. Retrieved March 4, 2017, from http://cityobservatory.org/how-should-cities-approach-economic-development/

Cubas, G., Ravikumar, B., & Ventura, G. (2015). Talent, labor quality and economic development. Working paper 2013–27D, Federal Reserve Bank of St Louis, May

De Wit, H., & Ripmeester, N. (2013) Increasing the stay rate of international students. University World News 259. Retrieved December 16, 2015, from http://www.universityworldnews.com/article.php?story=20130213165216138

Docquier, F., & Machado, J. (2016). Global competition for attracting talents and the world economy. *The World Economy, 39*(4), 530–542.

Dodani, S., & LaPorte, R. E. (2005). Brain drain from developing countries: How can brain drain be converted into wisdom gain? *Journal of the Royal Society of Medicine, 98*, 487–491.

Dumont, P., & Spielvogel, G. (2008). Return migration: A new perspective. In OECD. International Migration Outlook 2008. Paris: 161–22.

Embong, A. R. (2012). Micro-perspectives: Ideas, practices and challenges. In S. Y. Tham (Ed.) *Internationalizing higher education in Malaysia: Understandings, practices and challenges* (pp. 113–131). Singapore: Institute of Southeast Asian Studies.

European Union (EU). (2016). Best practices in talent attraction, development and retention. Paris: EU. August.

Fariza, H. (2006). Tacit knowledge: The role and effectiveness in acquiring knowledge in international strategic alliances in Malaysia. *Journal of International Studies, 2*, 115–130.

Gaillard, J., & Gaillard, A. M. (1997). Introduction: The international mobility of brains—Exodus or circulation. *Science, Technology and Society, 2*(2), 195–228.

Gibson, J., & McKenzie, D. (2011). Eight questions about brain drain. *Journal of Economic Perspectives, 25*(3), 107–128.

Gill, I., & Kharas, H. (2007). *An East Asian renaissance: Ideas for economic growth*. World Bank.

Griliches, Z. (1997). Education, human capital and growth: A personal perspective. *Journal of Labor Economics, 15*(1), S330–S334.

Hanushek, E. A. (2013). Economic growth in developing countries: The role of human capital. *Economics of Education Review, 37*, 204–212.

Hawthorne, L. (2012) Designer immigrants? International students and two-step migration. In D. K. Deardof, H. de Wit, J. D. Heyl, & T. Adams (Eds.), *The SAGE handbook of international education Los Angeles* (pp. 417–435). Sage.

Heidrick & Struggles. (2015). The global talent index report: The outlook to 2015. London: Economist Intelligence Unit.

Hogan, D. (2014). Why is Singapore's school system so successful, and is it a model for the West. The Conversation. Retrieved November 14, 2015, from http://theconversation.com/why-is-singapores-school-system-so-successful-and-is-it-a-model-for-the-west-22917

Institute for Management Development (IMD). (2016). IMD World Talent Report 2016. Lausanne: IMD World Competiveness Center.

IMD Competitiveness Center (IMD). (2014). IMD world talent report 2014. Lausanne, Switzerland.

Jorgensen, D. W., & Fraumeni, B. M. (1992). Investment in education and US economic growth. *Scandinavian Journal of Economics, 94*, S51–S70.

Khilji, S. E., Tarique, I., & Schuler, R. S. (2015). Incorporating the macro view in global talent management. *Human Resource Management Review, 25*(3), 236–248.

Kuputsch, C., & Pang, E. F. (2006). Introduction. In C. Kuputsch & E. F. Pang (Eds.), *Competing for global talent* (pp. 1–8). ILO.

Lavendran, G. (2013). Foreign students in a dilemma. Free Malaysia Today, September 6. Retrieved December 16, 2015, from http://www.freemalaysiatoday.com/category/nation/2013/09/06/foreign-students-in-a-dilemma/

Lee, J. K. Y., & Gomez, E. T. (2014). Advancing tacit knowledge: Malaysian family SMEs in manufacturing. *Asian Economic Papers, 13*(2), 1–24.

Malaymail. (2015). TalentCorp: harder to lure Malaysians to come back home with current political, economic climate. *Malaymail*. http://www.themalaymailonline.com/malaysia/article/talentcorp-harder-to-lure-malaysians-to-come-back-home-with-current-politic

Martin, R. L. (2014). The rise (and likely fall) of the talent economy. Harvard Business Review, October. Retrieved March 4, 2017, from https://hbr.org/2014/10/the-rise-and-likely-fall-of-the-talent-economy

Mellander, C., & Florida, R. (2012). The rise of skills: Human capital, the creative class and regional development. Paper 266, Center for Excellence in Science and Innovation Studies, Royal Institute of Technology, Sweden, March.

Merican, J. (2014). Attracting Malaysian talent home is tough for Johan Merican. *Din Merican blog*. https://dinmerican.wordpress.com/2014/04/09/attracting-malaysian-talent-home-is-tough-for-johan-merican/

Miller, B. (2013) Essential tools of talent management. *Forbes*, April 24. Retrieved December 16, 2015, from http://www.forbes.com/sites/forbesinsights/2013/04/24/essential-tools-of-talent-management/

Mincer, J. (1958). Investment in human capital and personal income distribution. *Journal of Political Economy, 66*(4), 281–302.

Mincer, J. (1974). *Schooling*. Columbia University Press.

Ministry of Education, Malaysia. (2015a). *Malaysia Education Blueprint 2013-2025 (MEB)*. Putrajaya: Ministry of Education.

Ministry of Education, Malaysia. (2015b). *Malaysia Education Blueprint 2015–2025*. Putrajaya.

Mukherjee, H., & Wong, P. K. (2011). The National University of Singapore and the University of Malaya: Common roots and different paths. In P. G. Altbach & J. Salmi (Eds.), *The road to academic excellence: The making of world-class Research Universities*. Washington DC: World Bank.

National Economic Advisory Council (2010) New Economic Model for Malaysia: Part 1. Putrajaya: Percetakan Nasional Malaysia Berhad.

O'Neil. K. (2003). "Brain Drain and Gain: The Case of Taiwan" Migration Policy. September 1. At http://www.migrationpolicy.org/article/brain-drain-and-gain-case-taiwan.

Pathak, A., & Pathak, S. (2015). Towards building a model of education success: A situated inquiry. *International Journal of Educational Science and Research, 5*(3), 17–28.

Perkins, D., Rasiah, R., & Woo, W. T. (forthcoming). Explaining Malaysia's Economic growth. In R. Rasiah, K. Salih, & K. C. Cheong (Eds.), *Malaysia's leap into the future: The building blocks*.

Polaski, S. (2006). *Winners and losers: Impact of the Doha round on developing countries*. Carnegie Endowment for International Peace.

Psacharopoulos, G., & Patrinos, H. A. (2004). Returns to investment in education: A further update. *Education Economics, 12*(2), 111–134.

PWC. (2014). The talent challenge: adapting to growth. London: Price Waterhouse Cooper (PWC).

Raddon, A. (2012). Singapore Workforce Development: SABER Multiyear Country Report, Washington D.C.: World Bank.

Rasiah, R. (2002). Systemic coordination and the knowledge economy: Human capital development in Malaysia's MNC-driven electronics clusters. *Transnational Corporations, 11*(3), 89–129.

Rasiah, R., Lin, Y., & Muniratha, A. (2015). The role of the diaspora in supporting innovation systems: The experience of India, Malaysia and Taiwan. In P. Shome & P. Sharma (Eds.), *Emerging economies*. Springer.

Ready, D. A., Hill, L. A., & Conger, J. A. (2008). Winning the race for talent in emerging markets. *Harvard Business Review*, November. Retrieved December 16, 2015, from https://hbr.org/2008/11/winning-the-race-for-talent-in-emerging-markets

Rohana, N., & Kamaruzaman, J. (2009). Tacit knowledge sharing and SMEs' organizational performance. *International Journal of Economics and Finance, 1*(1), 216–220.

Salmi. J. (2012). Attracting talent in a global academic world: How emerging research universities can benefit from brain circulation. *The Academic Executive Brief*, 2(1). Retrieved December 16, 2015, from http://academicexecutives.elsevier.com/articles/attracting-talent-global-academic-world-how-emerging-research-universities-can-benefit

Saxenian, A. L. (2005). From brain drain to brain circulation: Transnational communities and upgrading in China and India. *Studies in Comparative International Development, 40*(2), 35–61.

Schellekens, P. (2011). "Whither Malaysia's brain drain", World Bank Blogs April 27. At https://www.worldbank.org/eastasiapacific/whither-malaysia-s-brain-drain.

Schultz, T. W. (1961). Investment in human capital. *American Economic Review, 51*(1), 1–17.

Schwab, K. (2015) The new key to economic growth is unlocking latent talent. *The Globe and Mail*, May 4. Retrieved March 4, 2017, from http://www.theglobeandmail.com/report-on-business/rob-commentary/the-new-key-to-economic-growth-is-unlocking-latent-talent/article24424439/

Sianesi, B. (2003). Education and economic growth: A review of the literature. *Journal of Economic Surveys, 17*(2), 157–200.

Siti Khatizah, A., & Mohd, Anuar, A. R. (2014). The use of tacit knowledge and school innovation in Malaysian secondary schools. *International Journal of Evaluation Research in Education, 3*(1), 45–52.

Solow, R. (1957). Technical change and the aggregate production function. *Review of Economics and Statistics, 39*, 312–320.

Song, H. (1997). From brain drain to reverse brain drain: Three decades of Korean experience. *Science Technology Society, 2*(2), 317–345.

Stahl, G. K., Bjorkman, I., Farndale, E., Morris, S. H., Paauwe, J., Stiles, P., Trevor, J., & Wright, P. (2012). Six principles of effective global talent management. *MIT Sloan Management Review*. Retrieved December 16, 2015, from http://sloanreview.mit.edu/article/six-principles-of-effective-global-talent-management/

TalentCorp. (2010) PM Najib announces policies to attract and retain talent. Press Release, December 6.

Thiruchelvam, T., & Kamarul, Z. A. (2008). Attracting scientific and technical talents from abroad: The Malaysian experience. *Asian Journal of Technology Innovation, 16*(2), 113–132.

Tyson, A. (2017) Introduction. In A. Tyson (Ed.) *Talent war in Southeast Asia: The political economy of talent and ethnic hierarchies*. Institute of Southeast Asian Studies, forthcoming.

Wang, H. (2013). China's return migration and its impact on home development. *UN Chronicle, 1*(3). Retrieved December 10, 2015, from http://unchronicle.un.org/article/chinas-return-migration-and-its-impact-home-development/

World Bank. (2011). *Malaysian economic monitor——Brain drain*. Washington D.C.: The World Bank.

Ziguras, C., & Gribble, C. (2015). Policy responses to address student 'brain drain': An assessment of measures intended to reduce the emigration of Singaporean international students. *Journal of Studies in International Education, 19*(3), 246–264.

Cheong Kee Cheok is currently Senior Advisor, Asia Europe Institute, University of Malaya. A graduate of the University of Malaya, obtained his Ph.D. at the London School of Economics. Upon his return from studies, he joined the Faculty of Economics and Administration, University of Malaya, where he held the positions of Deputy Dean and Dean of Faculty. After a decade at UM, he spent 16 years at the World Bank in the capacity of Economist and subsequently Senior Economist. At the Bank, he was Coordinator for China and Vietnam in the Economic Development Institute, now the World Bank Institute. After returning to Malaysia in 2000, he has continued as Consultant for the Bank and UN agencies. Back with the University of Malaya since 2010, he has coauthored books, book chapters, and published numerous papers in top-tier academic journals as well as successfully supervised Ph.D. students, both international and local.

Than Lee Lee is a doctoral student at the Faculty of Business and Economics, Universiti Malaya. She specializes in the economics of education and economic growth.

Chapter 10
Cities, Urbanization and Infrastructure

Kuppusamy Singaravelloo and Kamal Salih

Abstract Malaysia's urbanization rate in 2020 was nearing 80%, with the rate varying across the thirteen states and the three federal territories. At the central conurbation of the Malaysian peninsula, what used to be different boundaries of cities before, have now emerged as large metropolitan areas. The population density has almost doubled from 42 persons per sq km in 1980 to 83 persons per sq km in 2010. Rapid urbanization has continued unabated because of public policies targeted at supporting rapid physical development, which has brought both positive and negative consequences. While it is undeniable that economic growth, employment and urbanization are inter-related, the negative consequences of rapid urbanization has necessitated city managers and decentralized agencies to painstakingly address them. Among them are urban poverty, inequality, crime, provision of housing, and public transportation infrastructure. Accordingly, we argue that planning policies, such as Local Plans, Structure Plans, and National Physical Plans, as well as the National Urbanization Policy are reviewed as an ongoing process to manage urbanization. This Chapter ends with strategies and measures for Malaysia to address and counter critical urbanization issues in the coming decades.

Keywords Urbanization · Physical infrastructure · Housing and public transport · Malaysia

Introduction

A country is considered urbanized when over half of its population resides in urban centres. Why do people move to urban centres? The answers could be—in search of jobs, prosperity, and better access to quality of life including health and education.

K. Singaravelloo (✉)
Faculty of Business and Economics and Administration, University of Malaya, 50603 Kuala Lumpur, Malaysia
e-mail: kuppusamy_s@um.edu.my

K. Salih
Malaysian Institute of Economic Research, JKR 606, Jalan Bukit Petaling, Kuala Lumpur, Malaysia

R. Rasiah et al. (eds.), *Malaysia's Leap Into the Future*, Dynamics of Asian Development, https://doi.org/10.1007/978-981-16-7045-9_10

Urbanization is a process where large numbers of people from the rural areas move to cities for various reasons, and they decide to reside in the cities for a long period of time.

McGranahan and Satterthwaite (2014) explored different ways the term urban is defined by different countries, most based on a catchment population size and at times this would include density, regions of administrative responsibility, but is not directly associated with the physical infrastructure. In many countries, "urban" is spatial and looks into a cut-off population size that resides in, while some countries also include day-trippers, this spatial area. Malaysia is somewhat trapped into this definition of urban, and although it had overcome this problem in the last two decades, it has reverted into this definition trap as there are parties that challenge the existing definition. In the past, an area is termed urban when it reaches a population of 10,000 persons and above. This forms the denominator in the estimation of the total national population who reside in urban areas. Only with a sound definition of the term urban can one decide the urbanization rate at a particular time. The Malaysian urbanization rate may be altered in the future if there is a significant shift in the definition of the term.

Urbanization is commonly seen quantitatively in terms of the increase in the population size in an area, but it can also be viewed qualitatively as changes in the lifestyle of the society. Urbanization has social, political, and economic growth dimensions that spur the development of cities. The latter creates opportunities for wealth and social development that becomes attractive for the rural population to improve their wellbeing by migrating to urban areas. Most parts of Europe have witnessed industrialization as the factor that increases rural–urban migration. Today, this is witnessed in China where the number of cities has increased from 467 in 1990 to 652 in 2008. Thus, China had its rate of urbanization increase from only 20% in 1980 to over 50% by 2011.

From the institutional point of view, cities have to manage the migration process that continues to introduce greater social problems but it is the city managers who have the ability and power vested in them to innovate, generate wealth and enhance the quality of living among its population, and this is best managed through agglomeration of cities (Turok & McGranahan, 2013), especially in the developing regions of Asia and Africa. While it is accepted that different levels of urbanization suit different countries, a major driver for the growth of many capital cities is the support system and redistribution network, rather than economic development in these cities.

We define urbanization as the process that results in the shift of rural population into urban settlements for economic and personal wellbeing reasons with the intent of remaining there.

Theoretical Considerations

There are a number of theories advanced to explain the urbanization phenomenon. First, Modernization Theory promotes the view that societies seek to change from traditional to modern ways of living. Globalization, coupled with the advancement of technology attracts rural people to move to urban centres. The theory views urbanization as driven by industrialisation, culture, advancement in technology, and the thirst for information. Thus, urbanization is seen as a natural process of rural population shifting their interests at modern urban areas. The theory states that society will change, within their own time, given there is technological support and advancement in production and consumption (Chaudhary, 2013). These elements would bring in a spill over effect onto the social and political development of the society concerned.

Lipton's (1977) Urban Bias Theory takes a different view—that there is a natural bias of society and governments in favour of cities, which contributes to a higher standard of living for urban dwellers. This attracts the rural poor to migrate to urban areas. Following this theory, it is evident that, again naturally, and by economies of scale, investment spent on urban areas results in higher economic efficiency than in rural areas.

Cities and urban centres are economic concentrations that arguably offer the most sophisticated infrastructure to country's populations, which are increasingly powered by micro-electronics-based information and communications technologies (ICT) (Castells, 2005: 3). The ICT-driven infrastructure has since the turn of the millennium increasingly been characterized by digitalization, which has inter alia, stimulated the introduction of Industry 4.0 technologies in which artificial intelligence is increasingly leading the way robots and drones assist humans in their day to day activities, both in the professional domain of work and in households (Dayita & Priya, 2019). Krugman (1995) argues that urban centres should not only be looked up by economists as power houses for full employment per se but instead urban centres are interconnected spatial systems that provide an economic stimulus to the national economy. Krugman states that the natural state of a spatial location will be underemployment and underinvestment unless measures are taken to induce the opposite. Instead of just looking into parameters such as transportation costs, economies of scale, and factor mobility, Krugman (1995) sees the necessity to formulate policies that would identify and promote site-specific economic activities, which is increasingly taking place in developing countries through industry localization. The trend and economic emphasis are now very much on regional specialization which is supported by specialized suppliers and skills. This was heavily manufacturing industry focussed. Krugman (1995) also professes that developing economies tend to focus very much on export-oriented clusters unlike in the past. This supports further robust economic activities in urban centres that draw more rural people to the fore. Economic theory states that foreign investments would be directed towards areas that are economically feasible for them to invest at as they usually focus on areas that are developed, and equipped with satisfactory infrastructure, political stability and security, and availability of labour to appropriate profit maximization opportunities (Rasiah, 1995, 2007).[1] This urban focus is the result of agglomeration of industries, capital investment, and abundance of workers that allow for easier planning and implementation of policies that benefit urban areas (Bradshaw, 1987). Price of properties is also higher in urban centres. On the other hand, distance to urban centres inversely affects the cost of such properties in rural areas. Housing becomes a continuous and strenuous problem to governments as an outcome of urbanization.

While urbanization results in economic and physical transformation, accompanied with the concentration of infrastructure and utilities, it has social and environmental consequences. Population is concentrated in certain parts of cities that provide condensed housing especially for the middle and the lower-income groups (Venkatesham, 2015). These result in the formation of heat islands in urban areas (Venkatesham, 2015) and heavy usage of energy resources. The state of rapid urbanization caused environmental degradation that includes deforestation; shortage of water resource and supplies; air pollution; adaptation to noisy surrounding; land; and excessive disposal of wastes that further compound the difficulty to counter these environmental menaces. It is a known fact that urban areas are heavy consumers of the products of the hinterland. Large cities and megacities are thus heavy consumers of food produced by the farmers in rural areas, but people are too attracted to the urban living. Thus, food production may not be sustainable in the future. Poor urban–rural connectivity and infrastructure cause inadequate supplies to urban dwellers leading to consumption of lower quality food and exposure to health risks (Matuschke, 2009). Consequently, it is not wrong if one claims that urban areas cause more damages to rural areas. Urbanization causes optimization and consumption of urban land, and urban resources that lead to the need for closer monitoring and management of the environment. As a result, many cities apply restrictive measures to discourage further rural to urban migration. Following this, urban planners tend to focus on second-tier cities to cater for these migrants and at the same time prepare their cities for investors.

With the intense growth in ICT which boosts the use of technology, and enables in the future the absorption of disruptive technologies, there is a need to ensure that development focuses on reduced use of natural resources, and space, and to maximize production of outputs and services. Experiences across the globe, through respective good practices, tend to force developing cities to capture the growth in adopting renewed ICT and technology in urban living and minimize use of energy resources. A failure to adapt to this would render the cities outdated, wasteful and stand the chance of being left behind in the unnecessary and unwilling chase towards development.

[1] See Rasiah et al. (2017) for a lucid account of the role of sub-national states in the agglomeration of industrial activities in Northern Malaysia.

Urbanization in Malaysia

United Nations Human Settlements Programme (2016, 2019) reported that 55% of the world's inhabitants were residing in urban areas in 2018, having grown rapidly from 746 million only in the 1950s to 4.0 billion by 2015. In 1950, 70% of the world's population resided in the rural areas, and this trend is set to reverse by 2050 when 68% of the world's population is expected in urban areas (United Nations, 2019). By 2018, urbanization rates in Africa and Asia have reached 43% and 50%, respectively; and this is slated to be 56% and 64%, respectively, (United Nations, 2019) by 2050.

Cities are defined as urban centres with a population of over 1 million persons. Megacities are those with over 10 million inhabitants, while large cities are those having between 5 and 10 million inhabitants. London and Beijing were the only cities over 200 years ago, and by 1950, there were already 77 and by 2016 there are 548 (United Nations, 2018). The significant point is that most of the cities are in Asia, Africa, and Latin America. The first megacity was New York by about 1940, but by 1990 there were 12 with seven in Asia alone, and three in Latin America. By 2018, this number has reached 33. The largest mega cities are Tokyo (with 37 million inhabitants), Delhi (28 million), and Shanghai (26 million), among others.

While in recent decades, these megacities expanded in Asia, the largest cities in the developed nations have shrunk due to slower economic growth and the inability of these cities to attract investments, trade liberalization and more significantly decentralization due to the merging of cities into metropolitan regions. This had enabled, through efficient transportation systems that now allow people to travel daily to cities to work or to perform other activities and to return home in the shortest period of time. Furthermore, population size has also dwindled in most cities due to reduced fertility rates.

By international standards, Malaysia has only one city, i.e. Kuala Lumpur with less than two million people in 2019, but many other large townships are moving closer to achieve this status. This includes Petaling Jaya, Subang Jaya, Selayang, Klang, Kajang, George Town, Johor Bahru, and Johor Bahru Tengah. Most of these large townships, with the exception of George Town, and those in Johore are located in the Klang Valley. What used to be large towns with distinct features in the past has become connected as if all these now form one large city, as exemplified by the growth of Greater Kuala Lumpur in the Klang Valley which would have a population size approaching just under 10 million by 2020.

At the national level, Malaysia's urbanization rate stood at 71% by 2010, implying that 71% of the population were residing in urban areas (Table 10.1). Selangor contributed the highest proportion of urban to national population at 20.4% followed by Sabah (12.0%) and Johor (9.5%) in 2010. The population growth over the decades shows that Pahang registered 5.4% growth between 1970 and 1980, and this is the time when Tun Razak led the country as the Prime Minister, with Pahang likely to have benefitted from economic growth in the state. Within the same period, Sabah, Selangor, and Kuala Lumpur also enjoyed high population growth during this period. The fast population growth is evident only in Sabah and Selangor in the 1980–1991

Table 10.1 Level of urbanization and population, 1980–2010

State	Level of urbanization (%)					% Urban population to national urban population					Population								
											Total (million)					AAGR (%)			
	1970	1980	1991	2000	2010	1970	1980	1991	2000	2010	1970	1980	1991	2000	2010	1970–1980	1980–1991	1991–2000	2000–2010
Johor	26.3	35.2	47.8	63.9	71.9	11.3	12.4	11.1	11.9	9.5	1.28	1.58	2.07	2.56	3.23	2.34	2.45	2.47	2.24
Kedah	12.6	14.4	32.5	38.7	64.6	4.1	3.5	4.8	4.4	7.3	0.95	1.08	1.30	1.57	1.89	1.37	1.72	2.09	1.85
Kelantan	15.1	28.1	33.5	33.5	42.4	3.5	5.4	4.4	3.1	5.3	0.68	0.86	1.18	1.29	1.46	2.65	2.89	0.96	1.26
Melaka	25.1	23.4	38.7	67.3	86.5	3.4	2.3	2.2	3.0	3.0	0.40	0.45	0.51	0.60	0.79	1.25	1.14	1.98	2.65
Negeri Sembilan	21.6	32.6	42.0	55.0	66.5	3.5	4.0	3.3	3.3	3.2	0.48	0.55	0.69	0.83	1.00	1.46	2.08	2.00	1.84
Pahang	19.0	26.1	30.4	42.1	50.5	3.2	4.5	3.6	3.8	5.4	0.50	0.77	1.04	1.23	1.44	5.40	2.79	1.80	1.61
Perak	27.5	32.2	53.6	59.5	69.7	14.6	12.5	11.3	8.8	7.4	1.57	1.74	1.88	2.03	2.26	1.08	0.67	0.55	1.35
Perlis	-	8.9	26.6	33.8	51.4	-	0.3	0.5	0.5	0.9	0.12	0.14	0.18	0.20	0.23	1.67	2.17	0.84	1.35
Pulau Pinang	51.0	47.5	75.0	79.5	90.5	13.4	9.5	9.0	7.1	5.9	0.78	0.90	1.06	1.22	1.52	1.54	1.52	1.62	2.11
Sabah	16.9	19.9	33.2	48.3	54.0	3.6	4.1	6.5	8.6	12.0	0.64	0.93	1.73	2.45	3.12	4.53	5.67	3.92	2.34
Sarawak	15.5	18.0	37.5	47.9	53.8	5.1	5.0	6.9	7.0	9.0	0.98	1.24	1.64	2.01	2.42	2.65	2.59	2.24	1.86
Selangor	26.2	34.2	75.2	88.3	91.4	8.7	10.8	19.4	25.4	20.4	0.98	1.43	2.30	3.95	5.41	4.59	4.31	6.03	3.17
Terengganu	27.0	42.9	44.5	49.4	59.1	3.7	5.0	3.8	3.2	3.9	0.40	0.53	0.77	0.88	1.02	3.25	3.43	1.54	1.43
Kuala Lumpur	100.0	100.0	100.0	100.0	100.0	21.9	20.5	12.9	9.5	6.1	0.65	0.92	1.14	1.30	1.63	4.15	2.00	1.46	2.20
Malaysia	**28.4**	**34.2**	**50.7**	**61.8**	**71.0**	**100.0**	**100.0**	**100.0**	**100.0**	**100.0**	**10.44**	**13.14**	**17.56**	**22.20**	**27.57**	2.59	2.64	2.60	2.17

Sources Malaysia (2001, 2011), Population and Housing Census of Malaysia, Department of Statistics Malaysia 2000, 2010, Kuala Lumpur: Percetakan Nasional Malaysia Berhad; Malaysia (2010), Preliminary Count Report 2010, Department of Statistics Malaysia 2010, Kuala Lumpur: Percetakan Nasional Malaysia Berhad
Note Excludes the Federal Territories of Putrajaya and Labuan

period. In the following decade of 1991–2000, population growth reduced to 3.92% in Sabah but increased to a high of 6.03% in Selangor. However, during the period 2000–2010, all states registered lower AAGR with the highest being 3.17% by Selangor. These support the view that Selangor, being the most populous and industrialized state in Malaysia continues to attract population growth from other states, including from urban areas. This resulted in lower population growth in nearby states. For instance, it can be seen that the neighbouring Perak registered a growth below one percent point between 1980 and 2000. On the other hand, Negeri Sembilan and Pahang continue to register a decline in population growth over the four decades. These relate to job opportunities offered by states such as Selangor, Kuala Lumpur, Pulau Pinang, and Johor which recorded steady growth rates. Malaysia's urbanization rate is estimated to have reached 74.3% in 2015 and is slated to hit 80% by 2025.

Rapid urban growth in spatial terms has been unabated in the past two decades as public policies have shown greater interest in developing areas as fast as possible. There are now 250 urban settlements in Peninsular Malaysia alone covering about 4,200 km^2, occupying 3.18% of land surface in the peninsula. Population density has also increased from 42 persons per sq km in 1980 to 83 persons per sq km by 2010. Opposite to controlled development is urban sprawl such as those in the Klang Valley where development is initiated at low-density areas due to high costs of development in city centres. Guneet (2008) sees urban sprawl as the spread of an urban area onto the outer edges of a city. Instead of concentrating development in urban centres, many areas have been cleared to introduce new townships in the Klang Valley to the extent that townships like Rawang—Sg Buloh—Kuala Lumpur—Shah Alam—Klang and Seremban are physically connected to form one conurbation of major urban development corridor. Many feel urban sprawl is not healthy as more green areas are converted for continued development instead of attempting urban renewal mechanisms to house more people in the city itself.

Consequences of Urbanization

Urbanization can be seen as a boon or a bane. In current times, urban areas are seen as a source of opportunities aplenty for all, especially for those from the hinterland and the rural areas. It is seen as a source of job creation and diverse economic activities. Investors see urban areas, especially cities, as potential locations for their investment. Thus, it is not surprising to note that less developed geographic areas in the past in Asia, Africa, and Latin America have now become host to more than two-thirds of the world's urban population. The World Bank sees urban land use will triple by 2030 compared to what it was in 1987. Although the cost of doing business is highest in the central business districts, people are willing to invest in urban centres as the returns are also likely to be optimized. Cities are also places where the rich and the famous would like to locate themselves. Thus, one could see the cities having different classes of hotels, shopping malls, and restaurants catering for the different class of the society. Once a place for industries and small scale industries, many cities have seen these industries move naturally or being moved away from the settlements nearby to places elsewhere cheaper for their operations. In the very beginning, these economic activities drive people from elsewhere to site their settlements nearby these economic activities. But when the settlements circle these places, the industries become a threat to these settlements urging local governments to entice the industries to move out with incentives thrown-in.

Urban areas become a bane too. As good as it attracts everyone with a basket of goodies, it also offers a string of negative elements. Cities attract the less fortunate from the rural and the hinterland to try their luck looking at the economic cake at the urban areas, they undergo a serious lifestyle as they need shelter, food and water, and sanitation. In the early years of their attempt to penetrate into being an urbanite, they also face housing, income deficits, and high costs of living leading many to build makeshift homes spreading the space at slum areas. These cause consistent problems for city governments to move them to proper housing which they are ill-equipped, unable to purchase or pay rental, and thus squatter or slums areas continue to exist and become a political domain for many. Urban areas are also centres for the promotion of good and healthy lifestyle as well as centres for health problems among those who regard it as unimportant. The World Bank also sees 40% of the urban population will have no access to water by 2030. Energy and food consumption also exceed supplies thus leading to dependency on the hinterland.

Urban Economic Growth Centres and Employment

Cities, as generators of income growth contributing to national output and employment, are also centres of commerce, culture, education, and government. Businesses tend to operate more in cities than in rural areas. Large cities are usually identified with dynamic growth centres for production and consumption of goods and industries that are supported by financial and other business services. Large cities are also the loci of domestic and international trade. Thus, large cities work on better economics of scale and thus are more stable than those in the rural areas.

Chan (2011) has shown evidence of this positive relationship between urbanization level and economic performance (measured by GDP per capita) among states over the decades 1990–2010, as reported in the Malaysia Human Development Report 2013 (UNDP, 2014). He found that per capita GDP growth is accompanied by increased urbanization, where highly urbanized states like Penang and Selangor have much higher GDP per capita. There is on the other hand less urbanization in Johor, Negeri Sembilan, Malacca, and Pahang, where over the past 20 years, these states saw significant increases in their urbanization rates as their GDP per capita grew. Obviously, the rise of GDP over time tends to come from urbanization. With more urbanization there is higher GDP per capita, but the link between them is not the same across the various states.

Following the lower economic growth in other states, as compared to the west coast states of Selangor and Penang, and to encourage spread effects to other states in its economic opportunities, the Federal Government had established economic zones. For instance, Kedah, and northern Perak are clustered together with Pulau Pinang to leverage on Pulau Pinang's strength in the northern Peninsular Malaysia. Kelantan, Terengganu, Pahang, and part of north eastern Johor are grouped together to form the East Coast Economic Region (ECER). In the southern part, Western Johor forms the major part of the Iskandar region. Likewise, there are the Sarawak Corridor of Renewable Energy (SCORE) and Sabah Development Corridor (SDC) at Sarawak and Sabah, respectively. The economic regions, as supported by Krugman (1995), are to function as economic zones for job generations at local areas so as to arrest the migration especially of the younger population out of their states. Introduction of economic zones may explain the changes that could be seen in the AAGR by the state for 2000–2010. The economic regions, especially in Iskandar and SCORE have seen the introduction of many educational institutions that generate population growth and jobs.

Social Effects of Urban Growth, Inequality, and Urban Poverty

The rural to urban migration causes serious problems to city managers who have to continuously manage and provide the required needs for these migrants. With various tiers of government located within the same locality, there exists disharmony in the role and scope of each tiers of government here. Each tier attempts to outdo the other causing disruption and inconsistency in services and facilities provided. Furthermore, different levels of urbanization rate across the country cause further disparity between states and regions. In 2014, the Gini coefficient in Malaysia was 0.391 and 0.355 for urban and rural areas, respectively, showing inequality in the distribution of economic wealth between urban and rural centres. Urban and rural demography also explains the incidence of poverty in the country. Even with more economic activities in urban areas, the incidence of poverty stood at 0.2% in 2016 as against 1.0% in rural areas (Table 10.2). The table illustrates a clear urban–rural divide in the incidence of poverty, suggesting that economic factors have resulted in lower incidence of poverty in urban areas. The rural sector had a rate of 58.5% in 1970 as against less than half of this rate at 25.5% in urban areas. The corresponding rates have been reported to be almost nil by 2016. The influx of rural to urban migrants have caused a pressure on the urban economy to absorb the constant arrival of migrants, and pose pressure to city administrations in constantly providing the required facilities year by year. Over time, the national capital has seen the rise in the homeless living on the streets, evident from the number of such persons assisted daily by soup kitchen food donors. Such an incidence contradicts the reported very low rates of incidence of poverty by the government. In August 2019, United Nations special rapporteur stated that the actual poverty rate could be between 15 and 20%

Table 10.2 Incidence of urban and rural poverty rate, Malaysia, 1970–2016 (%)

Year	Urban	Rural	Total national
1970	25.5	58.5	49.3
1976	15.4	45.7	37.7
1979	17.5	45.8	37.4
1984	8.5	27.3	20.7
1987	8.5	24.8	19.4
1989	7.1	21.1	16.5
1992	4.7	21.2	12.4
1995	3.6	14.9	8.7
1997	2.1	10.9	6.1
1999	3.3	14.8	8.5
2002	2.3	13.5	6.0
2004	2.7	11.9	5.7
2007	2.0	7.1	3.6
2009	1.7	8.4	3.8
2012	1.0	3.4	1.7
2014	0.3	1.6	0.6
2016	0.2	1.0	0.4

Sources Economic Planning Unit (2012), Department of Statistics Malaysia (2016)

currently. There is always disagreement with the poverty line being RM980 per household of four persons as the figure appears to be far too low and unrealistic.

Poverty rate was highest at 64.8% among the Bumiputeras followed by 39.2% for ethnic Indians in 1970 but this has been reduced to 2.2% and 1.8%, respectively, by 2012 (UNDP, 2014). Similar observations were made in terms of hardcore poverty rate which dropped from 9.9% (1984) to 0.3% (2012) for Bumiputeras and from 1.9% to 0.2% for ethnic Indians, respectively (UNDP, 2014). Between 1970 and 2012, average annual income grew at 6.91% for Top 20%, 7.54% for Middle 40%, and 7.89% for Bottom 40% of the population (see UNDP, 2014, p. 34), made possible by national policies that targeted the lower income households, which also saw Bumiputeras benefitting through the highest growth. Rapid urban growth has recorded a rise in median monthly income from RM4238 in 2010 to RM5156 in 2014 at the national level. The figures for rural areas are RM2372 and RM3123, respectively. In tandem with rising costs of living, the urban household size has also dwindled from 5.2 in 1980 to a mere 4.32 in 2010. UNDP (2014) reports that reforms in the labour market such as ensuring a minimum salary of RM900 per month reduces inequality by almost 8%. Reforms in education will reduce inequality by 4%, and income transfers of a minimum RM500 to the lower income group will reduce the inequality gap by one percent. If all these reforms were put together, one could expect a contraction of inequality by seven percent. On 10 July 2020, the government raised the poverty line to RM2208, acknowledging that the poverty rate is 5.6% in 2019, raising the number of poor households from 24,700 in 2016 to 405,441 in 2019 (The Star, 19 July 2020).

Ill-Effects on Rural Areas

Like in other international cities, rural to urban migration and foreign in-migration also invite crime that has become a menace in urban centres in Malaysia. Migration has caused some small towns to be abandoned as youngsters flock to urban centres leaving their old parents to mend paddy fields, which are eventually abandoned due to old age. Some towns have also faced negative growth, especially due to the introduction of new infrastructure development like a highway that is built across towns.

Cities Are Centres for Crime

Faced with the challenges in lifestyle of urban dwellers and those who flocked to urban centres, a number in the city turn to street crime to earn a fast living, some even threatening the lives of others. However, the Malaysian Royal Police have claimed that crime rates have lowered over the years. Such crimes are said to involve Malaysian citizens as well as foreigners alike. Most of the reported crimes (see Fig. 10.1) are incidents at urban areas.

Total reported crime in 2018 is highest in Kuala Lumpur (The Star, 13 June 2020) commensurate with the highest population per sq km being 7,366, economic factors, social problems in the society, and unemployment rates. Consistent with population density, reported crimes are highest in major cities. Incidence of crime was reported to decline from 2011 as the police reportedly made serious efforts to combat the problem. Many of the crime reports are symptoms of economic pressure onto urban dwellers who could not cope with the demands of urban living.

Health Issues

The prevalence of mental disorders in urban areas was 80.8% as compared to 48.9% in rural areas (Reddy & Chandrasekhar, 1998) which was largely associated with urbanization (Srivastava, 2009). Environmental degradation also causes more impact on the urban dwellers than rural residents. Given the larger proportion of residents in urban areas, it would be more efficient to provide health facilities in urban areas, where there is also the incidence of poverty and the lower-income group needs attention. Following Paul Samuelson's theory of public expenditure, the public provision is best

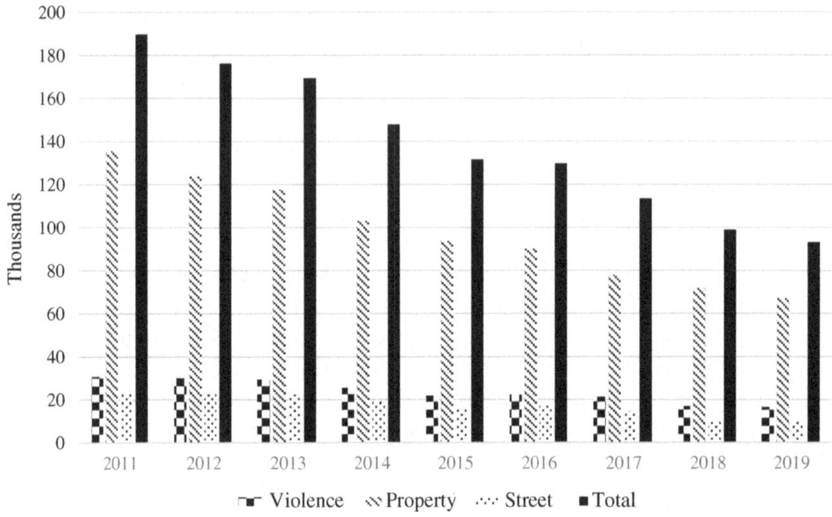

Fig. 10.1 Incidence of reported crime, Malaysia, 2011–2019. *Source* PDRM, by official request

by the public sector for goods that are not rivalled and non-excludable. Samuelson's theory fits when there is market failure that disallows citizens equitable access to services, and healthcare. Stiff competition between private healthcare requires these institutions to operate for profit and offer efficiency. Public healthcare institutions, on the other hand are laden with heavy overcrowding of urban and rural people who could not afford the expensive private healthcare services. The public sector continues to bear the costs of healthcare, especially in urban areas. It is thus sensible that healthcare institutions are found at urban centres than otherwise.

Urban Growth and Housing

With rural–urban migration comes the issue of housing, especially for the poor and those with low income. In the Ninth Malaysia Plan, 80% of the houses were built by the private sector but these targeted the middle and upper-income groups. The poor and the less fortunate have had their houses built by the public sector or the private sector by means of public policies that dedicate certain proportion of the development for low-cost housing. Due to risk-taking, private developers too continue to strain public funds when they abandon housing projects leaving many, who have paid deposits and have taken loans from financial institutions, in trouble. In its intention to provide more housing units, the Malaysian government has had a number of institutions to provide low-cost and affordable housing, including the *Perumahan Rakyat 1Malaysia* (PRIMA), which comes under the purview of the Prime Minister's Department despite there being a dedicated ministry for this purpose.

In the provision of urban housing, the government plays both the role of a planner and a developer. Insufficient provision of housing in urban areas can cause further problems to urban settlers who have to pay high rentals to reside although there are also public programmes such as those under City Hall of Kuala Lumpur which offers cheap rentals to them. Many seek slum areas to avoid paying high instalments and other payments to authorities. As this could affect their wellbeing and health in the long run, it is important that the government provides transition homes that become temporary housing for these people before they are moved to permanent housing. Nonetheless, these homes must be maintained. Of late, findings show that these units have been leased out to foreigners to the extent that local residents feel unsafe of their presence. Urban poverty must be contained so as to ensure that these do not turn into social issues in urban areas.

Wan Nor Azriyati et al. (2014) showed that the government (including the SEDCs) could not complete the targeted numbers of housing units especially for the poor, over the various Malaysia Plans where it took the role of a developer. The best performance of the government was during the 8th Malaysia Plan when it completed 188,189 houses including for the hardcore poor, which is its main focus. The government has had to depend on the private developers to provide the required numbers. As can be seen in Table 10.3, over the various Malaysia Plans, the government could only provide about 20% of required housing while the private sector built the rest. The private developers are entrusted to provide low-cost housing as part of their responsibility when they develop housing for the middle and the high-income group. The overdependence on the private sector in the provision of low-cost housing whose price is controlled by the government causes shoddy finishing work on the units while some are built at locations far from centre of economic activities. The government will increasingly continue to plan housing for the poor and the hardcore poor with the private sector being the main implementer under its National Housing Policy launched in 2011. This follows the international pressure on governments to adopt neo-liberalism concept that empowers the private sector in the provision of government products and services while the public sector facilitates implementation and the policymaker. Nonetheless, the pressure to build for the poor and the hardcore poor appears to continue despite the number of units provided over time, made worse by the migration of people from the rural to urban centres, and coupled with the influx of foreign migrants, both legal and illegal, across the national borders. Another focus is now taking a strong footing in the country—not only to provide housing for the poor and the hardcore poor, but also affordability, which poses a more serious challenge for the government.

Urban living has become more gated or going vertical. The former has become a lifestyle for the affluent communities, which also augurs well to better protection against crime. Others resort to vertical living in apartments, condominiums, and service apartments for various reasons. In addition, urban living has caused neighbours to be strangers to each other as most urban dwellers have devoted time and effort in search of financial resources. This has increasingly become a social issue for the government to address, at least for now.

Table 10.3 Provision of housing by public and private sectors, Malaysia (1991–2010)

	6MP (1991–95)	7MP (96–2000)	8MP (2001–05)	9MP (2006–10)	Total (1995–2010)
Public					
Hardcore poverty housing	15,376	62,812	9,536	31,700	104,048
Low-cost housing	8,075	7,188	81,108	42,300	130,596
Government quarters/staff housing	18,776	12,015	47,505	27,200	86,720
SEDC housing projects/land settlement schemes	42,315	39,609	50,040	9,600	99,249
PR1MA, PPA1M, RUMAWIP	Na	Na	Na	Na	
Total	84,542	121,624	188,189	110,800	420,613
Private					
Low-cost housing	212,003	127,514	94,029	53,500	275,043
Low-medium-cost housing	0	0	53,607	25,000	78,607
Medium- and high-cost housing	339,010	596,639	484,587	369,700	1,450,926
Cooperative housing	11,905	13,703	23,151	0	36,854
Total	562,918	737,856	655,374	448,200	1,841,430
Total public and private	647,460	859,480	843,563	559,000	2,262,043
% Public housing	13.1	14.2	22.3	19.8	18.6
% private housing	86.9	85.8	77.7	80.2	81.4

Sources Adapted from Wan Nor Azriyati et al. (2014), Economic Planning Unit (2011), Exhibit 4-4, pp. 4–7, and Strategy Paper 6
Note Figure for 10 MP and beyond were not available

Urban Growth and Environment

Cities are good consumers of resources, including food, water, supplies, and agriculture products which are produced by the hinterland. Each Malaysian consumes about 226 L of water per day, a figure that is higher than their neighbours in the region—90 L in Thailand, 130 L in Indonesia, and 155 L in Singapore.

With rapid urbanization comes its detrimental effect on the size of green cover and increase in the emission of pollutants. Development that takes place has been at the cost of the number of trees in the cities although local governments have been entrusted by law to protect the trees, or to ensure that such trees are replaced once any particular development is completed. With more people travelling from outskirts of cities into the city centres for employment, emission of pollutants causes negative impacts to the environment, unless they use public transportation. Many Malaysians still use private vehicles as it is cheaper, faster and brings them to the doorstep of their destination, which most other public transportation could not offer.

Urban wastes contribute about two-thirds of all solid waste materials in Malaysian urban areas. Of this, between 70 and 80% originate from household wastes alone. The other sources of wastes come from commercial (8%), industrial wastes (25%), and construction wastes (3%). With increasing urbanization, it is common that industrial operations other than in industrial estates are forced out of urban areas, and with that the contribution of industrial wastes to total urban waste production in the future may be lowered but this may increase the production of wastes at the outskirts of cities and large towns. The process will continue to exist in cycles over time when new settlements are established around the new industrial sites as such. Although urban solid waste disposal services have been privatized in some states in the peninsula to private consortia by region, the federal government could only fund about 70% of the solid waste disposal fee of the consortia, thus still requiring local authorities to pay about 30% of the remaining fee. To some local authorities, their proportion to pay the private fee is too high, and some have had to seek the help of Ministry of Housing and Local Government. With more people moving into urban areas, more funds have to be allocated to fund urban services and to pay fees to private consortia. On average, a household generated 1.64 kg of wastes a day, a figure that is higher than the international average, this contributed 16,247 tonnes of wastes per day in 2013. This is expected to become 11 million tonnes a year by 2020. The more people moving into urban areas, the more wastes will be generated.

Governing Urbanization

Urban matters are mainly the responsibility of local governments as the latter is made responsible on it. As enshrined under the Federal Constitution, local government is placed under the purview of state government. Malaysia embraces a federal system comprising a three tier government system.

Urbanization certainly requires the involvement of various parties of the government and civil society. Urban governance in that sense requires an environment that has adequate legal framework, and the administrative tools to manage the issues at the urban ground, be it political, social, or economic. Urban governance involves various institutions and individuals with a common goal of administering the city's administration, development, and growth. Often becomes more important in large cities, and many impinge on the issues of accountability, transparency, democratic and inclusiveness. Local governments play a pivotal role in exemplifying these.

Local Government

Among the three tiers of the government, local government has the biggest role in managing, rather than addressing, urbanization. Local authorities in the peninsula are guided by the Local Government Act 1976 in empowering the administration of the city, while the Town and Country Planning Act 1976 empowers the local authorities to be the local planning authority. These are supported by the third legislation, i.e. the Streets, Drainage and Buildings Act which was passed by the parliaments much earlier than the former two, in 1974. Local governments in Sabah and Sarawak are governed by their respective ordinances. As a government, a local authority is vested with powers to establish its own bylaws to assist in its administration and enforcement of the law. Under these legislations, local authorities are the urban administrators and all inhabitants including other institutions are bound to comply with the rules set by their local authorities. However, the state government has full control over land matters, while the federal; government governs over most national concerns including income tax, enforcement, national physical planning, and coordination.

With more people migrating to urban areas and cities, local governments, more aptly called local authorities in Malaysia, have to deal with the pressure for public housing, urban transportation, traffic congestions, urban services, urban health and hygiene services, and recreation. Local government too has to manage illegal traders including unlicensed hawkers, street living, slum settlements, and pollution. These add further costs and challenges to the operations of the local authorities, most of which are in need of additional revenue sources to fund their operations. Other federal agencies also manage the issue of acknowledging urban migration, and this includes addressing crime and illegal trades, job creations, economic growth, and pollution. With the pressure for better urban management, local governments must be placed on a stable and strong financial platform, which is usually not the case (Kuppusamy, 2007, 2008).

Urbanization must be handled in a manner that all positive effects are nurtured and counter actions are taken against the negative effects. Although various government agencies and ministries are working towards addressing urbanization issues, they tend to work in silos. With multiple agencies working at local levels, physical development comes under the purview of local authorities and the Town and Country Planning Department (TCPD), which operates at federal and state levels.

Furthermore, development at the local level is of interest not only to the local authority but also to the higher two tiers of the government. The federal government also depends on grassroots support of the local people. However, the development is located under the jurisdictional area of the local government, which falls under the powers of the state government. As land is a state matter, infrastructure development at the local level is a complex issue often leading to power struggles. It is pertinent that all three tiers work hand in hand to provide and coordinate development, infrastructure, and amenities required by the local people. This would also provide for guided investment at local levels.

Infrastructure and Urban Planning

Prior to 2005, urban planning was piecemeal depending on directives and plans of individual authorities. Local authorities have had to process planning permissions based on applications to the local authorities for approval. However, local authorities rely on Local Plans and district Structure Plans as a legal framework to approve or reject the application. Over time, Structure Plans were relegated to state level planning documents while Local Plans focus on district level land use development. With its functions and jurisdictions, TCPD was instrumental in introducing the National Physical Plan (NPP-1, 2005). NPP-1 established the economic conurbations and also set the hierarchies of townships towards supporting the conurbations, most of which became the economic zones now labelled as National Growth Conurbation (Kuala Lumpur), Regional Growth Conurbations (George Town, Johor Bahru, Kuantan), Intermediate Growth Conurbations (Ipoh, Melaka), and Urban Growth Centres (Kota Bharu, Alor Setar, Kuala Terengganu, Kangar). It also registered small and intermediate towns. For the first time, the NPP-1 also coordinated cross-district and cross-state infrastructure projects such as highways and freeways and garnered support from various states and local authorities.

The revised National Physical Plan 2010–2020 (NPP-2) was endorsed in August 2010 with its goal stated as "*the establishment of an efficient, equitable and sustainable national spatial framework to guide the overall development of the country towards achieving developed and high-income nation status by 2020*". NPP-2 sets out a development strategy for Peninsular Malaysia known as "concentrated decentralisation" where it is estimated that by the year of 2020, urbanization in Peninsular Malaysia would be 75% and 70% of urban population will be in four major conurbations known as the Kuala Lumpur Conurbation, George Town Conurbation, Kuantan Conurbation and Johor Bahru Conurbation (Fig. 10.2). A third version of the NPP (i.e. NPP-3) which is already in place looks at detailing out and strengthening policies in NPP-2. The fourth NPP was launched in mid-November 2021.

Although not directly related to Krugman's (1995) work, one of the key strategies is to concentrate the nation's scarce resources to a few priority urban areas with the greatest growth potential for job creation along the key economic corridors (while protecting the rural areas and natural environment). Another strategy is to focus on the future new urban development and regeneration in selected urban conurbations and key urban areas (which indirectly generate spin-offs to catalyze the development of surrounding areas in the regions), and eventually, to support the growth through the implementation of high-impact flagship projects or key infrastructure facilities.

The Sabah and Sarawak side of the infrastructure strategy is to attain a more balanced rural–urban spatial development, with the basic amenities covering water, energy, and transportation and telecommunications which is still lagging behind the peninsula.

Multi-tier Federal-State-Local Relationship

Urban development did not rely completely on local governments alone. A large part of it is funded through fiscal federalism. Over the years, the dependence of state and local governments on federal transfers has increased. Federal government

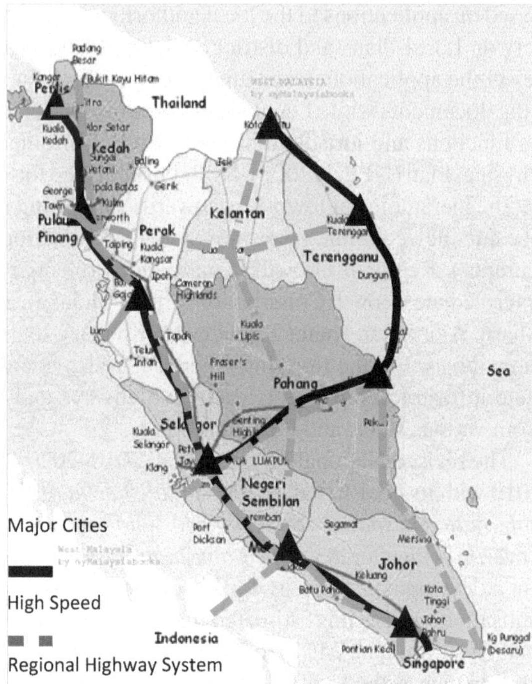

Fig. 10.2 Malaysia: major conurbations by 2050

development expenditure per capita has only risen from the Seventh Malaysia Plan and peaked at the Ninth Malaysia Plan, but still maintained a difference between East and West Malaysia in absolute per capita terms (UNDP, 2014).

While the pressure of urbanization falls mainly onto local governments, it is highly common to witness state agencies and federal agencies operating at the local level. However, as independent institutions, federal and state agencies neither consult nor coordinate their developmental activities with the local government as the latter is deemed lower in hierarchy of power. Each tier of government is in charge of respective responsibilities at the local level. In some cases, there have been numerous instances whereby the higher tiers tend to bypass the need to obtain the approval of the development plan by local government. With heavy dependence of local government on legislated annual federal equalization grant and that for development, federal agencies tend to disregard the need to get approval of local government of the development plans, as they are guided by the Ministry of Works and the Ministry of Finance guidelines. There have been cases where the federal government through its Public Services Department attempts to appoint the President of local authorities while the state government has the executive jurisdiction to do so. Having a federal appointed presidency allows for the assimilation of federal policies into the local level, which often irks state governments. This is however limited to the Federated Malay States and the Straits Settlements in the peninsula. The Unfederated Malay States have full authority in such appointment in their states. The public service department also rightfully controls the creation of posts in the local government administration. The state government on the other hand controls local governments in budgetary matters, planning approvals, being collateral for loans, adoption of federal directives and laws, implementation of revaluation exercise and revised rates, demarcation of local authority jurisdictional area (Kuppusamy, 2013).

In addition, the state government appoints the councillors who represent political affiliation rather than the local residents. There has been experience where the federal government took away some of the functions of local government with the claim that local governments are unable to meet the current expectations of the people. Topping this in the list is the urban cleaning services and sewerage services. The state governments, tended to agree that services across the boundaries of each local authority area must be synchronized. Thus state governments feel the services such as public car parking rates must be standardized, thus "snatched away" to a private consortium, such as in Selangor when it was government by National Front. During the same era, the Menteri Besar presented a broom to each non-performing local authority. In another instance, the current Selangor state government objected to the federal government's renewal of the solid waste disposal contract to Alam Flora Sdn Bhd, which reverted the solid waste disposal back to its local authorities. Although this was said to avoid over charging onto local governments in the state by the consortium, the public is wary that this is part of the political tussle between the Selangor state government and the federal government. These illustrate the weak systemic nature of the third tier government as against that of the federal and the state governments. Yet, the third tier government has to bear the brunt of urbanization and continues to serve the local area.

While local governments could enact by laws as its right, this is only to be exercised with its boundaries and coordination with neighbouring local authorities fall under the purview of their state government. However, coordination of local government matters across the state boundaries fall under the power of the federal government as the key local government legislations (the empowering acts for local authorities i.e. Local Government Act 1976; Town and Country Planning Act, 1976; and the Streets, Drainage and Buildings Act 1974) were enacted by the parliament.

These show the complex nature of the federal-state-local government relationship which also affects the manner in which urbanization issues at the local level are handled. These often lead to finger-pointing between the tiers of government.

The way urban centres are managed depends very much on the financial stability of various agencies, especially the local government. This may depart from the key role of local government as the city managers but with poor financial standing are unable to address urbanization issues. There is only good coordination through the formulation of Structure Plans, Local Plans, and Special Area Local Plans where all local parties are consulted for policy formulation and decisions. In addition, it is claimed that various agencies in the city meet sparingly to coordinate local activities. The other tussle is always with the leadership of the district and land office which believes that rapid urbanization side steps its power over the land, thus posing another challenge to local authorities. However, the latter only appears an important issue more in rural settings. In sum, urban politics and inter-agency relationships do not augur well to urban management, at least at present.

Urban Leap into the Future

Urban centres are well connected through road and rail networks that allow for ease of transportation of urban stakeholders. With the concentration of the people in urban areas, there is a better use of funds to provide transportation infrastructure in cities. This is now evident in large cities in Malaysia, especially at Kuala Lumpur. With the introduction of new transportation infrastructure, there is now more vertical development around transportation hubs in Kuala Lumpur while the price of properties has escalated compared with those further from major transportation hubs. It is now feasible to consider that people are willing to stay faraway but travel to major cities to work and return home using transportation infrastructure that is already considered efficient. Some public transportation systems such as KTMB Komuter and the LRT systems are highly congested during peak hours. As a result, economic growth is spread away from major cities to urban centres in the peripheries. Examples of these are Seremban, Nilai, Klang, and Bentong. In the future, this trend is likely to be fortified further as the people find it unaffordable to own a house especially in major cities like Kuala Lumpur, Johor Bahru, and Pulau Pinang. Looking at this, the Malaysian Ministry of Transportation has targeted a 40:60 modal split to encourage and foster the shift to use public transportation, i.e. achieving 40% use of public transportation by 2030. Kuala Lumpur, the most developed city in the country has only achieved 20% despite having started initiatives towards this intent for over a decade, while Johor Bahru at the southern gateway, has only met 15% by 2015 (Sinniah et al., 2021). Road users complain that connectivity with new and existing public transportation systems is problematic and question the efficiency of the system which lacked punctuality to schedules.

By 2050, the world population is projected to be 9.7 billion compared with 2.5 billion in 1950 and 6.9 billion in 2010 (United Nations, 2015a, b). Asia alone is expected to have 55% of the total population of the world in 2050. The United Nations (2015a, b) also projects the world to have a smaller population growth than 1.18% experienced in 2015, i.e. 0.6% by 2050 caused by a drop in the fertility rate that is expected to fall to 2.25 by 2050 compared to 3.87 in 1980.

Within this broad framework, Malaysia is heading towards 40.7 million people by 2050 compared with 30.5 million in 2015 (Table 10.4). The population growth is expected to dip too from 2.8% between 1950 and 1955 to 1.5% between 2010 and 2015 and to 0.4% between 2045 and 2050 (United Nations, 2015b, p. 479). Fertility rate in the country has dipped from 6.23 children per woman between 1950 and 1955 to only 1.9 by 2016 and is expected to fall further to 1.7 between 2045 and 2050. Population density is expected to grow from 19 per sq km in 1950 to 92 per sq km in 2015 and to 124 per sq km by 2050.

Table 10.4 Malaysia, population projections till 2050

	2015	2020	2025	2030	2035	2040	2050
Total population (mil)	30.5	32.6	34.5	36.1	37.4	38.4	40.7
% urban population	72.5	75.0	78.5	81.9	83.0	84.1	85.9
% rural population	27.5	21.0	21.5	18.1	17.0	15.9	14.1

Sources Tey et al. (2016), United Nations (2015a, b)
Note For 2050, uses United Nations (2015b), Medium Variant

In 2050, the whole country will be much more developed than that achieved by 2020 as envisaged by the NPP-2. The growth in transportation and urban development will emphasize inter-city connectivity including new high-speed rail systems to complement the parallel double-tracking system that will connect nine new cities as new growth centres enhancing the development of the three growth corridors first introduced in the Ninth Malaysia Plan, together with the Greater Klang Valley conurbation which was the focus of the Eleventh Malaysia Plan. At the same time, environmental considerations will ensure the impact of industrialization, urban development and housing will not jeopardize the quality of rivers, which would be enhanced over the thirty-year period from 2020, as well as the continued supply of water through efficient catchment area development. Rivers especially in Sarawak will also be playing revived roles for inland transport. Sabah and Sarawak will also be linked not just by the new Pan Borneo Highway, but also by a new railway system linking their major cities. Energy supply would have to be provided by major hydropower projects currently being developed, but also supplemented by mini-hydroelectric systems to ensure environmental integrity. Biodiversity, climate change, and land use considerations would be addressed by reference to Agenda 21 on Sustainability, Convention on Biological Diversity, Convention on Climate Change and the strategies mandated by the UN Habitat II. Malaysia has pledged a reduction of carbon emission of up to 45% by 2030 (Ministry of Urban Wellbeing, Housing and Local Government, 2016). This envisages many green technology initiatives to address climate change in Malaysia by means of low carbon and resource effectiveness and reduction of greenhouse gases, reducing air pollution that would help reduce climate change and environmental disasters. The objective of the development in the whole country by 2050 will be to maximize not only the productivity per worker in the country but also productivity per square kilometre in the peninsular, Sabah and Sarawak, while maintaining environmental sustainability. By 2050, Sabah and Sarawak cities are expected to attain the infrastructure levels experienced by the peninsula today. Kota Kinabalu, and Papar; as well as Sandakan and Tawau should be nearing city sizes, along with Kuching, Samarahan and Serian in Sarawak.

As per Table 10.4, the urbanization level would be approaching 86% by 2050. It would mean that almost nine in ten persons would be residing in urban centres by 2050. This would require more space to cater for the population growth, perhaps at the expense of the environment. It is not expected that people in rural areas would move further inland to retain their rural status as almost all current rural areas would have become suburban or fully urban centres. Following this, urban centres will be facing scarce land for development while older townships will increasingly undergo urban renewal and land readjustment schemes to rejuvenate townships. What is abundant now such as water, may be difficult to be taken that way. Malaysians will have no options other than accepting the fact that they have to conserve water and energy. Malaysians will be more environmental conscious. It can be expected that water will be more efficiently managed through inter-state connections—a measure that has already begun now, and this resource would be more expensive in the future, and water tariff would thus be consistent between states.

Within the filling of the geographic space with transport and telecommunication facilities, no community urban or rural in Malaysia 2050 will be more than an hour away from a major city or regional centre. Malaysia then will be a truly integrated economic space and elevating itself on track away from being an upper middle-class society.

Additional conurbations shall emerge by 2050 incorporating Penang, Johore and the Iskandar Region, Greater Kuantan, Kuala Terengganu and Kota Kinabalu in Sabah, and Kuching-Mukah-Bintulu as the centre of the SCORE region in Sarawak.

Urbanization in the future should be guided by six key themes: high-tech living; healthy living; urban wellbeing; citizen empowerment; fostering mutual respect and tolerance; and good urban governance. Attention has to be given in controlling urbanization outcomes and provision of efficient and effective services in urban centres and roping in the citizens towards meeting common targets and needs.

Based on the foregoing discussion, some of the expected urbanization outcomes in 2050 are as follows:

- Growth in urbanization rate may dampen—due to slower population growth and dependence on urban renewal and reduction of urban sprawl.
- There will be more numbers of large cities in Malaysia. There may also be a megacity in the Klang Valley due to the agglomeration of a few major cities.
- More international and cosmopolitan cities will emerge. Together with these, crime may co-exist.
- Cities will be impressively managed well, deviating from the current system in local authorities, by city managers who are elected for performance.
- Metropolitan local government may be formed as another tier to coordinate and manage large neighbouring cities like in Rawang, Selayang, Kuala Lumpur, Petaling Jaya, Subang Jaya, Shah Alam, Klang, Nilai, Seremban in Greater Kuala Lumpur; Melaka would have one metropolitan city management managing all its four local authorities; and one in Johor to govern Kulai, Iskandar Puteri, Johor Bahru, Pasir Gudang, Pontian, and Kluang. Sarawak is likely to own a metropolitan city managing both North Kuching and South Kuching cities, Samarahan and Serian. Sabah is not anticipated to have a metropolitan city management by then.
- Local government will need to be financially stable and strong. This will also be one of the reasons that local governments are shifted under the scope of federal government, though it should not be.

- Cities will use ICT and modern technology in its operations. In turn, the performance of cities will be measured in terms of how efficient city operations optimize the use of technology and automation.
- City management will leverage smart administration and living. This will involve enforcement through smart surveillance, smart traffic management, smart detection of urban problems, and many more aspects of city administration will be done without the need for stakeholders to face the officers at the office.
- More emphasis into modern public transportation—as cities are provided with better public transportation system and infrastructure. Thus more people will turn to public transportation.
- Population growth will be slower in urban areas—due to scarcity of space and high cost of living, and the intention to have a child will be affected by high cost of living factors besides fertility.
- There will be more emphasis on urban wellbeing. Citizens will be empowered, and local government system in the country will operate in a democratic manner, i.e. local councillors will be elected.
- Private cars may be too expensive to operate, and it may be owned only by the rich. Perhaps, it may not be impossible to see flying cars, which will change the way roads are to be used.
- People will be more willing to travel from far away to work in large cities, using more efficient and connected public transportation.
- People will be more concerned with environmental protection, and they will be highly concerned with green living. Citizens will be very concerned with environmental degradation, and the need to abate global warming and deforestation. All their activities will be checked against the need to arrest pollution, environmental degradation, and minimizing wastes.
- More residential units will be built towards high-technology living, and employing green technology and green living. This is already evident in some new housing developments in the peninsula.

The future also has threats as the last decade has witnessed the rise in crime in urban areas, including those by foreign migrants. This has somewhat impacted the urban wellbeing and satisfaction of urban dwellers, including those who carry out economic activities here. While the authorities have claimed that crime rates have lowered, there is mistrust among the public on these claims. It is believed that crime prevention will elevate higher and achieve a better satisfaction level consistent with greater and efficient enforcement systems in the public service.

The success of urbanization would depend on whether urban dwellers are happy and satisfied with their quality of urban living. To this end, by 2050, Malaysia would see urban areas having large scale urban green canopies and recreational areas, and where the older generation will be empowered to manage some of these infrastructures and services.

Nevertheless, the country will be facing the following critical issues:

- Malaysia will be almost a century old by 2050 as an independent country. Most of the existing infrastructure will be too old by then, which would inevitably require considerable refurbishment. There will thus be a continuous need to maintain or

renew existing infrastructure that includes network or transportation, telecommunication, and physical assets. This would require heavy investment to be at least partially financed by heavier taxes on the people.
- Public transportation and the transportation infrastructure will need continuous attention to ensure that people are happy to use them rather than relying on their own vehicles.
- The proportion of the aged in the population will be high, and cities will require more infrastructure and support systems built and managed for them.

Urbanization Strategies for the Future

Among the key strategies for Malaysia's urban future are the need for high-tech lifestyles, including employing potentials of ICT; intensification of green canopies in urban areas; arresting pollution; highly integrated underground public transportation systems; enforcement of law and well maintained facilities and amenities. As such, there is a need to minimize the negative impact of urban development on the environment. This can be undertaken by concentrating growth in existing urban centres, and by supporting compact city development, and vertical growth centres (which would support reduction of greenhouse gases). In addition, there is a need to enhance efficient use of resources: water, electricity, fuel (green fuel); as well as ensuring efficient use of technology: green technology in buildings, street lights, intelligent traffic systems, underground power cables, fibre optics; increase in green cover towards reducing greenhouse gases.

Towards this end, there will be a dire need to move towards urban wellbeing policies to ensure the functioning of urban dwellings to attain satisfaction in terms of liveability, happiness, competitiveness for the development of an inclusive society. This will require having an excellent and integrated public transportation system, which will assist the movement of human capital who could travel from home to workplaces without having to drive through congested roads. To encapsulate all these, there is a serious need to have an efficient city management through able managers and by full empowerment of local elected governments as city managers at the grassroots level. Communities must be empowered and engaged to ensure they play a role and take responsibility over their environment.

Some of the dysfunctional developmental issues as crime, new urban poverty, insufficient housing, and slum development, lack of recreational facilities, and lack of community empowerment, can be arrested if development is focussed and confined to "compact and green development" in existing cities as this also brings about a reduction in greenhouse gases (GHG) while saving the forests from human encroachment. The role of state governments in these matters is highly important. With more government emphasis on transit-oriented development, compact development would serve best with high connectivity and integration with technology and infrastructure to produce efficient and optimal use of natural resources. The government has moved towards increasing the modal split to the favour of public transportation, and this can be tapped further with more serious efforts and concerted urban planning. There is room for greater participation of the private sector in urban sectors including transportation and housing whereby the public sector could function as a facilitator of controlled development to provide subsidized services. For once, the move towards achieving a greater modal split in transportation must be supported by increased and efficient public transportation that would avoid concrete jungles and elevated highways in urban areas.

Communities in cities and large townships have shown to be actively involved in a variety of activities to meet their interests, though most of them are government-driven. There is large opportunities for the urban citizens to be empowered to determine their needs, including in choosing their own representatives to manage local governments. The advantages of ICT and digitalization should be appropriated by expanding its use in urban services. Efforts must be taken to raise the use of automation in public infrastructure facilities and amenities, including public transport, street lighting, and supply of water while at the same time optimizing the use of human power.

Conclusions

Malaysia is already a model Muslim-majority multi-ethnic and multi-cultural country where people of different faith and culture live in harmony. By the fifth decade of this century, save untoward major crises, the country is slated to be a modern high-income cosmopolitan country that would leverage on maximizing use of technology in the nation's administration. It will continue to attract migrants not only from rural areas, but also from neighbouring urban cities as well as international immigrants. The urbanization process will continue to be challenging for city managers and deconcentrated central agencies. Poverty will continue to be a major issue but in urban living rather than those in the traditional rural set-up.

The nation and cities would need leaders who are more dedicated, accountable, and compassionate to achieve efficient and effective urban governance. In the next three decades, the current and previous infrastructure systems would have to be renewed, repaired, or replaced including on systems that are obsolete by then. Financial resources will never be enough for any city administrator. Financial resources will have to be optimized. By then, city administrators must have the systemic applications that would alert issues and information richer than what city dwellers would have, consistent with Modernization Theory. City administration would need to be more proactive in administration and maintenance rather than being reactive. Not too far from now, accountability of city managers and councillors will be reverted and directed to the people rather than to the political masters. It is very likely that current local governments will fall under metropolitan city management structures soon, thus, the inability to perform in which lackadaisical attitudes shown by policy implementers can only be considered as lame excuses that should not be tolerated. There will also be more regional growth centres that would be dedicated to support the balanced development of clusters and integrated value chains in the country so that the outcomes will be in sync with Krugman's (1995) expectations. However, the role of local government shall always remain, and it should be independent of state and federal governments, at whatever costs so that it continues to play its role to benefit future generations of the country.

References

Bradshaw, Y. (1987). Urbanization and underdevelopment: A global study of modernization, urban bias, and economic dependency. *American Sociological Review, 52*(2), 224–239.

Castells, M. (Ed.). (2005). *The network society: A cross cultural perspective*. Edward Elgar.

Chan, H. C. (2011, August). Making a city liveable: The secret is economic growth from below. *Penang Monthly*.

Chaudhary, A. (2013). Modernization: Impact, theory, advantages and disadvantages. *International Journal for Research in Education, 2*(2), 34–38.

Dayita, & Priya, R. (2019). *Social network to monitor Malaysian living standards*. Final year project paper approved by Malaysian University of Science and Technology (MUST), Kuala Lumpur

Guneet, G. (2008). *Urban Sprawl, an issue of growing concern*, 44th ISOCARP Congress 2008. Retrieved December 31, 2016, from www.isocarp.net/Data/case_studies/1360.pdf

Department of Statistics Malaysia. (2016). *Household income and expenditure survey*. Prime Minister's Department, Putrajaya.

Economic Planning Unit. (2011). *Eleventh Malaysia Plan 2016–2020: Anchoring growth on people*. Economic Planning Unit.

Economic Planning Unit. (2012). *Socio-economic statistics—Household income and poverty*. Economic Planning Unit, Prime Minister's Department, Putrajaya.

Krugman, P. (1995). *Development, geography, and economic theory*. MIT Press.

Kuppusamy, S. (2007). Local governance and its role in socio-economic development—Lessons from Malaysia. In Park, E. K., & Klitz, W. (Eds), *Good local autonomy & governance, Seoul: Center for Local Autonomy*. Seoul; and Friedrich Naumann Foundation, Korea Office.

Kuppusamy, S. (2008). Local government in Malaysia: Back to basics and the current scene. *Journal for Malaysian Chinese Studies, 11*, 77–96.

Kuppusamy, S. (2013). Local government and intergovernmental relations. In Siddiquee, N. A. (Ed.), *Public management and governance in Malaysia: Trends and transformation*. Routledge.

Lipton, M. (1977). *Why poor people stay poor: urban bias in world development*. Cambridge: Harvard University Press.

Matuschke, I. (2009). Rapid urbanization and food security: Using density maps to identify future food security hotspots. Paper presented at the *International Association of Agricultural Economists Conference*, 16–22 August, Beijing. Retrieved April 21, 2017, from http://www.fao.org/fileadmin/user_upload/esag/docs/RapidUrbanizationFoodSecurity.pdf

McGranahan, G., & Satterthwaite, D. (2014). *Urbanisation concepts and trends*. IIED working paper. International Institute for Environment and Development Press.

Ministry of Urban Wellbeing, Housing and Local Government Malaysia. (2016). Dasar Perbandaran Negara Kedua: Semenanjung Malaysia & Wilayah Persekutuan Labuan. Town & Country Planning Department.

Rasiah, R. (1995). *Foreign capital and industrialization in Malaysia*. Basingstoke: Macmillan.

Rasiah, R. (2007). The systemic quad: Technological capabilities and economic performance of computer and component firms in Penang and Johor Malaysia. *International Journal of Technological Learning, Innovation and Development, 1*(2), 179–203.

Rasiah, R., Yap, X. Y., & Salih, K. (2017). Sub-national governments and technological upgrading in the integrated circuit cluster in Northern Malaysia. *Innovation and Development, 7*(2), 287–307

Reddy, M. V., & Chandrashekhar, C. R. (1998). Prevalence of mental and behavioural disorders in India: A meta-analysis. *India Journal of Psychiatry, 40*, 149–157.
Sinniah, G. K., Li, X., & Abdul Karim, S. (2021). The framework for assessing public transportation by using competitiveness index indicators. Paper presented at *Regional Conference in Civil Engineering and Sustainable Development Goals in Higher Education Institutions 2020*, The Everly Hotel, Putrajaya, 23–25 January 2021. https://doi.org/10.1088/issn.1757-899X
Srivastava, K. (2009). Urbanization and mental health. *Industrial Psychiatry Journal, 18*(2), 75–76.
Tey, N. P., Ng, S. T., & Tan, P. P. (2016). Population projection for development planning in Malaysia. In Peng, T. N., Cheong, K. C., & Rasiah, R. (Eds.), *Revisiting Malaysia's population-development Nexus*. University of Malaya Press.
The Star, *Interactive: From KL to Kinabatangan, a look at Malaysia's crime per capita*, 13 June 2020.
The Star, *Annuar: Address high crime rate in KL*, 14 June 2020.
The Star, *The path to poverty eradication*, 19 July 2020.
Turok, I., & McGranahan, G. (2013). Urbanization and economic growth: The arguments and evidence for Africa and Asia. *Environment & Urbanization, 25*(2), 465–482. https://doi.org/10.1177/0956247813490908
United Nations. (2015a). *World population prospects: The 2015 revision, Volume I: Comprehensive tables*. United Nations.
United Nations. (2015b). *World population prospects: The 2015 revision, Volume II: Demographic profiles*. United Nations.
United Nations. (2018). *The world's cities in 2018—Data booklet*. Department of Economic and Social Affairs, Population Division.
United Nations. (2019). *World Population Prospects 2019*. New York: United Nations.
United Nations Human Settlements Programme. (2016). Urbanization and development: Emerging futures. *World Cities Report 2016*. UN-Habitat.
United Nations Human Settlements Programme. (2019). *Addressing urban and human settlement issues in national adaptation plans—A supplement to the UNFCCC technical guidelines on the national adaptation plan process, Nairobi*.
United Nations Development Programme. (2014). *Malaysian Human Development Report 2013*. UNDP.
Venkatesham, V. (2015). The problems and issues in urbanization in India. *Indian Journal of Research, 4*(8), 277–278.
Wan Nor Azriyati, W. A. A., Kuppusamy, S., Doling, J., & Noor Rosly, H. (2014). Towards a housing policy in Malaysia. In Doling, J., & Romald, R. (Eds.), *Housing East Asia: Socioeconomic and demographic challenges*. Palgrave MacMillan.

Kuppusamy Singaravelloo is Associate Professor at the Faculty of Economics and Administration, Universiti Malaya. He specializes in local government management, urbanization, and finance.

Kamal Salih Ph.D. is an Executive Chairman of Ankar Corporation and Chairman of Malaysia Institute of Economic Research (MIER). He has served as Senior Technical Advisor to UNDP Malaysia and was Adjunct Professor of Economics and Development Studies and Senior Advisor to Asia Europe Institute in University Malaya.

Chapter 11
Future of Labour

Cheong Kee Cheok and Yong Chen Chen

Abstract Since attaining independence, Malaysia has undergone structural transformation of its economy. The labour force has also undergone major changes, the most important being that the share of those in the agricultural sector declined even as that in manufacturing rose. Better education and health also saw the quality of Malaysia's workforce improve. But the Asian Financial Crisis in 1997 exposed several workforce vulnerabilities that left the country in a "middle-income trap". The first is reliance on a low-skill model built around imported labour from less developed countries. Low-skills abetted low wages and discouraged industrial upgrading. A second challenge is Malaysia's low female labour force participation. Greater participation is important given the ageing of Malaysia's population and the gender-based occupational discrimination women face at work. A third labour force issue relates to the limited supply of science and technology (S&T) graduates from the educational system. Affirmative Action education policies coupled with Bumiputra employment in government have de-incentivized science and technology study. Another challenge is the outflow of skilled human capital discussed elsewhere. Premature deindustrialization in which manufacturing employment is shrinking since the 2000s is another issue. Related to the above is the shift to services which has been policy-induced. Although aware of these challenges, the government has produced no specific recommendations to address these challenges. It is uncertain if the political will exist to overcome these challenges. But in an idealized world, Malaysia will have nurtured the required human capital to break free of the middle-income trap.

Keywords Labour force · Low-skill model · Labour force participation · Science and technology · Brain-drain · Deindustrialization

---

C. K. Cheok (✉)
Asia-Europe Institute, University of Malaya, Kuala Lumpur, Malaysia

Y. C. Chen
Faculty of Business and Economics, University of Malaya, 50603 Kuala Lumpur, Malaysia
e-mail: ccyong@um.edu.my

R. Rasiah et al. (eds.), *Malaysia's Leap Into the Future*, Dynamics of Asian Development, https://doi.org/10.1007/978-981-16-7045-9_11

Introduction

Since attaining independence as the Federation of Malaya in 1957, Malaysia has undergone structural transformation that has earned its membership to being what the World Bank lauded as a "high performing Asian economy" (HPAE) (World Bank, 1993) among a group of similarly successful Asian economies. This transformation has seen the Malaysian economy progress from one of the world's leading producers of primary commodities—rubber, tin, palm oil, oil and liquified natural gas (Drabble, 2004)—to a successful light industry manufacturing base. A brief stint of import substitution was replaced by a strategy of export promotion that saw Malaysia well on the way to joining the ranks of newly industrialized countries (NICs), with a solid base of light manufacturing in textiles, electrical and electronic goods and components, rubber products, food processing, etc., (Drabble, 2004). A potent mix of generally sound macroeconomic management and good external developments—foreign direct investment (FDI) from NICs' readiness to offshore production, led by Japan in a "flying geese" formation (Akamatsu, 1962) and a flood of portfolio investment to "emergent markets"[1] like Malaysia with the end of the Cold War in 1990—contributed to this outcome (Wade, 2004: xxix).

Together with the changing structure of the economy, Malaysia's labour force has also undergone major changes, the most important being that the share of those in the agricultural sector declined even as that in manufacturing rose. Labour force surveys show the number of persons engaged in manufacturing increasing from 158 thousand persons in 1970 to 845 thousand in 1990, and further to 1,812 thousand in 2010 (Malaysia, Department of Statistics, 2017). Better education and health also saw the quality of Malaysia's workforce improve. Vision 2020, launched by then Prime Minister Mahathir in 1990 with the aim of transforming Malaysia into an advanced country by 2020, envisages Malaysia's workforce becoming part of the "knowledge" economy.

But economic growth, together with these ambitious plans, was brought to an abrupt end with the onset of the Asian Financial Crisis in 1997. This Crisis laid bare a host of the economy's vulnerabilities that, in the heydays of economic boom in the 1980s and early 1990s had been left unattended. Some of these vulnerabilities apply to the labour force, with the result that the heady growth experienced earlier never returned. Indeed, labour force challenges became a part of the larger challenge to Malaysia's future growth and development (see, for instance, Lee & Tham, 2007).

The current challenge Malaysia faces represents a good starting point to discuss Malaysia's labour future. The next section details Malaysia's predicament of being snared in the "middle-income trap". It is a situation the government is fully aware, so that the constraints it faces are, as Doner and Schneider (2016) had indicated, more political than economic. This puts efforts to escape the "trap" a contest between the government's rhetoric and what it can actually accomplish. We conclude this chapter

[1] The term "emerging market" has been attributed to World Bank economist Van Agtmael and refers to a market in a transitional phase between developed and developing, it being presumed that the market will eventually be developed. See Cox (2017).

on a more optimistic note in visualizing a Malaysian labour future in which major challenges have found solutions and in which Malaysia is endowed with a workforce that can power the country to developed country status.

Malaysia Today—Caught in the "Middle Income Trap"

The "middle-income trap" phenomenon was first articulated by Gill and Kharas (2007) to describe a situation faced by many middle-income countries whose advance to high-income status is hampered by a combination of competitive wage pressure from countries lower down the development ladder and also unable to upgrade technologically to challenge those countries more technologically advanced than they.

Malaysia is a classic example of a middle-income country ensnared in this "trap". After achieving impressive growth for over a decade, the country appeared ready to make the transition to high-income status. In anticipation of this eventuality, then prime minister Mahathir launched in 1991 "Vision 2020"[2] with the year 2020 being targeted for Malaysia to become an advanced economy. This growth rate was never achieved, especially after the arrival of the Asian Financial Crisis in 1997. What happened to derail a growth model that seemed, from past experience, eminently achievable?

A number of interrelated factors have conspired to prevent its achievement. Overall, according to Donner and Schneider (2016), it is as much politics as it is economics. Gomez, Cheong, and Wong (2021) saw Malaysia "trapped … in an economic system that relied on cheap labour and foreign capital to create goods for export,[3] while well connected conglomerates grew by establishing ties with political elites to obtain rents. A state-business alliance based on a well-embedded patronage system was a constituent feature of the economy by the 1990s".[4] But it is also the case that Malaysia lacks the economic fundamentals to advance to advanced country status. At the very time an increasingly technological workforce is needed to ensure international competitiveness, "Malaysia was deeply short of knowledge- and technology-based competencies required by a highly industrialized economy" (Gomez, Cheong, & Wong, 2021). Malaysia's problems have also been highlighted elsewhere (Perkins, 2019).

A low-skill model built around imported labour. But beyond patronage relationships is a set of structural distortions of the labour force that will take years to rectify. The first is reliance on a low-skill model built around imported labour from countries lower down the development ladder.

---

[2] "Vision 2020" was launched during the tabling of the Sixth Malaysia Plan in 1991. This would require annual growth of 7% from 1990 to 2020.

[3] Commodity exports were the other primary source of public revenue for growth.

[4] For an in-depth discussion on the political economy of patronage, see Gomez and Jomo (1999).

Long before independence as the Federation of Malaya in 1957, Malaysia's economy had benefited from migrants to the country. In modern times, the import of low-skill foreign workers to support Malaysia's rapid growth and to relieve rural labour shortages on account of rural–urban migration began in the 1970s when foreign workers were brought in to work in the plantation and construction sectors, and in the 1980s when rapid industrialization and economic growth witnessed widespread skill shortages and rising wages, setting the stage for the import of documented as well as undocumented foreign workers. These arrivals eased production pressures and were compatible with the demand for low-skill labour at the time.

Yet despite the fact that Malaysia's share of migrants in the country's population was higher than most of its regional peers (Ang et al, 2018: 2), policy on them was only formulated in the 1990s (Del Carpio et al., 2015: 3). Even then, despite economies like Australia, Hong Kong SAR, and Singapore having in place policies to attract skilled migrants, the Malaysian stance then was to permit them as an interim measure while a long-term strategy was put in place to upgrade the workforce. This long-term strategy never materialized.

Instead, the share of documented foreign workers to the country's labour force rose sharply from an already substantial 10.8% in 2002 to 18,8% five years later before settling back to 12% in 2017 (Ang et al., 2018; 2). By then, foreign labour accounted for over a fifth of employment in agriculture, construction, and manufacturing. And as their numbers swelled—from 380,000 in 1990 to 2.1 million in 2010 according to the Labour Force Surveys and from 3.2% of the working population to 7.4% over the same period (Del Carpio et al., 2015: 5–6)— their role in labour-intensive sectors became increasingly entrenched, with Malaysian employers themselves resistant to any change in this low-cost model (Lai, 2019).[5] Economic Census data also show foreign workers to be 30% of the workforce and that their presence has doubled since year 2000 in manufacturing (Del Carpio et al., 2015: 13) a clear indication of the reliance on foreign labour in manufacturing. Malaysian policymakers thus face pushback both from the factory floor and from the employers doing business using the low-skill model.

Defenders of immigrant labour have referenced their productivity and their positive impact on the employment of local workers (for instance, Jordaan, 2018). However, even with these positives, the main argument against relying on them is that their widespread presence, as Ang et al (2018) noted: "distorts domestic factor prices, and thus discourages industrial upgrading". The examples from the wave of Newly Industrialized Economies (NIEs) outsourcing production to Southeast Asia while simultaneously upgrading their productivity through technology are powerful models for Malaysia to emulate (Table 11.1).

As for the argument on the shortage of local workers that required foreign workers to fill, a plausible explanation may be the low wages Malaysian employers are willing to offer. Ang et al. (2018; 3) cite the example of Malaysian workers commuting daily

[5] Nowhere is this more apparent than the Malaysian Employers Federation's resistance to the imposition of a higher minimum wage (MEF, 2019). In its press release, the MEF refers to foreign workers as "a necessary evil" and not due to "the addiction to foreign workers".

Table 11.1 Low wage foreign workers allow employers to keep salaries low

Malaysian standard classification of occupation 2013	Malaysian	Foreigners
High-skilled		
Managers	5,000	10,000
Professionals	3,653	5,556
Technicians and associate professionals	2,581	3,650
Mid-skilled		
Clerical support workers	1,750	1,440
Service and sales workers	1,488	1,000
Skilled agri., forestry, livestock, fishery workers	1,500	1,000
Craft and related trade workers	1,700	1,165
Plant and machine operators and assemblers	1,530	1,006
Low-skilled		
Elementary occupations	1,025	970

Source Ang et al. (2018) Chart 4. Data from National Employment Returns 2016

to Singapore employed in mid- to low-skill jobs, except at wages much higher than in Malaysia. This was cited as evidence that low wage levels rather than unpleasantness were what dissuaded Malaysians from taking up "dirty, dangerous and difficult" (3D) jobs.

The employment of foreign workers and paying low wages leads to a vicious cycle that signifies a race to the bottom for Malaysian industry. For employers, low wages thus become a substitute for and disincentivizes productivity enhancement. As Table 11.1 shows, foreign workers invariably are paid less than local workers in mid-skilled and low-skilled occupations.

In summary, dependence on a low-cost foreign worker model has implications for technology upgrading (see the section on negative de-industrialization), the blossoming of the service sector (see the section on the shift to services) and for the occurrence of brain drain (see the section on brain drain). In formulating a coherent policy to diminish the use of such labour, it must be also be remembered that the pool of foreign workers also includes a large number of illegal immigrants, who are subject to Malaysia's harsh laws and work under unsatisfactory conditions while having little protection from abuses (Hunt, 2019). Unless these undocumented migrants are incorporated into labour force planning, dealing with documented migrants alone will not suffice.

Low female labour force participation. A second labour force challenge for Malaysia is its low female labour force participation rate (FLFPR). Despite recent gains in the FLFPR,[6] Schmillen et al. (2019: 38) noted that Malaysia's FLFPR is slightly low in comparison with countries at a similar level of development, such as Brazil and Kazakhstan. Malaysia's Gender Gap (the difference in LFPR between

[6] From 2010 to 2017, Malaysia's FLFPR gained 8% points, from 45.5% to 53,5%, compared to the 0.9% point gain between 1995 and 2010.

Table 11.2 Global gender gap index and economic participation and opportunity sub-index, Asian countries rankings, 2018

	Gender gap index—total	Economic participation
Brunei	90	26
Cambodia	93	45
Indonesia	85	96
Lao PDR	26	1
Malaysia	101	84
Myanmar	88	35
Philippines	8	14
Singapore	67	24
Thailand	73	22
Vietnam	77	33

Source World Economic Forum (WEF) (2018)

males and females) Index in 2018 ranks below all its ASEAN peers, particularly its neighbours Singapore and Thailand,[7] and its Economic Participation and Opportunity Sub-index[8] ranks below the same group of countries except Indonesia (Table 11.2). The lower FLFPR is also manifested in their being "single peaked", dropping off during the prime ages of 30 to 54 while males worked throughout their prime ages 25–54 (KRI, 2018: 81). This pattern of FLFPR, which has remained unchanged up to the present, stands in sharp contrast to the situations in Korea and Japan where women re-entered the labour force after marriage and childbearing (Schmillen et al., 2019: 39). This meant that despite the extension of the retirement age for men and women from age 55 to 60 in 2013, only just over 40% of women aged 55 to 59 continued to participate in the labour force. Given the greater presence of females in the country's school system and hence their higher education attainment, their non-participation in the labour force especially during prime ages represents significant underutilization of the human capital the government had expended considerable effort and resources to nurture.

Greater female participation in the labour force is also important given the progressive ageing of Malaysia's population. This has implications for both the labour force as well as those outside it. Outside the labour force, an obvious implication is the progressive increase in the old-age dependent population that needs to be supported by a smaller proportion of working population. The implications for female LFPR are unclear. On the one hand, as care givers, females may have to spend more time at home caring for elderly members of their families. On the other, women may be forced to re-enter the workforce to support their families, in the absence of social protection institutions (Chan et al., 2010), ore women at work will not only increase the size of the workforce but also ensure better burden-sharing in the care of the

[7] Schmillen et al. (2019: 38) noted that Malaysia's gender gap of 25.2 percentage points is about a third more than the 14.1 and 15.2% points of Singapore and Thailand respectively.

[8] The Economic Participation and Opportunity Sub-index covers FLFPR, wage equality, earned income, number of legislators and senior officials, and professional and technical workers.

Table 11.3 Net changes in labour force by educational level, and employment by skill level, Malaysia, 2010–2017

Net change ('000)	Local workers	Foreign workers	Total workers
Labour Force, by Education			
Tertiary	1,328	29	1,358
Secondary	1,200	423	1,623
Primary or none	−438	105	−332
Employment, by Skill Level			
Skilled	713	−17	697
Semi-skilled	1,286	96	1,383
Low-skilled	−2	473	471

Note Some numbers do not fully add up because of rounding
Source KRI (2018): Figs. 2.44 and 2.45

aged and ageing. A less obvious implication is the ageing of the workforce itself. A negative consequence of this is a negative perception that may lead to discrimination against the ageing workforce (Anisah et al., 2018).[9] Given the low participation of females at that age, the problem appears to be faced more by the male workforce, however.

As to whether higher FLFPR would diminish the inflow of foreign workers, this prospect is unlikely. Foreign labour tends to fill unskilled or low-skill work (see Table 11.3), while Malaysian women, to the extent they enter the job market, tend to possess better education than even Malaysian men.

KRI (2018: 90) noted that women made up almost 90% of the prime-age population outside the labour force, explaining their absence from the workforce in terms of "the disproportionate care responsibilities shouldered by women in the family" (KRI, 2018: 95).[10] While not disputing that family responsibilities also represent productive work, it nevertheless argued that "to alleviate women's challenge to balance family and work, … a fairer distribution of housework between men and women is crucial" (KRI, 2018: 95). In confirming the important role of "housework", Schmillen et al. (2019: 47) also added schooling as an important factor in women not participating in the workforce.

It also bears noting that even as women join the workforce, they face greater gender challenges compared to men. For one, "women are not only less likely to participate in the labour force, but when they do, they are also (slightly) less likely than their male

[9] Chan and Jariah (2007) found the perceptions of Malaysian human resources personnel regarding the older workers to be generally negative.

[10] This view is contested. Siah and Lee (2015: 613) found that "women's child bearing decisions are unaffected by their employment situation. In addition, we do not find evidence that presence of children hinders re-employment and continuous female employment." However, Lim (2017: iv) finds that "fertility has a larger negative effect on female labour force participation for planned births as compared to unplanned births… (with) a larger negative effect among the *Bumiputera* than the *non-Bumiputera* women".

counterparts to find a job" (KRI, 2018: 99). And among those employed, they tend to be concentrated in service and sales, professionals, and clerical support workers, with only a nominal proportion fill positions as managers. While not necessarily indicative of explicit gender discrimination, women at work still suffer from limitations on career and remuneration advancement imposed by their occupational choices (KRI, 2018: 102).

Schmillen et al. (2019: 51) also opined that "women's economic empowerment will require not only closing the gender gap in labour force participation but also removing barriers to more productive employment for women. Noting that despite outnumbering and outperforming their male counterparts in education, Malaysian women tended to enrol in courses traditionally considered as "female" after their secondary education, thus raising the question of whether they have equal access to productive employment opportunities to men (Schmillen et al., 2019: 12). This question appeared to be answered by the rising share of women employed in the informal sector and as own-account workers or unpaid family workers, all of which are characterized by low productivity and poor working conditions (Schmillen et al., 2019: 52).

Beyond unequal access to productive employment opportunities, this occupational concentration also leads to misallocation of human capital resources. As a specific example, increased female enrolment in tertiary education in the face of a progressive reduction of school-age children has seen Malaysia's already generous student–teacher ratio decline further, and causing education personnel to move into administration, with expenditures for salaries dominating the recurrent budget.[11]

Shortage of STEM graduates. A third labour force issue relates to the limited supply of science and technology (S&T) graduates from the educational system. This phenomenon has been documented elsewhere and its causes also elaborated (CIPD, 2019). A politicized education system has been used as a key instrument to promote affirmative action in favour of the majority *Bumiputera* students. This has taken the form not only of Bumiputera only schools[12] but also in the setting of different standards for admission to tertiary institutions. *Bumiputera* students in their colleges sit for "matriculation" examinations that are set and marked internally while all other students have to pass the nationally set examination, the Malaysian Higher School Certificate (*Sijil Tinggi Persekolahan Malaysia*, STPM) (Kaur, 2019a, b). They are also the recipients of most of the loans and scholarships. Thus, affirmative action has swept aside meritocracy as a guiding principle for admission to university study, creating two classes of students of different intellectual capabilities.

But different admission standards also lead to imbalances in subjects studied. Those with an easier entry qualification would naturally gravitate to the "softer subjects" in the social sciences rather than the "hard" physical sciences. Student

[11] IIEP (2018: 12–14) noted that in 2013, the pupil-teacher ratio was only 11.5 pupils and 13 pupils per teacher at primary and secondary levels respectively. It also noted that administrators accounted for one in five of the Ministry of Education workforce, with salaries taking up 80% of education's recurrent budget.

[12] The best example is the Universiti Instituit Teknoloji MARA (UITM) and MARA's elite residential schools Maktab Rendah Sains MARA.

choices would also have been abetted by the government's decision to absorb Bumiputera graduates into public service. In a system that provides few incentives to pursue the physical sciences, it is little wonder that only a small proportion of university students opt for STEM (Science, Technology, Engineering and Mathematics) studies (Kaur, 2019a, b).

That the limited output of S&T graduates would ultimately constrain the country's long-term advance is unquestioned. The challenge is whether this human capital also imposes limits on its short-term growth. To the extent that adherence to a decidedly low-tech model permits Malaysia's limited supply of S&T graduates to meet the demand of industry seems plausible for the moment. Certainly, as Table 11.2 shows, the net change in skilled workers in the employed workforce between 2010 and 2017 is less numerous than the increment to the labour force of those with tertiary education. This suggests that the number of university graduates is more than sufficient to meet labour market demand. Indeed, the excess supply of university graduates may mean some graduate unemployment (D'Silva, 2020). At the same time, this excess supply of S&T graduates has led to higher than average graduate unemployment (Dass, 2019) that in turn can be a cause of reduced demand for STEM studies.

That the number of women students outnumbers the number of male students in tertiary education has not helped boost STEM enrolment. The bulk of Malaysian women enrol in courses traditionally characterized as "female".[13]

Brain Drain. One other labour force challenge facing Malaysia is its outflow of skilled human capital even as it imports a large number of unskilled or low-skill foreign workers (Cheong et al., 2019). This "brain drain" is triggered by a confluence of two sets of factors, one contextual and the other policy-oriented. Among the first group of factors are Malaysia's traditional open economy, the country being no stranger to migration flows throughout its ancient and modern history (Cheong et al., 2019; 22). More salient contextually is the proximity of high-income Singapore which has become a magnet for emigrating Malaysians and their kin (Table 11.3). The labour-intensive model built upon imported unskilled labour, discussed above, has also depressed wages while limiting the need for talent and reducing the incentive for firms, both Malaysian and foreign, to upgrade their technology. Highly educated or trained Malaysians thus saw their career prospects diminished and demand for their talent limited. Thus, even the modest supply of STEM graduates looked overseas to fully utilize their talents and skills.

Another contextual factor is Malaysia's highly internationalized tertiary education system. Since the colonial era, higher education and teacher training has seen Malaysian students and trainees undertake their studies in the UK and Commonwealth countries through a variety of scholarships and subsidies. Students studying overseas could then easily find opportunities to find work in their study locations. This tradition has continued, although study destinations have diversified with the internationalization of tertiary education. With Malaysia intending to be an international education hub, international universities have set up branch campuses and/or

[13] Schmillen et al. (2019: 33) reported women making up 73% of courses in education and 66% of courses on health and welfare.

Table 11.4 Malaysia's brain drain and diaspora, by countries of destination, 2010

Destination	Diaspora (%)	Brain drain (%)	Brain drain as % of diaspora
Singapore	57	54	31.5
Australia	10	15	50.8
Brunei	7	3	13.4
United Kingdom	6	5	25.4
United States	6	10	55.7
Canada	2	4	53.2
New Zealand	2	2	41.9
Total all destinations	100	100	34.2
Total numbers	1,023,000	335,000	

Source World Bank (2011) Data from pp. 98, 103–104

collaborated with Malaysian tertiary institutions to offer joint degree programmes (The Sun Daily, 2015). While not a full substitute to studying overseas, these joint programmes nevertheless create awareness and sensitize students to the possibility of migration.

Arguably a most important contextual factor is the proximity of Singapore. With per capita income several times Malaysia's, Singapore is clearly a magnet for Malaysian migrants. And with a body of water barely a mile separating the two territories, there is practically no social distance for migrants to Singapore. Indeed, an estimated 300,000 Malaysians commute daily from the Malaysian state of Johor to work in Singapore (The Star, 2020). It is therefore little wonder that half Malaysia's migrants are found in Singapore (Table 11.4). It also explains the large proportion of diaspora among migrants to Singapore.

But policy also played a role. The low-skill model represents a policy choice. Likewise, the implementation of pervasive affirmative action that compromises meritocracy in admissions to public sector tertiary education institutions programmes have reinforced perceptions of push factors like "social injustice" and issues related to inter-racial harmony ranking quite high as contributory factors to migration (Table 11.5). Unless a degree of "brain circulation" in the manner of China, South Korea, and Taiwan is achieved, resources expended to nurture these emigrated talents would have been lost to the home country.

However, even if TalentCorp were to persuade emigrants to return to Malaysia, they would have to successfully navigate the country's highly fragmented and bureaucratic immigration management system that seem not to recognize the existence of the country's talent shortages. Multiple ministries handle immigrant labour approvals (PwC, 2017). The World Bank (2015) has also complained that Malaysia's fragmented immigration management system has resulted in difficulties with monitoring control and law enforcement.

Table 11.5 Drivers of brain drain from migrants' perspectives

Cause of migration	% of respondents in diaspora survey listing item as one of three top reasons for brain drain in Malaysia			
	World bank[1]	Wake up call Malaysia[2]	Independent survey[3]	
Career prospects	66	76	55	Malaysia's future
Social justice	60	80	58	Inter-racial harmony
Compensation	54	73	56	Malaysia's current situation
Study & stay on	50	–		
Safety & security	28	–	–	
Politics	23	–	63	
Study & return	19	–	69	
Liveability	12	–	–	
Better education	–	54	62	
No. respondents	194	518	854	

Notes [1]World Bank (2011), p. 121
[2]Wake Up Call Malaysia (2012)
[3]Wong (2010)
Source Cheong et al (2019) Table 2.3

Premature deindustrialization. Two other areas responsible for Malaysia's predicament are policy-induced but also have bearing on the country's deployment of its labour force. One is premature deindustrialization, first raised by Rasiah (2015: 714), who observed "a trend slowdown in manufacturing value added, trade performance and productivity since 2000. Not only has the trade performance of manufacturing been falling, manufacturing labour productivity has also slowed down, with the key sectors such as electric-electronics, textiles and transport equipment showing either negative or low productivity growth since 2000."

Rasiah et al., (2015: 86) pointed to the year 2000 as when negative deindustrialization began in Malaysia, arguing "that manufacturing has started to fall in significance from the mid-1990s with the contraction being the most serious since 2000. Critically, manufacturing industries have faced a slowdown or a fall in trade performance and productivity since 2000. The chronic contraction trends suggest that manufacturing growth in Malaysia has indeed plateaued and is facing negative deindustrialization since 2000".

They made four arguments to show that Malaysia has begun the process of premature deindustrialization (Rasiah et al., 2015: 79–80. First, the contribution of the manufacturing sector to GDP had begun to contract since 2000, at a time when Malaysia's GDP per capita showed the country was still an upper middle-income country (Table 11.6). Second, the mainstays of Malaysia's manufacturing growth and engines of exports, i.e. the light electric and electronics and textile and garment industries, had experienced a slowdown beginning from 2000 and extending over

Table 11.6 Selected indicators showing deindustrialization, Malaysia, 1990–2010

Indicator/sector	1990–1994	1995–1999	2000–2004	2005–2010
GDP Growth (%)	9.6		4.6	4.4
Agriculture	0.4	0.7	3.3	2.7
Manufacturing	11.7	5.9	4.6	2.6
	1990	2000	2005	2010
GDP structure (%)	100.0	100.0	100.0	100.0
Agriculture	15.2	8.6	8.4	10.4
Manufacturing	24.2	30.9	29.6	24.6
Services	42.5	44.0	42.5	48.5
Employment structure (%)	100.0	100.0	100.0	100.0
Agriculture	26.0	16.0	12.9	11.6
Manufacturing	19.9	27.1	28.7	28.3
Services	34.5	37.2	51.0	53.3
Export structure (%)	100.0	100.0	100.0	100.0
Agriculture	19.1	3.7	7.1	10.8
Mining	15.9	6.1	9;3	11.5
Manufacturing	58.8	90.1	81.6	76.2

Source, Rasiah et al. (2015) Tables 1 to 4

the period 2000–2010. Third, the import-substituting automobile industry that was promoted through heavy protection from 1981 has also begun contracting, not having achieved the minimum scale to become a competitively efficient producer. Fourth, Malaysia's leading export-oriented manufacturing sectors have been continuously facing a downward slide in revealed comparative advantage while manufacturing exports as a share of total exports have eroded (Table 11.5). Indeed, no better indicator of Malaysia's deindustrialization is the retreat from high-tech exports towards agricultural and extractive-based industries (*The Edge* 27 August 2018).

A more recent symptom of negative deindustrialization is declining competitiveness of Malaysia's manufactured exports to China, Malaysia's top trading partner since 2009. Malaysian has seen its share of domestic value added in manufactured products and total exports to China falling while the share of Chinese inputs in Malaysia's exports has been growing (Tham & Kam, 2019: 13).

Rasiah et al. (2015: 77) attributed this to Malaysian industrial policies' failure to move industries to high value added activities, the consequence of "failures to coordinate policies, enforce standards, sustain high productivity growth and stimulate transition to higher value-added activities. Manufacturing as a whole has registered slow wage growth since the late 1990s, with labour markets characterized by heavy presence of low-skilled foreign workers, increased contract labour and outsourcing and declining worker organization. The focus on perspiration-based low-skilled foreign labour rather than on expanding professional and skilled labour has driven Malaysia down the low industrialization road… and with labour market practices constraining instead of facilitating positive change" (Rasiah et al., 2015: 77).

Shift to services. More recent developments accelerated the negative deindustrialization process by shifting production away from industry to services. These developments were as much policy-induced as externally driven. Since 2009, the Malaysian government had encouraged its GLCs to cooperate with China's enterprises in property development (Gomez et al., 2017: 62), The result was inflated property values throughout the country. Externally, prices were buoyed further when high international oil prices added to the construction boom. Property speculation drove property values even higher. Policymakers, driven by the prospect of high returns from real estate investment, saw this sector, not manufacturing, as the driver of growth. Even the sovereign wealth fund, Khazanah, tasked with searching for technology and investing in productive activities, instead led the charge in investing in real estate businesses. Little wonder, then, that government initiatives to compete in the global market for high-value construction and engineering services, have failed to produce the desired outcomes (Wong & Foo, 2018: 15).

At the same time, emerging businesses employing new technologies such as the Internet of Things (IoT), artificial intelligence (AI), and robotics are not attracted by Malaysia with its reliance on low-skilled labour which is also handicapped by a shortage of technological manpower. Meanwhile, in the absence of a coherent policy to promote technological diffusion, foreign firms investing in Malaysia have not been keen to transfer technological know-how to local companies. Importantly too, the electronics industry on which Malaysia relies has not seen much progress while policy commitment to link FDI to local firms is waning (Ohno, 2013: 239). These two factors combined mean that negative deindustrialization began even before the country had acquired the technological capability to move out of low-skill labour-intensive industries to those generating more value added.

Rising to the Challenges and Responses

Despite official denials of some of the above challenges, the government acknowledges their existence, if only some of them explicitly. As Najib began his term as prime minister, he constituted the National Economic Action Council (NEAC) in 2010 which was entrusted with drafting a New Economic Model (NEM). The NEM Report stated that "we are not developing talent and what we do have is leaving" (NEAC, 2010a: 54). The NEM Part 1 identified a list of challenges the economy faced, with the expectation that Part 2 would surface bold solutions to address these challenges. But Part 2 (NEM, 2010b) proved to be much less radical in its recommendations compared to Part 1. For instance, instead of dealing decisively with affirmative action, Part 2 referred to "market friendly affirmative action", a concept that is logically contradictory.

The Tenth Malaysia Plan (10 MP) launched shortly after the NEM (Malaysia, 2010) likewise recognizes that a private sector role is vital for long-term growth, and that a knowledge-intensive approach that is powered by rising productivity and innovation, rather than by labour-intensive methods of production, will be essential. However, unlike previous five-year plans which were full of implementation plans, the 10MP has been long on rhetoric but scanty on details. Even within the broad framework of the 10MP. Nambiar (2011) has found areas that need improvement.

The midterm review of the next Malaysia Plan, the Eleventh, 2016–2020 (Amir, 2019: 6), have been effusive of its, and the previous Plan's achievements, celebrating successes in reforming the labour market, improving labour efficiency and productivity, enhancing access to quality education and training, and fostering greater industry—academia linkages. Yet few of the issues mentioned above have been mentioned let alone addressed.

Other policy documents that address Malaysia's labour future have been no more specific. For example, Talent Corp's *Visioning Malaysia* (2017: 6), while identifying relevant issues, has the limited objective of starting "conversations with key stakeholders in a series of engagements we have planned involving the Government, industry, learning institutions and talent", the objective being the drafting of "a national talent action plan for the future". And in place of specifics are self-congratulatory platitudes like "Given that Malaysia has already made commendable strides in the area of talent development, overcoming the above challenges is definitely achievable. By addressing these areas, the country will be poised to become a global talent destination that fulfils the needs of both local and global talent" (TalentCorp, 2017: 25).

From developments so far, it would appear that to the extent that major challenges are known to policymakers, lack of remedial action stems from a lack of political will. It is, as Doner and Schneider (2016) say, more politics than economics. Given this reality, it may be too much to expect a shift to an idealized labour force system in the near future.

Out of the "Trap"—An Idealized Long-Term Scenario

In taking a forward look at Malaysia's talent future (CIPD, 2019), experts assembled by the Chartered Institute of Personnel and Development (CIPD) and Human Resource Development Fund (HRDF) Malaysia listed the drivers required to take full advantage of the 4th Industrial Revolution (IR4) (CIPD, 2019: 5) and the challenges the country must confront—including all the issues cited earlier in this chapter (CIPD, 2019: 5–22). Based on these observations, the report came up with several scenarios for 2035 (Table 11.7).

Interesting though these scenarios are, they are based on numerous assumptions and their likely outcomes. For the purpose of this chapter, arguably the most relevant is Scenario 1, which assumes the continuation of existing trends. Unlike that scenario which predicts that Malaysia attains high-income status which cannot be sustained, we argue that the issues discussed would ensnare the country in a middle-income trap from which it cannot escape. While the issues and remedies needed to deal with

Table 11.7 Scenarios for Malaysia's talent landscape 2035

Assumptions/implications	Scenario 1 Groundhog Day	Scenario 2 Cog in the Wheel	Scenario 3 Elephant in the room	Scenario 4 Nature's revenge
Assumptions	Status quo	In supply chains	Technology & socio-political drivers	Technology & socio-political drivers
Economic/technology/environment	High income by 2025 FDI from China	Western protectionism ASEAN integration Low-cost model bypassed China builds supply chains SMEs adopt technology or move to lower cost	Specialists recruited End of NEP for private sector	Environmental crisis, natural hazards Environmental refugees Environ. Threat to economy Push for renewable energy
Political	NEP retained Low-cost model Education stagnates	Education overhauled English used	NEP only in public sector	Sustainable dev. Agenda, promote fair distribution
Social	FLFPR below men Religious-secular divide Ageing population		NEP actively debated Work flexibility stressed High-skill immigration	
Implications state	Struggle to keep high-income status Human capital deficit Education falling behind	ICT infrastructure investments Education overhauled Pro-innovation	Phasing out NEP Managing socio-gaps require some NEP retained	Fiscal strain to deal with ecological crisis Govt criticized for neglect, needs crisis management
Society	Ethnic divide continues	AI embraced	Social divide debated Need to rebuild intra-ethnic trust	Sensitivity to sustainability Stronger NGO role
Organizations	SMEs do not invest in technology Skill shortages Organizations behind neighbours	FDI arrives Professional services	Labour market competitive Gender gap closed Companies agile	Sensitive to ecological issues

(continued)

Table 11.7 (continued)

Assumptions/implications	Scenario 1 Groundhog Day	Scenario 2 Cog in the Wheel	Scenario 3 Elephant in the room	Scenario 4 Nature's revenge
Individual	NEP drives brain drain Shanghai, etc. attract talent	Brain drain slows Singapore still favoured	Brain drain slows	No more polluting jobs

Source CIPD (2019): 24–34

these issues are recognized both within and outside government, whether and when policies are put in place remains a big question mark. The government-favoured approach has been to issue well-crafted documents that are replete with identified issues but contain scant specific measures to deal with them.

In this our concluding section, we propose to bypass all these unanswerable questions and assume that in the long run an ideal situation will prevail when the right policies will have been put in place and Malaysia can at last escape the "Middle-income Trap". This can be considered Scenario 5.

A long-term idealized scenario will see the country less dependent on immigrant labour as an engine of production. This will require the progressive imposition of disincentives for the use of imported labour. To an extent, as incomes in source countries of labour import rise, such imports will become more expensive. And to the extent that some jobs will not be filled by local labour, some foreign workers will still be required. However, the point is not to encourage, through policy or lack thereof, reliance on low-skill imported labour as the core of the country's industrial production. Some pain will result as the economy attempts to compete at a higher point in the value chain, but the longer this is delayed, the greater will be the pain as the country attempts to catch up on international competitiveness.

Greater FLFPR will also be part of this idealized scenario. To the extent this is already occurring, as fertility continues to fall as the population ages, and with continuing rural–urban migration, this trend will likely continue and may even strengthen. Over time, perceptions in favour of women in the workforce will become more prevalent. Occupational concentration in lower-paying work, whether voluntary or socially enforced, will take longer to change, however.

A more challenging scenario is an increasing proportion of STEM graduates. To the extent that this is at the core of the nation's affirmative action, abandoning it after being implemented for decades will be a major leadership challenge. Yet the alternative of assisting weaker students to bring them up to the performance of the other students represents no less a feasible approach as giving weak students preferential access to university, and by levelling the playing field, preserve the vital role of meritocracy in human capital formation while avoiding incentivizing non-STEM study.

Beyond achieving a better balance of students in STEM subjects, reform of the country's technical and vocational education and training (TVET) system has been repeatedly announced but precious little has been done (Cheong et al., 2013). Calls to increase university autonomy, now heavily controlled at the ministerial level, have also been made (Wan, 2017).

The brain drain problem is a long-term phenomenon that is not easy to reverse even with proactive policy. As the earlier examples of South Korea and Taiwan and the recent example of China show, brain drain reversal will occur if the home country achieves strong economic growth and gives opportunities for returnees to prosper in business. In this respect, the continued pursuit of affirmative action represents a disincentive for return migration among migrants who typically cite this as a reason for their migration.

Finally, premature deindustrialization needs to be reversed through industrial policies that promote the growth of technologically enabled industries. For this to happen, the education system (including TVET) needs to ensure an adequate supply of STEM graduates to augment the nation's knowledge-based workforce. An environment should also exist in which the talented in the workforce is willing to remain in the country while companies that are competitive are willing to recruit them at attractive wages.

The target date for the realization of optimum labour force utilization is 2050. That is when demographic projections show Malaysia's working age population (age 15–64) reaching its maximum. By that year Malaysia will have "come towards the tail end of the demographic window of opportunity known as the 'first demographic dividend', and … will enter the stage of an aging nation." (IIEP, 2018: 9).

In this idealized world, Malaysia will have a workforce that is ready to take on all challenges as it emerges from the "middle-income trap". The key to this optimistic situation is success in nurturing and retaining the country's human capital.

References

Akamatsu, K. (1962). A historical pattern of economic growth in developing countries. *The Developing Economies, 1*, 3–25.

Amir bin Omar (2019). Labour market dynamics and future of work. In *Presentation at the Human Resource Conference, Cyberjaya.*

Ang, J. W., Murugasu, A, & Chai, Y. W. (2018). Low skilled foreign workers' distortions to the economy. *Bank Negara Malaysia.*

Anisah, A. H., Aliza, A. H., & Fadilah, P. (2018). Ageing workforce—a challenge for Malaysia. *Journal of Administrative Science, 15*(3), 1–13.

Chan, Y. F., Laily, P., Jariah, M., & Hamid, T. A. (2010). The future of the Malaysian older employees: An exploratory study. *International Journal of Business and Management, 5*(4), 125–132.

Chan, Y. F., & Jariah, M. (2007). *Perception of human resource personnel towards elderly workers.* Paper presented at the 7th Biennial Conference 2007, Asian Consumer and Family Economic Association. Malaysia.

Chartered Institute of Personnel and Development (CIPD) (2019). *The future of talent in Malaysia 2035.* Singapore: CIPD.

Chartered Institute of Personnel and Development (CIPD) & Human Resource Development Fund (HRDF) Malaysia (2019). The future of Talent in Malaysia 2035. Kuala Lumpur.

Cheong, K. C., Kuppusamy, S., Lee, H. A., & Abdillah, N. (2013). *Malaysia workforce development—SABER country report 2013.* World Bank.

Cheong, K. C., Goh, K.L., & Li, R. (2019). Brain drain and talent capture in Malaysia: rethinking conventional narratives. In A. Tyson (Ed.), *The political economy of brain drain and talent capture: Evidence from Malaysia and Singapore.* Abingdon: Routledge, Chapter 2.

Cox, S. (2017). *Defining emerging markets.* The Economist. At https://www.economist.com/special-report/2017/10/05/defining-emerging-markets. Accessed 11 May 2020.

D'Silva, V. (2020). More and more graduates are facing unemployment in Malaysia. *New Straits Times.* At https://www.nst.com.my/news/nation/2020/02/562309/more-and-more-graduates-are-facing-unemployment-malaysia. Accessed 15 May 2020.

Dass, R. (2019). *Stop pushing STEM and giving false hopes to the young.* FMI News, March 20. At https://www.freemalaysiatoday.com/category/opinion/2019/03/20/stop-pushing-stem-and-giving-false-hopes-to-the-young/. Accessed 4 June 2020.

Del Carpio, X., Ozden, C., Testaverde, M., Marouani, M., Nilsson, B., & Wagner, M. (2015). Foreign workers in Malaysia: Labour market and firm level analysis. *Malaysian Journal of Economic Studies, 52*(1), 1–19.

Doner, R. F., & Schneider, B. R. (2016). The middle-income trap: More politics economics. *World Politics, 68*(4), 608–644.

Drabble, J. H. (2004). The economic history of Malaysia. In R. Whaples (Ed.), *EH.Net Encyclopedia*. At http://eh.net/encyclopedia/economic-history-of-malaysia/. Accessed 31 May 2020.

Gill, I., & Kharas, H. (2007). *An east Asian renaissance: Ideas for economic growth*. World Bank.

Gomez, E. T., Padmanabhan, T., Kamaruddin, N., Bhalla, S., & Fisal, F. (2017). *Minister of finance incorporated: Ownership and control of corporate Malaysia*. Basingstoke: Palgrave-Macmillan.

Gomez, E. T., Cheong, K. C., & Wong, C. Y. (2021). Regime change, state-business ties, and remaining in the middle-income trap: the case of Malaysia. *Journal of Contemporary Asia*.

Gomez, E. T., & Jomo, K. S. (1999). *Malaysia's political economy: Politics, patronage and profits*. Cambridge University Press.

Hunt, L. (2019). Can Malaysia solve its big migrant worker challenge? *The Diplomat*. At https://thediplomat.com/2019/12/can-malaysia-solve-its-big-migrant-worker-challenge/. Accessed 13 May 2020.

International Institute for Educational Planning (IIEP). (2018). *Malaysia—The closing window of demographic opportunity: Adapting the education system to support Malaysia's first nation agenda*. UNESCO.

Jordaan, J. A. (2018). Foreign workers and productivity in an emerging economy: The case of Malaysia. *Review of Development Economics, 22*(1), 148–173.

Kaur, B. (2019a). Shortage of STEM students at universities. *New Straits Times*. At https://www.nst.com.my/news/nation/2019/09/518914/shortage-stem-students-universities. Accessed 15 May 2020.

Kaur, M. (2019b). Matriculation an easier path to public universities than STPM, says don. *FMT News*. At https://www.freemalaysiatoday.com/category/nation/2019/04/24/matriculation-an-easier-path-to-public-universities-than-stpm-says-don/. Accessed 16 May 2020.

Khazanah Research Institute (KRI) (2018). *Part 2: The Malaysian workforce—a changing landscape*. Kuala Lumpur: KRI.

Lai, A. (2019). Employers Federation unhappy with labour law reforms. *The Star*. At https://www.thestar.com.my/news/nation/2019/10/24/employers-federation-not-happy-with-labour-law-reforms.

Lee, P. P., & Tham, S. Y. (2007). Malaysia ten years after the Asian financial crisis. *Asian Survey, 47*(6), 915–929. Accessed 13 May 2020.

Lim, B. F. Y. (2017). The effects of education and fertility on female labour force participation in Malaysia. Ph.D. Thesis, University of Wollongong.

Malaysia, Economic Planning Unit (2010). *Tenth Malaysia plan 2011–2015*. Putrajaya: Prime Minister's Department.

Malaysia, Department of Statistics (2017). *Malaysia Economic Statistics—Time Series 2016*. At https://www.dosm.gov.my/v1/index.php?r=column/ctimeseries&menu_id=NHJlaGc2Rlg4ZXlGTjh1SU1kaWY5UT09.

Malaysia Employers Federation (MEF) (2019). Raising employers' concerns on increasing minimum wages to RM1,200 for 57 bigger cities and towns is not fear mongering. *Press Release*. At http://www.mef.org.my/news/pr_article.aspx?@ID=34. Accessed 2 June 2020.

Nambiar, S. (2011). *The labour market and economic growth in Malaysia*. Paper presented at the 26th Pacific Economic Community Seminar, Taipei, October 13–14.

National Economic Advisory Council (NEAC) (2010a). *A new economic model for Malaysia part I*. Putrajaya: NEAC.

National Economic Advisory Council (NEAC) (2010b). *New economic model for Malaysia concluding part: Strategic policy measures*. Putrajaya: NEAC.

Ohno, K. (2013). *Learning to industrialize: From given growth to policy-aided value creation*. Routledge.

Perkins, D. H. (2019). Malaysia: The challenge of avoiding the middle-income trap. Available at https://www.ehm.my/publications/articles/malaysia-the-challenge-of-avoiding-the-middle-income-trap

PWC (2017). Malaysia: East Malaysia immigration requirements and practices. *Insights from global mobility.* At: www.pwc.com/gx/en/services/people-organisation/global-employee-mobility/globalmobility-insights/east-malaysia-immigration-requirements-and-practices.html. Accessed 4 June 2020.

Rasiah, R. (2015). Is Malaysia facing negative deindustrialization? *Pacific Affairs, 84*(4), 714–735.

Rasiah, R., Crinis, V., & Lee, H. A. (2015). Industrialisation and labour in Malaysia. *Journal of Asia Pacific Economy, 20*(1), 77–99.

Schmillen, A. D., Tan, M.L., Abdur Rahman, A., Shahrul Natasha, H., & Sandig, W. N. (2019). *Breaking barriers: Toward better economic opportunities for women in Malaysia.* Washington, D.C.: World Bank Group.

Siah, A. K. L., & Lee, G. H. Y. (2015). Female labour force participation, infant mortality and fertility in Malaysia. *Journal of Asia Pacific Economy, 20*(4), 613–629.

The Star (2020). Malaysians to resume work in Singapore. At https://www.thestar.com.my/news/nation/2020/03/21/malaysians-to-resume-work-in-singapore. Accessed 3 June 2020.

TalentCorp (2017). Visioning Malaysia's future of work: A framework for action. Petaling Jaya: TalentCorp.

Tham, S. Y., & Kam, A. (2019). US-China trade war: possible trade and investment spill-overs into Malaysia. *Economics Working Paper* No. 2019-03, Singapore: Yusuf Ishak Institute.

The Sun Daily (2015). Malaysia has one of the highest proportions of international students pursuing higher education. At https://www.thesundaily.my/archive/1314991-XRARCH293390. Accessed 17 May 2020.

Wade, R. (2004). *Governing the market: Economic theory and the role of government in East Asian industrialization* (Paperback). Princeton University Press.

Wake Up Call Malaysia (2012). Wake up call Malaysia report. Formerly available at: http://wakeupcallmalaysia.com/wuc-malaysia-memorandum/

Wan, C. D. (2017). The history of university autonomy in Malaysia. IDEAS Policy Paper 40, Kuala Lumpur, May.

Wong, E. L., & Foo, K. Y. (2018). Reversing premature deindustrialization. *The Edge Financial Daily.* At https://www.theedgemarkets.com/article/reversing-premature-deindustrialisation. Accessed 21 May 2020.

Wong, E. (2010). Will you come back to Malaysia? Available at: https://pluggingthebraindrain.wordpress.com/about/.

World Bank. (1993). *The east Asian miracle: Economic growth and public policy.* Oxford University Press.

World Bank. (2011). *Malaysian economic monitor: Brain drain.* World Bank.

World Bank. (2015). *Malaysia economic monitor: Immigrant labor.* World Bank.

World Economic Forum (WEF). (2018). *The global gender gap report 2018.* World Economic Forum.

Cheong Kee Cheok is currently Senior Advisor, Asia Europe Institute, University of Malaya. A graduate of the University of Malaya, obtained his Ph.D. at the London School of Economics. Upon his return from studies, he joined the Faculty of Economics and Administration, University of Malaya, where he held the positions of Deputy Dean and Dean of Faculty. After a decade at UM, he spent 16 years at the World Bank in the capacity of Economist and subsequently Senior Economist. At the Bank, he was Coordinator for China and Vietnam in the Economic Development Institute, now the World Bank Institute. After returning to Malaysia in 2000, he has continued as Consultant for the Bank and UN agencies. Back with the University of Malaya since 2010, he has coauthored books, book chapters, and published numerous papers in top-tier academic journals as well as successfully supervised Ph.D. students, both international and local.

Yong Chen Chen is Associate Professor at the Faculty of Business and Economics, Universiti Malaya. She specializes in the economics of human capital development and talent.

Chapter 12
Poverty and Inequality

Rajah Rasiah

Abstract This chapter seeks to evaluate the impact of poverty alleviation programmes in Malaysia against the main policies introduced by the Malaysian government. Although the strategies adopted to address absolute and relative poverty inevitably required engagement in several social and economic programmes, this chapter focuses largely on the main direction of poverty alleviation and economic restructuring policies, which were the two key prongs of the NEP. Following a review of the extant poverty literature, the chapter examines the key strategies to alleviate poverty, i.e. rural development, export manufacturing, and ethnic restructuring. In doing so, the chapter also examines how these broad strategies affected economic restructuring, education, and other sectors in the economy. The chapter subsequently examines the consequences of these strategies on poverty and inequality by looking at the relationships between income growth and absolute and relative poverty. The chapter finishes by acknowledging the success achieved in addressing both poverty and inequality in the country. However, it also flags the need to shift food farming focus to intensive farming with the use of IR4.0 technologies, and dynamic technological upgrading policies in all sectors, from patronage to merit-based policies, and the abandonment of ethnic policies to support sustainable development that can be shared evenly by the population.

Keywords Poverty · Inequality · New economic policy · Export manufacturing · Rural development · Malaysia

Introduction

The Young, Bussink, and Parvez (1980) classified Malaysia as a successful model of a developing economy that has experienced rapid economic growth with equity. At the time of independence from British colonialism, the country was characterized by ethnic divides by geographic and economic concentration (Abraham, 1970; Amin &

R. Rasiah (✉)
Asia-Europe Institute, University of Malaya, 50603 Kuala Lumpur, Malaysia
e-mail: rajah@um.edu.my

R. Rasiah et al. (eds.), *Malaysia's Leap Into the Future*, Dynamics of Asian Development, https://doi.org/10.1007/978-981-16-7045-9_12

Caldwell, 1977; Sultan Nazrin Shah, 2019). The bulk of the indigenous *Bumiputeras* were engaged in sedentary agriculture. Malaysia was characterized by severe social imbalances caused by ethnic differentiation occupationally, rising unemployment, and poverty particularly among the rural poor throughout the 1960s. Consequently, the Malaysian government launched the New Economic Policy (NEP) through the Second Malaysia Plan in 1971 (Malaysia, 1971). As with most restructuring policies, the first objective of the NEP was to alleviate poverty—both absolute and relative (Ishak, 2000a, b; Jomo, 2019; Ragayah, 1996).

The Second Malaysia Plan focussed on poverty alleviation and ethnic restructuring to remove economic identification, which was targeted at addressing ethnic imbalances that increased social and political tensions in the country culminating in bloody ethnic riots in 1969 (Malaysia, 1971). Such was the truncation in the social and political structure in the country that ethnic restructuring was acknowledged as an unavoidable policy instrument. Rasiah and Ishak (2001) had argued that political stability was a key trade off with economic growth in the formulation of the NEP. Malaysia became one of several examples later that Langer et al. (2012) used to emphasize that horizontal inequalities are politically more explosive than vertical inequalities. Consequently, countries where such political divides through clearly identifiable cultural, geographic and social lines are used by politicians to mobilize support along such divides have remained vulnerable to social and political conflicts.

Despite remaining controversial among scholars (see Cham, 1975; Toh, 1982; Jesudason, 1989), the NEP received mass among the poor, particularly from the *Bumiputeras*. However, as with development planning in general it required effective implementation and calibration to take account of new information and random events. The Malaysian planning framework provided for it through mid-term reviews of the five-year Malaysia plans. However, we would argue that much of its instruments were already being compromised from the 1980s and the extension of ethnic-based policies undermined nation building. This chapter seeks to evaluate the efforts and effects of poverty alleviation initiatives in Malaysia against the main policies introduced by the Malaysian government. Although the strategies adopted to address absolute and relative poverty inevitably required engagement in several social and economic programmes, this chapter largely focuses on the main direction of poverty alleviation and economic restructuring, which were two key prongs of the NEP. The individual strategies pursued to address the broader goals of the government are discussed in detail in other chapters in this volume.

Theoretical Considerations

Arguably, the central focus of economic development among the developing economies is on absolutely poverty alleviation. However, addressing relative poverty has become increasingly critical owing to the trend worsening of income inequality among developed economies, such as the United States and Britain (Galbraith, 2012). Because economic resources are scarce, the unequal distribution of income and wealth often unduly reduces access for the poor to those resources, which often results in a skewed distribution of resource allocation thereby denying the poor basic essentials. Indeed, the alleviation of both poverty and inequality has remained a key focus on economic development plans in most countries. Langer et al. (2012) subsequently discussed the implications of horizontal and vertical inequalities making the case that the first can potentially generate political and social upheavals. Horizontal inequality refers to inequality across groups that can be identified politically, regionally, or ethnically, while vertical inequalities refer to inequality within groups. Rasiah and Ishak (2000) had flagged this point to show that political stability figured strongly in the formulation of the NEP as a consequence of serious ethnic divides that existed in Malaysia then. Lee (2021) makes a similar argument when comparing Malaysia and South Africa, though the focus is much more on higher education and higher level occupations. To some extent, the Young, Bussink, and Parvez (1980) recognized the government's role to avert further political conflict in Malaysia after the May 1969 bloodshed.

In contrast to the original argument on the causes of poverty that was claimed by Malthus (1798) and Ehrlich (1971), empirical evidence shows that population growth rates decline as countries become more developed. Using longitudinal statistical data and rich demographic evidence on the OECD countries, Kuznets (1955) found an inverted "U" shaped relationship between income inequality and per capita GDP (Logarithm) growth. However, Rasiah, Ishak and Jomo (1996) produced empirical evidence on East Asia to show that Kuznets' evidence applied to the OECD countries at a time when both birth and mortality rates were high. This was not the experience of the developing countries where mortality rates began to fall sharply during the early stages of economic growth as medical breakthroughs in the OECD countries diffused into these countries. In addition, poverty and economic inequality have been checked through deliberate government policies. While economic growth was pursued aggressively by some governments direct efforts were also made to address poverty. For example, land reforms by the American occupied administration in the second half of the 1940s played an important role in alleviating poverty and reducing income inequality in South Korea and Taiwan.

Countries that managed to achieve long-term economic growth also either pursued export-oriented industrialization from the outset, (such as Singapore) or import-substitution industrialization for export-orientation, (such as South Korea and Taiwan), both of which has had positive impact on falling unemployment levels, improvements in wages, and falling poverty incidence (Rasiah, 2020; Helpman & Krugman, 1985; Krugman, 1991). The main pillar of the argument is that the initial insulation offered through protection must be removed to expose firms to global competition for industrial upgrading to take place, which is also consistent with Hirschman's (1958, 1970) argument that exposure to external markets will offer firms the scale to evolve backward linkages within developing countries.

Subsequent evidence from Anand and Segal (2008), Fields (2001), and Palma (2011) using global data found no such systematic historical relationships. Palma (2014) then found that the most significant relationship to observe when examining inequality among countries is the Palma ratio, which refers to movements in incomes between the top 10% and bottom 40%. To these points, Piketty (2015) added the need to assess wealth distribution over time, which is an interesting observation but prevailing data makes such an assessment difficult because of the lack of consistent time series data.

Another significant point to examine is the measurement of poverty incidence, which has gained traction following criticisms by the United Nations Special rapporteur, Alston (2019) is a need to revise the classification of the poor as countries develop. Malaysia began to address these problems in 2020 but is unclear if the changes have taken into account of: one, changes in the composition of goods used to measure the poverty line as countries become more effluent; two, enumeration of households without address and the homeless; and three, household size. These are some of the criticisms that have been directed at Malaysia. Hence, the building blocks of poverty and inequality for Malaysia will have to review the measurement instruments to ensure that projections are scientifically robust, as well as, policy directions to reduce absolute and relative poverty over the future, which is a point alluded to also by Ravallion (2020).

Prime Pillars of Poverty Alleviation

The government targeted three prime strategies to address poverty and inequality in the country, namely rural development to raise farm output, export manufacturing to create jobs, and education to raise human capital in the country. In this section, we discuss these developments.

Rural Development

The NEP's two prongs were the eradication of poverty, and the elimination of occupational identification of ethnic groups. A third objective, which was often pursued both politically and economically was the raising of *Bumiputera* participation in corporate equity to 30% by 1990. However, Tun Abdul Razak had suggested that the NEP to be ended after 1990 so that the ethnic groups could integrate smoothly after inter-ethnic inequalities have largely been levelled (Rasiah & Salih, 2019).

Divide and rule policies and a focus on surplus appropriation to feed the industries of Britain and the West led to the development of basic infrastructure to support tin mining and rubber cultivation over the nineteenth and twentieth centuries. Subsequent work on how the configuration of ethnic groups influenced the formulation of the NEP and its consequences on occupational and class structures in the country can be found in Amin and Caldwell (1977) and Khong and Jomo (2009). Rising socioeconomic, cultural, and geographic differences with most Malays in rural locations, Indians in Plantations, and the Chinese either at tin mines or in control of commerce at urban locations exploded in the May 13 1969 ethnic crisis. Such was the tensions that it appeared impossible to conceive of non-ethnic restructuring policies to re-establish political stability in the country, which is a prerequisite for nation building.

The launching of the NEP by the Government through the Second Malaysia Plan in 1971 was masterful as it presented Malaysia with an opportunity to target poverty reduction and to integrate the then truncated living of the ethnic communities that had evolved during British colonialism into a plural society (Malaysia, 1971). While this was the actual aim of the NEP, its implementation was not easy as the Malays were not only largely poor but were also little integrated with the commercial sector (Ishak, 2000a, b; Rasiah & Ishak, 2001). The ruling coalitions, i.e. Alliance until 1970, and the National Front since 1970, have been constituted of political parties that largely represented particular ethnic groups, the overzealous pursuit of garnering votes led to heavy hiring of Malays in the civil service. Political negotiations to attract opposition parties, such as Gerakan to obtain the two-thirds majority required to make amendments required in parliament and to govern with autonomy meant that the interests of the electorate in formerly opposition states, such as Penang were met. Hence, while there were successful forays into restructuring ethnic concentration in plantations, and in professional occupations, such as doctors, engineers, accountants, and lawyers, the civil service (including the military and police) and government linked companies became dominated by the Malays. Also, we will argue in the chapter that political polarization by ethnic groups, especially since the late 1980s undermined nation building and aggravated further ethnic divisions in the country.

However, The NEP's implementation began along ethnic lines owing to the massive distance created between the major ethnic groups by the late 1960s. The majority of *Bumiputeras* were vocal with their view that Malaysia belonged more to the indigenous peoples of the country rather than to the immigrants. Indeed, some of these arguments can be found in Silcock and Ungku Aziz (1953; see also Muhammad Ikmal, 1995).

Consequently, the government focussed on rural development by investing heavily on basic infrastructure after the NEP was launched. Roads, canals, drains, power lines, water pipes, hospitals and schools connected the rural community (Malaysia, 1976). Specific areas of focus included the Muda Agricultural Development Authority (MADA) where physical infrastructure was developed and double cropping using high yield fertilizers, and mechanization were introduced to raise productivity. The government also introduced interventionist mechanisms and organizations to stabilize demand and prices for the poor farmers. It was during this time that Ungku Aziz (1956, 1962, 1964, 1965) introduced alternative measures of poverty that were easier to use to identify and target the hardcore poor for assistance, such as the sarong index, which also went beyond prevailing measures of poverty (see Ragayah, 1996, 2014; Rasiah & Salih, 2019). By distinguishing the number of sarongs per capita, Ungku Aziz was able to distinguish the poorest from the poor.

The government sought to introduced intermediary organizations to connect and coordinate between rural farmers with urban markets (Rasiah & Salih, 2019). The government launched the Farmers Marketing Authority (FAMA), Lembaga Padi dan Beras Negara (LPN), Malaysian Rubber Development Corporation (MARDEC), and the land tenure schemes of Federal Land Development Authority (FELDA),[1] Federal Land Consolidation and Rehabilitation Authority (FELCRA), and Rubber Industries Smallholder Development Authority (RISDA), among other things to strengthen the link between farmers and markets. Price controls were also introduced to stabilize prices in some activities, (such as rice and palm oil). The Majlis Amanah Rakyat (MARA) was founded in the 1960s with the focus of promoting Bumiputera economic advancement (Khaeruddin & Arshad, 2019).

Heavy focus was also placed on agricultural diversification to reduce problems posed by the fallacy of composition syndrome,[2] which was undertaken through export diversification. The aggressive promotion of oil palm to reduce dependence on rubber began in the 1970s. The government not only began diversifying agriculture but also started to promote smallholder cultivation on a large scale by coordinating their cultivation, processing, and marketing activities.[3] Hence, a massive exercise to diversify the economy began to take root from 1971. Oil palm cultivation began to expand rapidly along with efforts to increase self-sufficiency in rice production, which reached 87% in 1975 (Rasiah & Salih, 2019: 129). The Farmer's Marketing Authority (FAMA) began to connect directly with the poor Malay farmers so as to eliminate middlemen exploitation. The Fisheries Development Authority of Malaysia began to play a similar role to assist poor fisherman. In addition, the government also modernized peasant operations with supplies of subsidized gadgets, machinery, fertilizer, boats, and seeds (Rasiah & Salih, 2019).

Palm oil became a major export of Malaysia from the 1970s as the government's price stabilization policy, as well as its stable export market provided by the major edible importers insulated the commodity from wild price swings. Also, the Soybean lobby against palm oil had little impact among the major importers of China, India and the African economies.

Initiatives to modernize agriculture took place following the Fifth, Sixth, Seventh, Eighth, Ninth, Tenth and Eleventh Malaysia Plans over the period 1991–2020. However, the lack of enforcement and the easy availability of foreign labour resulted in few plantations and farms shifting to automation and other labour saving production technologies. Oil palm plantations and smallholder acreages under the Rural Industry Development Authority (RISDA) and the Federal Land Consolidation and Rehabilitation Authority (FELCRA) resorted to massive hiring of foreign low skilled workers. The substitution of local labour with foreign labour lowered the wage bill and labour turnover for the land tenure dwellers. Consequently, the incidence of poverty continued to fall in the 1980s.

However, despite the launching of the first, second, and third National Agricultural Policies (NAP) since 1984, agricultural value added grew slower than the targets. Despite the focus on the Eleventh Malaysia Plan to raise agricultural value added

[1] See Ikmal (2019) for a lucid account of poverty alleviation achieved through FELDA.

[2] Prebisch (1950) and Singer (1950) had argued that specialization in a narrow range of commodities that are characterized by long gestation periods are prone to falling terms of trade.

[3] Close coordination allowed smallholders to appropriate economies of scale to enjoy collective efficiency.

to 3.5% per annum over the period 2016–2020, the sector's contribution to GDP still contracted from 8.3% in 2015 to 7.3% in 2019 (World Bank, 2020). While the emphasis by NAP1, NAP2, and NAP3 on introducing agro-business to turn agriculture into a business has been helpful, value added growth in the sector continued to fall short of its target. While the Saemaul Undong programme in South Korea and land development programmes in Taiwan raised value added in gross output despite the continued fall in agriculture's share in GDP (ADB, 2012; Taiwan, 2010), the lack of significant technological transformation resulted in the sector in Malaysia facing stagnation (Rasiah, 2018).

Instead of focussing on a shift to intensive small-scale farming that relied on knowledge-intensive methods and high yielding varieties, as well as, focussing on spreading the use of robots and drones, the swift decline in the contribution of agriculture to GDP was largely a consequence of outmoded extensive farming methods used. This was not feasible as arable land was increasingly replaced by industrial and commercial interests (see also Rasiah & Salih, 2019; Chamhuri, Rospidah, and Mohamad, 2022).

Export Manufacturing

Export manufacturing was established as the engine of growth when the Second Malaysia Plan was launched in 1971. The government took advantage of foreign multinational corporations (MNCs), which were seeking politically stable and secure sites endowed with good basic infrastructure to relocate the labour-intensive stages of production (Sciberras, 1977; Lim, 1978; Rasiah, 1993a, b).

Export processing zones (EPZs) the opening of Free Trade Zones (FTZs) and its equivalent for some industries, (such as textiles and clothing), that were better located at specific sites in 1972 helped the relocation of a large number of MNCs in Malaysia. The government's aim behind this strategy was to attract foreign direct investment and to create jobs. Since skills requirements of assembly workers in the early 1990s focussed on dexterity, both urban and rural literate but lowly educated workers found jobs at these export processing zones. Employment grew rapidly to reduce unemployment levels between 1970 and 1984 (Fig. 12.1). The development of FTZs and LMWs were among the several instruments that the government deployed to reduce poverty levels in the country. From 21,243 in 1973, employment in FTZs rose to 81,688 in 1984, with the highest rise occurring in the period 1973–80 (Rasiah, 2019: 202).

However, the lack of emphasis on technological upgrading exposed export-oriented manufacturing to wild fluctuations in employment as the vicissitudes of volatile economic swings caused several retrenchments. For example, the global recession following the second oil crisis of 1979–80 and the 1984–85 cyclical downturn in the electronics industry resulted in firms retrenching massive numbers of workers in 1981–82 and 1985–86. Overall, EPZ employment levels were not too

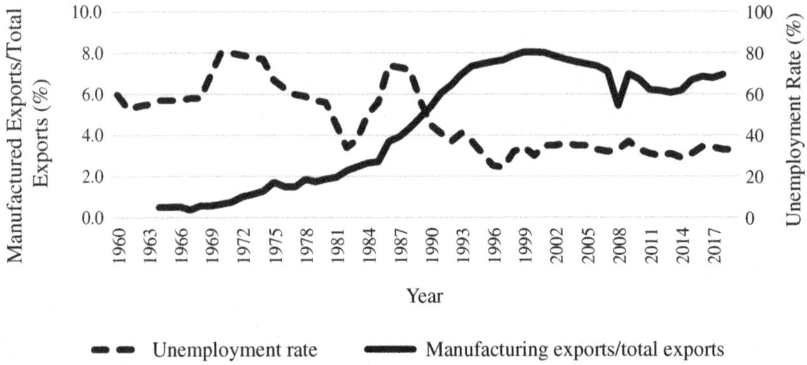

Fig. 12.1 Export manufacturing and unemployment, Malaysia, 1960–2019. *Source* Plotted from World Bank (2020) data

badly affected in 1981, mainly because of the relocation in Malaysia of labour-intensive firms after Singapore restructured its incentives to promote knowledge-intensive and higher value added industries (Salih & Young, 1985; Rasiah, 1987). The contraction in EPZ employment in 1985 was much sharper, falling by 16.8%, which was mainly in the electronics components industry, which is reflected in rising unemployment in 1984–87 (Fig. 12.1).

Nevertheless, the electric and electronics industry has remained a major employer over the years. This was the case even when economic overheating in the country failed to discourage a new massive influx of firms from Japan, Taiwan, South Korea, and Singapore from relocating in Malaysia in the early 1990s (Rasiah, 1995).

However, the proliferation of knowledge-intensive activities—driven largely by automation and flexible production systems—began to lower mean permanent employment of firms, which fell sharply from the late 1980s (1988). From 759 in 1973, mean firm-employment, which rose to 863 in 1981, had fallen to 636 in 1986, rising only marginally to 689 in 1987 (Rasiah, 2019: 202).

In the 1970s until the late 1980s, workers generally enjoyed better wages during industry booms, (as they gave them overtime opportunities) and lower wages during busts. Retrenchments were accompanied by the hiring of new workers with lower wages, which was common in electronic components firms in the period of 1979–82, and in mid-1984 and early 1987 (Rasiah, 1988, 1993a, b). Nevertheless, huge inflows of FDI over the period 1987–93 helped export manufacturing to provide massive employment in the manufacturing sector, which not only lowered national unemployment rates to 5.1% in 1990 and 3.7% in 1991, the exhaustion of labour surplus also drove wages up despite production experiencing increased automation (Rasiah et al., 2015).

The ethnic breakdown of FTZ employment in 1987 show that the *Bumiputras* (57.1%) almost proportionately represented the national breakdown then, with the Chinese (24.8%) considerably lower, and the Indians (17.3%) significantly higher than their respective national demographic proportions (Rasiah, 2019: 2013). The high share of *Bumiputeras* in FTZ employment helped meet the NEP criterion set by the government, though at the management level, *Bumiputeras* were largely confined to human resource management. Nevertheless, by the end of the 1990s, *Bumiputras* did helm the managing director's job at Advanced Micro Devices (Bayan Lepas) and Motorola (Petaling Jaya). While low-wage labour dominated the female labour force, FTZs and LMWs also served as major platforms for female employment in Malaysia. Despite the rapid introduction of knowledge-intensive technology in FTZ firms since the 1980s, the survey showed that the overall gender breakdown was still strongly skewed towards female labour (73.2%). Electronics firms had the biggest proportion of female workers (76.4%), followed by textile and garment firms (69.5%). That Bumiputeras dominated the lower stratum of EPZ employees at least met the government's efforts to lower unemployment levels.

Although a second round of import-substitution industrialization was launched since 1981 when the heavy industries of cement, iron, and steel, and transport vehicles were promoted, export-orientation was retained with strong emphasis resumed after 1985 (Rasiah, 1995). Electric and electronics exports in particular continued to grow, though its share in overall exports fell below 40% since 2010 (Rasiah, 2020).

Except for the periods 1997–98 and 2008–09 when the Asian Financial Crisis and the Global Financial crisis affected domestic firms, and exports respectively, export manufacturing has remained strong in Malaysia (Fig. 12.1). Consequently, the unemployment rate only rose slightly in 1997–98 and 2008–09. Also, the overall relationship between export-orientation and unemployment has been strong with an explanatory power of 66%, which demonstrates that export manufacturing has had a strong impact on lowering unemployment rates in Malaysia (Fig. 12.2). A one percent increase in the share of manufactured exports in total exports lowered unemployment by 0.05% in the period 1970–2019.

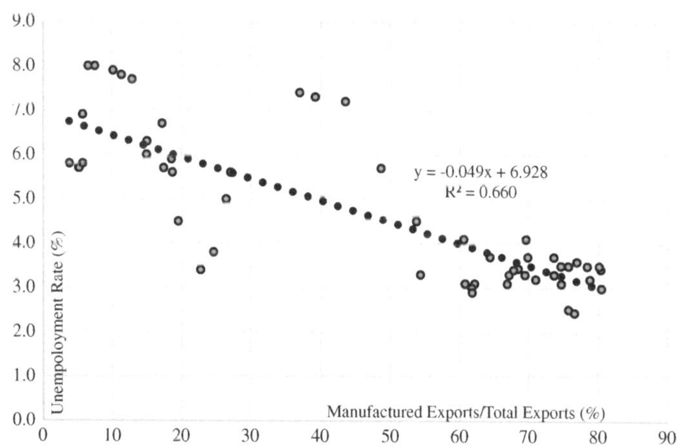

Fig. 12.2 Export manufacturing and unemployment, Malaysia, 1970–2019. *Source* Computed from data obtained from DOS and World Bank (2020) data

Ethnic Restructuring

Taking the cue from Langer et al. (2012) it is critical that any efforts to build a plural Malaysia that is integrated to insulate the country from potential political conflicts would require the government's focus on integrating the country from the truncated socio-political and regional structures that persisted in 1971. After all the May 13 1969 political bloodshed manifested ethnically. The *Rukun Negara* promised a great step towards pursuing it as it called for *Muhibbah* and *Perpaduan*, while advancing the role of the Royalty constitutionally to pursue the country's goals (Abdul Rahman, 2019). While the government acknowledged the need to build a nation, it justified ethnic restructuring through favouring the *Bumiputeras* over the period 1971–90 through the NEP only because the majority of them were poor, detached from modern living, and enjoyed little access to the basic amenities (Rasiah & Salih, 2019). However, it will be argued in this chapter that the government departed from this goal largely because of the ethnically defined dominated political parties who pursued their interests truncated at the expense of building a truly plural Malaysia.

While it was difficult to locate sufficient numbers of competent leaders in the 1960s and early 1970s, there were already a critical mass of qualified *Bumiputeras* by the 1980s. One major criticism by authors, such as Cham (1975), Toh (1982) Jesudason (1989), over the implementation of the NEP is the target of achieving 30% corporate equity for the Malays, which had led to the promulgation of the Industrial Coordination Act (ICA) in 1975 and subsequently the establishment of Permodalan Nasional Berhad. (PNB) in 1978. Under the ICA businesses registered in Malaysia above the mandatory registration floor were expected to show 30% *Bumiputera* equity. The term *Bumiputeras* refers to all those with indigenous roots, though, the dictionary only refers to it as "sons of the soil". The launching of PNB and the subsequent expansion of government linked companies (GLCs), especially since the first Mahathir administration to achieve this target have been viewed by some as to have diminished the capacity of corporations to compete in open markets, reduced government finance from its social obligations and crowded out the market from private interests in certain sectors (Jesudason, 1989). The excessive government focus on the development of one ethnic group led Jesudason (1989) and Yoshihara (1988) to contend that it had acted to discourage the Chinese from venturing into the industry on a large scale. The aggressive state forays into the private sector encouraged patronage above performance, which removed strict use of merit in the appointment of even capable *Bumiputeras* endowed with tacit and experiential knowledge in leadership positions.

In addition, it must be said that the lop-sided expansion of *Bumiputeras* into the civil service, including public universities, hospitals, and schools was a departure from the original aims of the NEP. Critics of the NEP claim that it is the prime reason as to why Malaysia did not record the extraordinary growth rates enjoyed by Singapore, South Korea, and Taiwan (Jesudason, 1989; Yoshihara, 1988). Supporters claim that the NEP framework offered a trade-off as growth with equity prevented political chaos (World Bank, 1980; Stewart, 2002), though others who shared this view criticized its implementation for the slower growth rates as the focus on creating a state-defined bourgeoisie from among both the *Bumiputeras* and non-*Bumiputeras* stifled the creation of a competitive industrial bourgeoisie (Rasiah & Ishak, 2001).

The lack of efficiency improvements in some of the key heavy industries became a serious drain to the Malaysian economy as Perwaja Steel collapsed because of bad management, while Proton only remained until the Geely takeover through heavy implicit subsidies (Rasiah, 2020). Construction companies nevertheless gained strongly from joint-venture operations to become internationally competitive. United Engineering Malaysia is an example. Efforts to corporatize important utilities, such as the National Electricity Board and Malaysian Telecoms, and promoting private ownership of power plants and hospitals had a negative impact on income distribution while at the same time restricting efficiency improvements owing to protracted privatization that targeted cronies (Jomo, 1995).[4]

The Government recognized that education is a major route to address poverty, and the exposure of *Bumiputeras* to science education through the creation of special science schools went a long way to stimulate their progression economically. Ungku Aziz's arguments to start special education routes for Bumiputeras on the premise that they lacked adequate facilities in their homes made sense in the 1970s (Rasiah et al., 2016). However, the continuation of such policies after 1990 exacerbated ethnic divides at the expense of aggravating ethnic polarization in the country. Consequently, I would argue that if only the government had abandoned such divisive instruments once sufficient progress was made by the *Bumiputeras*, the country could have enjoyed greater ethnic integration and progress as the circumstances experienced by the *Bumiputeras* from 1990 have been no different from the poor from other ethnic backgrounds (Rasiah & Salih, 2019). A detailed account of the role of NEP and the specific education policies is undertaken by Selvaratnam (2021), and the problems ethnic policies raised in the development of human capital is carried out by Cheong and Lee (forthcoming) and Cheong and Yong (2021) in this volume.

The massive inflow of FDI focussed on export manufacturing also helped create jobs, which reduced unemployment rates and raised real wages in the period 1990–97. For example, real wages in the export-oriented sub-sectors of electric-electronics and textiles grew on average by 4.3% and 3.1%, respectively, in 1990–97 (Rasiah, 2019). However, the huge inflow of FDI also attracted massive inflows of less skilled foreign labour in low value added activities, which undermined real wage growth 2000. Consequently, electric-electronics faced annual average growth of 1.4% and 1.8% per annum in 2001–05 and 2005–10 (Rasiah et al., 2015). Textiles experienced annual average real growth of −2.0% and 0.1% per annum over the period 2001–05 and 2005–10.

[4] Interview with Tan Sri Ani Arope on November 27, 1997 in Kuala Lumpur.

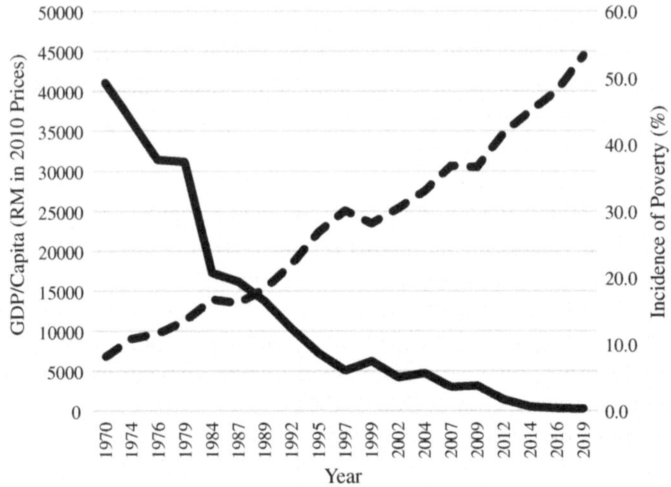

Fig. 12.3 GDP per capita and poverty incidence, Malaysia, 1970–2019. *Source* Compiled from DOS and World Bank (2020) data

Consequences on Poverty and Inequality

While the government revised its poverty line income from RM980 in 2016 to RM2208 in 2019 (Malaysia, 2020),[5] I use in this section the former to show time trend influences over the years. The overall performance of Malaysia on both absolute and relative poverty is remarkable when compared to most developing economies as its poverty incidence and income inequality fell in trend terms from 49.3% and 0.513 in 1970 to 0.3% and 0.407, respectively, in 2019.

Income Growth and Absolute Poverty

Except for the crisis years 1984–87, 1997–98, and 2008–09, GDP/Capita of Malaysia grew steadily over the period 1970–2019 (Fig. 12.3). Meanwhile the incidence of poverty fell drastically in the period 1970–1998 before rising slightly in 1999, 2004, and 2009. While rural development plans, and export-oriented manufacturing and export diversification were key drivers of both income expansion and poverty reduction in the period from 1970 and early 1980s, only the latter has remained important since. Land development programmes were highly successful in the 1970s in particular in reducing rural poverty but have largely been undermined since the 1990s in particular following a lack of technological transformation (Rasiah, 2018), encroachment of farmland from manufacturing and construction (Chamhuri, Rospidah, and

[5] The Malaysian government's new poverty line income is a welcome addition.

Mohamad, 2022; Kuppusamy & Salih, 2022), and corrupt mismanagement practices that came to light since 2018 (Nurisyal & Norhaninah, 2020).

Poverty incidence rose in 1999, 2004, and 2009 as the incomes of the poor wage earners fluctuated with the fortunes of export-oriented sectors. Nevertheless, the reliance of the economy on exports ensured that the incidence of poverty continued to fall in trend terms till 2019. Also, government assistance for the hardcore poor through microfinance instruments addressed some of the problems faced by the poor. For example, the Amanah Ikhtiar Malaysia begun in 1987, which was operated by Bank Negara Malaysia, offered small loans to the deserving poor (Malaysia, 2017a). Tabung Ekonomi Kumpulan Usaha Niaga (TEKUN) Foundation was established in 1998 to support Bumiputra entrepreneurs with funds ranging from RM500 to RM50,000. This organization was subsequently modernized and named as TEKUN Nasional by the government in 2008 (Malaysia, 2017b).

Meanwhile, poverty incidence fell sharply following the introduction of cash vouchers to the poor since 2012 under the *Bantuan Rakyat 1 Malaysia* (BR1M) to the poor starting from 2012 with a voucher of RM500, which declined from 3.8% in 2009 to 0.4% in 2016 and remained at that level in 2019.[6] Hence, the new poverty line income, is a valuable adoption by the government to ensure it targets the vulnerable segments of the population better but existing trends suggest that it will continue to go down.

The government also recognized in 2012 that significant sections of the Indians were in the bottom 20% income groups, and hence, extended government assistance programmes to them. Consequently, Indians were included in the TEKUN programme.

It can be seen in Fig. 12.4 that the trend growth in real per capita GDP in Malaysia has been achieved over falling poverty incidence. The explanatory power of the trend line equation is 92%, which is high. The results show that a one percent growth in the logarithmic GDP per capita income has brought a fall in poverty incidence by 0.3% over the period 1970–2019.

Income Growth and Income Inequality

In the period 1970–2019, income inequality in Malaysia worsened over the periods 1970–76, 1992–97, 2002–04, and 2016–19 in the face of strong real per capita GDP growth (Fig. 12.5). While the carrying effect of a skewed ownership structure from the 1960s was largely the reason why income inequality grew in 1970–76, the aggressive promotion of privatization can be considered the cause of a reversal in income distribution in 1992–97. There were no discernible developments in the periods 2002–04 and 2016–19, which did not experience a tangible worsening in income distribution.

As shown in Fig. 12.6, the inverse relationship between per capita GDP and income inequality is strong with an explanatory power of 78%. A one percent growth in the

[6] As of 2018, it was renamed as *Bantuan Sara Hidup Rakyat* programme.

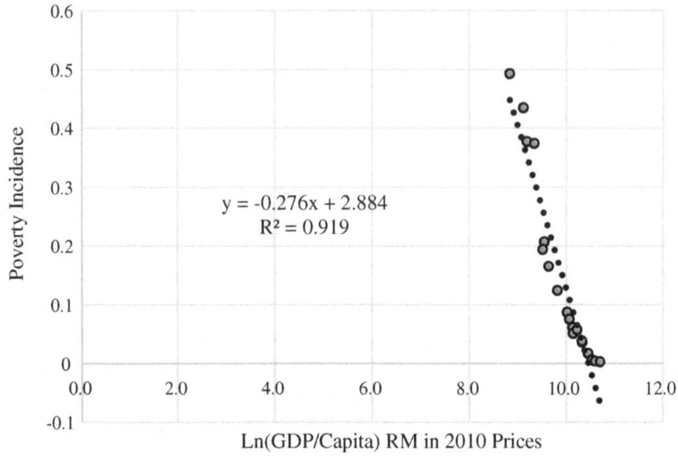

Fig. 12.4 GDP per capita and poverty incidence, Malaysia, 1970–2019. *Source* Computed from DOS and World Bank (2020) data

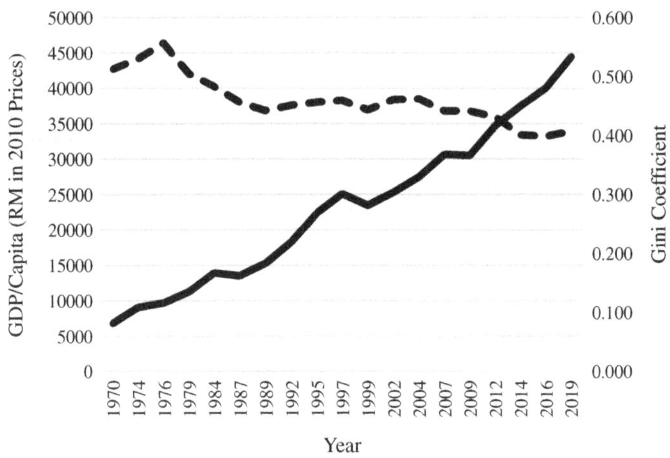

Fig. 12.5 GDP per capita and income distribution, Malaysia, 1970–2019. *Source* Plotted from DOS (2020) and World Bank (2020) data

logarithmic GDP per capita has been accompanied by a fall in income inequality of 0.07% over the period 1970–2019. Given that income inequality in Malaysia remains on a downward trend, it does not suggest a reversal with income growth in the near future all.

Taken together, both absolute and relative poverty in Malaysia have shown remarkable improvements over the period 1970–2019. However, it has to be noted that much of the improvements since 2012 have been a consequence of direct cash aid by the government through the provision of BR1M vouchers to the poor. Although such

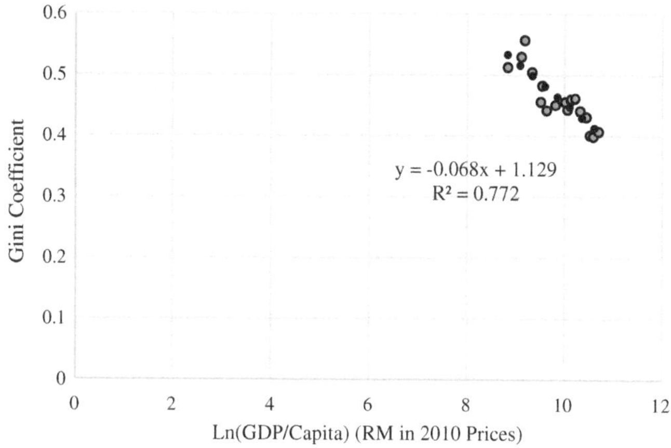

Fig. 12.6 GDP per capita and income distribution, Malaysia, 1970–2019. *Source* Computed from DOS (2020) and World Bank (2020) data

assistance has also been deployed by other countries, it is important to note that it is possible to improve further the absolute and relative poverty levels by correcting the policy failures that were discussed above, especially the nature of farm support facing small-scale poor farmers, and the emphasis on ethnic preferences.

Conclusions

No doubt that Malaysia has enjoyed a remarkable experience with economic growth and improvements in absolute and relative poverty over the period 1970–2019. Although one could argue that many programmes did not go according to plan, and some may even have undermined efficiency (Rasiah & Ishak, 2001), it is difficult to contend with its success in holding the social fabric of the Malaysian population from further ethnic explosions while at the same time propelling it to upper middle-income status. However, as argued by Perkins et al. (2021) in this volume the road to a developed economy requires significant changes in policy. Besides, the provision of government handouts through BR1M and its successor BSRH programmes, were instrumental in quickening the fall in both poverty incidence and income inequality after 2012, suggesting that the main economic activities on their own in the country done little to reduce further poverty. The coronavirus (COVID19) pandemic that erupted in 2020 has thrown up massive problems facing the B40 group and the vulnerable entrepreneurs, and those engaged in informal work (Lin, 2021; Paulo & Ikhwan, 2020).

While the focus on export-orientation, including export manufacturing must continue, three major developments are essential for Malaysia to make the transition to a developed economy with low levels of poverty incidence and income inequality.

Especially with improved measures of poverty to reflect better the living standards of the people, poverty incidence, (which was found to be 5.6% in 2019 rather than the 0.3% if the 2016 poverty line income estimates had been used), lowering real poverty will not be easy. As with poverty line income measures, the government should also review minimum wages from time to time to reflect better both the efforts of workers but also their incomes against fluctuations in consumer price inflation.

Firstly, food-based agriculture requires a sea change in farming methods. The continued promotion of extensive farming methods goes against the grain of advantages small farmers enjoy from specialization on the basis of scope. Intensive farming methods using IR 4.0 technologies *a la* Taiwan, including robots and drones, but collectively shared among a number of farmers, is critical to raise yield and lower wastage.[7] There should be targeting to raise self-sufficiency in rice and vegetable cultivation to 90% by 2050, with strong appraisal, monitoring, and calibration of policies to effect its achievement. The achievement of collective efficiency from such an approach can not only lower reliance on imported food, but also help raise the incomes of the small farmers.

Secondly, the key parastatals supporting agriculture, mining, manufacturing, and services, and those that deliver public goods (e.g. schools and universities, R&D labs) and public utilities (e.g. power, water, and health) must use merit as the basis for hiring and promotion. Unless the captains of such service providers carry the endowments to lead such organizations, it will have a negative knock-on effect on individuals, farms, firms, and organizations that compete internationally. The patronage system that the current framework has created has even denied capable Bumiputera talent from leading such organizations. The patronage system that has evolved has been so collusive that human capital development has been compromised at the expense of an expansion in low skilled foreign workers to support low value added activities. Instead of stimulating value added upgrading through human capital development, the policies in place have been focused on specialization in low value added exports through the use of low-wage foreign labour (Rasiah et al., 2015).

Thirdly, just as the NEP had the objective of creating the initial conditions to raise Bumiputera participation to appreciable levels before a non-ethic policy was to be followed, government policies should no longer be coloured by ethnic and region-based considerations. If the 1969 ethnic riots is to serve as a lesson, the government must break down ethnic divisions to start an integrated society so that all Malaysians, regardless of ethnicity and regional location can come together to build a plural nation. In doing so, it is absolutely important for the government to abandon ethnic divides by pursuing a needs-based approach to alleviate poverty, which is also similar to calls by Sultan Nazrin Shah (2019). A needs-based approach will offer all Malaysians falling below a meaningful estimate of poverty line income to access the essential resources to live a decent life. As it is now, that target group for assistance will obviously be concentrated by the poor in East Peninsular Malaysia, and the states of Sabah and Sarawak in Eastern Malaysia. Land tenure programmes

[7] Taiwan had actually managed to raise rice and vegetable self-sufficiency levels to 97% and 80% respectively in 2011 (Lee, 2011: 8).

must emphasize the need to include all ethnic groups in sync with the principles of Rukun Negara that promote the spirit of *Muhibbah* and *Perpaduan*. It is only in this way that the country can expect to break away from mere sloganeering of this multi-ethnic social spirit to stop the ethnic coloration that Malaysia's ethic-driven political parties, such as the United Malays National Organisation (UMNO), *Parti Islam Se-Malaysia* (PAS) and Bersatu have pursued.

References

Abdul Rahman, E. (2019) Nation building and inter-ethnic integration. Rasiah, R. and Salih, K. (eds), *Driving development: Revisiting razak's role in Malaysia's economic progress*. Kuala Lumput: University of Malaya Press.

Abraham, C. E. R. (1970). *The political economy and race relations in Malaya: A historical perspective*. University of Wisconsin.

Alston, P. (2019). Statement by Professor Philip Alston, United Nations Special Rapporteur on extreme poverty and human rights, on his visit to Malaysia, 13–23 August 2019. Retrieved September 10, 2020, from https://www.ohchr.org/EN/NewsEvents/Pages/DisplayNews.aspx?NewsID=24912&LangID=E

Amin, M., & Caldwell, M. (Eds.). (1977). *Malaya: The making of a neo-colony*. Spokesman Books.

Anand, S., & Segal, P. (2008). What do we know about global income inequality? *Journal of Economic Literature, 46*(1), 57–94.

Cham, B. N. (1975). Class and communal conflicts in Malaysia. *Journal of Contemporary Asia, 5*(4), 446–461.

Chamhuri, S., Rospidah, G., & Mohamad, I. (2022). Agriculture and food security. In Rasiah, R., Salih, K., & Cheong, K. C. (Eds.), *Malaysia's leap into the future: The building blocks*. Springer.

Cheong, K. C., & Yong, C. C. (2022). Future of labour. In Rasiah, R., Salih, K., & Cheong, K. C. (Eds), *Malaysia's leap into the future: The building blocks*. Springer.

DOS. (2020). Unpublished data, Department of Statistics, Malaysia, Putrajaya.

Ehrlich, P. R. (1971). *The population bomb*. Universal Books.

Fields, G. (2001). *Distribution and development: A new look at the developing world*. MIT Press.

Galbraith, G. K. (2012). *Inequality and instability: A study of the world economy just before the great crisis*. Oxford University Press.

Helpman, E., & Krugman, P. R. (1985). *Market structure and foreign trade: Increasing returns, imperfect competition, and the international economy*. MIT Press.

Hirschman, A. (1958). *Strategy of economic development*. Yale University Press.

Hirschman, A. O. (1970). *Exit, voice, and loyalty: Responses to decline in firms, organizations, and states*. Harvard University Press.

Ikmal, M. S. (2019). FELDA and rural development. In Rasiah & Salih (Eds.), *Driving development: Revisiting Razak's role in Malaysia's economic progress* (pp. 95–122). University of Malaya Press.

Ishak, S. (2000a). Globalization and economic disparities in East and Southeast Asia: New dilemmas. *Third World Quarterly, 21*(6), 675–693.

Ishak, S. (2000b). Economic growth and income inequality in Malaysia, 1971–1995. *Journal of the Pacific Economy, 5*(1–2), 112–124.

Jesudason, J. V. (1989). *Ethnicity and the economy: The State, Chinese business, and multinationals in Malaysia*. Oxford University Press.

Jomo, K. S. (Ed.). (1995). *Privatizing Malaysia: Rents, rhetoric, realities*. Westview.

Jomo, K. S. (2019) Malaysia's new economic policy. In Rasiah & Salih (Eds.), *Driving development: Revisiting Razak's role in Malaysia's economic progress* (pp. 57–74). University of Malaya Press.

Khaeruddin S., & Arshad, A. (2019). The role of MARA in developing Bumiputeras. In *Driving development: Revisiting Razak's role in Malaysia's economic progress* (pp. 141–156). University of Malaya Press.
Khong, H. L., & Jomo, K. S. (2009). *Labour market segmentation in Malaysian services*. Singapore University Press.
Krugman, P. R. (1991). *Geography and trade*. MIT Press.
Kuppusamy, S., & Salih, K. (2022). Cities, urbanization and infrastructure. In Rasiah, R., Salih, K., & Cheong, K. C. (Eds.), *Malaysia's leap into the future: The building blocks*. Springer.
Kuznets, S. (1955). Economic growth and income inequality. *American Economic Review, 45*(1), 1–30.
Langer, A., Stewart, F., & Venugopal, R. (Eds.). (2012). *Horizontal inequalities and post-conflict development*. Palgrave Macmillan.
Lee, C. W. (2011). Promoting self sufficiency in food. *Taipei Times*. Retrieved September 15, 2020 from https://www.taipeitimes.com/News/editorials/archives/2011/03/04/2003497297#:~:text=Currently%2C%20Taiwan's%20general%20food%20self,it%20is%20above%2080%20percent
Lee, H. A. (2021). *Affirmative action in Malaysia and South Africa: Preference for parity*. Routledge.
Lim, L. Y. C. (1978). *Multinational firms and manufacturing for export in less-developed countries: The case of the electronics industry in Malaysia and Singapore*. Ph.D. dissertation. University of Michigan, Ann Arbor.
Lin, L. L. (2021). *The socioeconomic impacts of COVID-19 in Malaysia: Policy review and guidance for protecting the most vulnerable and supporting enterprises*. Working paper. Retrieved March 26, 2021, from http://ilo.org/wcmsp5/groups/public/---asia/---ro-bangkok/documents/publication/wcms_751600.pdf
Malaysia. (1971). *Second Malaysia Plan, 1971–1975*. Government Printers.
Malaysia. (1976). *Third Malaysia Plan, 1976–1980*. Government Printers.
Malaysia. (2017a). *Amanah Ikhtiar Malaysia*. Downloaded on 12 December 2017 from http://www.usaawan.com/pinjaman/amanah-ikhtiar-malaysia.html/
Malaysia. (2017b). *TEKUN Nasional*. Downloaded on 12 December 2017 from http://www.usahawan.com/pinjaman/tekun-nasional.html/
Malthus, T. R. (1798). *An essay on the principle of population*. Chapter V, 39–45, Oxford World's Classics reprint.
Muhammad Ikmal, S. (1995) Malay Nationalism and National Identity. *Suomen Antropologi (Helsinki), 2*, 11–31.
Nurisyal, M., & Norhaninah, A. G. (2020). A decade of corruption studies in Malaysia. *Journal of Financial Crime, 27*(2), 423–436.
Palma, J. G. (2011). Homogeneous middles vs. heterogeneous tails, and the end of the 'Inverted-U': It's all about the share of the rich. *Development and Change, 42*(1), 87–153.
Palma, J. G. (2014). Has the income share of the middle and upper-middle been stable around the '50/50 Rule', or has it converged towards that level? The 'Palma Ratio' revisited. *Development and Change, 45*(6), 1416–1448.
Paulo, D. A., & Ikhwan, R. (2020). Can Malaysia cope with the challenges posed by the COVID19 pandemic? *CNA Insider*. Retrieved March 26, 2021, from https://www.channelnewsasia.com/news/cnainsider/poor-malaysia-cope-challenges-posed-covid-19-pandemic-poverty-13303070
Piketty, T. (2015). About capital in the twentieth century. *American Economic Review, 105*(5), 48–53.
Prebisch, R. (1950). *Economic survey of Latin America*. United Nations Economic Commission for Latin America.
Ragayah, M. Z. (1996). Policies and strategies for poverty alleviation in Malaysia. In Vyas, V. S., & Bhargava, P. (Eds.), *Poverty reduction in developing countries: Experiences from Asia and Africa*. Rawat Publications.
Ragayah, M. Z. (2014). Poverty eradication and income distribution. In Hill, H., Tham, S. Y., & Ragayah, M. Z. (Eds.), *Malaysia's development challenges: Graduating from the Middle*. Routledge.

Rasiah, R. (1988). The semiconductor industry in Penang: Implications for the New International Division of Labour Theories. *Journal of Contemporary Asia, 18*(1), 24–46.

Rasiah, R. (1993a). *Pembahagian Kerja Antarabangsa: Industri Separa Konduktor di Pulau Pinang.* Persatuan Sains Sosial.

Rasiah R. (1993b). Free trade zones and industrial development in Malaysia. In Jomo, K. S. (Ed.), *Industrializing Malaysia: Policy, performance, prospects.* Routledge.

Rasiah, R. (1995). *Foreign capital and industrialization in Malaysia.* Macmillan.

Rasiah, R. (2018). *Developmental states: Land schemes, parastatals and poverty alleviation in Malaysia.* Universiti Kebangsaan Malaysia Press.

Rasiah, R. (2019). Export manufacturing. In Rasiah & Salih (Eds.), *Driving development: Revisiting Razak's role in Malaysia's economic progress.* University of Malaya Press.

Rasiah, R. (2020). Industrial policy and industrialization in Southeast Asia. In Arkebe, O., Cramer, C., Chang, H. J., & Wright, R. K. (Eds.), *Oxford handbook of industrial policy.* Oxford University Press.

Rasiah, R. (2022). Manufacturing transformation. In Rasiah, R., Salih, K., & Cheong, K. C. (Eds.), *Malaysia's leap into the future: The building blocks.* Springer.

Rasiah, R., & Ishak, S. (2001). Markets, government, and Malaysia's new economic policy. *Cambridge Journal of Economics, 25*(1), 57–78.

Rasiah, R., & Salih, K. (2019). Connecting farmers and fishermen with markets. In Rasiah & Salih (Eds.), *Driving development: Revisiting Razak's role in Malaysia's economic progress* (pp. 123–140). University of Malaya Press.

Rasiah, R., Crinis, V., & Lee, H. A. (2015). Industrialization and labour in Malaysia. *Journal of the Asia Pacific Economy, 20*(1), 77–99.

Rasiah, R., & Ishak, S. (2000) Markets, government and Malaysia's new economic policy. *Cambridge Journal of Economics, 25*(1), 57–78.

Rasiah, R., Ishak, S., & Jomo, K. (1996). Globalization and liberalization: Implications for growth, inequality and poverty in East and Southeast Asia. In Woodfield A. (Ed.), *Globalization and liberalization and its implications for growth, poverty and inequality.* UNCTAD.

Rasiah, R., & Muhammad Shujaat, M. (2020). Energy consumption and greening: strategic directions for Pakistan. *Lahore Journal of Economics, 25*(1), 59–88.

Rasiah, R., Norma, M., & Chandran, V. G. R. (2016). Royal Professor Ungku Abdul Aziz: A key pillar in Malaysia's development. *Institutions and Economies, 7*(3), 1–19.

Ravallion, M. (2020). Ethnic inequality and poverty in Malaysia since May 1969, Parts 1 and 2, *World development*, forthcoming.

Salih, K., & Young, M. L. (1985). Penang's industrialization: Where do we go from here? Paper presented at *Malaysian Economic Association (Northern Branch) Convention on The Future of Penang*, 6–8 May.

Sciberras, E. (1977). *Multinational electronics companies and national economic policies.* JAI Press.

Selvaratnam, V. (2022). Malaysian education: The past and the future. In Rasiah, R., Salih, K., & Cheong, K. C. (Eds.), *Malaysia's leap into the future: The building blocks.* Springer.

Silcock, T. H., & Ungku Aziz, A. (1953). Nationalism in Malaya. In Holland, W. L. (Ed.), *Asian nationalism and the west.* Macmillan.

Singer, W. H. (1950). The distribution of gains between investing and borrowing countries. *American Economic Review, 40*, 473–485.

Sultan Nazrin Shah. (2019). *Striving for inclusive development: From Pangkor to a modern Malaysian State.* Oxford University Press.

Toh, K. W. (1982). *The state in economic development: A case study of Malaysia's new economic policy.* Doctoral thesis approved by University of Malaya.

Ungku Aziz, A. (1956). The causes of poverty in Malayan agriculture. In Lim T. B. (Ed.), *Problems of the Malayan economy.* Donald Moore.

Ungku Aziz, A. (1962). *The sub-division of estates.* Department of economics, Universiti Malaya, monograph, Kuala Lumpur.

Ungku Aziz, A. (1964). Poverty and rural development in Malaysia. *Kajian Ekonomi Malaysia, 1*(1), 75–105.
Ungku Aziz, A. (1965). Poverty, proteins and disguised starvation. *Kajian Ekonomi Malaysia, 2*(1), 7–48.
World Bank. (2020). *World development indicators*. World Bank Institute.
Yoshihara, K. (1988). *The rise of Ersatz capitalism in South-East Asia*. Oxford University Press.
Young, K., Bussink, W.C.F., Parvez, H. (1980) Malaysia: growth with equity in a multiracial society, baltimore: John Hopkins University Press, published for the World Bank.

Rajah Rasiah Ph.D., is Distinguished Professor of Economics at the Asia-Europe Institute, University of Malaya. His research interests include technology and international development, foreign investment, human capital, public health, and environment. He holds external positions at UNU-MERIT, Oxford University, Cambridge University, and Universiti Tenaga Nasional. He is the 2014 recipient of the Celso Furtado Prize awarded by the World Academy of Sciences for advancing the frontiers of social science thought.

Chapter 13
Natural Environment

Melvin Terry Gumal, Christina Yin, Yunus Yasin, Elvinson Rosedy, Douglas Tan, and Sylvia Ng

Abstract In the first quarter of 2016, a qualitative survey of 451 Malaysians was conducted to examine their views of what their future environment would be in 2050. Of these, 172 (38.1%) responded to the focused surveys with 52.3% indicating that the future was negative and only 19.8% believing that the future would be positive. The surveys were conducted on student-debaters, young professionals, and environment specialists. The top three reasons for their concern for the future were environmental deterioration, deforestation, and increased pollution. Towards improving the future environment, the focused group listed environmental awareness and stricter laws and better enforcement as potential solutions. The concerns of Malaysians for the future of the environment in 2050 appear to be similar to those shown in the United States and the United Kingdom. The chapter finally discusses the building blocks to stem the decline and rebuild a better environment.

Keywords Environment 2050 · Environmental concerns · Malaysia

Introduction

Twenty-four years ago, in 1992, the word environment was akin to an anti-establishment, left-wing, and perhaps even a socialist term, not just in Malaysia, but worldwide where conservationists or environmentalists were basically seen as anti-development. At that time, most governments worldwide, including Malaysia's were also gearing up for the Earth Summit of June 1992, a United Nations (UN)-led

M. T. Gumal (✉) · C. Yin · E. Rosedy · D. Tan · S. Ng
Kuching, Malaysia
e-mail: melvint@sarawakforestry.com

C. Yin
e-mail: cyin@swinburne.edu.my

S. Ng
e-mail: sng@wcs.org

Y. Yasin
Petaling Jaya, Malaysia

R. Rasiah et al. (eds.), *Malaysia's Leap Into the Future*, Dynamics of Asian Development, https://doi.org/10.1007/978-981-16-7045-9_13

event, attended by 172 governments, but with the exclusion of non-governmental organizations (NGOs) (Parson et al., 1992; United Nations, 1997).

A parallel, non-government event was also convened on-site, which saw the attendance of about 2,400 NGOs from all over the world (Parson et al., 1992; United Nations, 1997). In total, about 10,000 on-site journalists who reported environmental discussions on a daily basis for 14 days, covered the two globally-important events. Among the many policies agreed on and general messages communicated to the rest of the world were the need to halt the destruction of irreplaceable natural resources; reduce pollution on the planet; identify alternative sources of energy to replace the use of fossil fuels which are linked to the depletion of the ozone layer and global climate change; and address human consumption of natural resources, so as to have a planet that can support life in a positive, fulfilling, and sustainable manner.

Fast forward to 2016, and it appears that the same message is still being regurgitated, albeit at an urgent pace, not just by NGOs (now called civil society) and government agencies but also by a string of celebrities such as Harrison Ford (Sales, 2015; Skojec, 2016), Leonardo de Caprio (Goldenberg, 2016; Mooney, 2016), Sting (Shapiro, 2012; Suchecki, 2015), and Arnold Schwarzenegger (Harvey, 2015; Neslen, 2015). The messages are now instantaneous and come in many new forms, including via the pervasive social media that invade and permeate our daily lives. While we can instantaneously know or even take part in globally significant events and ask environmental questions to prominent people such as Prime Ministers or Presidents at "Town-Hall events", the general mood on the environment appears sombre and gloomy. An indication of this sombre mood is the time of the "environmental doomsday clock" which has the state of the earth's environment moving closer to a critical level at 12 o'clock. In 1992, it was listed at the "worrying level" of 7:49 p.m. while in 2015, it was cited at the "fearful" level of 9:27 p.m. (The Asahi Glass Foundation, 2015). Do note, however, that Gring and Woodin's Environmental Doomsday Clock is different from the World Doomsday Clock (includes nuclear events) which was listed at three minutes to midnight in 2016 (Eden et al., 2016; Leopold, 2016).

In the last few decades, humans have made huge scientific progress. In spite of this progress, the environmental calamities projected in 1992 have taken various trajectories. Among the peer-reviewed, scientifically validated calamities are extinctions (e.g. wild rhinos in Malaysia) (Clements et al., 2010; Havmøller et al., 2015; Taylor, 2015; Walston et al., 2016), steady declines (e.g. losses of natural forest cover and overharvesting of pangolins and tigers) (Duangchantrasiri et al., 2016; Miettinen et al., 2016; Spracklen et al., 2015; Walston et al., 2016; Zhang et al., 2015), and even negative increases, such as the proliferation of exotics, e.g. oil palm and acacia plantations (Brown & Jacobson, 2005; Koh & Wilcove, 2008; Miettinen et al., 2016). Sadly, there has also been an increase in pseudo-science, paid for by land clearance experts, fossil fuel hunters, and development practitioners to try to counter such empirically validated, scientific publications by attempting to influence the social masses (McDonald, 2013; Smith & Whiteley, 2014; Wilson et al., 2016).

Given the streams of mixed messages, good and bad science, implementable and non-implemented policies, what indeed will 2050 (24 years from now) look like in terms of the environment in Malaysia? We followed the adage of "many heads are better than one", and posed several qualitative and quantitative questions to 451 people living and working in Malaysia. These included school and university students aged between 14 and 24 years, young professionals aged between 25 and 35 years, and mature environmental specialists or conservationists (36 years old and above). This chapter is about the views of 172 (38.1% response rate) people, i.e. those who responded to questions on Malaysia's environmental future in 2050.

Contemporary Environmental Issues

The issues highlighted in the scientific publications in the previous paragraph are slightly different from those listed in the media, and also in the grey literature often found in internal reports by government agencies, non-governmental or civil society reports, or private consultancies. The focus in this chapter is largely on what are the environmental issues, and how are they to be achieved from the perspective of the younger generation in Malaysia. Such a focus inevitably takes us away from critical contemporary environmental issues, such as the shift from fossil fuels to renewable energy. Interested readers can read already published or forthcoming papers in this area (e.g. Rasiah et al., 2017, 2021; Santha & Rasiah, 2021). These papers also discuss the Malaysian government's efforts to expand the supply of renewable energy in the country, including the four large-scale solar (LSS) projects since 2018.

Malaysian-led scientific publications on the Malaysian environment appear to avoid addressing sensitive issues or practise self-censorship in their criticism or recommendations. Examples of these include the general absence of internationally accepted, high-impact, peer-reviewed studies which focus on losses of biodiversity due to oil palm; limited or contradicting reporting on the extent of forest coverage in Malaysia (Bryan et al., 2013; Gaveau et al., 2014); or the current expansions of monoculture crops into the Permanent Reserved Forests or the Permanent Forest Estates due to confidentiality issues (Meijaard et al., 2012; Gaveau et al., 2016). In part, this could be not only due to a lack of current data or little research interest by Malaysians but also because researchers have to be compliant with their Government-approved research permits or local corporate/donor requirements and thus become less critical of these issues. Unfortunately, where critical recommendations are found in internal documents, the authors also do not want them published as these are considered confidential or too sensitive.

There have also been disputes between Government-linked science and their recommendations, with those of international scientists. A case in point is where the Government-linked science indicated that peat swamps can be developed for agriculture without causing much negative environmental impact. This then resulted in a globally led publication with 139 scientific co-authors (115 international institutions) asserting that there was strong denial by governments of devastating consequences of converting peatlands for agriculture (Wijedasa et al., 2017).

Regardless of arguments for and against the devastation of the environment as summarized in the previous two paragraphs, in the last 20 years, the main issues in the environment in alphabetical order are: climate change; forestry and agriculture; land conversion (dams); marine-related issues; pollution; terrestrial wildlife issues; and water issues (see Appendix 13.1—https://rb.gy/gbakao). The issues have evolved over time, ranging from unsustainable logging (in a biological sense where productivity of the forest is surpassed by logging offtake) and forestry issues in the 1980s to the current ones of illegal logging, pollution and poaching of targeted animals such as elephants, tigers, and pangolins.

A case in point of the evolving issues in sustainability can be seen in forestry. Ecological or biological diversity requirements for sustainability in forestry is now considered "passé" as the forestry fraternity looks at plantation forestry as a substitute for natural forestry, disregarding the view that a monoculture is not a substitute for the biodiversity found in natural forests. In this sense, "economic sustainability" takes precedence over ecological or biological sustainability. In discussions with the elders of the forestry fraternity, there is acceptance that they could not maintain the "age-old and holy-grail" requirements of forestry, i.e. natural growth of trees to replace the ones logged.

Apart from the move from ecological sustainability is the increase in issues concerning legality. Again, within the forestry fraternity, there had been views that in the 1970s to 1990s, humans had tended to be compliant to laws and thus appeared to be in general, more law-abiding (Green et al., 2005) compared to the 2000s. This is in contrast to the views of Pinker (2011) and Wente (2015) (http://www.theglobeandmail.com/opinion/the-worlds-nicest-most-law-abiding-generation/article25249936/) who indicated that over time, humans have become much more law-abiding and violent crimes have reduced. Despite the contrasting views, current conservation policies have tended to favour the theories proposed by Green et al. (2005) as the issues have moved away from voluntary sustainable compliance to that of "private regulation compliance" prior to access to markets, e.g. FLEGT (Forest Law Enforcement Governance and Trade), RSPO (Roundtable Sustainable Palm Oil), FSC (Forest Stewardship Council), MTCC (Malaysian Timber Certification Council), etc. It is as if compliance of Malaysian policy and laws are flouted to the extent that local and international markets are now trying to make natural resource extraction companies comply with their own, private regulations or certification schemes.

Environmental issues in Malaysia are diverse. It is impossible to treat each of these issues with the summary accorded to those mentioned for Forestry above. However, to give the reader a general summary of environmental issues within Malaysia, we compiled these issues in Appendix 13.1. The compilation is based on reports that are readily available over the trustworthy sources on the internet or in scientific publications.

Mitigating Environmental Threats

The implementation agencies should have access to these readily available materials just as the authors had access to them. As noted in Appendix 13.1 (in the right-most column), awareness is sometimes not an issue as there has been a lack of political will, inadequate staffing, and an unwillingness to enforce the regulations. Of course, there are instances where a lack of awareness has led to environmental issues and these include emerging ones such as micro-beads and pollution (Malaysian Digest, 2016).

Nonetheless, there also are instances of complicit negligence by Malaysians and these include the public purposely throwing rubbish on roads, politicians ignoring scientific reporting, and laws pertaining to issues such as eating turtle eggs (Free Malaysia Today, 2015) or ignoring the fact that sharks are killed by large numbers in Sabah (Chan, 2015).

The recommendations to mitigate these environmental threats are listed in Appendix 13.2. A summary of some of the mitigation efforts include: (a) increased environmental awareness; (b) better enforcement; (c) improved legislation; (d) better planning; (e) increased staffing; and (f) reducing the threats such as pollution, logging, and overharvesting of the natural resources. The mitigation effort is dependent on the threat and not all the efforts are needed to mitigate each threat.

Capturing the Future

This chapter focuses on what Malaysians who are likely to live till 2050 see as the future of the environment in Malaysia and what they believe are the solutions essential to achieve a positive future. The methodology was aimed at Malaysia's younger populace without focussing on achieving specific targets for countries, such as capping carbon dioxide and greenhouse gases to check climate change and global warming (Rasiah et al., 2017). The methodology elicited responses that appear as general targets of the United Nations' sustainable development goals (SDGs) that emphasize dealing with the environment so as to ensure that the globe's inhabitants enjoy a secure future.

There are numerous survey methods used in asking sensitive conservation questions (Conteh et al., 2015; Cross et al., 2013; Nuno & St. John, 2014). In all these published literature, the underlying themes were to try to elicit as many responses as possible and to be unbiased and truthful in the response (Nuno & St. John, 2014). The questions and their delivery should also be tailored so that they are culturally acceptable and easily understood. A pilot test should also be conducted to examine whether the survey questions would be understood and not ambiguous (Schade, 2015; Thabane et al., 2010; van Teijlingen & Hundley, 2002).

Three different age groups were surveyed, i.e. 14 to 24-year-old student-debaters from throughout Malaysia; 25 to 35-year-old young professionals, and environmental or conservation specialists (36 years old and above). The authors targeted the student-debaters as they were selected from their respective schools as being the most eloquent students and had the best grasp of a multitude of issues. Two hundred and sixty-seven debaters were identified and asked three questions (see Appendix 13.3 for the detailed method). The students were asked to respond on different coloured recycled "paper leaves" and the final output of their responses is shown in the following URL (https://www.facebook.com/WCS.Malaysia/videos/vb.138129426245896/1042380369154126/?type=2&theater).

One hundred and sixty-one young professionals (25 to 35-year-olds) were emailed the questions. The questions were only given to local and foreign-trained professionals living in Malaysia and ranged from fresh graduates, post-graduate students, teachers, uber-drivers, staff of major corporations, and NGOs. The young professionals were selected as they appeared to understand environmental issues when asked preliminary questions by the researchers. A list of questions is shown in Appendix 13.4.

Finally, 23 specialists were emailed questions pertaining to the environment in Malaysia in 2050. These individuals were selected as they had worked in this field for over 15 years. The background information question format is shown in Appendix 13.5.

This focussed-survey is biased in that the young debaters are educated, opinionated, and vocal young people; the young professionals are all university-educated people as are the mature specialists. Thus, this survey is not conducted in a random fashion to the various age groups and is not meant to be reflective of views of a true, random cross-section of the Malaysian community. It is a survey of people from various age groups who are opinionated and have a grasp of current Malaysian and possibly world issues. A pilot test was also conducted with the various groups prior to the surveys. The respondents in that pilot understood the qualitative nature of the surveys and also the questions posed.

The data from the 172 respondents is qualitative; the respondents were also informed that they would remain anonymous, and the responses were also grouped into broad categories to enable the authors to analyse them in a descriptive sense. No major statistical analyses were conducted on the grouped categories beyond the descriptive statistics as the purpose of the surveys was to examine a simple snapshot of what the various age groups' views of the future of the Malaysian environment would be in 2050.

Some qualitative quotes are highlighted and these are included with the respondents' consent (see Appendix 13.6).

Seeing the Future

The overall response rate was 38.1% as 451 people were asked for their views with 172 responding. This response rate falls within the bandwidth of responses between online surveys (33%) and paper-based surveys (56%) (Kaplowitz et al., 2004; Nulty, 2008; Royal Society for the Protection of Birds, 2015). The breakdown of respondents from the various groups is as follows: student-debaters = 40.4% (108 respondents); young professionals = 33.5% (54 respondents); and specialists = 43.5% (10 respondents). Student-debaters had direct contact with the authors and were given questions on paper or leaves to respond to, whereas the young professionals and the specialists were emailed questions.

From the 172 respondents, 52.3% indicated that the future of the environment in 2050 was negative, whereas 19.8% viewed that the future would be positive (see Table 13.1). Meanwhile, 27.9% were neutral or uncertain as to what the future holds. Thus, slightly more than half of the respondents viewed the future to be bleak, double that of positive responses.

A breakdown of the responses according to the different groups is shown in Table 13.2. As can be seen, the young professionals and the specialists were much more negative in their outlook as 90% of these respondents viewed that the future of the environment in 2050 would be bleak. The overall view from the student-debaters

Table 13.1 Future of the environment, Malaysia, 2016

Categories	Respondents	%
No. of people who think that the environment is going to be positive	34	19.8
No. of people who think that the environment is going to be negative	90	52.3
No. of people who are not sure/neutral	48	27.9
Grand total	172	100

Note $N = 172$; Number of respondents and the percentages on whether they view that the condition of the environment in 2050 would be positive, negative, or are uncertain
Source Authors' Survey

Table 13.2 Future of the environment according to group, Malaysia, 2016

Age group	Percentage of positive response	Percentage of negative responses
(14–24 years) via Tree of Life	43	57
(25–35 years) Young professionals via emails	10	90
Mature Professionals via emails	10	90

Note $N = 172$; Breakdown of the ratio of responses according to the groups on whether the future of the environment in 2050 would be positive or negative
Source Authors' Survey

Table 13.3 Reasons for a Negative Future, Malaysia, 2016

Negative	No. of responses	Percentage
Environmental deterioration, general natural resource depletion (not including logging or deforestation), leading to doomsday predictions, natural disasters, or global warming	85	30.4
Deforestation	46	16.4
Increased pollution and use of non-environmentally friendly technology	39	13.9
Species extinction	37	13.2
Human negligence and negative mindset	22	7.9
Increased illegal activities	16	5.7
Miscellaneous	13	4.6
Not applicable	12	4.3
Human population explosion	10	3.6
Total	**280**	**100**

Note $N = 172$; Rankings on respondents' reasons as to why the Malaysian environment in 2050 would be negative. Each respondent was not limited to one response
Source Authors' Survey

was also slightly negative with 57% indicating that they believed the future would not look good.

Based on all these overall responses, the breakdown of reasons as to why the future was viewed as negative is shown in Table 13.3. Environmental deterioration/natural resource depletion (30.4%) and deforestation (16.4%) were the most cited reasons. Beyond these, the next two most cited reasons as to why the future was predicted to be negative were pollution (13.9%) and species extinctions (13.2%).

The overall response for those who viewed the future environment being better is shown in Table 13.4. The most common reasons given were because there will be increased environmental awareness and greater citizen action (25%), better use of technology as the country becomes more developed (23.9%), more protected or green areas being created (19.3%), and miscellaneous (11.4%, but not giving any reason).

The overall solution as provided by all 172 respondents to improve the future of the Malaysian environment in 2050 is shown in Table 13.5. According to the respondents, there has to be more education and increased environmental awareness (26.6%) followed by increased enforcement of regulations (19.1%). The next two solutions are "others" (14.6% but no actual solutions given) and the use of environmentally friendly development where the people benefit (7.5%).

Table 13.4 Reasons for a positive future, Malaysia, 2016

Positive	No. of responses	Percentage
Increased environmental awareness and positive citizen action	22	25.0
Technological advancement, developed country, and green energy use	21	23.9
Increased protected and green areas and flourishing natural environment	17	19.3
Miscellaneous	10	11.4
Cleaner environment, decreased pollution, and more beautiful	9	10.2
Not applicable	3	3.4
Current conditions maintained	2	2.3
Responsible use of natural resources	2	2.3
NGOs are effective caretakers	2	2.3
Total	**88**	**100**

Note N = 172; Respondents and why the future of the Malaysian environment in 2050 would be positive. Each respondent was not limited to one response
Source Authors' Survey

Table 13.5 Solutions for improvement, Malaysia, 2016

Solution	No. of responses	Percentage
Education, awareness and empowerment, and increasing environmental awareness	53	26.6
Stricter laws and better enforcement	38	19.1
Others	29	14.6
Green development by government	15	7.5
Reforestation and tree planting	13	6.5
Conservation of green areas	12	6
Not applicable	11	5.5
Advanced green technology	10	5
Effective NGO action	10	5
Green consumption pattern	8	4
Total	**199**	**100**

Note N = 172; Respondents and their solutions on how to improve the Malaysian environment in 2050. Each respondent was not limited to one response
Source Authors Survey

What Does the Evidence Say?

> … But then, if the critical mass doesn't realize the ascension of the consciousness across the globe soon, there may not be a civilization in 2050.
>
> That's why I say: saving the tiger is a test and if we pass, the planet will keep us.
>
> -Kae Kawanishi, Specialist

More than half of the respondents (52.3%) indicated that the future of the environment in 2050 was negative and it is more than double those (19.8%), who indicated that the future was positive. For the different age groups, only the 14- to 24-year-old student-debaters appeared less pessimistic about the future. The feeling of pessimism about the future of the environment has been evident, particularly in the developed world for more than 60 years. For example, in 1948, Fairfield Osborn published a book "Our Plundered Planet" about the environmental destruction of the planet and humanity's inherent hand in its slow demise (Osborn, 1948). This book predated "Silent Spring" by Rachel Carson (Carson, 1962) who became a poster child for environmentalism, winning numerous awards about humankind's wanton behaviour leading to pollution and the degradation of our planet. Both these seminal books on the environment, going back past 50 years, described a difficult or even an apocalyptic future where the natural environment of the world is degenerating or degrading. By the late 1990s, beyond the gathering of world leaders at the Earth Summit of 1992, experienced conservationists were still predicting dark days for the environment, unless much is done to halt the destruction, e.g. in the *Last Stand* (Kramer et al., 1997) or *Requiem for Nature* (Terborgh, 1999).

The "dark and difficult environmental future" has since seeped beyond scientific publications and has been popularized by movies like "*Waterworld*"[1] in 1995 and in the 2000s by "*The Day After Tomorrow*[2]", "*The Day the Earth Stood Still*[3]", and "*Avatar*[4]".

If Google is the eminent search engine for computer literate or computer-savvy people, a potential explanation could be to examine the changes in the "results" for Google searches on "Environment", "Environmental disasters", or "Environmental solutions" since 1993. In a Google search done on 21st June 2016, comparing the views of the environment since 1993, globally and in a Malaysian context (see Fig. 13.1), it can be seen that over the last 23 years, there has been an increasing number of "results" on Google carrying the words "Environment", "Environmental disasters", and "Environmental solutions".

Comparing the searches on "Environmental disasters" and "Environmental solutions", it can be seen that there has been a large increase in the results of the latter in the last five years (Fig. 13.2). If searches in Google are a barometer of trend, this is in convergence to the optimism shared by the younger respondents (14–24 year olds).

---

[1] http://www.imdb.com/title/tt0114898/.

[2] http://www.imdb.com/title/tt0319262/?ref_=tt_rec_tt.

[3] http://www.imdb.com/title/tt0970416/.

[4] http://www.imdb.com/title/tt0499549/.

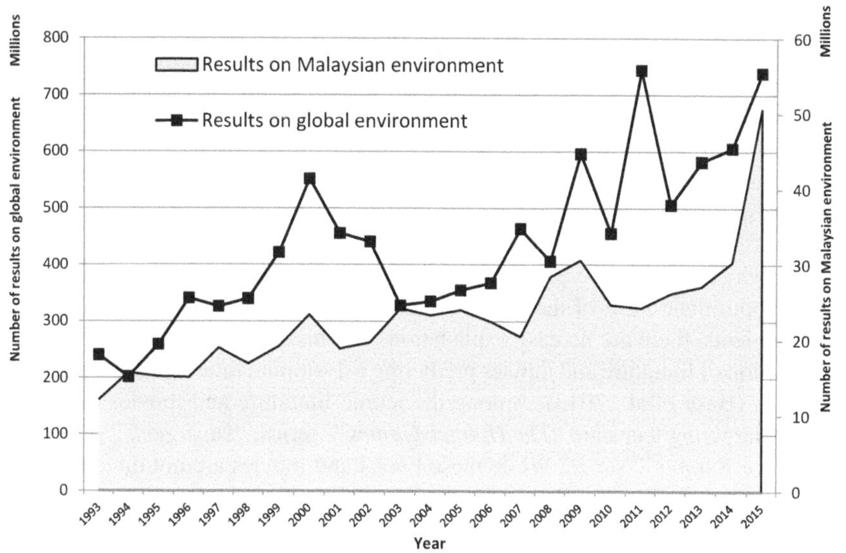

Fig. 13.1 Results from keyword searches of "environment" and "Malaysian environment", 1993–2015. *Source* Authors compilation (2016)

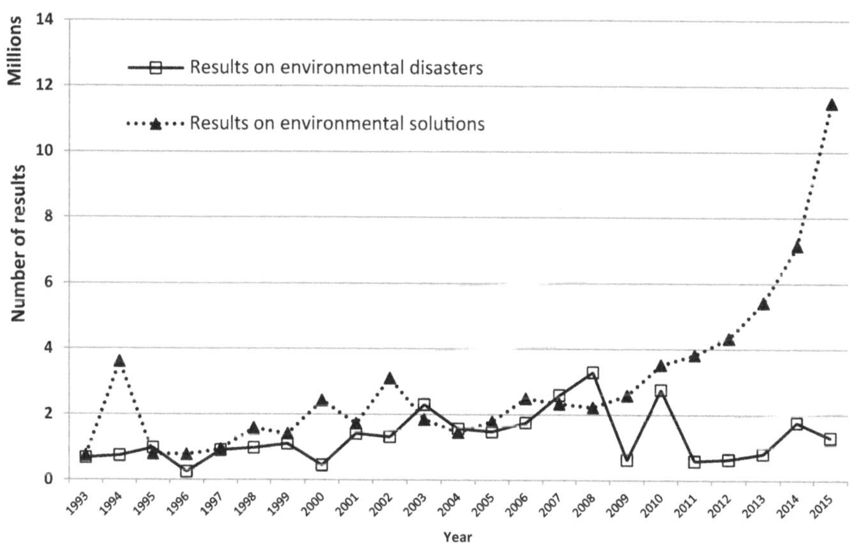

Fig. 13.2 Google results on global searches on "environmental disasters and solutions", 1993–2015. *Source* Authors compilation (2016)

However, it is difficult to ascertain what "results" mean as these are information, pages, and links (including keywords that they have in their database) related to the query (Blachman & Peek, 2007). In general, what it probably means is that in the last 23 years, there are more "results" of these keywords. It also probably means that there are more "results" of "environmental solutions" in the last five years, compared to "environmental disasters". While there has been an increase in "results" it does not necessarily mean that Google has guided the perceptions of respondents as the causal reasons for their perceptions were not asked in the surveys.

As to why the 14- to 24-year-old student-debaters tended to have a less pessimistic or more optimistic view of the future of the environment than the other categories of respondents, there are no easy explanations for this. This is in spite of the recent proliferation of literature and movies predicting a dystopian future targeting youthful audiences (Basu et al., 2013). Among the iconic literature and movies in the last 10 years targeting teens are "*The Hunger Games*[5]" series, "*Divergent*[6]" series, and "*The Maze Runner*[7]" series. While these books and movies are not directly linked to environmental disasters, their themes are certainly apocalyptic although all have tended to have an optimistic conclusion. Perhaps an explanation for part of their optimism is that the student-debaters share a view by Anair in Donston-Miller (2014) that "in almost all dystopian worlds, young people hold the values that the adults have forgotten. The adults left them a horrible world. They learn what is important and make moral choices and see themselves in it" (Donston-Miller, 2014). Perhaps as well, this optimism is based on the fact that younger people are generally much more optimistic (Adams, 2013) or have an optimistic bias (Sharot, 2011, 2012). Perhaps it is also possible that our respondents, due to our selection criteria, are confident and high achievers who see themselves as agents of change who can alter the world for the better.

Most of the responses have tended to concentrate on issues linked to the natural, terrestrial environment as the main environmental disaster. Issues such as wildlife-linked epidemics and human health, lack of creation of marine parks, or oceanic pollution were hardly mentioned, even though these issues have been highlighted globally (Portier et al., 2010; U.S. Environmental Protection Agency, 2016). For example, environmental pollution is also currently discussed in quite a few international publications such as Hardesty et al. (2015), Lavers and Bond, (2016), Li et al. (2016), Lohmann and Belkin (2014), Song et al. (2015), Steen et al. (2016), Wilcox et al. (2016), and Zalasiewicz et al. (2016). It has also been mentioned in Twitter (search on marine pollution; microplastics [#microplastics—72 mentions from 2009 to 2016] and microfibers [#microfibers—6 mentions from 2007 to 2016]) as well as in Malaysian newspapers such as The Star ("microplastic" six results from 2014 to 2015 and "microfiber" zero result) and New Straits Times ("microplastic" one result in 2015 and "microfiber" zero result). Even Malaysia-centric marine issues such as loss of tourism revenue related to marine wildlife watching such as sharks and

[5] http://www.imdb.com/title/tt1392170/.

[6] http://www.imdb.com/title/tt1840309/.

[7] http://www.imdb.com/title/tt1790864/?ref_=nv_sr_1.

dolphins were not mentioned by the respondents. These appeared several times in the Malaysian newspapers (Star, NST) and in international publications (Moreno & Amelung, 2009; Topelko & Dearden, 2005; Vianna et al., 2012). Perhaps the lack of such responses by the respondents is in part due to the general paucity of reports on these issues in both the social and general print media as they are not considered as "mainstream" as are loss of forests, iconic species such as tigers and great apes, etc. There is also a view that these issues are complex and not easily understood (United Nations Environment Programme, 2016).

Furthermore, the main solutions proposed by all the respondents were education (which would promote better environmental awareness), and better or stricter law enforcement. The combined percentage of education and enforcement responses totalled 45.7%. The former can be a short and long-term solution as education takes time. Stricter enforcement is a shorter-term solution although it can be debated that the penalties can be a good long-term deterrent. Some studies have provided good evidence for a deterrent effect created by increases in the certainty of punishment, at least in the short-term (Moffatt & Poynton, 2007). As for increasing the fines or sentences, there is uncertainty of the utility of this as some studies have indicated that "crime is not deterred, generally, by harsher sentences" (Doob et al., 2014; U.S. Department of Justice, 2014). Please note that certainty of punishment is different from harsher sentences as the latter could be just the written law, whereas the former reflects the certainty of being caught.

There is a general view that the authors and conservationists should be happy that so many respondents DO think about the environment (Mathai pers. comm. 2016) as there is socio-environmental research indicating that city folks or urban dwellers have tended to be apathetic and millennials are less interested in social and environmental issues (Cai et al., 2012; Juneman & Pane, 2013). But, this could be the result of a much simpler explanation; that these educated, socially and environmentally conscious respondents are indeed more aware than the general city person or the general millennial.

The conclusion that authors have reached after examining the feedback from this small survey is that most respondents fear for the environmental future of Malaysia in 2050, much like surveys carried out worldwide, e.g. in the USA (The Nature Conservancy, 2011) and in the UK (A Focus on Nature, 2016; Royal Society for the Protection of Birds, 2015) where those respondents also feared for the future of the environment in 2050 in their countries.

There is also a view by those respondents in the UK and the USA that they, the youth, will inherit potential environmental problems in 2050 and these would have been caused by the irresponsible activities of the current mature generation. These environmental problems, the youth believe, would be left for them to fix or repair. While much does appear bleak, the recommendations of the youth from the USA and the UK, as in their counterparts of this survey, also highlight that there may be solutions to alleviate the potential environmental problems projected to exist in 2050.

As written in a dystopian future envisioned by Pittacus Lore in "*I am Number 4*".

> When you have lost hope, you have lost everything. And when you think all is lost, when all is dire and bleak, there is always hope.

Conclusions: The Building Blocks

There have been ongoing concerns about our environmental future globally, as seen in the publications in the USA (The Nature Conservancy, 2011) and the UK (A Focus on Nature, 2016; Royal Society for the Protection of Birds, 2015). In Malaysia, the Ministry of Youth and Sports started inviting ideas from Malaysian youth to contribute to the formulation of a long-term plan on what the youth want Malaysia to be in 2050. This bottom-up involvement of the youth's aspirations linked with reviews of global trends, scenario planning, and input from experts is supposed to include long-term targets and achievable milestones. The targets will benefit all Malaysians and the plan itself is to be a successor to Vision 2020 (Prime Minister's Office, 2010).

There are numerous building blocks towards achieving a better environment in 2050. However, approaching the idea from just building blocks without a plan of implementation, timelines, accountability, designated responsibilities, milestones of achievable targets, financing, and scenario planning for success or scenario planning of what to do in terms of failures would be an exercise in futility (Aileron, 2011; Bustin, 2014).

In essence, to be successful, these building blocks must not be seen in isolation, but must be carried out in partnership with all the various points raised in the previous paragraph. The list of building blocks is shown in Table 13.6.

Perhaps the take-home message for the reader, politicians, and public administrators is that we need to do something about the pessimistic views and give our young Malaysians hope. As indicated by conservationists in Malaysia and overseas, it is not too late. We need to conserve now and inject hope in Malaysians to work towards a better future. Finally, together with hope, we also need to care, inculcate a consciousness for the environment, and ultimately internalize a moral obligation (Osborn, 1948; Ripple et al., 2016; Terborgh, 1999) that we all have to save the environment for its sake and for the sake of all the species it is home to, including our own.

Table 13.6 Building blocks for improving the environment, Malaysia, 2016

Building blocks
Management structures
• Greater accountability and responsibility in the implementation of policy
• Improved flexibility to work with the most appropriate implementation or governance structure
• Appropriate usage of both bottom-up and top-down management systems
• Identifying the most appropriate and optimal planning for the resource, whether it is via the use of regional, landscape, or local planning authorities
Working with communities, government agencies, and NGOs
• Greater education and awareness for the environment
• Greater participation by all stakeholders
• Establishing feedback loops and continuous engagement with the communities or interest groups affected by the environmental degradation
• Creating critical mass for protecting the environment and sustaining the public's interest (e.g. usage of social media platforms)
• Acknowledging the rights of communities and those of interest groups
Legislation and enforcement
• More pertinent and effective laws
• Improved enforcement and ensuring that they are adequately funded
• Better implementation of penalties
• Greater awareness by the judiciary
Programmatic focus linked with conservation of the environment. There has to be increased interest in:
• Human population growth
• Human consumption patterns
• Human urbanization and use of building materials
• Food consumption, waste handling, and disposals
• Water use by humans and wastage
• Energy production for the collective and energy consumption by individuals
• Catchments and green areas for human recreation
• Biological diversity requirements
• Climate change and floods affecting habitats, species distribution, and migration patterns
• Wildlife health and human health
Science and technological change
• Improved, up-to-date science for monitoring the environment, be it wildlife science, water quality, or social science
• Green industrial development and keeping up with technological changes, i.e. using better, more efficient and environmentally friendlier technology
• Adequate human capital with appropriate technological know-how within universities or institutions of higher learning

(continued)

Table 13.6 (continued)

Building blocks
• Reforestation and tree planting using appropriate species. Fast-growing species for certain areas for the timber market and native flowering and fruiting species for others. The choice is dependent on the situation
• Appropriate funding for research and development for green technologies in local universities, especially for tropical climate use, as well as monitoring on their deliverables
Sustained financing and budgets
• Estimating costs of mitigating environmental degradation, e.g. climate change (see, e.g. Rasiah et al., 2016a,2016b)
• Identifying sustained sources of funds for mitigation against environmental degradation
• Reviewing budgets to ensure that funding streams are adequate to address environmental degradation

Note The ideas for improving the environmental future towards 2050 have been divided into sections ranging from improving management so that the work can be implemented to actual programmatic requirements to improving the environment
Source Authors' compilation

Appendix 13.1

See attached Excel file at https://rb.gy/gbakao.

Appendix 13.2

Samples of environmental issues in the media and scientific publications (in alphabetical order)		
No	Environmental Indicators	Sample of recommendations to mitigate threats
1	Climate change	Strengthening environmental policies and legislation to reduce forest loss and land conversions
		Promote business opportunities or tax incentives for green industries such as production of solar panels, reduction of taxes for hybrid cars, etc.
		Encourage adoption of sustainable consumption and production, e.g. use of car-pooling in cities, imposing taxes on the use of non-biodegradable plastics and those that ultimately pollute the marine environment, etc.
		Identify locations that may be prone to flooding and identify whether the communities should be resited or sea-walls or flood walls built to protect them

(continued)

(continued)

Samples of environmental issues in the media and scientific publications (in alphabetical order)		
No	Environmental Indicators	Sample of recommendations to mitigate threats
		In locations where water shortage becomes an issue, dams have to be built to increase water storage. Educational activities on wise use of water may have to be promoted to discourage water losses or pollution
		Journalists should be encouraged to report on climate change and do so in a manner that is easily understood so that readers can better understand the issue and take greater responsibility
2	Forestry and agriculture issues	
	(a) Logging	In sites where logging is ecologically permissible, the activity should continue. However, there should be continued monitoring to ensure compliance of the laws
		Where logging is considered detrimental to the environment, it should be stopped. Alternative non-resource consumptive activities should be encouraged such as bio-banks or ecotourism (where possible or suitable)
	(b) Monoculture plantations	There should be continued monitoring and enforcement on growth of plantations, legal or otherwise. For the former, this is to ensure compliance of the laws. For the latter, these plantations should be removed
		The creation of plantations should be avoided in areas that have substantial biodiversity. This reduces the nation's overall biodiversity losses
		Future plantations should be at locations of low carbon stock. As such, carbon emissions will be reduced and climate issues avoided
		Private regulation, traceability, and greater responsibility for "zero deforestation" by large plantation companies may be a solution
		Substantial biodiversity losses will only be averted if future oil palm expansion is managed to avoid deforestation
3	Land conversion (Dams)	
	(a) Determining the location of the proposed dams	There is a need to examine the impacts of dams during the inception phase and mitigate the negative impacts

(continued)

(continued)

Samples of environmental issues in the media and scientific publications (in alphabetical order)		
No	Environmental Indicators	Sample of recommendations to mitigate threats
		Recommendations not to construct the dams include looking at: a. REDD; b. alternative values of the forest through medicinal plants, and c: ecotourism activities
	(b) Dam construction	The Government will review and act on recommendations to reduce the environmental damage caused during the construction of dams
4	Marine related issues	
	(a) Shark-finning	There should be more awareness campaigns to stop people eating shark fin soup and to encourage restaurant owners to stop offering shark fin soup on their menus
		As a signatory to the CITES (Convention on International Trade in Endangered Species of Wild Fauna and Flora), Malaysia has an international obligation to implement measures intended to ensure the international trade in products of the shark species protected under the Convention is both legal and sustainable
		Where possible, Malaysia should create more marine parks as this could help shark conservation
		Laws against shark hunting should be enacted especially for rare and endangered species
	(b) Over-fishing	There should be greater enforcement to stop encroachment by commercial trawlers, as well as the operation of Illegal, unreported, and unregulated fishing
		There is a need to implement action programmes to help reduce overfishing and rehabilitate fisheries resources in the coastal areas, including reducing pollution and stopping the destruction of coastal aquatic habitats
	(c) Illegal trade, e.g. illegal sale of turtle eggs	There should be greater enforcement and awareness to stop consumers from buying turtles' eggs
		There is a need for a joint management programme to reduce sale of turtle eggs over time
5	Pollution	There should be conservation education awareness programmes and these should include the separation of wastes

(continued)

(continued)

Samples of environmental issues in the media and scientific publications (in alphabetical order)		
No	Environmental Indicators	Sample of recommendations to mitigate threats
		Enforcement should be done in various locations where there is negligence
		Where laws are inadequate, they should be enacted and a greater political will to ensure compliance
6	Terrestrial wildlife issues	
	(a) Poaching	Conservation education should be conducted at sites where poaching is rampant
		For greater prosecution rates: there is a need for better forensic work on wildlife crime and the admission of other forms of defensible evidence to monitor online trade
		In general, there should be more education and awareness of the law, as consumers are generally unaware of these laws
		There should be continued monitoring of wildlife trade including those found online, and subsequent prosecution of illegal activities
	(b) Terrestrial wildlife management	Where necessary, more protected areas should be created
		Protected areas should be linked if possible and this includes the creation of wildlife corridors for the movement of wildlife
7	Water Issues	There is a need to improve delivery of clean and uninterrupted water supply to the population
		Alternatives used during periods of water shortage should not contribute to increased general pollution, e.g. use of polystyrene cups
		There is a need to ensure that water-polluting companies be compliant to clean water requirements

Appendix 13.3: Project Title-Tree of Life

Conducting the activity:

1. Each student was asked the following question: "In 2050, what do you think the future would be like for the Malaysian environment?"
2. Each student was given three leaves of different colours (Green/Amber/Red) made from recycled paper in a recycled envelope. Each student was given a

chance to respond to the question above following the guidelines below, with choices of answering all or any according to their opinions (it can be just one out of the three, two out of the three, or all three of them)

i. Green leaf: The future environment is positive and good. Why do you think that it would be good?
ii. Red leaf: The future environment is negative and poor. Why do you think that it would be poor?
iii. Amber leaf: Students are asked for suggestions and/or solutions to make the future environment a good or positive one.

3. All leaves were collected in the same envelopes.
4. The leaves were then assembled onto the "Tree of Life" and the contributions of each student that responded were displayed.

Appendix 13.4: Responses of Young Professionals

The Young Professionals were given three questions and the background information upon which their thoughts should be based.

Malaysia's Leap into the Future: The Building Blocks is targeted at analysing the existing scenario of the critical issues that are important to push Malaysia towards 2050. We are required to assume that we will already be developed by 2020. The focus then will shift towards health, environment, and knowledge-based activities in an environment where Malaysia's population growth will slow down, dependence on natural resources will fall from resource exhaustion, and greater demand by the people to have freedom, clean air, and access to capabilities. Hence, thoughts are to be centred on the following.

In your opinion:

1. Discuss where you think the Malaysian environment will be in 2050 (over 30 years from now).
2. Describe your thoughts by answering the following questions:
   - Will it be better, the same, or worse?
3. What do you think can be done by the Government to change the situation?

Appendix 13.5: Questions Emailed to Specialists

All the specialists were given the same background information and asked the accompanying questions. The questions were in-depth to enable the specialists to convey their understanding of the environmental conditions they faced.

Malaysia's Leap into the Future: The Building Blocks is targeted at analysing the existing scenario of the critical issues that are important to push Malaysia towards

2050. We are required to assume that we will already be developed by 2020. The focus then will shift towards health, environment, and knowledge-based activities in an environment where Malaysia's population growth will slow down, dependence on natural resources will fall from resource exhaustion, and greater demand by the people to have freedom, clean air, and access to capabilities. Hence, thoughts are to be centred on the following:

1. What is the current state of the environment in your field site or place or issue where you are working towards resolving [In all the questions, please be descriptive. I am not compiling a quantitative assessment.]. One or two paragraphs would be fine.
2. Discuss the threats and opportunities—both internal and external to your field site or place or issue [Again be descriptive].
3. Discuss how government agencies and Malaysia in general can address the threats and appropriate opportunities or NOT. If you think the agencies have the capacity, great. Describe how the agencies can do so. If you think the agencies do not have the capacity, also say so. Describe who else can address the threats. Again be descriptive.
4. Discuss where we will be in 2050 in your field site or place or issue if:
    (a) it is business-as-usual, contribution by the Government agencies;
    (b) Your perfect future—if agencies pick up and put a whole lot of energy into the environment.
    (c) If the agencies are not doing the job, are there separate entity/entities, apart from the Government agencies who can do the job? What would it be like in 2050?
5. Bonus question—Imagine what the young now would want in 2050.

Appendix 13.6: Sample of Quotes from Respondents

Names of those who wanted anonymity are not provided. The quotes are ad libitum. No changes were made to correct their English grammar. Please note that the quotes need to be read in context of the questions posed to the respondents (Appendices 1 to 3) or else their meaning could be misconstrued.

	Student-debaters	
1	Anonymous	*"Youth needs to be more proactive & creative & innovative in giving into sustainable technology. Youth should be given more chances to perform and create."*
2	Anonymous	*"Many aspects conserved by past generations like the wildlife will be gone and the future generations would not even know what a rainforest is because there're no more rainforest in this world."*

(continued)

(continued)

	Student-debaters	
3	Anonymous	*"If deforestation continues, it is most definite that our environment would worsen. Plants and animals would die and face endangerment."*
4	Anonymous	*"Our air and water would become polluted and we would slowly run out of usable resources."*
5	Anonymous	*"Malaysia will remain a heavy polluter, especially in CO2 emissions. A lot of flora and fauna will go extinct. Several places will be submerged underwater."*
6	Anonymous	*"The current situation could obviously be improved if the govt actually focused more than just economy but instead work more on greener forms of urban development."*
7	Anonymous	*"Many endangered species in Malaysia will be extinct. There will be less trees, less clean water and less species of animals."*
8	Anonymous	*"In 2050, less native forests will be exploited as people will make use of existing vacant lands and build integrated townships to accommodate population growth."*
9	Anonymous	*"I think if we take action now, in the future I believe our wildlife will flourish."*
10	Anonymous	*"The environment will be so bad. I have no word to describe it."*

	Young professionals	
1	Anonymous	*"We are taking their homes away thus the animals cannot be blamed for the increase in animal-human conflicts because we are the trespassers."*
2	Anonymous	*"Exotic species or our valuable wildlife such as tiger, elephant, clouded leopard may become extinct or just can be seen in zoo."*
3	Anonymous	*"It might reach to a stage that our land being replaced by more "concrete forest" and wild animals soonly extinct."*
4	Anonymous	*"Lack of enforcement, corruption among officers, outdated environment law, uncontrolled development, public mentality would be main factors to the demolition of natural environment in Malaysia."*
5	Anonymous	*"Although there are efforts made to improve or help the environment, the population is growing rapidly with increasing demands, development and waste. The small scale effort will mostly be cancelled out."*
6	Anonymous	*"Young people striving to become doctors, lawyers, and accountants because they perceive environmental practitioners as second class and low-waged profession."*

(continued)

(continued)

	Young professionals	
7	Win Sim	*"Mitigation efforts are then taken but the causes of the environmental issues often remain unaddressed. Without a vigilant government oversight on environmental issues, the Malaysian environment will get worse over time."* *"In a nut shell, the government must raise their game if they are serious about conserving and preserving what little is left of the Malaysian environment. With the government's current direction, I despair at the thought of the Malaysian environment in 2050. All is not lost, however. It took Qin dynasty twenty years to build the Great Wall of China. How long will it take to usher Malaysians to a more environmentally-friendly path in the twenty-first century? I am optimistic."*
8	Wong Pui May	*"If the government can't provide funds for conservation, they should at least set aside their egos and be more open to collaborating with civil society."*

	Specialists	
1	Anonymous	*"It remains uncertain, if the future generation will bring conservation into mainstream national development, however, it requires a monumental improvement of the education in Malaysia, from primary school to graduate level."*
2	Anonymous	*"The young consists of different groups, probably largely defined by their upbringing and family backgrounds. Unless we raise them to see humanity's need and dependence on nature, it would not be greatly different from their predecessors."*
4	Kae Kawanishi	*"When everyone is compassionate to everything and everyone around them, and is mindful of the consequence of every action, then there no need for law enforcement. Sustainable nature conservation is not arming the nature to the teeth and fencing her"*
5	Anonymous	*"The government certainly has the capacity to overturn the foolish policy decision to allow plantations inside forest reserves. A concerted public campaign would force the government to stop clearing natural forest. At least a clear policy could be adopted so that there would be no "nett" loss of natural forest. As a developed nation this would be the only responsible step to take."*
6	Anonymous	*"Even the severe flooding at the end of 2014 did not result in greater appreciation of biodiversity conservation/natural resource management, as the official conclusion appears to be that climate change was to blame and the appropriate response should be to allocate more resources for technical/engineering solutions."*
7	Anonymous	*"The 'business-as-usual' scenario will see the interests of connected parties taking precedence over the interests of communities and the interests of the environment. The rivers will be polluted, the natural resources depleted and the iconic wildlife lost. Forests will be converted to an ever-expanding mono-culture of plantation species."* *"The involvement of non-resident officials and non-resident communities claiming rights to the area in resource use decisions is a threat as the basis for their decisions do not include environmental services as benefits."*

(continued)

(continued)

	Specialists	
8	Anonymous	*"The politics of water supply and water pollution may be the key factors that finally alert the general public to the government-led land changes. it is possible that the romance of wildness which attracts many elsewhere, carries a connotation of "uncivilised" and is therefore rejected by the wealthy and increasing middle classes."*

References

A Focus on Nature. (2016). Vision for nature. *A Focus on Nature.* Retrieved July 25, 2016, from http://www.afocusonnature.org/wp-content/uploads/2016/07/Vision-for-Nature-report-1.pdf

Adams, C. (2013). Teenagers are more optimistic about future than adults, survey finds. *Education Week*, 23 September.

Aileron. (2011). 10 reasons why strategic plans fail. *Forbes.* Retrieved May 22, 2017 from https://www.forbes.com/sites/aileron/2011/11/30/10-reasons-why-strategic-plans-fail/#73a0437f86a8

Basu, B., Broad, K. R., & Hintz, C. (2013). *Contemporary dystopian fiction for young adults: Brave new teenagers.* Taylor & Francis.

Blachman, N., & Peek, J. (2007). Part II: Understanding results. *Google Guide.* Retrieved March 30, 2016, from http://www.googleguide.com/category/understanding-results/

Brown, E., & Jacobson, M. F. (2005). *Cruel oil: How palm oil harms health, rainforest and wildlife.* Center for Science in the Public Interest.

Bryan, J. E., Shearman, P. L., Asner, G. P., Knapp, D. E., Aoro, G., & Lokes, B. (2013). Extreme differences in forest degradation in Borneo: Comparing practices in Sarawak, Sabah, and Brunei. *PLOS ONE, 8*(7), e69679.

Bustin, G. (2014). Why most company strategic plans fail. *Forbes.* Retrieved May 22, 2017, from https://www.forbes.com/sites/forbesleadershipforum/2014/09/15/why-most-company-strategic-plans-fail/#439777f46a38

Cai, H., Kwan, V. S. Y., & Sedikides, C. (2012). A sociocultural approach to narcissism: The case of modern China. *European Journal of Personality, 26*(5), 529–535.

Carson, R. (1962). *Silent Spring.* Houghton Mifflin.

Chan, J. (2015). No shark-fin industry in Malaysia, says minister in dismissing need for ban. *The Malay Mail Online.* Retrieved February 18, 2017, from http://www.themalaymailonline.com/malaysia/article/no-shark-fin-industry-in-malaysia-says-minister-in-dismissing-need-for-ban

Clements, R., Rayan, D. M., Zafir, A. W. A., Venkataraman, A., Alfred, R., Payne, J., & Sharma, D. S. K. (2010). Trio under threat: Can we secure the future of rhinos, elephants and tigers in Malaysia? *Biodiversity and Conservation, 19*(4), 1115–1136.

Conteh, A., Gavin, M. C., & Solomon, J. (2015). Quantifying illegal hunting: A novel application of the quantitative randomised response technique. *Biological Conservation, 189*, 16–23.

Cross, P., St. John, F. A. V., Khan, S., & Petroczi, A. (2013). Innovative techniques for estimating illegal activities in a human-wildlife-management conflict. *PLOS ONE, 8*(1), e53681.

Donston-Miller, D. (2014). Why young adults 'hunger' for The Hunger Games and other post-apocalyptic dystopian fiction. *Forbes.* Retrieved March 30, 2016, from http://www.forbes.com/sites/sungardas/2014/11/20/why-young-adults-hunger-for-the-hunger-games-and-other-post-apocalyptic-dystopian-fiction/#3abf017bcdd2

Doob, A. N., Webster, C. M., & Gartner, R. (2014). Issues related to harsh sentences and mandatory minimum sentences: General deterrence and incapacitation. *Centre for Criminology & Sociolegal Studies.*

Duangchantrasiri, S., Umponjan, M., Simcharoen, S., Pattanavibool, A., Chaiwattana, S., Maneerat, S., Kumar, N. S., Jathanna, D., Srivathsa, A., & Karanth, K. U. (2016). Dynamics of a low-density tiger population in Southeast Asia in the context of improved law enforcement. *Conservation Biology, 30*, 639–648.

Eden, L., Rosner, R., Ewing, R., Krauss, L. M., Kartha, S., Pickering T. R., Pierrehumbert, R. T., Rajaraman, R., Sims, J., Somerville, R. C. J., Squassoni, S., & Titley, D. (2016). It is still three minutes to midnight. *Bulletin of the Atomic Scientists*. Retrieved March 30, 2016, from http://thebulletin.org/it-still-three-minutes-midnight9107

Free Malaysia Today. (2015). Federal minister, Sabah leaders eating turtle eggs goes viral. *Free Malaysia Today*. Retrieved February 18, 2017, from http://www.freemalaysiatoday.com/category/nation/2015/11/04/federal-minister-sabah-leaders-eating-turtle-eggs-goes-viral/

Gaveau, D. L., Sloan, S., Molidena, E., Yaen, H., Sheil, D., Abram, N. K., Ancrenaz, M., Nasi, R., Quinones, M., Wielaard, N., & Meijaard, E. (2014). Four decades of forest persistence, clearance and logging on Borneo. *PLOS ONE*, 9(7), e101654.

Goldenberg, S. (2016). How Leonardo DiCaprio became one of the world's top climate change champions. *The Guardian*. Retrieved March 30, 2016, from http://www.theguardian.com/environment/2016/feb/29/how-leonardo-dicaprio-oscar-climate-change-campaigner

Green, D. G., Grove, E., & Martin, N. A. (2005). *Crime and civil society: Can we become a more law-abiding people? Civitas: Institute for the Study of Civil Society*. St Edmundsbury Press Ltd.

Hardesty, B. D., Good, T. P., & Wilcox, C. (2015). Novel methods, new results and science-based solutions to tackle marine debris impacts on wildlife. *Ocean & Coastal Management, 115*, 4–9.

Harvey, F. (2015). Arnold Schwarzenegger says climate campaigns need to focus on 'right now' not 2050. *The Guardian*. Retrieved March 30, 2016, from http://www.theguardian.com/environment/2015/dec/07/arnold-schwarzenegger-climate-campaigns-need-focus-right-now-not-2050

Havmøller, R. G., Payne, J., Ramono, W., Ellis, S., Yoganand, K., Long, B., & Burgess, N. (2015). Will current conservation responses save the critically endangered Sumatran rhinoceros Dicerorhinus sumatrensis? *Oryx, 50*(02), 355–359.

Juneman, A., & Pane, M. M. (2013). Apathy towards environmental issues, narcissism, and competitive view of the world. *Procedia Social and Behavioral Sciences, 101*, 44–52.

Kaplowitz, M. D., Hadlock, T. D., & Levine, R. (2004). A comparison of web and mail survey response rates. *Public Opinion Quarterly, 68*(1), 94–101.

Koh, L. P., & Wilcove, D. S. (2008). Is oil palm agriculture really destroying tropical biodiversity? *Conservation Letters, 1*(2), 60–64.

Kramer, R., van Schaik, C., & Johnson, J. (1997). *Last stand: Protected areas and the defense of tropical biodiversity*. Oxford University Press.

Lavers, J. L., & Bond, A. L. (2016). Selectivity of flesh-footed shearwaters for plastic colour: Evidence for differential provisioning in adults and fledglings. *Marine Environmental Research, 113*, 1–6.

Leopold, T. (2016). Doomsday clock stays at three minutes to midnight. *Cable News Network*. Retrieved March 30, 2016, from http://edition.cnn.com/2016/01/26/us/doomsday-clock-feat/

Li, W. C., Tse, H. F., & Fok, L. (2016). Plastic waste in the marine environment: A review of sources, occurrence and effects. *Science of the Total Environment, 566–567*, 333–349.

Lohmann, R., & Belkin, I. M. (2014). Organic pollutants and ocean fronts across the Atlantic Ocean: A review. *Progress in Oceanography, 128*, 172–184.

Malaysian Digest. (2016). Microplastics should be Banned in cosmetics to save oceans, MPs Say. *Malaysian Digest*. Retrieved February 18, 2017, from http://www.malaysiandigest.com/world/628644-microplastics-should-be-banned-in-cosmetics-to-save-oceans-mps-say.html

McDonald, L. (2013). Crimes against ecology. *Alternatives Journal*. Retrieved March 30, 2016, from http://www.alternativesjournal.ca/policy-and-politics/crimes-against-ecology

Meijaard, E., Wich, S., Ancrenaz, M., & Marshall, A. J. (2012). Not by science alone: Why orangutan conservationists must think outside the box. *Annals of the New York Academy of Sciences, 1249*, 29–44.

Miettinen, J., Shi, C., & Liew, S. C. (2016). Land cover distribution in the peatlands of Peninsular Malaysia, Sumatra and Borneo in 2015 with changes since 1990. *Global Ecology and Conservation, 6*, 67–78.

Moffatt, S., & Poynton, S. (2007). Deterrent effect of higher fines on recidivism: Driving offences. *NSW Bureau of Crime Statistics and Research Bulletins*, 15.

Mooney, C. (2016). Leonardo DiCaprio's Oscars speech was about climate change, which could be worse than we thought. *The Washington Post.* Retrieved March 30, 2016, from https://www.washingtonpost.com/news/energy-environment/wp/2016/02/29/leonardo-dicaprios-oscar-speech-was-about-climate-change-which-could-be-worse-than-we-thought/

Moreno, A., & Amelung, B. (2009). Climate change and coastal & marine tourism: Review and analysis. *Journal of Coastal Research, 56*, 1140–1144.

Neslen, A. (2015). Arnold Schwarzenegger terminates tusk for anti-poaching campaign. *The Guardian.* Retrieved March 30, 2016, from http://www.theguardian.com/environment/2015/nov/13/arnold-schwarzenegger-terminates-tusk-for-anti-poaching-campaign

Nulty, D. D. (2008). The adequacy of response rates to online and paper surveys: What can be done? *Assessment & Evaluation in Higher Education, 33*(3), 301–314.

Nuno, A., & St. John, F. A. S. (2015). How to ask sensitive questions in conservation: A review of specialized questioning techniques. *Biological Conservation, 189*, 5–15.

Osborn, F. (1948). *Our plundered planet*. Little, Brown.

Parson, E. A., Haas, P. M., & Levy, M. A. (1992). A summary of the major documents signed at the Earth Summit and The Global Forum. *Ciesin.* Retrieved March 30, 2016, from http://www.ciesin.org/docs/003-312/003-312.html

Pinker, S. (2011). *The better angels of our nature: Why violence has declined*. Viking Press.

Portier, C. J., Thigpen Tart, K., Carter, S. R., Dilworth, C. H., Grambsch, A. E., Gohlke, J., Hess, J., Howard, S. N., Luber, G., Lutz, J. T., Maslak, T., Prudent, N., Radtke, M., Rosenthal, J. P., Rowles, T., Sandifer, P. A., Scheraga, J., Schramm, P. J., Strickman, D., Trtanj, J. M., & Whung, P. Y. (2010). A human health perspective on climate change: a report outlining the research needs on the human health effects of climate change. *Research Triangle Park, NC: Environmental Health Perspectives/National Institute of Environmental Health Sciences.*

Prime Minister's Office. (2010). Challenges to realising Vision 2020. *Government transformation programme: The roadmap,* 41–52. Performance Management and Delivery Unit (PEMANDU).

Rasiah, R., Ahmed, A., Al-Amin, A. Q., & Chenayah, S. (2016a). Climate change mitigation: Comparative assessment of Malaysian and ASEAN scenarios. *Environmental Science and Pollution Research,* 1–11.

Rasiah, R., Al-Amin, A. Q., Ahmed, A., Leal Filho, W., & Calvo, E. (2016b). Climate mitigation roadmap: Assessing low carbon scenarios for Malaysia. *Journal of Cleaner Production, 133,* 272–283.

Rasiah, R., Al-Amin, A. Q., Nazia, H. M., Anwar, H. C., Santha, C., Ferdous, A., & Leal Filho, W. (2017). Assessing climate change mitigation proposals for Malaysia: Implications for emissions and abatement costs. *Journal of Cleaner Production, 20*, 163–173.

Rasiah, R., Siti Indati M., & Amar Hisham, J. (2021). Energy efficiency and greening: Strategic direction for Malaysia. In R. Rasiah, V. Gopi Krishnan, & O. R. Azleen (Eds.), *Financing sustainable development in East and Southeast Asia.* Springer (forthcoming).

Ripple, W. J., Lopez-Bao, J. V., Durant, S. M., Macdonald, D. W., Lindsey, P. A., Bennett, E. L., Beschta, R. L., Bruskotter, J. T., Campos-Arceiz, A., Corlett, R. T., Darimont, C. T., Dickman, A. J., Dirzo, R., Dublin, H. T., Estes, J. A., Everatt, K. T., Galetti, M., Goswami, V. R., Hayward, M. W., & hedges, S., Hoffman, M., Hunter, T. B., Kerley, G. I., Letnic, M., Levi, T., Maisels, F., Morrison, J. C., Nelson, M. P., Newsome, T. M., Painter, L., Pringle, R. M., Sandom, C. J., Terborgh, T., Treves, A., Valkenburgh, B. V., Vucetich, J. A., Wirsing, A. J., Wallach, A. D., Wolf, C., Woodroffe, R., Young, H. & Zhang, L. (2016). Saving the world's terrestrial megafauna. *BioScience, 66*(10), 807–812.

Royal Society for the Protection of Birds. (2015). Response for nature: Evidence report. *Royal Society for the Protection of Birds*. Retrieved March 30, 2016, from http://www.rspb.org.uk/Images/responsefornature_evidencereport_tcm9-408345.pdf

Sales, L. (2015). Harrison Ford hits out at global inaction on climate change, warns of 'disastrous' consequences. *ABC News*. Retrieved March 30, 2016, from http://www.abc.net.au/news/2015-12-09/harrison-ford-hits-out-at-global-inaction-on-climate-change/7015380

Santha, C., & Rasiah, R. (2021) Energy sustainability policies in Malaysia: Addressing energy efficiency and environmental greening. In E. Quah & R. Shubert (Eds.), *Sustainability and environmental decision making*. Springer.

Schade, A. (2015). Pilot testing: Getting it right (before) the first time. *Nielsen Norman Group*. Retrieved March 30, 2016, from https://www.nngroup.com/articles/pilot-testing/

Shapiro, G. (2012). Sting's S.O.S. for the environment. *The Wall Street Journal*. Retrieved March 30, 2016, from http://www.wsj.com/articles/SB10000872396390443507204578022613484133902

Sharot, T. (2011). *The optimism bias: A tour of the irrationally positive brain*. Pantheon Books.

Sharot, T. (2012). Optimism bias: Why the young and the old tend to look on the bright side. *Washington Post*. Retrieved March 30, 2016, from https://www.washingtonpost.com/national/health-science/optimism-bias-why-the-young-and-the-old-tend-to-look-on-the-bright-side/2012/12/28/ac4147de-37f8-11e2-a263-f0ebffed2f15_story.html

Skojec, C. (2016). WATCH: Julia Roberts, Harrison Ford and Kevin Spacey lead all-star lineup for eye-opening video series on the environment. *Alternet*. Retrieved March 30, 2016, from http://www.alternet.org/environment/nature-speaking-star-studded-video-series-highlights-importance-conservation

Smith, E. I. & Whiteley, A. (2014). The false politics and faulty science of climate change. *Wake Up World*. Retrieved March 30, 2016, from http://wakeup-world.com/2014/12/08/the-failed-politics-and-faulty-science-of-climate-change/

Song, Y. K., Hong, S. H., Jang, M., Han, G. M., Rani, M., Lee, J., & Shim, W. J. (2015). A comparison of microscopic and spectroscopic identification methods for analysis of microplastics in environmental samples. *Marine Pollution Bulletin, 93*(1–2), 202–209.

Spracklen, B. D., Kalamandeen, M., Galbraith, D., Gloor, E., & Spracklen, D. V. (2015). A global analysis of deforestation in moist tropical forest protected areas. *PLOS ONE, 10*(12), e0143886.

Steen, R., Torjussen, C. S., Jones, D. W., Tsimpidis, T., & Miliou, A. (2016). Plastic mistaken for prey by a colony-breeding Eleonora's falcon (Falco eleonorae) in the Mediterranean Sea, revealed by camera-trap. *Marine Pollution Bulletin, 106*(1–2), 200–201.

Suchecki, P. M. J. (2015). "Every breath you take." Sting's big cause is protecting rainforests. *Inside Philanthropy*. Retrieved March 30, 2015, from http://www.insidephilanthropy.com/home/2015/3/26/every-breath-you-take-stings-big-cause-is-protecting-rainfor.html

Taylor, A. P. (2015). Sumatran Rhino goes extinct in the wild in Malaysia. *Live Science*. Retrieved March 30, 2016, from http://www.livescience.com/51965-sumatran-rhino-extinct-in-malaysia.html

Terborgh, J. (1999). *Requiem for nature*. Island Press.

Thabane, L., Ma, J., Chu, R., Cheng, J., Ismaila, A., Rios, L. P., Robson, R., Thabane, M., Giangregorio, L., & Goldsmith, C. H. (2010). A tutorial on pilot studies: The what, why and how. *BMC Medical Research Methodology, 10*(1), 1.

The Asahi Glass Foundation. (2015). Gring and Woodin's environmental doomsday clock. *The Asahi Glass Foundation*. Retrieved March 30, 2016, from http://www.af-info.or.jp/en/gw_clock/index.html

The Nature Conservancy. (2011). Connecting America's youth to nature. *The Nature Conservancy*. Retrieved March 30, 2016, from http://www.nature.org/newsfeatures/kids-in-nature/youth-and-nature-poll-results.pdf

Topelko, K. N., & Dearden, P. (2005). The shark watching industry and its potential contribution to shark conservation. *Journal of Ecotourism, 4*(2), 108–128.

U.S. Department of Justice. (2014). Five things about deterrence. *National Institute of Justice*. Retrieved March 30, 2016, from http://nij.gov/five-things/pages/deterrence.aspx

U.S. Environmental Protection Agency. (2016). Climate impacts on human health. *U.S. Environmental Protection Agency*. Retrieved March 30, 2016, from https://www3.epa.gov/climatechange/impacts/health.html

United Nations. (1997). UN conference on environment and development (1992). *Earth Summit*. Retrieved March 30, 2016, from http://www.un.org/geninfo/bp/enviro.html

United Nations Environment Programme. (2016). UNEP frontiers 2016 report: Emerging issues of environmental concern. *United Nations Environment Programme, Nairobi*. Retrieved March 30, 2016, from http://web.unep.org/frontiers/sites/unep.org.frontiers/files/documents/unep_frontiers_2016.pdf

van Teijlingen, E., & Hundley, V. (2002). The importance of pilot studies. *Nursing Standard, 16*(40), 33–36.

Vianna, G. M. S., Meekan, M. G., Pannell, D. J., Marsh, S. P., & Meeuwig, J. J. (2012). Socio-economic value and community benefits from shark-diving tourism in Palau: A sustainable use of reef shark populations. *Biological Conservation, 145*(1), 267–277.

Walston, J., Stokes, E. J. & Hedges, S. (2016). The importance of Asia's protected areas for safeguarding commercially high value species. In L. N. Joppa, J. E. M. Baillie, & J. G. Robinson (Eds.), *Protected areas: Are they safeguarding biodiversity?* Wiley

Wente, M. (2015). The world's nicest, most law-abiding generation. *The Globe and Mail*. Retrieved February 18, 2017, from http://www.theglobeandmail.com/opinion/the-worlds-nicest-most-law-abiding-generation/article25249936/

Wijedasa, L. S., Jauhiainen, J., Könönen, M., Lampela, M., Vasander, H., Leblanc, M.-C., & Andersen, R. (2017). Denial of long-term issues with agriculture on tropical peatlands will have devastating consequences. *Global Change Biology, 23*, 977–982.

Wilcox, C., Mallos, N. J., Leonard, G. H., Rodriguez, A., & Hardesty, B. D. (2016). Using expert elicitation to estimate the impacts of plastic pollution on marine wildlife. *Marine Policy, 65*, 107–114.

Wilson, K. A., Auerbach, N. A., Sam, K., Magini, A. G., Moss, A. S. L., Langhans, S. D., & Meijaard, E. (2016). Conservation research is not happening where it is most needed. *PLOS Biology, 14*(3), e1002413.

Zalasiewicz, J., Waters, C. N., & Ivar do Sul, J. A., Corcoran, P. L., Barnosky, A. D., Cearreta, A., Edgeworth, M., Gałuszka, A., Jeandel, C., Leinfelder, R., McNeill, J. R., Steffen, W., Summerhayes, C., Wagreich, M., Williams, M., Wolfe, A. P. & Yonan, Y. (2016). The geological cycle of plastics and their use as a stratigraphic indicator of the Anthropocene. *Anthropocene, 13*, 4–17.

Zhang, H., Miller, M. P., Yang, F., Chan, H. K., Gaubert, P., Ades, G., & Fischer, G. A. (2015). Molecular tracing of confiscated pangolin scales for conservation and illegal trade monitoring in Southeast Asia. *Global Ecology and Conservation, 4*, 414–422.

Melvin Terry Gumal is an Adjunct Professor at Swinburne University of Technology Sarawak Campus and until 2020, was the Director for the Wildlife Conservation Society, Malaysia Program. In 2014, he won the Whitley Award for Conservation in Great Ape Habitats.

Christina Yin is Senior Lecturer at the Swinburne University of Technology, Sarawak. She also works with students on conservation, creative writing, and debate activities. Her research and fiction and nonfiction writing have appeared in *Anak Sastra, eTropic Journal, New Writing* and *Ombak*.

Yunus Yasin is President of the Association of Science, Technology and Innovation (ASTI). He obtained his doctorate in Engineering from Cambridge University. He has been active in designing and implementing start-ups particularly in the areas of education and sustainable development.

Elvinson Ak Rosedy is an Environmental Executive in a private environmental consultancy firm in Malaysia since 2018. He was previously a Researcher at the Wildlife Conservation Society (WCS), Malaysia Program.

Douglas Tan a business graduate of the Swinburne University of Technology, Sarawak Campus, was the communication executive of Wildlife Conservation Society—Malaysia Program.

Sylvia Ng is a graduate in animal resources science from University Malaysia Sarawak and also social research from the University of Edinburgh. Her current work focuses on conservation education and social research in the Wildlife Conservation Society, Malaysia Program.

Chapter 14
Healthcare and Wellness

Sharifah Muhairah Shahabudin and Yap Su Fei

Abstract Health status has been linked with future income, consumption, and welfare. More importantly health is the basic capabilities that should not be undertaken on the basis of presumed economic benefits. Its public good characteristic mandates a role for government to ensure satisfactory health to all including the disadvantaged. This chapter examines the Malaysian public and private health systems, together with the issues arising therefrom and analyses the opportunities and threats facing the sector today. Public healthcare being the main provider, has been encountering difficulties in providing speedy delivery of healthcare owing to less provisions made for geriatric healthcare and a lack of basic medical programmes for immigrants. Private healthcare providers are profit driven and largely cluster in the large towns and cities. It is suggested that Malaysia 2050 health and wellbeing can be advanced following a more Realistic and Intermediate Pathway of the Australian health system with a suggested growth rate of 5–6%. As health and social wellbeing is the major goal of Envisioning Malaysia 2050, it is proposed that every person residing in Malaysia shall not be deprived of quality healthcare, that every person enjoy the maximum life expectancy and advance level of healthcare becomes the norm for both primary and secondary preventive medicine.

Keywords Healthcare · Health-income · Health model · Health intervention · Malaysia

That every person residing in Malaysia will have affordable, accessible and quality health care and that no-one shall be deprived of the best chances to live to their fullest potential, physically, mentally, spiritually and emotionally

S. M. Shahabudin (✉) · Y. S. Fei
Faculty of Business and Economics, University of Malaya, 50603 Kuala Lumpur, Malaysia
e-mail: muhairah@um.edu.my

R. Rasiah et al. (eds.), *Malaysia's Leap Into the Future*, Dynamics of Asian Development, https://doi.org/10.1007/978-981-16-7045-9_14

Introduction

The relationship between health and economic development appears clear enough. It is hard to argue against the Economist's (2008) statement that appears to make perfect sense:

"Healthy people can work longer and harder than sick people. Healthier children are likely to stay in school longer and learn more, earning more when they enter the workforce. Even across countries the relationship seems clear: those with better health are generally richer, and those that improve their citizens' health grow faster".

But this relationship is far more complex than such a statement suggests. For instance, is this a statement of association or of causation? And if so, which causes which? Extant research provides only a partial answer. Until the last decade of the twentieth century, while there has been extensive research to show the impact of rising income on health, not a lot had been written on the impact of health on income and/or economic development (Rosensweig, 1988). This asymmetry is surprising, considering the extensive research that had been undertaken. This situation has since been rectified, with an increasing amount of work explaining health's contribution to economic development.

An early example of this genre is Leibenstein (1957) who argued that better nutrition increased productivity. Sorkin (1977) also showed that declining mortality raised economic growth in developing economies early in the twentieth century, explaining this link through enhanced productivity, lengthened hours of work, the development of previously unsettled or undeveloped regions, and facilitating the capability to innovate and be entrepreneurial (Aguayo-Rico et al., 2005). But it was likely the publication of the World Bank's report on health in 1993 (World Bank, 1993) that galvanized research in this area. Around this time, theoretical work was undertaken that incorporated health into human capital (Barro, 1996; Bloom et al., 2001; Mankiw et al., 1992). But studies were also undertaken that linked health directly to economic outcomes that fostered rising income and economic growth. For instance, health indicators were shown to impact productivity by Bloom and Canning (2000), and Strauss and Thomas (1998).

A life cycle approach was used by Smith (1999) to relate health status to future income, consumption, and welfare. A third approach is to marshal historical evidence to establish this link. For instance, Sorkin (1977) supported his argument using data from the early years of the twentieth century. More recently, Strittmatter and Sunde (2011: 1) used data on the introduction of public healthcare systems in Europe to support their findings of decreases in infant mortality rates and crude death rates, leading eventually to growth in income per capita and increased population growth. With this growing body of research, members of the Commission on Macroeconomics and Health were able to confidently proclaim in their report to the Director General of the World Health Organization (Sachs et al., 2001: 23):

"The macroeconomic evidence confirms that countries with the weakest conditions of health and education have a much harder time achieving sustained growth than do countries with better conditions of health and education".

The report also alluded to health improvement's indirect impacts (Sachs et al., 2001: 25):

"Longer-lived households will tend to invest a higher fraction of their incomes in education and financial saving, because their longer time horizon allows them more years to reap the benefits of such investments".

Despite this confidence, questions have been raised as to the extent of this impact. Sorkin (1977) was of the view that such a link worked only in developing but not developed countries. Evidence has also emerged that the health-income/economic growth relationship is not necessarily monotonically positive. This is because improved health was also found to lead to higher population growth until a fertility transition occurs. For developing countries, this may take a while to materialize (Bloom & Canning, 2008). Indeed, Acemoglu and Johnson (2007) produced evidence that health's impact on population growth led to a fall in per capita income when life expectancy increased—a larger population had to share the same stock of income and wealth. Deaton (2003) also warned against assuming that higher income alone is associated with better health, citing studies that show income inequality also poses risks to health (Lynch et al., 2001; Wilkinson, 2000). According to him,

"equal societies have more social cohesion, more solidarity and less stress; they offer their citizens more public goods, more social support and more social capital; and they satisfy humans' evolved preference for fairness" (Deaton, 2003: 113).

What are the takeaways for policy from all this research? First, it is important to remember that whatever the nature of the relationship between health and income/economic growth, attaching overwhelming weight to this relationship is no more warranted than believing that education is all about human capital. As important as health is to economic growth, it is, as constantly reminded by Nobel Laureate A. K. Sen, "health is among the basic capabilities that gives value to human life." (Sachs et al., 2001: 21). The Economist (2008) is therefore spot-on in stating that "It may be best to make a case for improving health because it is a good thing in itself, rather than on the basis of presumed economic benefits that may not appear for generations". Its public good characteristic mandates a role for government, especially in its role of poverty eradication, the poor being invariably disadvantaged by unsatisfactory health.

Second, the nature of the health situation in any country is highly contextual, and the many studies offer at best a broad guide to best practices and lessons. Issues, challenges, and opportunities, and how best to respond to them, have to be framed within a specific context. This context includes the geography and climate in which a country is located which is material to the nature and likelihood of specific health risks, the history and institutions of health care which speak to the success of health interventions, and the socio-economic conditions facing the population, which are the products of a host of factors.

The context for this chapter is Malaysia, which has had a long history of public, and a briefer but growing history of private, health care. It has also in place a slew of policies relating to health care. This is the context which frames this chapter's discussion.

In the next section, Malaysia's public and private health systems are reviewed, together with the issues arising therefrom. Section 14.3 then looks at the opportunities and threats facing the sector today. The substance of these two sections sets the tone for what the health sector needs to be, as discussed in Sect. 14.4. Section 14.5 ends the chapter with some thoughts on the priorities and initiatives to be implemented to get there.

Historical Backdrop

The Malaysian health sector has a strong framework which was drawn from its colonial roots and further strengthened by the First to Eleventh Malaysia 5–Year Plans (Ministry of Finance, various years). After independence, Malaysia's healthcare system was predominantly government led. It was not until the 1980's that private healthcare services emerged changing the healthcare system to a dual-tiered parallel system.

Health has always been a key component of National Development plans as it forms a pillar of an important input to production, that is, human capital. Healthcare spending was 4.2% of GDP in 2017 (Ministry of Health Malaysia, 2019) which places it below the average for upper middle-income countries of 5.7% based on the World Bank data.[1] Total health expenditure was RM57.4 million in 2017 for Malaysia with consistent increases each year.

Private health expenditure (as a percentage of GDP) in Malaysia was 1.8 as of 2013. Its highest value over the past 18 years was 1.8% in 2013, while its lowest value was 1.2% in 1997. However, compared the period until the early 1990s, health care in Malaysia was largely borne by the government. This figure began to change dramatically when the government embarked on a massive healthcare privatization programme since so much so that the share of government expenditure of total healthcare expenditure rose to 50.6% in 2017 (Rasiah et al., 2009, 2010; World Bank, 2020). This alarming fall in government funding of health, which coincided with aggressive promotion healthcare commercialization attracted mounting opposition by civil society organizations (Rasiah et al., 2017). Private health expenditure by definition (WHO) includes direct household (out-of-pocket) spending, private insurance, charitable donations, and direct service payments by private corporations. The availability and affordability of private healthcare remain the chief constraints that limit demand.

However, challenges inherent in the system stem from both external and internal sources, the former linked to global epidemics and immigration, the latter from environmental pollution and lifestyle and occupational diseases among many (ILO, 2013).

[1] https://data.worldbank.org/indicator/SH.XPD.CHEX.GD.ZS?locations=8S.

Malaysian Health Sector: "SWOT" Analysis

The Malaysian Healthcare system has been effective to a certain extent in providing healthcare to the public. The vision to provide high-quality healthcare for the people is still a "work in progress" as there is a need to constantly review the existing strategies and process to maximize the existing resources as well as potential assets. A review of the current healthcare system is crucial, and this can be realized by identifying the strengths, weaknesses, opportunities, and threats of the existing system.

Strengths and Weaknesses

Medical Personnel

The Ministry of Health (MOH) is at the forefront monitoring and providing services including health promotion, disease prevention, curative and rehabilitative care delivered through clinics and hospitals. The satisfactory health allocations and planning has generated a relatively healthy society. The harnessing of doctors through a compulsory service requirement has ensured sufficient medical personnel over the years while nursing staff are trained in various centers in the country. However, there remains insufficient specialists in specific disciplines, such as pathology, emergency medicine, radiology, neurosurgery, oncologists, and pediatric surgery (Ministry of Health, 2014). Malaysia is still below the Vision 2020 target of supplying 1 doctor for every 600 persons. In 2016, the doctor-patient ratio was 1.58:1000 (Ministry of Health, 2019).

Medical facilities are fairly well distributed particularly within urban areas. The overall healthcare system shows the public sector as the main provider of inpatient care (about 80%) and the rest are provided by the private sector (Jaafar et al., 2012).

Neonatal, Maternity, and Infant Care

There is efficient support for neonatal, maternity, and infant care in the country. The current system of Midwifery clinics, Government clinics, and Public Hospitals at both the rural and urban areas have resulted in relatively low infant mortality of 7 in 1000 (Jaafar et al., 2012; World Bank, 2019) (see Figs. 14.1 and 14.2). Malaysia is one of the three countries in the ten ASEAN nations to reach infant and mortality rates below 10 per 1000 live births (Jaafar et al., 2012).

However, support for new mothers and the breastfeeding programme follow-up has not reached the levels of awareness as in developed countries. This has been to some extent due to aggressive promotion of producers of cow's milk and alternative industries for obvious reasons.

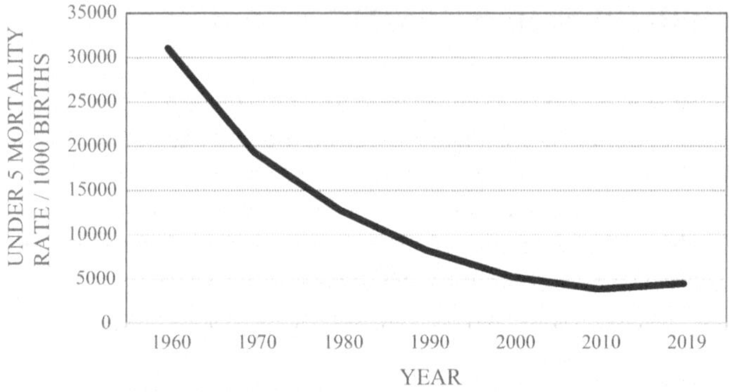

Fig. 14.1 Infant under five mortality rate, 1960–2019. *Source* The World Bank (https://data.worldbank.org)

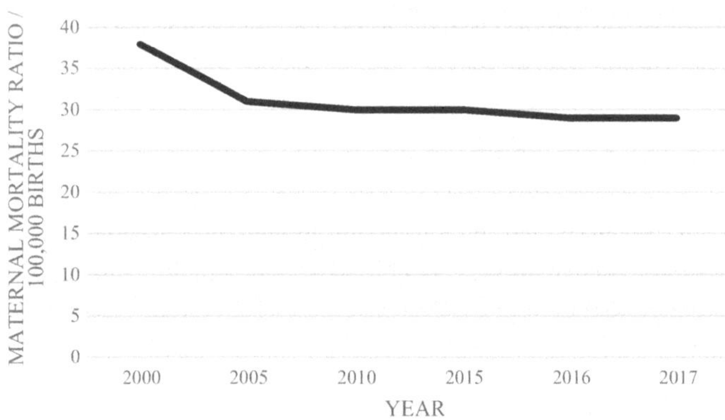

Fig. 14.2 Maternal mortality ratio, Malaysia, 2000–2017. *Source* The World Bank (https://data.worldbank.org)

Long waiting periods are the bane of those seeking healthcare particularly in Pediatric and Emergency Departments (incorrectly abused as a means to cut queues). This inherent weakness needs to be quickly addressed via a more systematic delivery that circumvents unnecessary administrative procedures. In spite of the good supply of doctors, this has not translated itself to speedy delivery of health care at most government hospitals.

Free Immunization for Children and Preventive Medicine

Free immunization is available for children and preventive medicine. Currently, newborns are immunized against major diseases such as TB, Rubella, Chicken pox, measles, Hepatitis and given the HPV vaccine at the appropriate intervals. However, this can be expanded to include other prevalent diseases especially for the old and very young. Alternatively, the government could subsidize those seeking supplementary protection at private clinics.

Another recommendation is to at least tax-exempt fees paid for immunization. Investigative processes such as scans, tests, and other related procedures should also be tax-exempt because it will encourage early detection and good monitoring in-line with first world practices. Preventive medicine is currently not actively pursued and this should form the next thrust of national plans as a healthy workforce and consistent productive input is crucial for the achievement of the nation's ideals.

Immunization for immigrants has not yet been implemented. A critical weakness facing the country is the lack of basic medical programmes for immigrants. Malaysia receives a large number of migrants from neighbouring countries amounting to 11% of the population, legally and illegally and in addition about 90,000 refugees and asylum seekers (Jaafar et al., 2012). This posts as a strain to the country's health systems and exposes the local population to contagious diseases such as typhoid, tuberculosis, dysentery, and hepatitis. For refugees and asylum seekers, health care services are provided mainly by non-government organizations and by local government health clinics and visiting medical personnel.

Civil Servants Health Programme

The one million civil servants in the country are provided with heavily subsidized healthcare. The upper tiers of officers, panel doctors in private practice support general healthcare, though the provision is not universal. Free dental care is only available in government clinics, which is often subjected to long queues.

Family Core-Unit Still Strong but Challenged

First care of infants, children, and the aged are basically managed by families, with core families and extended families existing as strong institutions providing physical, mental, and emotional support. However, the traditional systems are increasingly corroded as rural–urban migrations and emigrations accelerate. Consequently, reliable babysitting and childcare, medical facilities for the aged and handicapped, and supplementary support will do much to circumvent avoidable health threats and strengthening such care should receive attention. As such, preliminary work on childcare by Amin et al. (2015) shows that this area is relatively neglected in Malaysia. The importance of this area to both complement and supplement the formal healthcare sector cannot be overstressed.

Old Age Health Care

Current provisions are not adequate. The healthcare provided does not focus on geriatric health or palliative care. In a system where limited allocations have to be optimally distributed, the more productive segment of population below 60 years of age receives more consistent care.

Handicapped Persons

While the regulatory structure promises handicapped person-friendly premises, the implementation leaves much to be desired. For example, limited parking bays, absence of lifts, too-steep ramps, door widths not according to specifications, locked toilets, too-high drinking fountains, and so forth are common. Facilities should be seamless and flowing, enabling convenient access by the handicapped, the old, and very young. All drains should be covered, specific walking paths and corridors connected, and shielded. Hospitals should shorten waiting periods for consultation and medicines, especially for special-needs persons. Human rights for this marginalized segment of the population as enshrined in the UN charter has to be acknowledged.

Private Healthcare Sector

Private healthcare is fairly well distributed within urban areas but sporadic in the rural areas. Primarily profit driven, clustering of private practitioners and specialists are found in the larger towns and cities. Hence, these are not easily accessed by those living in rural areas which usually arises when particular expertise is not available in public hospitals.

Access to Generic Drugs

There is inadequate funding for high-end drugs and elective/preventive care, such as fertility treatments. Moreover, access to generic drugs is threatened by TPPA and its successor and this should be looked into by the authorities.

Healthcare Personnel

So far supply of healthcare personnel is largely considered sufficient, though the long queues at government hospitals suggest that more personnel, especially specialists, will be necessary (see Rasiah et al., 2017).

Also, as with the public sector, shortages in highly narrow health fields suggest the need to strategize planning at the national level. Imbalances in the provision of healthcare are also geographic with challenges facing East Malaysia and the East Coast of Peninsular Malaysia in health care provision.

Incomplete Insurance Coverage of Population

Insufficient insurance coverage for the population is apparent, particularly among the lower-income families. Currently, there is the free National Health Protection Scheme, mySalam for the bottom 40% household income (B40) group to cover for 36 critical illnesses. However, the penetration of insurance coverage for the low-income segment is still meagre as there are others who have no access to the coverage and those borderline middle-income households that need protection. High cost of healthcare includes consultation, procedures, surgical/medical treatment. Current tax exemption levels should be raised or given full tax exemption to encourage protection and more effective patient care.

- Health programme coverage

There are limited allocations for old age health care and care of the disabled. Moreover, infrastructure for the disabled is not universally available due to lack of enforcement.

Legislation and Regulations/Intellectual Property

Legislation and regulations with regards to intellectual property are insufficient to prepare the nation for first world medical care.

Opportunities

While acknowledging the successes of the current health development of the country, potential threats of new and unknown diseases that constantly appear bring more challenges to the community through the rapidity with which they can spread. New challenges bring opportunities for new discoveries that will lead to an improved health system.

Rapid development of new drugs and new methods of combating diseases through biotechnology and nanotechnology.

Malaysia has ventured into nanotechnology and has developed its own nanotechnology policies and initiatives since 2001. Nanotechnology has been identified as one of the critical fields among 14 other priority research areas for potential breakthroughs in manufacturing, agriculture sector, biotechnology, medicine, energy, and environment (Hashim et al., 2009). Due to its new technology, Malaysia lacks behind in terms of insufficient experts in the area, brain drain, competition with other Asian countries like China and India and lack of investments from the private sector (Hashim et al., 2009). Recognizing the significance of this new technology and the current weaknesses in the system, the government under the Ministry of Science, Technology and Innovation (MOSTI) has allocated RM868 million from the 2006 national budget to fund R&D.

Traditional Herbal Medicine and Alternative Medicines as Complementary Medicine

At present, traditional and alternative medicine such as by Chinese and Malay practitioners and products are becoming increasingly popular in treating human diseases in developed countries. For example, more than 60% of the drugs used for cancer treatment are of medicinal plant based (Jahan et al., 2009). The fact that these plants are easily available, easy to prepare, inexpensive, and have fewer side effects on humans and the environment makes it a sort after medicine (Van Hai, 2015). Malaysia has developed a good foundation for this sector. Various agencies were established for funding, R&D, and commercializing of products. However, more progress can be made if the focus is given to producing quality herbal products that meet internationally acceptable standards in the pharmaceutical industry (Muhammad & Awaisu, 2008). To date, under Malaysian Pharmacopoeis (directory for quality medicinal substances), only five products have been listed. More can be done through proper guidelines and control over the manufacturing of these products and seamless integration of traditional medicines into the national healthcare systems.

Health Education

Health literacy among the general publics of utmost importance as increasing health literacy among patients and public can significantly reduce hospitalization, reduce early mortality and improve quality of life (Butterworth, Gray, Butterworth, & Allam, 2011). Malaysia has progressed well in terms of reaching the public through school-based health education and also creating awareness in sexual education, health protection, family planning, and disease prevention through immunization. However, the present health education running in Malaysia lacks depth as the general public are merely being informed rather than being educated. The knowledge on the health needs to be embedded from young at all levels of socio-economic group. The lack of knowledge in health has affected young adults in their attitude and practice towards mental health issues and sexually transmitted diseases (Shahar et al., 2019). Moreover, the issue of malnutrition and poor diet is associated with low socio-economic group particularly among the older adults and children.

A transfer of knowledge should be the main objective not only for the general public but also the clinical staff. The use of electronic media through an efficient and easy to use interactive system or even a booklet for the non-IT literate would be useful in explaining difficult terms and to answer questions often asked by the clinical staff. This would shift the mindset of the general public from the culture of "doctor knows best" to a more learned public.

Threats

Contagion of Diseases and World Pandemic

An outbreak of diseases especially contagious diseases such as SARS and Covid-19 is considered as a major threat to the public health security. An outbreak of a disease is inevitable as urbanization and international travel increase the risk of spreading diseases further. Malaysia's level of health system and systematic control programmes for contagious diseases has yet to be tested entirely. The most contagious virus that was detected locally is the Nipah virus in 1998/99, where 105 cases of deaths were reported (World Health Organization, 2007). There were uncertainty and confusion in diagnosing the disease which caused delayed detection, inappropriate control measures that caused high mortality. In case of SARS and H1N1, there was a shortfall in influenza vaccine production that made it more difficult to contain the pandemic.

Resistance to Antibiotics

Bacteria can develop resistance to antibiotics. This can happen through over prescribing or under prescribing of drugs, poor compliance of the recommended dosages and by taking counterfeit drugs. The consequences are severe, requiring more complex and longer treatments. Patients are not aware of the importance of completing the prescribed antibiotics when they discontinue taking it after the symptoms disappear but before the pathogen is eliminated. Malaysia like many other developing countries, have problems with counterfeit drugs and detection of these type of drugs is very difficult because we import generic drugs in large amount.

Legislation WTO and Intellectual Property Rights

The WTO sets standards and technical regulations of trade and one of its main roles is control over market access for goods. The Agreement on Trade-related Aspect of Intellectual Property Rights (TRIPS) which is one of the most controversial agreements, is one strategy that is being used by powerful states and multinational companies in bargaining for access and distribution of vital drugs. This poses a problem for the developing countries, Malaysia included, through the setting of trade restrictions and distortions. Large companies with economies of scale directly reap economic gains from the agreement which encourage and support the existing pharmaceutical cartels.

Environmental Health

Environmental pollution is a major issue in public health. In Malaysia, health issues arise from air pollution from mobile sources, industrial production processes, and open burning sources. In addition, there is a problem arising from lead content in herbal traditional medicine preparations such as Tongkat Ali, which is used for fever, aches, sexual insufficiency, and health supplements that weaken the immune defence system. Contamination during the manufacturing process, can bring in metals from polluted soil.

Lifestyle Diseases

Lifestyle diseases are rising because of the modern way of life. Noncommunicable diseases such as heart and pulmonary circulation diseases are the leading causes of adult mortality in Malaysia (Jaafar et al., 2013). The Third Health and Morbidity Survey in 2006 has found that 29.7% of males and 28.6% of females in the country are overweight and this is alarming as 3 of 5 leading causes of deaths is related to obesity (Tan et al., 2011). Malaysian children are at risk to NCD as 22.8% children from the low-income group are obese (Shahar et al., 2019). Obesity is a predisposing factor for NCD, and related diseases are heart diseases, cancer, hypertension, stroke, and diabetes accounts for one third of medically certified death in Malaysia (Tan et al., 2011).

Malaysian love their food but there must be a concerted effort to promote healthier diets and a more active lifestyle to reduce obesity. Propagation of information and possible regulatory changes may be necessary. For example, availability of gymnasiums, strictly non-smoking zones, or healthy balanced food at workplaces.

Pathways into the Future

Alternative pathways that Malaysia might take are given in Fig. 14.3 (dubbed Utopian, Realistic, or Linear). Malaysia 2050 health and wellbeing can be advanced following the Scandinavian model which has been identified as a relatively advanced health model. To this end, Norway is currently holding the top position as the country with one of the highest health expenditure per capita of USD9,715 (World Health Organization, 2020). Norway has a government run and government financed universal health care system. The system is such that a special purpose income tax finances 8–10% of the public healthcare with a doctor-to-patient ratio of 4.2: 1000.

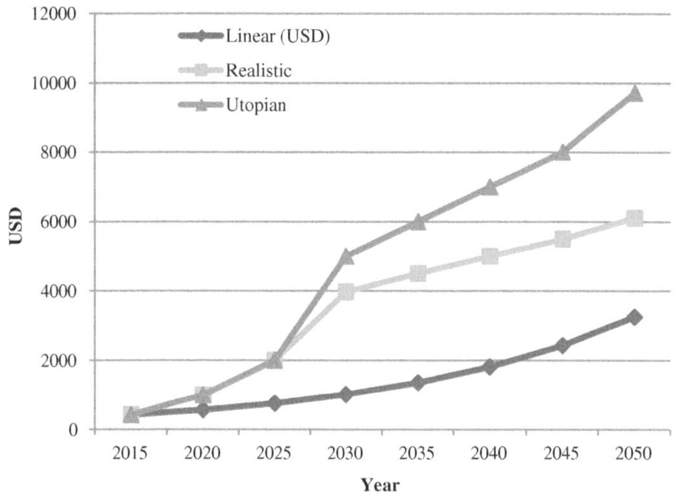

Fig. 14.3 Alternate Pathways for health per capita expenditure, Malaysia. Source: Authors

Malaysia's per capita expenditure on health is USD384, which is 4% of the country's GDP (World Bank, 2020). Malaysia's healthcare system is market-oriented. The lower-income earners are patrons to the public hospitals and clinics while the higher income earners spend on private healthcare services. Malaysia's doctor-to-patient ratio is now 1.58:1000.

In the event that minor intervention is made to our current healthcare system, Malaysia will evolve to a similar healthcare system that Singapore currently operates on. The current Singapore healthcare system focus on compulsory savings and price controls which ensures affordability to all with a doctor-to-patient ratio of 2:1000. The key principles of the health financing system are to ensure individuals are responsible for the healthcare costs but the community and government support are given to those in need and to practice patient co-payments with insurance companies to discourage extra-billing or over consumption. Singapore has three major sources of financing; Medisave (mandatory for all), MediShield and MediShield Plus (low premiums for voluntary backup to protect from major medical expenses), and Medifund (charity-style assistance financed from Medifund's interest income) (World Health Organization, 2002).

If weaknesses and threats affect the trajectory then a shortfall will take place and the probability that the utopian state will not be achieved is significantly higher. If so, then a mid-range target similar to the Australian Healthcare Model is more probable. Australia has a health expenditure per capita of USD6,110. The second possible realistic or intermediate target may very well be Japan with health expenditure of USD3,966 per capita.

Without intervention, Malaysia will go on a linear trajectory. In such a case, based on our extrapolation, Malaysia will reach a pattern similar to the current Singapore

Health Model by 2050. Health spending is anticipated to reach USD3,251 per capita by 2050.

The gap between the linear pathway and the utopian pathway is a gap of about USD6,000. The gap between the linear and the intermediate path is approximately USD3,000. A more Realistic and Intermediate Target would be to follow the Australian system. Central to Australia's healthcare system is a co-existing system between public and private. The system known as Medicare, is funded partly by a 1.5% income tax levy (with the exception for low income earners). Its doctor-to-patient ratio is 3.3:1000. Japan's healthcare system on the other hand, relies heavily on government funding. Currently, the government funds around 70% of the public healthcare costs. Japan's doctor-to-patient ratio is 2.3:1000.

The utopian pathway suggests a growth of 7–8% every year on a nonlinear path. The intermediate path results from a 5–6% growth rate or any exogenous shock displacing it from the most desired path above. The third linear path is when the current trajectory is just maintained.

Future Objectives of Healthcare Sector

Malaysia aims to be a nation of healthy individuals, families, and communities. Health and social wellbeing as the ultimate goal of Envisioning Malaysia 2050 has as its objectives the following outcomes:

- That every person residing in Malaysia will have affordable, accessible, and quality health care and that no-one shall be deprived of the best chances to live to their fullest potential, physically, mentally, spiritually, and emotionally.
- That every person will enjoy the maximum life expectancy inherited in their genetic composition and to not just add years to their lives but also add life to their years.
- To reach an advanced level of health care where both primary and secondary preventive medicine becomes the norm, whereby primary preventive medicine is defined as being circumventing problems before they even arise and to go beyond the present structure of just seeking health care for curative purposes and actively prevent diseases at the primary level. Secondary preventive medicine is meant to assist with the early detection of diseases when prognosis is still good. To go beyond the present structure of just seeking health care for curative purposes and actively prevent diseases at the primary level.

Social Protection as a Means of Healthcare Financing

Social protection in Malaysia is comprehensive enough as it covers beneficiaries from young to old. There are four approaches to social protection in the country, mainly social insurance, employer liability, social assistance, and provident funds and all approaches cover various healthcare benefits, employment injury, invalidity benefits, and family benefits.

For children, Malaysia currently has the National Immunization Programme which incorporates free vaccines according to immunization schedule. The immunization programme should be expanded to include other threatening infections.

It is estimated that school going children spend a quarter of their day in school and food eaten in the school setting contributes to the children's total diet (Lucas et al., 2017). Scandinavian Schools and schools in Japan have planned meals that are nutritionally balanced for children and raised health status of school going children. This can be implemented in pre-school and primary school, for children 12 years and below across the country. Malaysia currently has the School Milk Programme only for primary schools covered by the Supplementary Food Programme. A subsidized meal programme should be introduced to public primary schools and quality monitoring according to nutritional food group of the meals sold in school cafeterias should be thoroughly implemented. Basic nutrition may be more important than the use of devices such as computers or tablets as physical health is the first thing that must be nurtured.

For working adults, 1Malaysia Clinic and 1Malaysia Mobile Clinic comprises a chain of clinics aimed at providing accessible health throughout the country. The infrastructure and the overall idea is good, however, the human resource planning and staffing of these clinics can be improved. Moreover, pharmaceutical supplies have to be efficiently managed.

Additionally, working adults are given financial assistance for assistive devices, as well as cancer prevention via early screening and mammograms. The tax rebate procedures in Malaysia offer adequate claims to support such healthcare services.

For registered workers under the Employee Provident Fund (EPF), withdrawal from Account 2 savings are allowed to cover medical expenses for critical illnesses suffered by the members or members' family. The savings also cover healthcare equipment to treat illnesses. This is particularly useful for those without medical insurance; however, the amount permitted for withdrawal is not large. The amount is the equivalent of 6 months' basic wages and DA (dearness allowance) or employee share with interest. Moreover, for the minimum income group, if the EPF savings is RM100,000, 10% for healthcare is insufficient. Therefore, the government has to build a healthcare fund (Dana Kesihatan) for the elderly structured like PTPTN (student loan scheme).

Working adults who are registered with the Social Security Organisation (SOCSO) and their dependents are protected against contingencies which include disease that derives from occupational hazards and accidents that require physical and vocational rehabilitation under the Employment Injury Scheme and/or Invalidity Pension Scheme. Aside from the coverage, members who are 40 years and above are entitled to free health checkups under the SOCSO Health Screening Programme (HSP). Currently, only workers employed under a contract of service with salary of RM4,000 and below are registered members. However, many SOCSO members have low level of awareness of their eligibility to obtain free health screening and claim for protection against injuries even if they are not registered under SOCSO (Lai et al., 2017).

For the elderly, free medical consultations at all government hospitals and clinics are provided. However, the system is not well integrated among ministries and delivery of health services and financial assistance for assistive devices are inefficient. In addition, elderly day care centre and retirement homes are available in every state for those who need the assistance. However, more stringent supervision is required to ensure cleanliness and hygenic standards are attained.

Conclusions

Envisioning Malaysia 2050 demands serious effort on the part of government, the private sector and civil society working together in achieving a prosperous, peaceful, and harmonious future for future generations. Civil Society Organisations (CSOs) play an important role in the allocation of healthcare services to protect the interests of the poor. It is evident that with the growing numbers of commercialization of healthcare services since the 1990s, resource allocation for the public hospitals has decreased. The CSOs serve as the third force to ensure the state uses its power to safeguard the social needs of the poor. Thus, emphasizing the role of CSOs and its involvement in healthcare issues is crucial.

The strong presence of private hospitals is evident in urbanized towns in the country, which has resulted in easy access to healthcare services for urban dwellers. However, the access of commercialized healthcare has created a gap in the distribution of healthcare services between the rich and the poor and among the rural and urban population. The government should increase the resources of the public healthcare facilities and services in the rural and urban centres to serve the needs of the poor and to lessen the dependency on private hospitals. Failure to address the constraints in public hospitals may result in the poor having to wait in long queues to get treatments or take loans to pay exorbitant costs of medical fees from the private sector.

The uptake of healthcare insurance is low among the lower-income families. To encourage protection among the lower-income group, tax exemption levels should be raised, or full tax exemption should be given. Additionally, public–private partnerships for healthcare insurance should be encouraged, such as the recent example of mySalam protection programme, in which an alliance with Great Eastern Takaful, serves to provide protection of RM2 billion for 8 million disadvantaged adults through insurance scheme.

Opportunities to develop the current health system are evident as Malaysia ventures into nanotechnology and alternative medicine. With the right investments; funding for R&D, human capital development, and proper guidelines over processes and standards of products, Malaysia will garner more benefits.

The proposed Malaysian healthcare trajectory for 2050 considers the Australian system as a more realistic target to follow as Australia has a similar co-existing public–private healthcare system. This would require a growth rate between 5–6%

per annum. However, a shortfall in intervention would bring Malaysia to a linear trajectory that reflects the current Singapore Health model by 2050.

Implemented on the basis of confidence, trust, and integrity, such a vision for Malaysia in 2050, is realizable, and presents itself as a statement of hope for our country's future.

Appendix

In an ideal economic state, the following should have been acquired:

Future medicines 1–7 below capture the essence of out 7 point achievements of healthcare that will enable the Visions and Goals above to be attained.

Future Medicine (1)

Precision medicine

Tailoring of medical treatment and preventive interventions to the individual characteristics of each patient. Genomics, metabolomics and proteomics are encompassed within the larger panomics framework that specifically treats patients in a targetted manner depending on the genetic makeup and molecular characteristics of the patient.

Future Medicine (2)

Productive ageing

To engage the segment of population over 60 years of age in productive activities and worthwhile contributions towards the nations GDP. To harness the aged in our increasingly inverted V-population structure towards the development of our nation.

Future Medicine (3)

It is hoped that currently incurable diseases including cancer will be curable by 2050. In this regard, if Malaysia is to tap onto the global network of knowledge creation and expansion, the country's legislative and intellectual property must be ready to facilitate the flow of new drugs into the country that respect international patent rights.

Future Medicine (4)

The new norm of prevention as the preferred mode of health care. The current system sees the greater portion of patients seeking curative medicine. Ideally, in the future we will see more patients doing routine medical tests that are tailored for mainly maintaining good health.

Future Medicine (5)

To build a secure Malaysia that is ready to handle any potential epidemic with secure first world facilities from entry point detection, to containment, to hospital preparedness and to stem any spread. This is critical in face of rising threats in the past and which continue to afflict the world as mutated viruses and antibiotic resistance create new problems globally. Strategies: foster global partnerships, strengthens national disease surveillance and develop national action plans to permit early detection.

Future Medicine (6)

To integrate the handicapped into society in a manner that reflects our commitment to universal human rights and gives dignity to every sector of society.

Future Medicine (7)

To stem the current decline in environmental health threats and if possible, reverse it, to commit to sustainable living and growth and to recognize that the environment and future of man will be intertwined as we honour our pledge for a better world for coming generations.

References

Acemoglu, D., & Johnson, S. (2007). Disease and development: The effect of life expectancy on economic growth. *Journal of Political Economy, 115*(6), 925–985.

Aguayo-Rico, A., Guerra-Turrubiates, I. A., & de Oca-Hernández, R. M. (2005). Empirical evidence of the impact of health on economic growth. *Issues in Political Economy, 14*.

Barro, R. (1996). Three models of health and economic growth. Harvard University. Unpublished manuscript.

Bloom, D. E., & Canning, D. (2000). The health and wealth of nations. *Science, 287*, 1207–1209.

Bloom, D. E., & Canning, D. (2008). Population health and economic growth. Working Paper No. 24, Commission on Growth and Development. World Bank.

Bloom, D. E., Canning, D., & Sevilla, J. (2001). The effect of health on economic growth: theory and evidence. Working Paper 8587, National Bureau of Economic Research, Cambridge, Mass.

Butterworth, K., Gray, A., Butterworth, H., & Allam, O. (2011). Using education theory to design a patient e-health education system capable of increasing health literacy. Paper presented at the 24th International Symposium on Computer-Based Medical Systems (CBMS).

Deaton, A. (2003). Health, inequality and economic development. *Journal of Economic Literature, 41*, 113–158.

Economist. (2008). Health and wealth. Nov 20. Retrieved February 13, 2016, from http://www.economist.com/node/12637080.

Hashim, U., Nadia, E., & Salleh, S. (2009). Nanotechnology development status in Malaysia: Industrialization strategy and practices. *International Journal of Nanoelectronics and Materials, 2*(1), 119–134.

International Labour Organization. (2013). Repairing the economic and social fabric. Retrieved from https://www.ilo.org/wcmsp5/groups/public/---dgreports/--dcomm/documents/publication/wcms_214476.pdf.

Jaafar S., Noh K. M., Muttalib K., Othman N.H., Healy J., Maskon K., et al. (2012). *Malaysia health system review* (Vol. 3, No. 1). New Delhi: World Health Organization, Regional Office for the Western Pacific.

Jaafar, S., Noh, K. M., Muttalib, K. A., Othman, N., & Healy, J. (2013). Malaysian health system review. *Health System Transition, 3*(1), 15–80.

Jahan, S., Chaudhary, R., & Goyal, P. K. (2009). Anticancer activity of an Indian medicinal plant, Alstonia scholaris, on skin carcinogenesis in mice. *Integrative Cancer Therapies, 8*(3), 273–279.

Lai, E. P., Beh, C. Z., Heng, K. W., Liew, L. K., & Lim, J. X. (2017). The awareness of employees for the health screening benefits provided by Socso upon 40 years old (Doctoral dissertation, UTAR).

Leibenstein, H. (1957). *Economic backwardness and economic growth: Studies in the theory of economic development*. Wiley.

Lucas, P. J., Patterson, E., Sacks, G., Billich, N., & Evans, C. E. L. (2017). Preschool and school meal policies: An overview of what we know about regulation, implementation, and impact on diet in the UK, Sweden, and Australia. *Nutrients, 9*(7), 736.

Lynch, J., Davey-Smith, G., Hillemeier, M., Shaw, M., Raghunathan, T., & Kaplan, G. (2001). Income inequality, psychosocial environment and health: Comparisons across wealthy nations. *Lancet, 358*, 194–200.

Ministry of Health Malaysia. (2019). Malaysia National Health Accounts: Health Expenditure Report. Putrajaya.

Mankiw, N. G., Romer, D., & Weil, D. N. (1992). A contribution to the empirics of economic growth. *Quarterly Journal of Economics, 107*, 407–437.

Muhammad, B. Y., & Awaisu, A. (2008). The need for enhancement of research, development, and commercialization of natural medicinal products in Nigeria: Lessons from the Malaysian experience. *African Journal of Traditional, Complementary and Alternative Medicines, 5*(2), 120–130.

Rasiah, R., Abdillah, N., & Makmor, T. (2009). Privatizing healthcare: Power, profits and profits. *Journal of Contemporary Asia, 39*(1), 50–62.

Rasiah, R., Nik Rosnah, W. A., & Makmor, T. (2010). Markets and healthcare services: Critical issues. *Institutions and Economies, 3*(3), 467–486.

Rasiah, R., Makmor, T., Latifa, M. H., & Ndoma, I. (2017). Civil society organizations in opposition to healthcare commercialization: Protecting access for the poor and middle class in Malaysia. *Nonprofit and Voluntary Sector Quarterly, 46*(3), 1–19.

Rosensweig, M. R. (1988). Labor markets in low income countries. In H. Chenery & T. N. Srinivasan (Eds.), *Handbook of development economics*, (Vol. 1, pp. 713–762). North Holland.

Sachs, J. E., et al. (2001). *Macroeconomics and health: Investing in health for economic development*. World Health Organization.

Shahar, S., Lau, H., Wan Puteh, S. E., Amara, S., & Abdul Razak, N. (2019). Health, access and nutritional issues among low-income population in Malaysia: Introductory note. *BMC Public Health, 19*(Suppl 4), 552–557.

Smith, J. P. (1999). Healthy bodies and thick wallets: The dual relation between health and socioeconomic status. *Journal of Economic Perspectives, 13*, 145–166.

Sorkin, A. L. (1977). *Health economics in developing countries*. Lexington Books.

Strauss, J., & Thomas, D. (1998). Health, nutrition and economic development. *Journal of Economic Literature, 36*, 766–817.

Strittmatter, A., & Sunde, U. (2011) *Health and economic development: Evidence from the introduction of public health care*. Discussion Paper 5901, Institute for the Study of Labor, Bonn.

Tan, A. K., Dunn, R. A., Samad, M. I. A., & Feisul, M. I. (2011). Sociodemographic and health-lifestyle determinants of obesity risks in Malaysia. *Asia-Pacific Journal of Public Health, 23*(2), 192–202.

Van Hai, N. (2015). The use of medicinal plants as immunostimulants in aquaculture: A review. *Aquaculture, 446*, 88–96. https://doi.org/10.1016/j.aquaculture.2015.03.014

Wilkinson, R. G. (2000). *Mind the gap: Hierarchies, health and human evolution*. Weidenfeld and Nicolson.

World Bank. (1993). World development report: Investing in health. Washington DC.

World Bank. (2019). World Bank data retrieved from https://data.worldbank.org/indicator/SP.DYN.CDRT.IN?locations=MY

World Bank. (2020, August 14). Retrieved from https://data.worldbank.org/indicator/SH.XPD.CHEX.PC.CD

World Health Organization. (2002). *Medical savings accounts: Lessons learned from limited international experience* (Discussion Paper EIP/FER/DP.02.3). Retrieved from World Health Organization website. https://www.who.int/health_financing/documents/dp_e_02_3-med_savings_accounts.pdf

World Health Organization. (2007). A safer future: Global public health security in the 21st century. Retrieved from https://www.who.int/whr/2007/whr07_en.pdf.

World Health Organization. (2020). Health systems in transition. Retrieved from https://apps.who.int/iris/bitstream/handle/10665/331786/HiT-22-1-2020-eng.pdf?sequence=1&isAllowed=y.

Sharifah Muhairah Shahabudin is Senior Lecturer at the Faculty of Business and Economics, Universiti Malaya. She was previously Head of the Department of Development Studies, Universiti Malaya.

Yap Su Fei retired as Associate Professor at the Faculty of Business and Economics and Administration, Universiti Malaya. She had served as Head of the Economics Department, Universiti Malaya. She specializes in macroeconomics topics.

Index

R. Rasiah et al. (eds.), *Malaysia's Leap Into the Future*, Dynamics of Asian Development, https://doi.org/10.1007/978-981-16-7045-9

The manufacturer's authorised representative in the EU is Springer Nature Customer Service Centre GmbH, Europaplatz 3, 69115 Heidelberg, Germany. If you have any concerns regarding our products, please contact ProductSafety@springernature.com

Printed and bound by CPI Group (UK) Ltd, Croydon, CR0 4YY
06/10/2026
02225252-0012